Hines Ward faces off with Jerome Bettis after Super Bowl XL victory.

This book is dedicated to Bobby Layne and
Ernie Stautner, two of the greatest Steelers
of them all.

Cover photos by George Gojkovich/Getty Images

James P. O'Brien — Publishing
P.O. Box 12580
Pittsburgh PA 15241
Phone: (412) 221-3580

First printing: September 2006

Manufactured in the United States of America

Printed by Geyer Printing Company, Inc.
3700 Bigelow Boulevard
Pittsburgh PA 15213

Typography by Cold-Comp
91 Green Glen Drive
Pittsburgh PA 15227

ISBN 1-886348-13-8

Contents

Preface
The Promise

It began with a promise. And a daring dream. Ben Roethlisberger, a brash rookie quarterback, told Jerome Bettis, a battered and beleaguered 12-year running back who had spoken about retirement, that if he returned for one more season he would get him back to his hometown of Detroit for the next Super Bowl.

It was a bold statement, offered in the wake of a disappointing defeat to the New England Patriots in the American Football Conference championship game at Heinz Field. It was a blown opportunity and it hurt deeply. Bettis' body was telling him it was time to hang up his spikes.

Once Bettis felt better, and the soreness in his bones went away, he thought better of his decision and chose to come back for one more shot at the Lombardi Trophy, the Holy Grail of the National Football League. There were four of them on display in the replica of team founder Art Rooney's office at Three Rivers Stadium that is on the second floor of the Steelers' training complex on the South Side. Bettis had seen and admired them many times during his nine seasons with the Steelers.

It was too late to get "One for the thumb," as this was a new generation. Owner Dan Rooney repeatedly said the slogan no longer applied. "This is a new day, a new team," he said. "They need to win a Super Bowl for themselves." Bettis wanted to be part of a new Steelers' generation that could land a Lombardi Trophy to top off its own accomplishments.

Thanks to Big Ben and Bettis, Antwaan Randle El and Hines Ward, Joey Porter and Troy Polamalu, Jeff Hartings and Alan Faneca and the rest of the determined Steelers' cast, and the coaching of Bill Cowher and his staff, and the support of the most fervent football fans in the nation, the promise and dream were realized. In perhaps the greatest run in Super Bowl history, the Steelers stood atop the podium when it was all over. The franchise had claimed its fifth NFL championship.

Kevin Colbert, the director of football operations for the Steelers, could appreciate the magnitude of the accomplishment. He had grown up on the North Side and had come to the Steelers from the front office of the Detroit Lions. Colbert has contributed in a big way to getting Cowher the kind of players he needed to be successful.

"Every little play mattered," claimed Colbert. "We had no margin for error. Every play counted, every game to the end."

The journey to Detroit and Super Bowl XL was a difficult one for the Steelers. Chances of it happening were particularly bleak after Roethlisberger was hurt and missed several games, and the Steelers lost three in a row and found themselves with a 7-5 record.

They could not lose the next game, or, as it turned out, any game after that to realize Roethlisberger's boast. Thinking about it now, that drive for five remains so improbable. It was, indeed, an incredible stretch run, ranking right up there with those memorable finishes by horse racing legend Silky Sullivan.

"I'm not a guy to make those kind of promises," remarked Roethlisberger when it was all over. "I'm glad it worked out the way it did."

Cowher convinced his players to pay attention to the next game, and not to worry about anything else. It was quite a journey. They made the playoffs as the last wild-card entry. They were the sixth seed in the playoff and they were often reminded that no sixth seed had ever won the Super Bowl.

Along the way, I believe that Cowher and Bettis both completed their Pro Football Hall of Fame resume. So did Hines Ward, who won the MVP Award in the big game. He already had surpassed pass-catching records established by two other Hall of Fame members, John Stallworth and Lynn Swann, along with Louis Lipps. Roethlisberger didn't have the best game at Ford Field, but, as he'd done before, he found a way to win. No one is better at making something positive happen. He and wide receiver/passer Antwaan Randle El and Ward came up with big plays, and a Super Bowl victory will look good on Roethlisberger's resume when he completes a career that holds great promise. None of us had any idea at the time how precarious Big Ben's career status might be. That's another story.

Hines Ward had wept openly the year before after Bettis had spoken to the team after the disappointing loss to the Patriots, and revealed his retirement plans. Ward wanted Bettis to go out a winner. He had such great admiration for this beloved teammate who had taught him the ropes in his early years with the team.

Cowher had begun every one of his previous 13 seasons saying the team's goal was to win the Super Bowl. Nothing less would be satisfactory. No matter what the Steelers did, Cowher would say, "We haven't accomplished anything yet." At times it seemed he had set an unfair standard for himself and his troops.

He had gotten them to the Super Bowl once before, during the 1995 season, but the Steelers came up on the short end of the score against the Dallas Cowboys. I traveled to and from Arizona with the Steelers' party and I saw their disappointment up close. I had covered the Steelers in 1980 when they won their fourth Super Bowl in six years and I knew the stark contrast in the post-game interview rooms. The Steelers had lost three AFC championship games, and Cowher's critics pointed to those setbacks when expressing their disappointment in his overall performance. The Steelers were nearly always a contender under Cowher, except for the 1998 and 1999 seasons, but they had never won the Lombardi Trophy.

Cowher had grown up in nearby Crafton when Chuck Noll's teams won four Super Bowl titles in as many tries during the decade

Mike Longo

of the '70s. He knew that many Pittsburghers thought the Super Bowl was the last game on the Steelers' schedule.

Cowher said he never viewed the Steelers' legacy as a personal burden. "All we've tried to do is build on it," said Cowher. "We're in the second generation of the '70s fan base that was created with all the championships. We love that. We love going on the road and going to all the hotels and seeing the people sitting there. Those were the kids who followed the teams of the '70s, and they have their kids now.

"It's not being in the shadows. It's a privilege to be able to say, 'We did it our way, too.' I think it's been very motivating."

In the aftermath of the Steelers' Super Bowl victory the citizens of Crafton wanted to show their "Billy" how much they appreciated his achievements. They named an alley after him — Cowher Way — in his old neighborhood. They had already retired his football number at Carlynton High School.

The Steelers had to win their last four games of the regular season to qualify for the final wild-card spot in the playoffs. Then they had to beat the three top-seeded teams out there, with every game on the road, to win the championship. It's how they did it that makes it such a great accomplishment. It's why the town went wild in celebration of their feat.

Beating the Colts in Indianapolis was the key. Noll always said it didn't pay to play the what-if game. But what if?

What if Colts' defensive back Nick Harper had gone all the way with that Jerome Bettis fumble at the Colts' goal line in the late going of that game? What if Roethlisberger doesn't make that desperate shoestring tackle of Harper? His wife had stabbed Harper in the leg with a knife on the eve of the contest. Wouldn't he have been a great hero for the NFL to hail that week?

What if Colts kicker Mike Vanderjagt doesn't miss the game-tying field goal with seconds remaining? Do you think Pittsburgh fans would still be screaming about the interception by Troy Polamalu that was disallowed by an official's call? There are so many memorable moments like that, good and bad, that Steelers' fans will never forget. It was that kind of season, that kind of playoff series, that kind of Super Bowl.

The Steelers' highlight film for the 2005 season was entitled "Road To Glory," not exactly original, but fitting. There were two special moments involving Bettis that were captured in the film. In one segment, second-year running back Willie Parker is helmet to helmet with Bettis and saying, "This is your last stop. I want to say thank you. You made me what I am, which isn't much. I learned from you."

In another mushy moment, Roethlisberger is hugging Bettis and talking in his ear. "Thank you for everything you've done for me. I love you, Bussie."

The Cowboys were once known as "America's Team," but it appeared that the Steelers had stolen that role with the 2005 edition.

TV ratings were at a near-record level for the Steelers' post-season games.

"If anyone turned in a script to Hollywood like this," said Bettis, "it would get turned back. It was too unbelievable."

Others referred to it as a "dream come true" and "the ultimate thrill." It was more like a children's fairy tale.

It began with a journey. The destination was Detroit. The Steelers had played in the first NFL game ever played at Ford Field in Detroit, in the pre-season opener in 2004. When you refer to Ford Field, at least for a Pittsburgher, it sounds like Forbes Field. That's where it all started for the Steelers in 1933.

That's where they played in 1963, my senior year at the University of Pittsburgh, and Forbes Field was just two blocks away from the William Pitt Student Union. That was Andy Russell's rookie season and we share stories about it all the time. The Steelers came this close to winning the NFL East crown that season, but their quarterback Ed Brown had come apart in the final game against the Giants in New York. That was as close as the Steelers would get to any kind of championship game until Chuck Noll came to town in 1969.

Buddy Parker had talked grizzled veteran quarterback Bobby Layne into retiring after the 1962 season, and some thought that Layne could have led the Steelers to a championship if he had stayed for one more season. Parker and Layne had won NFL championships in Detroit before they brought their act to Pittsburgh.

The Steelers have a storied history. They were losers most of the time until Parker and Noll made them more respectable. They were always a tough team, and they were always Pittsburgh's team. They represented the city well. Fans often asked me how I would compare the Steelers' latest Super Bowl team to the Steelers of the '70s. My answer is that you can't compare the teams. It's a different game today. Great athletes meet the test of their times. No one should attempt to compare them until these Steelers win three more Super Bowl titles.

At the same time, I tell everyone that there are just as many good guys on this team as there were on the teams of that decade when Pittsburgh was hailed as "The City of Champions."

That's what is so appealing about these Steelers. There are a lot of good guys on this team. People like them. For the most part, they are good role models. They care about the fans and the community. They do their part to help wherever they can help. They do a lot of positive things in the city and its surrounding environs.

A fan only has to look across the state to the Philadelphia Eagles and see how one bad apple — take Terrell Owens, for instance — can spoil the whole barrel. One bad actor can tear a team apart.

Steelers' chairman of the board Dan Rooney believes the Steelers try to do it right and look for the right people to accomplish their lofty goals.

11

Rooney had to be wondering how the Steelers' No. 1 draft pick, wide receiver Santonio Holmes of Ohio State, managed to be arrested twice for off-the-field incidents in May and June. It didn't look good.

This is not a book about the games of the Steelers' super season. Others have produced those books. This is a book of stories and tales about these Steelers, and others associated with the team, that provides a broader picture of what this team means to Pittsburgh.

I've always been more interested in the people who play the games, more than the games themselves. What can we learn from these Steelers? That's what this book is about. It's about the Steelers who have the right stuff, Steeler stuff. Some of them were so honest in the stories they offered about themselves and their upbringing.

Among other things, we learned that it's okay for men to cry, it's okay for men to embrace one another. It's good to care and to share. It's important to be positive and pleasant, to set goals and go after them with all your heart and soul. It's important to count one's blessings and to be grateful for what others do for us. Try to smile more often. It's unlikely you can do many of the things that Jerome Bettis and Ben Roethlisberger and Antwaan Randle El and Hines Ward can do on a football field, but they've shown us the importance of a smile, a simple smile.

I watched this Super Bowl on television in my family room at my home in Upper St. Clair. My friend Myron Cope, who had retired as the Steelers' analyst and color man after the 2004 season, watched the game on television in his town house in neighboring Mt. Lebanon. The Steelers had invited him to go with them to Detroit, but he declined because of precarious health. I had traveled with the Steelers to Super Bowls twice before, once when they won their fourth Super Bowl in Pasadena, California and once when they lost a Super Bowl in Tempe, Arizona. I'd been to seven Super Bowls altogether.

I was tempted to attend the parade that celebrated the Steelers' Super Bowl triumph. But it seemed a little on the cool side when I stepped outside my door. I decided to watch it on television, and I am sure I got to see more of what went on than any of the estimated 200,000 fans who filled downtown Pittsburgh that Tuesday afternoon in February.

Then I decided to go to Atria's Restaurant & Tavern in Mt. Lebanon, hoping I'd catch some friends who'd gone downtown and would stop there on the way home to celebrate the Steelers' victory once more. When I got there, someone behind the bar informed me that Myron Cope was in the back room. He was watching the victory parade on TV with a friend.

There was something wrong with this picture. Had the parade passed us by? When the Steelers turned to playing basketball during the winter months and when they resumed their workouts in the spring I started visiting them and interviewing them. People really liked this team, its personalities, and I wanted to learn more about them. I wanted to find out what I had missed. I was not disappointed when I got up close and personal with them. We can be proud of these Pittsburgh Steelers. They've got the right stuff, Steeler stuff.

Aaron Smith
Determined to succeed in life

"I was completely lost my first year."

Aaron Smith said on Thursday that we could talk after practice on Friday. That was Friday, May 19, 2006. It was the third and final day of a mini-camp at the Steelers' South Side complex. The Steelers were scheduled to be on the field at the indoor training center from 9 a.m. till 10:15 a.m. That was nearly two hours earlier than they had practiced the previous two days.

Many of the players and coaches had committed to playing in two charity-related golf outings that Friday, a cool, dank day with temperatures in the 50s and the threat of more rain, not the best conditions for a fun golf outing. Former Steelers star Andy Russell was hosting his 30th Annual Celebrity Classic at The Club at Nevillewood and Diamond Run, while Marc Bulger, the Pittsburgh-bred quarterback (Central Catholic) of the St. Louis Rams, was hosting an outing at the Fox Chapel Golf Club.

I planned on getting to the practice facility around 10 a.m., so I could catch the tail end of the workout. That would suffice. Watching football practice is not my idea of morning entertainment. Most of the media spend the time exchanging rumors and complaints.

I recall a story about another Smith that sheds light on that observation. Chester L. Smith, the late sports editor of *The Pittsburgh Press*. He was near the end of a long and distinguished career when I was a student at the University of Pittsburgh in the early '60s. I helped him in the press box at several Pitt games, including a contest against Army at Yankee Stadium. He smoked cigarettes and swapped stories in rapid fashion.

Chester L. Smith was talking to the sports information director at Penn State University prior to a trip to State College and they were reviewing the agenda. The SID said something about attending practice on Friday afternoon. "Practice?" said Smith. "I'll go if you can tell me they're going to do something that hasn't been done at every other football practice in history."

Of course, Smith also once wrote that he wouldn't watch the college basketball championship game if they played it outside his bedroom window. "I'd close the blinds," wrote Smith.

It had been my experience, however, that if you watch practice closely enough you will see something you can use in a story to give it some immediacy, to make sure the readers (and your sports editor) knew you were there.

When I showed up to see Aaron Smith this Friday, however, the indoor facility was nearly empty. I should have known better. Bill Cowher has a habit of cutting the last practice of any session shorter

than advertised. That's one of the reasons his players call him "a player's coach."

Cowher and his assistants had put the players through some stretching exercises and dismissed most of them after twenty minutes. Some of the rookies and free agents were kept on the field to review some of the stuff they'd been introduced to the previous two days. They were still confused by the nomenclature, the numbers and colors and calls.

And Aaron Smith was still on the field. He was working with some of the new defensive linemen, helping them through a walk-through session. "I remember how difficult it was for me at my first camp," said Smith. "I was completely lost that entire first year. If I had been the coach I'd have cut myself. I'd come from a Division II college environment and just wasn't prepared for what I encountered here."

That scene showed the real Aaron Smith. So checking out the practice scene can be worthwhile. Smith could empathize with what the new guys were going through, and he wanted to help them. That's Smith's style. He remembered how helpful Kimo von Oelhoffen had been with him when he joined the Steelers in Smith's second season back in 2000.

Now von Oelhoffen, one of the most popular players on the team, was gone, signing as a free agent with the New York Jets. Jerome Bettis, the team leader, had retired to the broadcast booth. The Steelers needed new leaders and a lot of them to fill the void. Smith was stepping forward.

I didn't know much about Aaron Douglas Smith except that he was a solid, not sensational, starter at left end on the Steelers' three-four defensive alignment. He had been a starter since his second season and was preparing for his eighth season with the Steelers. He had been a big contributor to the Steelers' Super Bowl XL success story.

He had come a long way since he reported to St. Vincent College for summer training camp after being the Steelers' fourth round draft choice in 1999. He had come an even longer way from where he started, growing up under difficult circumstances in a trailer camp in Colorado Springs, Colorado.

He had signed a six-year contract in July of 2002 and seemed to have a secure status with the Steelers. Of course, all the players worry about what the future holds for them in professional athletics. "I've got to make the team and keep my job," said Smith. "That's my first goal."

I checked the Steelers' press guide before I went to see Smith at the Steelers' training complex, hoping to find some story possibilities. None jumped off the pages.

He was listed at 6-5, 298 pounds. He had gone to Northern Colorado, a small college in Greeley, Colorado. That community was named after Horace Greeley, a legendary newspaperman famous for saying, "Go west, young man."

14

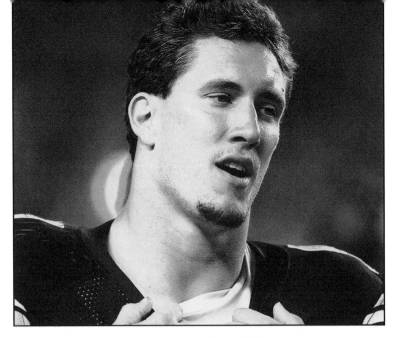

Aaron Smith

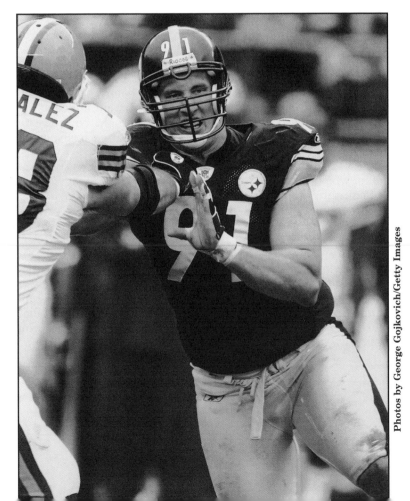

Photos by George Gojkovich/Getty Images

At Northern Colorado, Aaron Smith was a consensus Division II first-team All-American selection. He was the Most Valuable Defensive Lineman in the All-North Conference. He starred in basketball as well as football at Sierra High School and was all-conference in both sports. I had seen him playing for the Steelers' basketball team in earlier years and knew he had ability on the hardwood. "It was my first love," he said, "but I quit playing because I didn't want to risk an injury."

He was married to Jaimie and they had a daughter, Ellaina, who was four years old, and a son, Elijah, who was 2½. Smith told me they were expecting another daughter in early June.

There was nothing in the guidebook to spark a story idea. I didn't know what we were going to talk about, frankly. He had seemed friendly to me when we spoke a few days earlier, and that would help.

He joined me in the dining area of the Steelers' complex, one where the Pitt people next door also dine. It's also open to businesses nearby on a pay-as-you-go basis in order to maintain a year-round restaurant facility.

Smith wore the same kind of black T-shirt that Max Starks had worn the day before. He wore black shorts and black open-toed sandals. When he finished eating, he propped his feet up on the next chair to relax a little. He had many stories to share and he wanted to get comfortable.

Smith has brown hair, blue-gray eyes, and a wispy beard. His face is long and theatrical. It goes back and forth from looking sad to happy, kind of like the story of his life. He is thought to be a quiet guy.

I suggested that Smith tell me his story. He said he had shared his story at the same site just the night before with Pittsburgh businessmen. It's an annual "Here's My Story" event aimed at getting the Steelers introduced to businessmen who might be interested in employing them in some manner on a moonlighting basis, or during the so-called off-season.

Midway through my conversation with Smith I was aware that this man, who had turned 30 only a month (April 9) earlier, was being more forthright than most interview subjects. He was sharing the most personal of stories. I felt like a cross between a priest in a confession box or a 5 cents psychiatrist like Charlie Brown in the "Peanuts" cartoon.

Smith is definitely an old-fashioned rags to riches story, an inspiration for anyone who experienced a difficult childhood. He was driving a Cadillac he'd bought at Baierl Cadillac in Wexford, near where Smith lives. "I think anyone who has ever accomplished anything," said Smith when we were about to part company following an hour-and-a-half interview, "had to overcome some kind of adversity."

> *"Every payday is a good payday."*
> — **Rocky Bleier**

"I have lots of stories. How big is this book?"

Aaron Smith:

There are so many different facets to my life. My father was a construction worker — a dry-wall worker — and my mother was a nurse at a nursing home. She didn't make much money. My dad worked off and on, nothing regular. He'd work six months and then be out of work for six months. It was hit and miss. We lived in a trailer park. We were the family that got the Christmas turkeys, the government cheese, welfare coupons. Things were often tough.

Sometimes we had money; sometimes we didn't.

I was the youngest of four boys. So I had three older brothers to tag after. We lived, at first, in the Meadows Trailer Court in Colorado Springs. The Air Force Academy is in that city.

The funny thing about being poor is that you never knew you were poor until you went off to college. My dad was a diabetic. There was a long time when he was quite sick. He didn't take proper care of his diabetes. He was grumpy and irritable a whole lot. He was physically and verbally abusive. I didn't realize our family had problems. I can't remember when my father wasn't swearing at us. We were at the southern end of Colorado Springs so I didn't know anything different. I thought it was the American way.

You can talk to Kendall Simmons. He has diabetes and he can tell you that there are days he just feels lousy because of his diabetes.

My dad ended up losing his big toe on his right foot because of the diabetes. Later, he lost half his foot. Then he lost his right leg and he was having problems with his left leg as well. He was always home and he was miserable. He was always yelling and screaming, like it was our fault he felt so bad. My dad was a big man, 6-4, 280 pounds, and he towered over us then.

I was 12 when my mother divorced my dad. I remember that my mom called my oldest brother, David, and had him get all the firearms out of the house before she told my dad what she was doing. She was worried about what he might do. He scared all of us.

When I was eight, nine and ten I was so angry with my father. I told him every night I loved him because I was afraid he'd kill us, and I thought maybe he'd spare me if I told him I loved him. I slept with a baseball bat in my bed in case I needed to protect myself.

17

When my mother left my dad my brothers put their money together and bought her a Pinto for $100. It didn't have a defroster so you had to put a blanket over the window at night in the winter to keep the snow off the window. We had a space heater in the car. My brother Kevin spray-painted "The Beast" on one of the doors. Once the car went over 40 miles an hour it began to rattle like crazy.

You know what, though, I have to smile when I'm telling you this story. I have some good memories about that, to be honest. We moved to another trailer court. It was next to the trailer court where my father had his trailer. The new one was called the Candlelight Court, I think.

Life was fun there. There were always kids to play with. We couldn't afford much stuff, but there were always people out there playing.

My dad's name was Harold Smith. He died when I was 16. He had a heart attack and died in bed. He died alone. I saw him four to six months before he died. I went to my grandmother's house for some family function, and he was there. He stood up to hug me and I walked right past him. Talk about guilt. I thought about that for a long time after he died.

I played basketball by myself a lot. Other kids would shoot with their dads, but I'd be by myself, or with my brothers. I used to ask, "Why do I have a father? Why do I have the father I've got? Why wasn't my father interested in me? He never came to any of my games.

"My dad was never there."

Now that I'm a husband and father I am determined to be different than my dad. That's a big concern. I think I do a good job as a husband and father. There are days I get home tired at five, and my kids want to play. I'll go downstairs and sit in the middle of the playroom. I just want to be there. My dad was never there.

My wife Jaimie is from Frederick, Colorado. It's a small town. There were probably 50 in her graduating class in high school. She knows all my stories. She knows my concerns.

None of my kids ever met my father. I regret that I never got to tell him about my success or about my family. My daughter asks me about my dad. What am I going to tell her? I search for some good thoughts.

Then I get angry with him all over again. I have nieces and nephews and my father could have had such a wonderful life if he had looked at things differently.

When I came home from school I would take a longer route so I wouldn't have to pass my father's trailer court. I didn't want to see him. I've forgiven my father and myself for the whole thing. My faith has helped me in that respect.

My wife knows everything I went through. She's my redeeming factor. She's the only reason I'm going to make it to heaven. She's going to keep me straight.

I try to help other kids where I can. I'm involved with Urban Impact Foundation. They're headquartered on Union Avenue on the North Side, and nearby is the Allegheny Center Alliance Church on East Ohio Street. They have a lot of sports programs to keep the kids occupied and to get them off the streets. They get something to eat there and they hear the word of God. They have something going on six days a week.

I remember how lucky I was to have coaches and counselors when I was a kid. I didn't have any of these crazy coaches you read about now. These were good moral men and they taught me things that helped me grow.

My older brothers helped me, too. Dave is 39 now. He's married and has two kids. My brother Stephan is 36 and he's raising two boys. He's divorced. Brother Kevin is 35, and he has a son and daughter. He's divorced, too. So I guess they made some of the same mistakes. But they helped raise me, and I'm grateful for that. I love them and their families.

When I was a teenager I started to realize that our family situation was different from most other kids' experiences. Other kids had better clothes and sneakers than I did. They had Nikes and I was wearing something we got at Payless. I was wearing Pro Wing Eagles, and mine had holes in them. I was a tall, lanky kid, one of the biggest in the class, so it wasn't easy for me to hide or get lost in the crowd. The adidas models had three stripes and my Trek models had five or six stripes. The guys got a big joke out of my shoes. They were fake adidas. It doesn't seem important now but it was then.

I can recall one of the most shameful moments in my life. After my parents had separated, my dad came to one of my basketball games. He didn't want to see me. I knew my mother would be there and he wanted to confront her.

He came in wearing an all-orange jump suit, his hunting attire. He looked like a big orange. We were beating this team when my dad walks into the gym. My teammates didn't know he was my dad — he'd never come to any of my other games — and they started pointing at him and laughing about his outfit. I never said, "Hey, that's my dad." I didn't want them to know he was my dad. I didn't speak up.

I wasn't happy with him, but he was still my father. I should have said something. It was like that scene out of the movie "Hoosiers" where one of the player's dad (played by

Dennis Hopper), who helps coach the team, shows up drunk and makes a fool of himself.

Hey, I can tell you so many stories. How big is this book?

"We'd never gone on any vacations."

When I got to college at Northern Colorado, I found out that people came from different backgrounds. I learned that people went on vacations to nice places. We'd never gone on any vacations.

I was 6-5, 200 pounds when I reported to college. I was red-shirted my freshman year. I was eating more food and I put on 40 pounds my first year. I had never lifted a weight before I got there. I worked hard and believed in my ability. In my sophomore season, I beat out the guy who was in front of me and I started for four years. We won two national championships, and I was drafted in the fourth round.

When I went to college I was undersized but I was successful. When I went to the pros I was undersized. I was about 275 to 280 at the start, not as big as most defensive linemen in the National Football League.

My first year with the Steelers was strictly a learning experience. My roommate was Kris Farris, an offensive tackle from UCLA, and we both worried about our status. I went home every night that year figuring my days with the Steelers might be numbered. I felt like I was the worst player ever to be with the Steelers. I refused to give up. I had mental toughness. I think I've always had mental toughness. That's gotten me through a lot of challenges.

I held out two days for an extra $10,000 before I signed. I had missed the conditioning workouts. I was sitting in my apartment out near Ross Park Mall while I was holding out and I heard that Jamain Stephens had been cut after they had the players run around the field in the conditioning test the first day. He had been a No. 1 draft choice (in 1996). That got my attention. I called my agent. Peter Schaffer, and said, "Get it done; I want to sign. I want to be at camp."

When I got in I had so much to learn. I had played in a 4-3 defense at Northern Colorado. Now I had to learn to play in a 3-4 set. I'd never lined up inside a tackle before. I was going up against the likes of Dermontti Dawson, Bredan Stai, Roger Duffy and Jim Sweeney. Jim Sweeney helped me so much that year. He gave me advice. He had the strongest hands I've ever encountered.

I had a lot of bad days at St.Vincent. I had plenty of them. I felt completely lost. I'd come back from lunch and I'd see my

coaches — Jim Haslett and John Mitchell — coming toward me from the opposite direction. I'd run and hide so they wouldn't see me. I'd dodge them. They were on me 24/7. Haslett told me once that he would never draft anyone out of Northern Colorado. He said I was soft. He said some other things, too, but I won't repeat them. I like Coach Haslett and we're fine with each other now. Same with Coach Mitchell. They were playing mind games with me.

I can appreciate their approach now. They were trying to motivate me. They must have seen something worth salvaging that first season.

That's why I stayed out with the young guys today. I remember how awkward it is. We were out about an extra 40 minutes. I was with Lee Vicher, Scott Paxon, Oren Harris and Sean Nua. Yes, I know their names.

Brett Keisel and I are supposed to be the starting ends this year, with Kimo gone. Keisel and I have very similar personalities. He's a good basketball player, too. I used to like to play with the guys, but it got a little too dangerous. Too much at risk. But basketball was definitely my first love.

I was a Hawks fan when I was a kid. I loved Dominique Wilkins and Spud Webb. They were both spectacular players and were the best dunkers in the league. One was tall and one was small, but both could fly. People think when you drive a Cadillac you've got it made. People say that going to the Pro Bowl or the Super Bowl are life changing events. I feel the same. I think I disappoint people when I don't talk more about the Super Bowl. That's what they want to hear.

But those are not life changing events, as far as I'm concerned. Marrying my wife was a life-changing event. Having our children were life changing events.

I'll probably wear my Super Bowl ring once and now I've put it away. I wear my wedding band all the time, except when I'm on the football field. I was telling Lee Vikkers that if you're not motivated when you have a child then you're never going to be motivated. Having a kid makes you want to go the extra distance. You want to be able to give them a good life.

My outlook now is to go out there and keep my job. That's my first priority. Then I want to help the Steelers win some games.

We have a great situation here at our training complex. When we were at Three Rivers Stadium we had no windows. It was like working in a cave. We never knew if the sun was shining or not until we went out onto the field.

You don't see the sun that often in Pittsburgh to begin with, so you want every opportunity to enjoy it. This makes a difference in your day. Pittsburgh can be gray. We were so depressed when we first got here. You didn't see the sun for a

month. We love it now. This is our home. When I'm finished playing football, we want to live here. I want to raise my children here. I wouldn't change anything about my life. I made some mistakes. But my background is who I am today. My mother is coming to live with us. Her name is Ruth and she's 59. She'll be 60 in August. We have plenty of room for her.

With a third child on the way, my wife can use some help. My kids will get to enjoy having a grandmother around. That's part of the bigger picture. It's their heritage. It gives them a foundation. My wife and I had a home in Colorado for three years, but we got tired of moving back and forth. Now we've sunk some roots here. I'm optimistic about our future.

Jim O'Brien

Aaron Smith takes a break during summer camp session at St. Vincent College in Latrobe.

Books By Jim O'Brien

COMPLETE HANDBOOK OF PRO BASKETBALL 1970-1971

COMPLETE HANDBOOK OF PRO BASKETBALL 1971-1972

ABA ALL-STARS

PITTSBURGH: THE STORY OF THE CITY OF CHAMPIONS

HAIL TO PITT: A SPORTS HISTORY OF
THE UNIVERSITY OF PITTSBURGH

DOING IT RIGHT

WHATEVER IT TAKES

MAZ AND THE '60 BUCS

REMEMBER ROBERTO

PENGUIN PROFILES

DARE TO DREAM

KEEP THE FAITH

WE HAD 'EM ALL THE WAY

HOMETOWN HEROES

GLORY YEARS

THE CHIEF

STEELERS FOREVER

ALWAYS A STEELER

WITH LOVE AND PRIDE

LAMBERT: THE MAN IN THE MIDDLE

FANTASY CAMP

STEELER STUFF

To order copies of these titles directly from the publisher, send $26.95 for hardcover edition. Please send additional $3.50 to cover shipping and handling charges per book. Pennsylvania residents add 6% sales tax to price of book only. Allegheny County residents add an additional 1% sales tax for a total of 7% sales tax. Copies will be signed by author at your request. Discounts available for large orders. Contact publisher regarding availability and prices of all books in Pittsburgh Proud series, or to request an order form. Some books are sold out and no longer available. You can still order the following: Doing It Right, We Had 'Em All The Way, Hometown Heroes, Glory Years, The Chief, Lambert, With Love and Pride and Fantasy Camp.

Steeler Stuff

STORIES ABOUT A CHAMPIONSHIP SEASON AND A REMARKABLE JOURNEY

By Jim O'Brien

Jim O'Brien

Max Starks
He speaks from his heart

*"I like to be involved in good causes,
and help where I can be of service."*

Outlined against a blue-gray late May sky, Max Starks cast quite a shadow across the driving pad at the 14th hole of the Southpointe Golf Club in the Washington County community of Canonsburg, just over 20 miles south of downtown Pittsburgh and Heinz Field. Starks is 6-8, about 340 pounds and is the biggest Steeler of them all. He is the team's starting right offensive tackle.

Grantland Rice began a newspaper column like that once and created the legend of "the four Horsemen of Notre Dame." Granny would have liked Max Starks, who was bigger than any of those four famous football players in South Bend. The quarterback of Knute Rockne's team was Harry Stuhdreher, who became a successful executive at U.S. Steel in Pittsburgh and stood about 5-8.

Elmer Layden, one of the Four Horsemen and later the football coach at Fordham and Duquesne, wrote in his memoirs in 1969, "We were small by 1924 standards. We were almost midgets by today's standards."

Let it be said, that standing next to the likes of Max Starks, Marvel Smith and Alan Faneca, the Four Horsemen were midgets.

I first met Stuhdreher when he spoke at a Curbstone Coaches luncheon at the Roosevelt Hotel in the early '60s. I was a student at Pitt at the time. The Steelers' offices were in the Roosevelt Hotel back then and team owner Art Rooney was a regular at the Curbstone Coaches.

I first met Max Starks at the luncheon program of the Coaches Corner, which is what the Curbstone Coaches evolved into during the '90s. Starks spoke at the luncheon co-sponsored by Iron City Brewery and KDKA-TV as a rookie and made a positive impression on everyone. I spoke to Starks afterward and told him how good he'd been. He remembered that when I spoke to him this time around. Starks is an engaging, pleasant fellow and, better yet, a fine public speaker. He was demonstrating these same qualities in the best-ball outing on the tight, challenging course just off I-79 on the outskirts of Canonsburg.

Starks was wearing a chartreuse golf shirt, beige slacks he constantly hitched up, and had something to say to everyone he encountered along the way.

Canonsburg is best known as the birthplace of singers Perry Como and Bobby Vinton. Southpointe was just a green pasture around Western Center, a state mental hospital, when they were growing up.

Now it is a successful industrial park and includes Iceoplex, the practice facility of the Pittsburgh Penguins, as well as a beautiful 18-hole golf course. Sarris Chocolates is close by, and Frank and Athena Sarris have a beautiful home at Southpointe.

Many of the Pittsburgh Steelers were playing golf on a break during what are called "voluntary coaching sessions" at the Steelers' practice facility on Pittsburgh's South Side.

Starks was leaning on his driver while one of the members of the foursome he was accompanying on this Monday, May 22, 2006 was getting set to tee off. This was a break in his football routine as he prepared for his third season with the Steelers.

His heart is as big as his body. His name was on the banner back at the clubhouse for the Hoge-Starks-Ward Celebrity Golf Classic. He replaced Mark Bruener two years earlier when Bruener was released by the Steelers and signed with the expansion Houston Texans.

Starks and Ward were mainly responsible for rounding up teammates, including star quarterback Ben Roethlisberger, to come out to Canonsburg for a day of golf and community service. Since 1994, this event has raised over $2 million, including matching funds from Highmark Blue Cross Blue Shield of the Highmark Caring Foundation. These funds have provided hundreds of children with health care coverage, and offered hope and healing to children and families grieving the loss of a loved one.

Starks had made several appearances at the Highmark Caring Place in downtown Pittsburgh, in the old Hornes Building near the Gateway Center. The Southpointe Golf Club is managed by Jack Piatt III, son of the Jack Piatt who developed Southpointe and whose Millcraft Corporation had just been charged by Mayor Bob O'Connor to lend his golden touch to turning around the Fifth-Forbes Avenues Corridor in yet another renaissance for downtown Pittsburgh.

Max Starks has made a difference in his short stay with the Steelers. A year earlier he established a fund to promote childhood literacy and education at The Pittsburgh Foundation. He was only 23 at the time and one of the youngest ever to create such a fund.

Reading and speaking well are subjects close to Max Starks. He credits his mother, Eleanor Starks, for making sure he learned how to read early and emphasizing the need to know good grammar and express himself well. Max Starks is a huge monument to his mother's mission.

Max Starks is a great mixer, and knows how to engage people in conversation. One of the volunteers at the 12th hole had told him, "You're my second favorite Steeler, right behind Hines Ward. You both have such great smiles."

Starks smiled in response to the compliment. Ward is known for his constant smile, but Starks actually has a bigger smile than Ward.

Starks was wearing a dark blue ballcap with the USO logo on the front of it. During the previous month, Starks had gone on a 12-day USO Tour of U.S. military bases in Afghanistan and the Peninsula Gulf.

24

Max Starks has souvenir ballcap from his USO-sponsored trip to visit with troops in Mideast.

Max Starks

Photos by George Gojkovich/Getty Images

"There were Terrible Towels; there were flags; there were banners; it was unbelievable," Starks said upon his return to the States. "In Kosovo, on one of their helicopters, there is a Steelers logo painted on the belly that I got to autograph. It was pretty profound. It was very memorable for me."

In mid-April, Starks visited the USS Theodore Roosevelt stationed in the Atlantic Ocean, and was on the USS Ronald Reagan, the Navy's newest Nimitz-class nuclear-powered aircraft carrier that departed San Diego on its maiden deployment back in January.

"I truly appreciate what the armed forces are doing," said Starks. "Especially the Navy, giving air support to our men and women in Iraq and Afghanistan and in the Gulf region. It's really an honor to meet and interact with these men and women and sailors."

Starks went on the USO Tour with two other National Football League performers, defensive tackle Bryce Fisher of the Seattle Seahawks and defensive end Patrick Kerney of the Atlanta Falcons.

Starks serves on several boards of community service activities, and has to be one of the busiest Steelers in that regard. "Our guys are pretty good when it comes to giving back," said Michelle Rosenthal, in her second year as the first full-time community relations director for the Steelers. "Max does more than his share. He's great to work with."

I shared a ride with Max Starks for seven holes at the golf outing. He was the driver. I made one stipulation, asking him to drive carefully so he wouldn't turn over the golf cart. "And if you do, don't tip it over on my side," I said. The thought of a spill, with all 6-8, 340 pounds of Max Starks landing on me was a scary one." He smiled and said, "I promise to be careful." He did take a few curves on the cart path too fast, but did so with a smile on his face, assuring me that all was well.

As he squeezed his legs past the steering wheel to play one hole, he offered, "Getting in and out of the golf cart is the toughest part of me playing golf." All that green stuff gets to him at times, and he had a few sneezing fits.

Starks was playing with a foursome sponsored by UPMC and hosted by Mark Disco, who lettered in basketball in 1974-75, with teammates such as Billy Knight, Tom Richards, Jim Bolla, Keith Starr and Mickey Martin. "I was from Sherman, New York, a country boy, and everybody else was from western Pennsylvania." Disco is 6-8, 220, a leaner version of Max Starks. "He's easy to be with," Disco declared of Starks. "He's at ease and comfortable with everybody."

When Starks met his foursome, he warned them, "I just play golf. I'm not a golfer. I won't be on the PGA Tour any time soon."

When I asked Starks about his engaging manner, he said, "They remember your kindness. You never know when that person might be able to help you, when the tables are turned."

Starks said he had been playing golf since he was eight years old, but you wouldn't know it. He either crushes the ball, sending it to distant and disparate places, or he miss-hits and sends it scurrying

26

through the grass. He's a heavyweight hacker all the way, with divots as big as his size-19 black and white golf shoes.

He told me he also served on the board of Gateway Rehabilitation. I was familiar with its founder, Dr. Abraham Twerski, a Jewish rabbi and licensed psychiatrist. "Dr. Kenneth Ramsey is the president of Gateway," said Starks. "I saw his son, Major Jeff Ramsey, when I was on the USO Tour. I'm involved with a youth services project at Gateway. I've had counseling training, and I was an arbitrator to settle student disputes when I was in high school. I'm an honorary chairman for Community Partners which has a concert with the Pittsburgh Symphony. We're bringing The Temptations to Pittsburgh for a concert. I'm also with Nine Over Ninth, another community project. I'm on the board of directors."

He was also rehabilitating a knee injury. "I tore the lateral meniscus, and had to have arthroscopic surgery to repair the damage. It's coming along pretty good," said Starks.

I told Max Starks he was an inspiration. After watching him play golf, I thought I might get back to the game. I worried about not playing well, and making a fool of myself. Max Starks showed me that you shouldn't take yourself too seriously on a golf course.

"I get serious when I'm on the football field," he said. "I play right tackle and Ben likes to roll out to my side. He favors that side, so I have to keep him clean. It's a tough assignment, especially the way Ben moves around a lot. When I fail to do my job, he is never negative about it. He'll say 'Get 'em next time,' and that's what I try to do."

On the 17th hole, one sponsored coincidentally by Max & Erma's Restaurants, which had a food station just outside of the club house to provide lunch for everyone, Starks struck a mighty blow off the tee and sent his Nike One Platinum ball (for greater distance) straight down the center of the fairway. It was the ball everyone in the fivesome would hit next.

"Man, I felt like Barry Bonds on that one!" Starks sighed. He slipped a pinch of Skoal, the Apple Blend brand, under his lower lip and allowed a satisfied smile to crease his dark mustache and goatee. "It only takes one great shot to make your day. Or save the day."

His next shot was close to the pin. "You're looking like Tiger Woods," I suggested.

"I don't think so," Starks smiled back, "but thanks anyhow."

Max Starks was definitely enjoying his day off.

Starks is single. "There'll be no children until I get married," he promised. He grew up in Orlando, Florida. He made his first trip to Disney World when he was four years old, when he also started helping his mother at the family funeral home.

"You learn compassion, how to be mature in the face of adversity," he said. "You know you're helping someone at their lowest point."

That's also why he was such a perfect fit for The Caring Foundation and The Caring Place.

He began at age 4, dressed in a gray suit and a red Hawaiian shirt, by passing out programs to mourners at the family's funeral home. He later ushered visitors, served as a pallbearer if they were short of escorts, and drove the hearse. At 14, he and his brother Justin started their own gravestone business to make spending money.

In grade school, Starks was a patrolboy, wearing a badge and directing his schoolmates across busy streets. He won the American Legion Award as the top student in middle school. In high school, he tutored students at low-achieving schools in the city.

At the University of Florida, where he gained All-America second-team honors, Starks visited sick children, read to students and collected school supplies for students. "He always was a helper," said his mother, Eleanor Starks. Max Starks sounds almost too good to be true. Max credits his mother and his aunt, Ida Muorie, as the biggest influences in his life.

A third round draft choice, Starks wears the same number, 78, as former Steelers' standout Dwight White. It was White who introduced Starks to the Pittsburgh Foundation. White is a friend of Bill Trueheart, the foundation CEO.

"I'm very impressed with Max," said White, managing director of the Pittsburgh office of Mesirow Financial Services. "He has a maturity about him that you don't find in a lot of kids his age. He has a plan."

I had interviewed Starks the previous week following a practice session at the Steelers/UPMC Training Complex. He sat in the cafeteria, working on a Chef Salad as he spoke. I told him he had the biggest Afro I had seen since the ABA days of Dr. J and Darnell Hillman. I didn't know if he'd recognize those names or not.

"I played basketball with Darryl Dawkins after he had played in the NBA and was retired," said Starks. "We played at Lake Lorna Doone Park. I know he had an Afro in his playing days. He came out of high school in Orlando to play pro ball and I know he was a teammate of Dr. J (Julius Erving) in Philadelphia. Dawkins ("Chocolate Thunder" and "Dr. Dunk" were two of his many nicknames) could still dunk with the best of them when I was playing as a high school kid. I met Artis Gilmore, who played in the ABA and NBA after he came out of Jacksonville."

Max Starks:

"I think God has a specific purpose for all of us."

I was impressed with all the people I met on that USO Tour. It was interesting to see the different approaches and attitudes depending on whether they were in a peacekeeping mission in

Kosovo, or in a real hot spot like the Mideast. A lot of the guys want to be in it. They've gone over there to defend our country and free the civilians from oppression. They are doing humanitarian efforts. It's not just conquer and destroy. They are helping the people there to become self-sufficient and to establish a democratic government with free elections. Some of the guys just want to go home; they feel like they've been there long enough.

I'm glad I went. I think God has a specific purpose for all of us, and it's to leave this earth better than you find it. If you have an opportunity to help somebody, and change things in a positive direction, I think you ought to do it.

As an adult or as a parent, you want to be looked up to, and I think it's important to give back to the community and to obey the laws and stay out of trouble. You shouldn't be selfish.

Everyone has his or her own personal goals, and that's very important. With the status that you amass, you can promote literacy at schools, for instance. You want to get kids to read once in a while instead of watching television and playing video games. You can go back to your hometown and talk to kids at the community center. They have questions. Sometimes it's not socially cool to talk about certain things. A lot of kids think they have to fit in. But you've got to let them know it's okay to ask about certain things, to get some good advice.

"Everyone in life has an amazing story."

Family is important. I learned growing up with my mother and two brothers the importance of the family unit. I was 17 when I found out that my biological father was Ross Browner, who'd been a pro football player. I was raised by Max Starks who married my mother when I was quite young. Ross Browner is my father, but Max Starks is my dad. There's a difference. I have a relationship with both men now, but they're not in the same classification. I don't look to him as I do my dad and the man who raises you. There's a definite distinction. I treat them both with respect.

Ross Browner never married my mother. My namesake and my mother divorced.

It takes a village to raise a child. It's important to feel safe and be comfortable. My mother is No. 1 in my life, outside of God. I watched my mother trying to recover from cancer. She's a real warrior. I think I can empathize and sympathize with people with problems. I saw my mother trying to get over her battle with cancer and look after us at the same time.

My mother is my hero, my role model and my best friend. You can never truly repay your parents for what they do for you. I look up to my Mom. I try to live my life the way she'd want me to live. My mother is a very competitive person and she set high standards for all of us. She's always been supportive. She's always been willing to give me her two cents' worth, even when I didn't want to hear it.

I can relate to these guys with problems. Everyone in life has an amazing story. Everyone has done something they wish they hadn't done. But I wouldn't want anything to be different. There are lessons to be learned from difficulties. God has a plan for you. You don't know how to react to some challenges in your life. You have tough decisions to make.

Yes, I care about what people think about me. I'm a big guy and have that challenge of the dumb jock syndrome. There are a lot of preconceived notions about someone my size. Hey, not all of us are ignorant. I didn't go to school just to be an athlete. I majored in sociology. When I was growing up, I had people outside of my family that I looked up to. I had some good teachers and good coaches and counselors. They had high moral standards. I looked up to guys like Michael Jordan and Lawrence Taylor — Taylor for his football approach, not his lifestyle — and great athletes. Jordan lived his life as he believed he should.

But when I was in eighth grade and watching Super Bowl XXX on television, I couldn't have dreamed that someday I'd be playing football with those guys. You know Willie Williams played for the Steelers against the Dallas Cowboys, and he was a teammate of mine last year. We were on the same team.

"You should always set new standards."

I worked with my mother beginning at age four. She always said to be respectful of others unless they gave you a reason not to. She taught me never to be complacent, that you should always set new standards and new goals.

There's one thing I know about this team's general makeup. They believe in drafting individuals who are unselfish, sacrificing, dedicated and disciplined. No one is out for personal glory. Everyone did it for the guy next to him, a teammate, and a brother. If we had some bad guys they had to conform and get with the rest of the team. You had to give your best effort and do it for the good of the entire team.

"About halfway through the season, a lot of people were counting the Steelers out. They said you didn't have a chance. I know the feeling."
— **President George Bush at White House reception for champion Steelers, June 2, 2006**

It didn't matter if you were Ben Roethlisberger, Jerome Bettis, Hines Ward, Troy Polamalu, Joey Porter, James Farrior. You were a Steeler. You were representing Pittsburgh and the Steelers and the Rooneys.

They don't want negative people here. The Steelers don't want to draft guys like that. They're not interested in picking up other people's problems. They're big on character. They want guys who want to be a team player, who'll give you their best effort. They want guys with a good work ethic.

My mother was a speechwriter. She wanted to make sure I spoke well at all times. She said if you want to talk to anybody you want to make sure they understand what you're saying. If you can't talk clearly people won't know what you're trying to communicate.

I learned to read early. I always tested several grades ahead of my age. I was taught grammar and English very early. That's one of my biggest interests. It upsets me when I hear some kids talking and you can't make sense of what they're saying. This is a special problem with many African-American children. It's so important that they learn to talk properly.

I've been told that "you sound like a white person." I prefer it when someone says, "You talk real good," or rather "you talk well." I'm thankful to my mother and to my teachers for teaching me proper English. All Americans should know how to speak a proper sentence.

I can go into any environment and feel comfortable in conveying my thoughts. I can speak to businessmen at a luncheon program or I can speak to children in a school setting and feel equally comfortable. A lot of people can't get that. I still like to read books and learn more.

My Dad pushed that, too. My Dad spoke well and clearly. I'd see my Dad interact with people and picked up on how he did it. When you're running a funeral home you have to talk to all kinds of people about personal stuff.

My great-grandparents started the Max Starks Funeral Home back in 1934. They learned to relate to all kinds of people. I guess it rubbed off on me. I've watched those TV shows like "Six Feet Under" and "Family Plots." Hollywood and reality are different worlds, but "Family Plots" was more realistic.

I had a lot of interesting experiences working in the funeral home. We had a funeral involving one of my uncles where it turned out he had two separate families. The widows were carrying on so, and I was wondering why I had to wear a suit for that kind of affair. Another time, we were in a cemetery in Georgia, and we got the hearse stuck in that famous Georgia red clay. One of my uncles had a white dress shirt that ended up red from the tires spinning in the mud when we tried to move the hearse forward. That was kinda funny. But most funerals aren't funny at all.

Everyone feels the sense of loss. You don't get to where it doesn't matter.

You had to learn to respect other people's feelings. You have to be compassionate and you have to be a consoler. As a teenager, I was a grief counselor. I haven't lost any parents. I still have three of them. But I've lost an aunt and grandparents so I know how that feels.

I was a mediator in high school, helping to solve problems. I guess I've always had this gift. Being in the funeral business, I can relate to other people's problems. So it was a natural for me to get involved with the Caring Foundation when I came to Pittsburgh. I'm blessed and proud to be associated with Dr. Ken Melani and Judd Gordon and the people at The Caring Place. We show people how to deal with grief. It's an important mission.

When you suffer a personal loss you can soar above the sky, or you can sink below the bowels of the earth.

I was always big for my age. I wasn't allowed to play Pop Warner Football because it was by weight divisions, and I was over the weight limits. So I played a lot of other sports to stay active. Basketball was my first love. I had some chances to go to college for basketball until coaches found out I was also a blue-chip football prospect. The bigger colleges came after me for football.

When I was in eighth grade, I transferred from a private school to the public school. I showed up for class with a nice polo shirt tucked into my slacks, and I had a backpack. I was the biggest kid in the class. The kids came up to me and when I started talking to them they asked me if I was the teacher.

They thought I was an adult, the way I was talking and interacting with them. I was about 6-4 at the time. That's probably one of the reasons people always thought I was older than I was. Now I'm just bigger than everybody else. But I try to behave in a way so that nobody thinks that I think I'm bigger or better than anybody else.

> *"This has been an organization that prides itself on putting a good line on the field. You can dictate what you want to do."*
> — Max Starks

Jeff Hartings
Spiritual center of Steelers

"He's got a few more solid seasons in him."
— **Russ Grimm**

Jeff Hartings left our table in the Steelers' dining area to get something to drink. He had at least a dozen choices from spring water to raspberry iced tea to chocolate milk. I watched him as he walked toward the dispensers at the end of the serving line. He left a steaming shredded beef sandwich on his plate. It was lunchtime following a Steelers' workout session at the UPMC Sports Performance Complex.

He stopped for a moment to say hello to Dan Rooney, the owner and chairman of the board of the Steelers. Rooney was wearing a dark suit, a button-down white shirt and a green paisley tie. Rooney is round-shouldered and, at 74, he seems to shuffle when he walks. Rooney reminds me of his late father, Arthur J. Rooney Sr., who founded the franchise in 1933, when he walks among the Steelers these days. He moves with a similar motion. I saw Hartings extend his right hand and pat his boss on the back. Rooney smiled in reply and said something to Hartings. He does that in a quiet fashion with every one who approaches him.

Rooney had been sitting at the next table — that's how I knew the color of his tie — with two secretaries. That's his style. To him, everyone in the Steelers' organization is an important person. Ike Taylor, one of the team's starting cornerbacks, came and sat next to him for awhile. I'd seen Taylor in Rooney's company earlier in the week. I wondered what he was talking about to his boss. Taylor had been one of the team's restricted free agents and had signed a one-year contract. Maybe he wanted to get an extended contract so his future with the Steelers would be assured.

Hartings, for sure, wanted to stay with the Steelers until he retired. He was preparing for his 11th season in the National Football League and said he was now taking them one at a time, as far as deciding how long he wanted to continue to stay, just like his boss, Bill Cowher. It was nearly 90 degrees and quite humid outside, but Hartings said it had been perfect for practice. "This will help us get ready for summer camp at St. Vincent," he said. "I believe I have at least one more good year in me. There's nothing better than playing for this team right now."

Hartings was wearing a black T-shirt with a white Nike swoosh in the center of his powerfully built chest. He wore black shorts and black sneakers. Hartings is listed as 6-3, 299 pounds in the Steelers' press guide. He wears No. 64. He was considered a key to the team's strong running attack.

He had been one of two first round draft choices of the Detroit Lions in 1996 and had become an immediate starter at right guard. He was a mainstay at that position for four seasons with the Lions. Then he signed as a free agent with the Steelers in March of 2001. Kevin Colbert, who had worked in the player personnel department in Detroit, had come to the Steelers as the director of football operations and he thought Hartings could move to center and replace future Hall of Fame center Dermonti Dawson in the Steelers' starting lineup.

Colbert was correct in his judgment. Hartings had become a repeat Pro Bowl center with the Steelers. Colbert stopped by our table during our interview. This was on Thursday, June 1, 2006, and another week of "voluntary coaching sessions" had been concluded.

Hartings would join the Steelers the following day in Washington D.C., where they were being honored at a reception hosted by President Bush at The White House. When they returned to Pittsburgh, the Steelers would be presented with their Super Bowl rings at a private dinner for the team at Heinz Field that Sunday evening.

Dan Rooney had designed the ring with the help of Jerome Bettis and Ben Roethlisberger. They had talked Rooney into including four diamonds to mark the team's four Super Bowl titles from the '70s, to go with the diamond for their achievement. The five Lombardi Trophies were all on display in the Art Rooney Memorial Library upstairs in the Steelers' training complex on the South Side. Rooney had set the new one away from the other four because he believed this was a new day, a new team, and that the players deserved their own distinctive honor.

There was a time when Hartings may have thought this wouldn't be possible. Hartings had suffered a disabling knee injury in October of 2002 in a game against the Indianapolis Colts, and his career appeared to be in jeopardy. The injury ended a streak of 61 consecutive starts for Hartings, 39 with the Lions at right guard. He would miss five games that season because of the nagging injury.

He had bounced back big time. He had a 54-game streak of consecutive starts going for him as he approached the next season. He would be 34 years old in September when the 2006 season started in earnest. "He's playing great now," said his line coach Russ Grimm when I spoke to him earlier that same day. "He continues to get better. He's got a few more solid seasons in him if he stays healthy."

Hartings has good things to say about Grimm, too, and loves playing for him. Grimm had told me that he was fortunate to have played at Pitt and with the Washington Redskins where he was mentored by two outstanding offensive line coaches who shared Western Pennsylvania roots with him. Grimm came from Scottdale. Joe Moore of Mt. Lebanon (by way of Bloomfield) coached him at Pitt and then Joe Bugel of Munhall coached him and "The Hogs" with the Super Bowl champion Redskins.

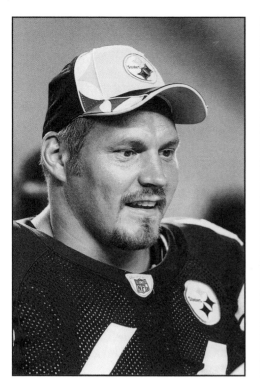

Jeff Hartings

Associate head coach Russ Grimm gives advice to center Jeff Hartings.

"I had the best coaches you could have for an offensive lineman," said Grimm, "and I learned a lot being with Joe Gibbs and here with Bill Cowher." Hartings felt the same way about working with Grimm and Cowher. And working for Dan Rooney and his oldest son, Art II.

Hartings took a pay cut following the Super Bowl victory in order to stay with the Steelers. They needed to restructure some contracts in order to stay under the team salary cap. They had done the same thing with Jerome Bettis the previous two seasons.

"You see the owners here and they come into our locker room every day," said Hartings. "That wasn't the case in Detroit."

I told Hartings that I had met and spoken with Bill Ford, the owner of the Ford Motor Co. and the Lions, when I was working on a story for *Sport* magazine about Pro Bowl defensive back Lem Barney of the Lions back in 1966, right after I had been discharged from the Army. Hartings was reminded of those days in Detroit when the Steelers worked out at the Pontiac Silverdome prior to playing the Seattle Seahawks in Super Bowl XL at Ford Field.

When Hartings was with the Lions, they played their home games at the Silverdome. They had moved to Ford Field in downtown Detroit two years earlier. Hartings didn't want to leave Ford Field after the Steelers had defeated the Seahawks, 21-10. He just wanted to stay and soak up the scene. It was surreal.

"It doesn't get any better than winning the Super Bowl," Hartings said of his distinguished ten-year pro career. He had played for Joe Paterno at Penn State where he was a two-time All-American guard, and had led a privileged life as far as football was concerned.

"It starts with the ownership here," said Hartings. "The Rooneys . . . they run the team like a business, obviously because it is a business. They're down in the locker room. They're out on the practice field occasionally. They're 100 percent involved. I think it just trickles down from there to the general manager, the coach and the players. It starts with the leadership and that's the owners, the general manager and the coach. They're the ones who keep us focused and in the right direction."

He liked to thank God for his good fortune. He disclosed that he planned on becoming a minister when his pro football days were over. Following our interview, he would attend a Bible Study session at a nearby table with several of his teammates, including Max Starks and Dan Kreider. I had spotted him at a similar post-practice session in the dining area the week before. Team chaplain Jay Wilson led the meetings.

I told Hartings that back in the '70s there were about 25 to 30 Steelers who met regularly for Bible study sessions, and they included Jon Kolb, Donnie Shell, John Stallworth, Terry Bradshaw, Mel Blount and Tony Dungy.

Hartings had participated in many fund-raising efforts for local charities since joining the Steelers. He had his most profound involvement with the Urban Impact Foundation, a faith-based non-profit organization on the North Side that seeks to help at-risk children spiritually, academically and physically. Hartings led a group of 19 Steelers who participated in the program during the 2005 season. He donated tickets and signed Steelers' memorabilia to be auctioned off to support the foundation. In the previous two years, Hartings had helped raise over $72,000 for the Urban Impact Foundation. He had also participated in the Urban Impact Football Clinic each of the last three seasons.

Hartings has close-cropped thinning hair and a receding hairline that makes his dark eyes even more penetrating when he talks to you. He looks you in the eye and has an earnest way about him. He offers a smile now and then. There's a lot more than meets the eye about Jeff Hartings, as I would learn during our hour-long session. We talked again a week later, after the Steelers had been honored with a visit to see President Bush at The White House and they had received their Super Bowl rings two days later at a dinner at Heinz Field.

Jeff Hartings:

"I did a lot of hard work early in my life."

I grew up on a farm in Ohio. We had a 40-acre farm with pigs and cows in a community called St. Henry. We became chicken farmers when I was in eighth grade. We built a hen house and produced a lot of layers. There were ten children in our family. I have five sisters and four brothers. I have two older brothers and four older sisters and I was No. 7 age-wise.

I learned something about hard work and team work, no doubt about it, growing up on a farm. I played sports with my brothers all the time, after we had done our chores, of course. I did a lot of hard work early in my life. That's why I'm in the NFL. I've always been willing to work hard at whatever needed to be done.

I learned a great work ethic from my parents. My father's name was Lester and my mother's name was Dolores. With them, nothing was ever too hard. My dad had a regular job. He put tile in farm fields around us to drain those fields. Then he worked our farm. He never missed a day's work.

One of the most profound things he taught me was this: You might not be born with the most talent so you have to outwork everyone else. That's served me well. If nothing else, I can outwork you.

If you learn your trade well you can out-think them as well. I always thought I could build myself into a great football player. So I do my drills and I do a lot of film study. One of my best characteristics is never being content. I'm never satisfied.

That's part of what defines me. I've never been satisfied. No matter how many honors I have gained, I never thought I'd arrived as a player. We've won the Super Bowl now, but now I want to win it again.

When I was growing up in St. Henry, I didn't think I'd be able to fulfill my dream of playing big-time college football. I didn't think I'd get noticed. Then I found out about Jim Lashey, who was nine years older than me and had played at St. Henry High School. He played with the San Diego Chargers and Washington Redskins (1985-1994). I saw him play in Super Bowl XXVI with the Redskins.

Jim Lashey is the guy who made me realize it was possible. When he got to the NFL, I started working harder to get better. I thought, "If he can do it, I can do it." And I started working even harder. We had another player come out of St. Henry High, quarterback Bobby Hoyings, who also made it to the NFL.

When I got hurt in 2002 my knee hurt more than you can imagine. It took a long time to get back after the surgery. My knee wasn't strong in 2003, either, and I couldn't function as the football player I wanted to be. I was proud of that season, and that I got through it as well as I did. My body just felt different, but I had to play. You build your character that way. I feel better now than I have in years.

I was in so much pain during the 2003 season it made me call out to God literally every single night in my bed. "How am I going to get through tomorrow," I thought aloud, "much less through a football game?" I have no idea how I played in some of those games. I had to take anti-inflammatory medications to get through those games.

I think the circumstances I grew up in helped me there. My father never took a day off. I never remember him lying on the couch with a headache. I love playing football, and it was very difficult to miss so many games during that 2002 season. It was a humbling experience. I had thought I was indestructible. God, no doubt, brought me through that. When I had that injury, it made me think about what I would be doing if I weren't playing football.

I paid more attention to the game. Russ Grimm is a great coach for me. He played the game, for starters, at a high level, and he didn't just rely on his athletic ability. He pushes us the way he pushed himself. He was never satisfied. He wanted to know what could give him an edge. He wanted to understand how defenses played. He's taught us to recognize our opponents and what they are doing. We understand what a defense is trying to do to us.

That's what's made me excel, and get to the level of play I need to play and stay in the NFL.

"They have high standards for excellence."

Everything here starts with Mr. Rooney. He and his son Art show the way. I respect him for the man he is. His reputation precedes himself. Even before I came here, I knew about the Rooney family, their lifestyle and their values. Players and coaches around the league know about it. Knowing they have a high standard for excellence, you want to be a part of that. They have high expectations for you on and off the field as far as your behavior is concerned.

There's a stability about the Steelers that you can appreciate as a player or as a fan. It's nice to know that the guy who signs your paycheck is in the locker room asking about your family and cares about every minute detail of the team. It sends a message through the ranks and it trickles down to the players. I don't know exactly how to put it. I don't want to say respect because I think in Detroit there's a great deal of respect for the Ford family and their willingness to spend any amount to bring a championship caliber team there.

We were very competitive when I was there, but things have changed. Whatever they've been doing hasn't been working. I knew changes were going to be made, and I didn't want to have to go through what has been a difficult transition. For me, it couldn't have worked out better.

My faith in God also serves me well. He's the only one I care about. I care about what he thinks of me. I read the Bible. I want to know how Jesus Christ wants us to live. Some people don't share my beliefs, but that's okay. I know what's important to me.

Football-wise, that's where my flesh gets in the way. We care what our teammates think of us. We all struggle with fear of letting our teammates down. My goal is that I play for God. If I do that I think it will be good enough for my teammates.

I understand that people have different beliefs, different priorities. Some guys don't make good decisions, and it can end in bad consequences. Sometimes they get away with it. When I hear about someone getting into trouble (we had been talking about top draft pick Santonio Holmes of Ohio State getting arrested in Miami that same week after an altercation with police), I pray that when they come through it they'll be a better person.

Plaxico Burress is a perfect example. He came from a different background — being in difficult and challenging circumstances in his youth — and he had some growing up to do when he came here. But he ended up being one of the best teammates I ever had. He learned that there was a purpose in life beyond football.

39

This organization understands that. Mr. Rooney treats us like we're his own kids. There has to be some firmness and there has to be some forgiveness. The Steelers do their best to get the best players and the best people. But that doesn't happen all the time. They let us know that certain behavior is not acceptable, and that it won't be tolerated too long. They make you face the consequences for your actions. With that in mind, they've had to do some things that are difficult for them to do.

I think the Steelers get the utmost from their players. That's one of the reasons I stayed here. I'd probably be retired if the Steelers didn't take me back. I will finish up here.

I enjoy the tremendous tradition and heritage they have here. This team has had many great centers, such as Ray Mansfield, Mike Webster and Dermontti Dawson (and before them, they had Bill Walsh), and I know that. You're expected to uphold the tradition. I've always been able to block out outside influences. To me, it can be a negative influence. I concentrate on what I can control. I just want to keep my focus narrow. I don't worry about what someone might write about me.

I'm very honored to play with the Pittsburgh Steelers and follow outstanding performers at my position. If I can be mentioned in the same sentence as some of those guys when I leave I'll know that I did my job.

They took a great risk when they signed me. I had practiced at center on a few occasions in Detroit, just in case I was needed, but it was strange to switch on a full-time basis. There's no way they would have signed me if they didn't think I was equal to the challenge. It took a while for me to get used to snapping the ball and blocking from that stance, and it was ugly for a while that first summer at St. Vincent. I had more than my share of bad exchanges with the quarterbacks.

I had a chance to think about where I've been and how things have gone when we practiced for the Super Bowl at the Pontiac Silverdome. That's where the Lions played when I was on the team. I knew those locker rooms. I remembered my teammates on the Lions. I knew how lucky I was to be with the Steelers. It helped put everything in its proper perspective.

I know where I'm headed now. I'm going to be a minister. My family is in Salt Lake City now. I'm involved in a non-denominational church there. A man named Luther Ellis, who played nine seasons with the Lions and one more with the Broncos, and his wife, Rebecca Ellis, are responsible for getting me to this place in my life. He gave me my vision. I played with him and he brought me to my first Bible study session. He changed my life. He's still in Michigan, but we hope to team up again.

I have been married for ten years to Rebecca, and we have five children. We adopted two of them. They are Sierra, 8; Michael, 6; Lucas, 5; Miamma, 4, and Isabella, 2. They keep us busy.

In 2002, I started to think about what I was going to do after football. Now I know. I want to work with young people who need help. That's what brings me the most joy. Seeing kids grow up and helping them develop is a very satisfying work. I want to help prepare them for life and for eternal life. That's simple enough, don't you think?

Bill Priatko

Jeff Hartings checks out familiar Pontiac Silverdome surroundings with his children during Steelers' practice session prior to Super Bowl XL at Ford Field in Detroit. The Lions played their home games at the Silverdome when Hartings played for them prior to signing with Steelers as free agent.

Bill Cowher
One game at a time

"We love the enthusiasm."

From Dare To Dream, 1996

During his first four seasons with the Steelers, Bill Cowher clearly demonstrated that he was an outstanding football coach, and certainly a worthy successor to Chuck Noll. They were the two most successful coaches in Steelers' history.

Noll set high standards for the Steelers, winning four Super Bowls in a six-year span in the '70s when the Steelers were heralded as "the team of the decade." Noll was not a tough act to follow, however, because his team qualified for the playoffs only once in his last seven seasons on the job, and the team's overall record during that span was 52-61. He finished up his 23 seasons as head coach of the Steelers with a 7-9 team in 1991, and he was drawing criticism from the fans and media. They felt Noll and a new breed of athletes were no longer on the same page.

Noll used to say about an over-the-hill ballplayer "it's time for him to get on with his life's work." Now Noll was getting the same sage advice, and he didn't like where it was coming from. It happens to the best of coaches as one of Noll's mentors, Don Shula of the Miami Dolphins, learned the hard way during the 1995 season.

Cowher came from Crafton, a middle class community on the outskirts of Pittsburgh and within 15 minutes of Three Rivers Stadium. So he knew well what Noll and the Steelers had accomplished in the '70s. That's the way Cowher recalled the Steelers, too, just like so many of the team's spoiled fans. So he knew it would not be an easy task, but he thought he was equal to the challenge of turning the team back into a perennial contender.

His dad had taken him when he was a child to see the Steelers play at Forbes Field and Pitt Stadium. So it seemed he would have a sense of history. What did he remember about those days, about the last game he'd seen at Pitt Stadium?

"I remember being at the game," said Cowher. "But I remember eating hot dogs and candy and everything else more than the game."

Cowher's first four teams all made the playoffs. His first team went 11-6. His third and fourth teams made it to the AFC championship game, and his fourth team made it all the way to Super Bowl XXX. Noll made it to the AFC championship game in his fourth year and the Super Bowl in his sixth year. His team's overall record of 17-2 in 1978 is the standard for success with the Steelers.

It is important to point out, however, that the 1994 and 1995 seasons were two of the outstanding seasons in Steelers' history.

George Gojkovich/Getty Images

How's that? The overall records of 13-5 in 1994 and 13-6 in 1995 were the sixth and seventh best records (percentagewise) in club history. Fans forget that before Noll came to Pittsburgh, the Steelers fielded mostly mediocre teams. The tenures of Noll and Cowher were clearly the best of times.

"There was a time," late owner Art Rooney often remarked, "when people didn't think we were smart enough to come in out of the rain."

In fact, the Steelers posted a winning season only three times in the team's first 25 years of operation, and only seven times in the first 37 years. The overall record during those 37 seasons was 164-268-19 — .380). That includes Chuck Noll's first season of 1969 when the Steelers were 1-13 — the worst record in Steelers' history. So Noll had the distinction of having the best and worst records for a spell.

Before Cowher came along, the Steelers had only three coaches who had winning records: Noll (209-156-1 — .572), Jock Sutherland (13-10-1 — .563, and Buddy Parker (51-48-6 — .514). During Parker's tenure, the Steelers traded off most of their top draft picks each year, and there was little or no excitement generated on Draft Day anywhere in the NFL back then. Cowher's record for the first four seasons on the job was unrivaled in club history.

"Maybe the time has come to carve Bill Cowher's chin on the side of the Clark Building," wrote Dave Ailes, the sports editor of the *Tribune-Review*. "Cowher's carving a phenomenal start for himself as coach of the Steelers. A guy named Chuck Noll is revered in these parts, with good reason. He brought the franchise back from 40 years of oblivion, ascending to the NFL throne four times. Compared to Cowher's success ratio, though, Noll was a slow starter."

It is important, however, to keep in mind that Noll took the Steelers to four Super Bowls and won them all, a trick Cowher can never match. It would be hard enough just to get to four Super Bowls, and Cowher and his team came up short against the Dallas Cowboys, 27-17, in Super Bowl XXX. They had their chance. Cowher and the Steelers came within one scoring drive of winning it. No one could fault Cowher or his club for their effort.

Cowher came away from Tempe a winner. Cowher had conducted himself well all week long at the Super Bowl XXX press conferences, smiled broadly and said all the right things and proved popular with the national media. I was there and attended all those media events, so I had a close-up look at Cowher and he was more expansive than usual. He would have gotten an "A" grade for all his efforts if he made sure his players appeared at all scheduled press conferences. There was a misunderstanding in respect to the team's obligations in that area and the team drew a $25,000 fine from NFL headquarters. In the game itself, the most important of his tasks, Cowher showed his competitive fire and gutsy approach in going for broke in the biggest game of his life. Had the Steelers won, they would still be applauding Cowher for his decision to go for an on-side kick in the second half, a tactic that worked and kept the momentum clearly on the Steelers' side. Defensively, the Steelers made adjustments at the intermission, and made a comeback possible. Cowher succeeded where so many AFC coaches had failed in recent times by making the Super Bowl a bonafide contest.

"Maybe Cowher will never return to this stage," wrote Gene Collier of the *Pittsburgh Post-Gazette*, "but he'll do so in the knowledge that he coached the kind of game critics have begged for most of its glorious-despite-itself 30-year history.

"Cowher gambled at almost every opportunity across the green felt of Sun Devil Stadium," continued Collier, "and the fact that his Steelers lost Super Bowl XXX to a superior Dallas Cowboys team should never tarnish his daring and his accomplishments."

"If you're not talking about x's and o's, you can lose Bill's attention in a hurry." — Kaye Cowher

Anybody who thought Noll was a focused coach — and he certainly was — might find it difficult to buy this observation, but Cowher might have been even more focused, or channeled, in relation to his football responsibilities. Noll prided himself on being a Renaissance man, with keen interests in diverse areas. Noll loved to chat with the media in the hallways and the kitchen area at Steelers' headquarters, and he loved to share his thoughts on many subjects, especially non-football subjects. His eyes glazed over in a hurry when anyone wanted to probe him too deeply about his football philosophies. History, politics, piloting airplanes, scuba-diving, photography, fine wines, gourmet meals, education, history, child-rearing . . . those topics all appealed to Noll. Noll was often portrayed as a cold individual, but that was not the case. He was a charming, decent man; he simply fell short of being what some people wanted him to be. Sometimes the media wants to put everyone in a mold that would make his or her job easier. Noll was not always as interesting or colorful, as they would have liked. He had a droll sense of humor. "I could never tell a joke," he confessed, which explained why his "Franco Who?" remark was mostly misunderstood. Noll was wary of the media, understandably, and was said to have made disparaging remarks about the media to his players behind closed doors. Even so, he didn't keep as much distance as Cowher does from the regular beat guys.

Cowher was not comfortable with the small talk. He seldom paused in the hallways to talk to members of the media. Some sportswriters said Cowher would lower his gaze as he approached them in the hallways at the stadium. It was easier to pass without a word that way. There were times he appeared paranoid about the press. For the most part, Cowher had received positive reviews during his initial four-year run, and the Pittsburgh press had generally been less critical than that to be found in most major markets. Cowher had thrown up a lot of roadblocks to make their jobs more difficult, but he had given them little to criticize as far as performance was concerned.

The Steelers had been successful on the field, but had more than their share of off-the-field difficulties. What Noll used to term "distractions" became commonplace. No matter what happened, Cowher stayed the course. That was to his credit. Nothing seemed to keep Cowher and his club from moving forward. They were undaunted in that regard.

Cowher could have been more cordial; he could have lightened up in his personal approach. He often found it difficult just to say, "Hello." Or, "Good morning." It's a shame, because I saw him with other people, and he could be downright charming and a wonderful ambassador for the Steelers and Pittsburgh. Noll assumed that role more after he retired from coaching.

Their styles could best be summed up by the way they handled their weekly press conferences. Noll sat at the end of a rectangular table in the midst of the media. It was like a card game. Cowher sat alone behind a table with the media sitting in student desks facing him in a classroom setup. There was an imaginary moat between the two parties.

Cowher was not easy to get close to. I mentioned to his wife, Kaye, one day in the press box at Three Rivers Stadium that I found it difficult to get into any kind of casual conversation with her husband.

"If you're not talking about x's and o's," confided Kaye, in a telling admission, "you can lose Bill's attention in a hurry."

Cowher concentrated on his job. No one could criticize him in that regard. The assistant coaches said he was extremely well organized. Former assistant coaches questioned his loyalty and fairness. Steve Furness, for one, felt he had done nothing to deserve being fired after his first two seasons of looking after the defensive line. The former Steelers' defensive standout seemed to have rubbed Cowher the wrong way. Ron Erhardt and Pat Hodgson had been with Cowher from the beginning, yet they were not rehired shortly after the team returned to Pittsburgh from its strong appearance in Super Bowl XXX. They were stunned. Where's the love, man? But few people who lose their jobs have much good to say about their former bosses, right?

Once asked what three words described him best, Cowher responded, "Loyal, dependable, confident."

Like everything else he had done since the Steelers hired him, Cowher did not look back or second-guess his decisions. He was so consistent in so many respects. That was the most impressive aspect of his approach. Cowher had an unrelenting resolve to keep on truckin'. He didn't dwell on past disappointments or setbacks. Like Satchel Paige, he didn't believe in looking back, somebody might be gaining on him. He was always looking forward to the next challenge. With him, taking a one-game-at-a-time approach did not sound like a cliché. It was a way of life. He was indomitable. He never seemed to waver from the philosophies he had picked up from the likes of Marty Schottenheimer and Sam Rutigliano, coaches he had worked for in his professional development days.

Merril Hoge, a holdover from the Noll days, played two seasons for Cowher before signing as a free agent with the Chicago Bears. He came back to Pittsburgh to serve as an analyst on WTAE Radio's coverage of Steelers' games in 1995.

"I remember when he came in to replace Chuck Noll, and I was thinking, 'Man, I'm glad I'm not in his shoes.' But he did an amazing job," said Hoge. "He built an attitude that continues to this day. And that's taking nothing away from Chuck Noll. But what Coach Cowher has done is extraordinary.

"He always promised us as players that he would take care of us. 'If you give me everything you've got, I'll take care of you.' Coach Cowher is not only a great coach; he's a great friend. He's been able to toe that line. He does it from the heart. You can see how it works."

That was how he was able to rally a team that had gotten off to a frustrating 3-4 start in the 1995 season — there was second-guessing from the media then — and drive them to Super Bowl XXX, winning 10 of 11 games before the Steelers came up short against the Cowboys at Sun Devil Stadium. And the Steelers should have won another game, as well, but didn't when normally sure-handed receiver Yancy Thigpen dropped a pass from Neil O'Donnell in the end zone on the final play at Green Bay. Cowher had the good sense to smile through that episode, hugging Thigpen as he came off the field. He did not want to end the regular season on a negative note, so he made light of it, since it did not affect the Steelers' standing or playoff position. Some day, Cowher might check his career record and wish the Steelers had won the last game on the schedule in 1994 and 1995, which the media labeled "meaningless" games. In the end, there are no meaningless games.

During Super Bowl XXX week, Cowher discussed the Steelers, his personal philosophies about football, Pittsburgh and its special fans, Dan Rooney, his boss, and other related subjects. It provided some insights into Cowher, and his marvelous success since Rooney tapped him as the man to resurrect the Steelers and return them to their glory days.

Cowher was younger and more demonstrative than Noll. Cowher was 34 years old when he was hired, and Noll was nearing his 60th birthday when he retired. Free agency, agents and attorneys, big money, too much media, and changing attitudes among athletes had all altered the pro sports scene, and Noll, like many of his contemporaries, found it difficult to deal with or accept many of the changes.

Cowher was certainly the equal of Noll when it came to demanding and receiving respect. He could freeze anyone with a steely glare. His face was more chiseled, and many noted his long chin, ear-to-ear mouth, and such features in characterizing the man. The local editorial cartoonists had a lot of fun with his face, much to Cowher's chagrin. His face was a caricaturist's dream. During his playing days, Cowher's nickname was "The Face." And if it's any consolation to Noll, Cowher can't tell a joke well, either. Most coaches can't.

"When Cowher is unhappy," wrote Alan Robinson of the Associated Press, "his eyes grow steel cold, his neck tightens, his jaw juts out and his voice hits a high decibel."

Bud Shaw, a columnist for *The Cleveland Plain-Dealer*, noted his fiery eyes and "a chin cut from brimstone." Shaw saw something else that characterized Cowher's approach to his position. "His news conferences are infomercials selling Pittsburgh to Pittsburgh," wrote Shaw. He credited Cowher for his promotional skills, and his ability to rally the crowd to his cause.

His approach to public relations and marketing was different from Noll. He appeared on radio and TV talk shows, had his own column in *Steelers Digest*, let NFL Films into his clubhouse before games and at halftime, was especially cozy with certain out-of-town writers, and appeared in print and TV commercials. Cowher became as identified with Pittsburgh as Iron City Beer, kielbassa, pierogies and babushkas.

Cowher was always promoting Pittsburgh and the Steelers' special place in his hometown and the surrounding environs, and the fans lapped it up. They loved Bill Cowher. He was one of their own. They believed in Cowher Power. Who could blame them? When he wanted noise at the stadium — NFL rules to the contrary against such petitions — Cowher had a way of getting the word out and the fans always responded to his cheerleading. Sportscaster Myron Cope called for Terrible Towel demonstrations and Cowher seconded the motion.

"Be loud," he said at the end of the press conference that preceded the AFC game with Indianapolis. "Please be loud. We have the energy. We love the enthusiasm."

Cowher always complimented the crowd on its efforts.

"I think we have the best fans in America," Cowher often commented. "People here can relate to this football team. And we can relate to them. There's an appreciation, and I think there's a respect that typifies this city."

It is no wonder Cowher was so popular. He was twice honored as Pittsburgh's Man of the Year in Sports by the Dapper Dan Club and, in May of 1996, he was named Man of the Year at the annual YMCA Dinner that recognized the special achievements of hundreds of Pittsburgh area student athletes. I was there that night, and Cowher told them he was a pretty fair athlete in high school, but he never had the grades this group could boast. He was a big hit.

He was not a gifted athlete in his youth, but he had a message that made sense to young people who enjoyed playing sports and wanted somehow to be successful.

"When you grow up here," Cowher told the crowd, "there is such a strong work ethic. I was never a great athlete. I've had to work hard for everything I've accomplished. Taking pride with the little ability I had and I tried to become the very best. It's something I was taught at an early age."

"There is a bonding that is taking place in this city."
— Bill Cowher

Cowher was aware of the team's rich tradition and its Hall of Fame history and while properly acknowledging the legacy he wanted everyone to know it was a different era. To his credit, Cowher has always paid proper homage to Noll and his teams — "we haven't accomplished anything yet," he would say — and had wisely discouraged comparisons.

"I don't think it's anything to get caught up in," said Cowher at his first press conference upon becoming coach of the Steelers, when asked how he felt about succeeding Chuck Noll. "What the man has done for this city, for this organization, speaks for itself. No one can ever emulate him. All you can do is have the same kind of success.

"Chuck Noll is a legend. He's brought tradition; he has brought pride to the city. And that's the thing I want to do also, in my own way. And I have no reservations about following Chuck Noll.

"We will bring back the pride and tradition that's long been associated with the Pittsburgh Steelers, and more appropriately, the great people of Pittsburgh." And Cowher kept his word.

Four years later, before Super Bowl XXX, he said, "The only pressure that we have is pressure we're putting on ourselves. And, really, I don't look at it as pressure. I mean, we have talked about a championship for four years and not just, you know, winning the division, getting to the playoffs, or getting to the Super Bowl. We have always talked about one thing: winning a championship.

"And so, while we have had that as our goal, I think it has been refreshing to see the city kind of resurrected again with a second generation of people that have come now and experienced the same excitement as they did with the teams of the '70s when they were kids. Now they're taking their kids to the games and talking to them about what it was like then. They've got their Terrible Towels twirling again. I think that is great. There is a bonding that is taking place in our city. When you can do that in a city, a city that's as special as Pittsburgh, it's very gratifying.

"You could see that at Three Rivers Stadium when we've been in the playoffs the past few years. I think that's what professional sports is all about. It's never been any more evident than in Pittsburgh."

Cowher has been complimented for being a players' coach, and extolled for his ability to relate to his charges.

"He's a great communicator," said quarterback Mike Tomczak. "He exhibits the personality of the city. He won't let us quit. He has that 'tough job, big chin' type of attitude. One time I made a mistake at camp, and he came marching across the field in my direction. He was still ten feet away from me and his chin was, like, right in my face.

"I played for Mike Ditka in Chicago. Like Bill, he grew up near Pittsburgh. There must be something about western Pennsylvania that gives coaches dramatic facial expressions and mustaches that make them disciplinarians. But the way I look at it, I played for one coaching legend in Ditka. Now I'm playing for an up-and-coming coaching legend."

Veteran linebacker David Little said of Cowher: "You can come in and talk to him about anything, like a father image. With Chuck, you always knew he was your boss." Little lasted just one season with Cowher.

Running back Bam Morris said, "Coach Cowher always tells us when you get the chance, you've got to make something happen."

Justin Strzelczyk, a holdover lineman from Noll's days, said, "Coach Noll was more intimidating. He was the Emperor. He was more like your grandfather. This guy is more like your uncle."

Linebacker Chad Brown wished Cowher could back up a little bit when he was chewing somebody out. "You almost can't hear what he's saying because you're thinking, 'He's entirely too close to me right now.' Maybe it's a coaching thing, but I'm from California — we like our space — and I've never experienced anything like it."

Reserve running back Steve Avery said, "He's so emotional when he speaks to us that even his lips start shaking. Thank God, he doesn't have halitosis."

"Fortunately, I've never been on the end of one of his butt-chewing," said linebacker Kevin Greene. "But I hear they're quite exhilarating. You get that spray going. He's drooling, he's slobbering . . . screaming. You got to love a coach like that."

Leon Searcy, an offensive tackle who departed Pittsburgh in favor of his home state of Florida as an unrestricted free agent after Super Bowl XXX, said of Cowher: "He's a players' coach. He's one you can trust, but one you can't take lightly. Because he's so intense with the game, when you go out and play, you better mean business."

Cowher was proud of his reputation as players' coach. "I am very open with them," said Cowher. "I think you've got to be in this business. I think you respect people that not only tell you what you have to do, but why you have to do it. And I think that is the case in talking to them, not talking down to them.

"You try to create that sense where they feel comfortable displaying or expressing what they feel; at the same time, you are going to tell them how you feel, and not necessarily giving in. But I think if they understand why you are doing things and the only prerequisite we ever use is what is in the best interest of the Pittsburgh Steelers to win a championship.

"They understand and respect that, and I have a great deal of respect for every player, and they understand that, so we communicate openly. We communicate at times maybe when there is a lot of emotion, but I think that is what this game is about, too. And I think there is a mutual respect between myself and the football team."

Defensive end Brentson Buckner said, "He lets players be themselves without getting carried away. But he'll never let anyone get bigger than the team."

Cowher said he was not a choreographed set on the sideline. What you see is the real Bill Cowher.

"I guess you've got to be yourself," said Cowher. "I have said before I am not very good at hiding my emotions. I am going to tell you how I feel; whether it is good or bad, and move on. I mean, I think in this business, if you try to harbor ill feelings, if you let things eat at you, you are not going to last very long.

"There are so many emotional ups and downs we go through every Sunday. You've got to enjoy it. You don't get too high with the highs; you don't get too low with the lows. It is such a great competitive form that we have in this business that you've got to enjoy it. And you know, I am not worried about getting burned out. Somebody mentioned that to me before. I enjoy it. I can see doing this for a long time." The crowning moment for Cowher had to come after the AFC championship game when he stood atop a hastily-assembled platform at midfield and accepted the championship trophy, along with Steelers' president Dan Rooney, from Buffalo Bills' owner Ralph Wilson. Cowher couldn't get over the scene, he continued cheering from the fans that filled the stadium and stayed around to witness the ceremony. Cowher kept holding the trophy on high to share it with all Steelers' fans and waving and saluting the faithful. It doesn't get any better for a hometown boy. I was standing below him and could feel his supreme joy.

"I'm just happy the city can go through this," he said after the game. "That's why it's great. It unites everybody. It's like one big happy family. That's the way we are right now."

Cowher had tears in his eyes, and he didn't deny it. "I'm an emotional guy . . . I was feeling a sense of achievement."

Dan Rooney was a reminder of the rich heritage of Pittsburgh's NFL franchise, which dates back to 1933 when his father, Arthur J. Rooney, obtained the team for the purchase price of $2,500. The Rooneys remained constant in their mode of operation through different eras that presented different challenges. This was the first time Dan Rooney was representing his family and the organization, rather than his father, for such a presentation. Rooney had recently undergone gallbladder surgery, and he looked pale and underweight, but was boosted physically and spiritually by the warm response to what the Steelers had achieved. Rooney should have been resting, but he wouldn't have missed this for the world.

"I think Dan is a unique individual," said Cowher at a press conference in Phoenix before Super Bowl XXX. "He is very down to earth. He is Pittsburgh. I mean this guy symbolizes the city. He has grown up there, and has inherited much from his father. I think with our football team that he has created a very family-like atmosphere. It is important that he does things to create that. He makes an ongoing effort to do that.

"You know he is a guy that while he is there every day, very hands on, you never know it. He's not trying to coach the team. He is a great guy, and the one thing he has been to me for four years — in addition to being my boss — is my friend. He is a guy you can talk to, and he is a guy that cares just as much about that guy up at the top of the stadium as he does the ones in the private boxes, and I think that says everything about the man."

"Mike Ditka is a guy I've always respected." — Bill Cowher

Pro Football Weekly graded NFL coaches in its New Year's issue of 1995 and gave Cowher an "A" and called him a great motivator. Don Shula got a B, Bill Parcells an A-. Marty Schottenheimer a C+. Dave Wannstedt also got an A. Wannstedt, from the Pittsburgh suburb of Baldwin, and a former Pitt player under Johnny Majors in the mid-70s, was a strong candidate for the Steelers' position when Noll surprised the team by retiring. The choice came down to Cowher and Wannstedt, and some in the Steelers' organization wanted Wannstedt. That was Tom Donahoe. Dan Rooney chose Cowher. He had also named Noll in 1969, who was then an assistant under Shula at Baltimore, so he appeared to be two-for-two in picking the right head coach for the Steelers. Just for the record, he also selected Bill Austin, who was a dismal failure as a head coach.

Wannstedt was with the Dallas Cowboys at the time, and was later chosen head coach of the Chicago Bears, succeeding Mike Ditka. Wannstedt had been interviewed for the Pitt job, too, but his alma mater went with Paul Hackett. That was a mistake, but it worked out for the best for Wannstedt.

Ditka, by the way, heaped praise on Cowher for "molding a no-nonsense team that the city of Pittsburgh wants."

Dick Hoak

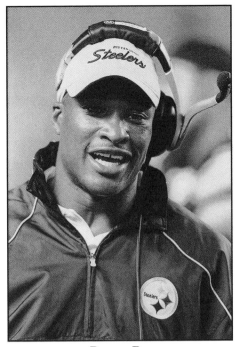

Darren Perry

Valued coaches

"Why should I retire," said Dick Hoak, who had spent 44 of the past 45 seasons with the Steelers as a player and a coach. "I enjoy what I'm doing, and the Rooneys have always been right with me."

Ken Whisenhunt

Russ Grimm

Cowher had a chance to return the compliment when he participated in the Mike Ditka Celebrity Golf Classic at Beaver (Pa.) Lakes Country Club a week before training camp opened in 1995.

"It's an honor for me to be here," Cowher said. "Mike Ditka is a guy I've always respected and had a lot of admiration for. He's one guy who really exemplified western Pennsylvania."

Asked what accomplishment as an athlete he was most proud of, Cowher said it was playing five years in the National Football League. He survived by scratching and clawing his way with the Philadelphia Eagles and Cleveland Browns. He was looking for players who wanted it just as badly, but had more talent than he did as a player.

Cowher was an emotional guy, much like Ditka. "It's one of the factors I considered a real plus," said Dan Rooney. "I think it had much to do with our selecting him as the head coach."

Tom Donahoe, then the director of football operations, said of Cowher soon after he was hired. "He's a coach with fire. He's going to be very demanding of the players. There's going to be one way to do it and there will not be any exceptions."

Donahoe had a history with Cowher. Donahoe was coaching the football team at South Park High School in 1975 when Cowher was in his last season as a player at Carlynton High School.

Cowher, in his final game at Carlynton, returned an interception 24 yards for a touchdown and caught two two-point conversion passes in a 47-7 victory over South Park on November 1, 1974. "He owes me," said Donahoe.

"The dignity of the team comes first."
— Dan Rooney

Chuck Noll and most of his players tell romantic tales of their days at training camp at St. Vincent College. Several said their best memories of their days with the Steelers were at the summer getaway when it was football 24 hours a day, and everyone was in the same boat, or dormitory or dining hall. They enjoyed the camaraderie. Randy Grossman, a reliable tight end on four Super Bowl winners, put it best: "Practice at the Stadium was like a 9-to-5 job, a more normal work day. At St. Vincent, we were completely removed from the real world. You were with a bunch of guys and you were sweating it out from morning till night. You didn't have to make your bed: somebody else did that for you. You didn't have to cook or make any schedule. You didn't have to worry about anything but football."

Cowher did not appear to care for camp as much as Noll. Maybe that had something to do with the fact that Cowher had an auto accident on his first trip to St. Vincent and had to have his car towed. That was no way to get initiated to the charms of his life in the Laurel Highlands.

"Training camp is one of those necessities you have to go through," said Cowher. "You have to hone up the skills, bring the football team together and develop a new chemistry. It's something you have to do. I'm not sure anybody likes it. It's just one of those things you have to go through during the course of the season."

Like Noll, Cowher did not care to discuss holdouts or players who were sidelined by injury when he was interviewed at his first camp: "We're going to coach the players who are here," said Cowher, cutting off any further discussion relating to holdouts. Writers paused in their note-taking to see which coach was addressing them.

"If you don't want to do what you're told, get out of here!" Cowher told the players at one heated camp session. The players circled around Cowher and Cowher read the riot act: "And that goes for everybody! You're here to play football! If you think otherwise, you'll be gone! Your job's on the line!" Cowher could have tied a Noll record there for most exclamations (!!!!!) in a 30-second spiel.

Later, reflecting on the outburst, he said, "This football team will always know how I feel."

After Cowher became the coach, veteran offensive tackle John Jackson commented on the coaching change.

"I think everyone knew that we needed to make some changes after last season. I don't think anybody ever came out and said that Chuck should retire, but I have to admit that getting Bill had been a nice change for all of us."

Later, after a loss to New Orleans in the pre-season, Jackson was surprised by Cowher's camp demeanor. "Chuck wouldn't have done it that way," said Jackson, perhaps having second thoughts on the subject. "Chuck would've just made us practice longer to let us know he wasn't satisfied. Chuck never lost his temper on the practice field."

Like Noll, Cowher had said, "I don't concern myself with things I have no control over."

They shared some sentiments regarding player personnel. For example, neither he nor Noll cared for Jeff Graham, the wide receiver from Ohio State. Cowher and Donahoe deep-sixed recalcitrant or problem players, getting rid of unhappy campers such as Bubby Brister, Eric Green and Barry Foster, among others.

Under Cowher, assistant coaches were working longer hours, with days beginning shortly after daybreak and sometimes lasting beyond midnight. Cowher's coaches were not going down the road at night to bars and restaurants as Noll's coaches often did. When they went down the road it was for good. Coaches came and went during his first four years. It appeared it was either his way or the highway.

Dick Hoak had a chance to go elsewhere. He was offered the post as offensive coordinator by Tony Dungy at Tampa Bay soon after Super Bowl XXX, but declined the offer in order to stay in his home

Bill Cowher's weekly press conference is shown live on Fox Sports. Stan Savran was the host announcer. He'd cue Cowher when the cameras were set to roll. "Am I okay?" Cowher said to Savran one day. "I don't know about that," responded Savran, "but you can start talking."

area. Hoak grew up in Jeannette and lived in Greensburg, not far from the team's summer training camp at Latrobe. He knew he could always get a corner table at DeNunzio's Restaurant in Jeannette, a block from his boyhood home.

Hoak, the only holdover assistant coach retained from the Noll era, said, "Camps are camps. You meet and you practice and you eat and you go to bed. The next morning you get up and do it again. Every day is the same. They just all run into each other."

Bryan Hinkle, a linebacker who had come up during the Noll regime and stayed for two seasons with Cowher before retiring, said, "Bill's camp is more structured than Chuck's camps."

Hinkle liked Cowher's intensity: "He focuses on the positive rather than the negative."

There were other more noticeable changes at training camp. Cowher put numbers on the players at camp, which was not the case when Noll was in charge. Noll used to stick two fingers between his teeth and whistle and wave the players to move. Cowher had Chet Fuhrman, the conditioning coach, set off an air horn to signal the start and finish of different drill sessions. Everything ran by the clock.

Cowher was more restrictive with the media, and where they could go and not go on the grounds. He moved media from between the practice fields; he wanted no one to get in the path of the players as they moved from one field to another. No one in the organization was permitted to chat with the media on the sideline during camp workouts. He drew the boundary lines his first year when he declined an invitation for him and assistants to attend a pool party with the beat reporters in nearby Greensburg.

Noll and his assistants used to have a "happy hour" with the media immediately after the second practice session of the day. It was an "off-the-record" social time. I thought it was valuable time and that it helped establish a better working relationship between the coaches and the media. You couldn't quote any of the coaches from conversations at "happy hour," but you learned a lot about what was going on at camp, and how the coaches were thinking. It kept you from making some mistakes about how the personnel were faring. Cowher discontinued the practice. Cowher was more concerned about spending time with his assistants and players. Noll was wary of the media, but Cowher kept them at a greater distance, by choice.

Cowher provided transportation for his players between the dormitories and the locker room and dining hall at St. Vincent College. He said he wanted to save their legs. It was heresy to old-time football people. Some insiders thought the camp was getting a lot softer, and that Cowher was pampering the players. Even some veteran players felt that way. It certainly made it more difficult for fans to get autographs between practice sessions.

Dan Rooney let Cowher do it his way. Noll was no longer the head coach at the camp. "He's not a ghost here," remarked Rooney.

Rooney realized he wouldn't have the same relationship, either, that he enjoyed for 23 years with Noll. "Bill Cowher is younger than three of my kids," said Rooney, who was 60 at the time. He could appreciate Cowher's appeal to the players. "He's young like they are and they like that. But that doesn't mean they're anti-Noll either.

"When Chuck came in everybody said he worked for Don Shula, Paul Brown and Sid Gillman, so he was going to do this or that. But Chuck was himself and that's why he was a success. I think that's the biggest thing Bill Cowher has to be. He has to be himself. The dignity of the team comes first."

Strong as he appeared, Cowher did not always get his way. He wanted to shift Greg Lloyd from outside to inside linebacker and Lloyd balked at the idea and wanted none of it, and brought little effort and no enthusiasm to the experiment, so Cowher conceded and went back to the old way. Cowher said it was an "in-house matter," and declined further comment. It was easy to appreciate his discomfort with that one.

He has had outbursts with players, NFL officials, staff, even his own boss. "If I need your attention, I usually know how to get it," said Cowher. He said some of the same things Noll used to say. "We're going to do whatever it takes." Or, "We feel very much that we're going to find a way to win."

Cowher often spoke about "finding a way to win," which seemed to have become a standard motto among many coaches in pro and college sports in 1995.

Bobby April, his special teams coach in 1994 and 1995, left the team after the Super Bowl to return home to coach the New Orleans Saints. April had done a great job in turning a weakness into a strength, and he and Cowher seemed a lot alike in their emotional approach to the game.

"He's good because he gets the best out of players," said April. "His whole week of preparation is pretty technical. We have a psychological message and a motivational message. He likes to build up the team for the entire week, but he always speaks to them at least a couple of minutes a day. He bases everything we do on the Pittsburgh Steelers. He'll recognize an opponent, but his main concern is what we do and how we do it."

Aaron Smith on Coach Bill Cowher:

"He's got the respect of the players, yet the players enjoy having him as a coach. He does a good job of keeping a fair balance between that."

"I would love to spend years
and years in Pittsburgh."
— Kaye Cowher

Cowher lived in Fox Chapel. Cowher never looked better than when his wife and their three daughters were at his side. They made for a handsome family. There were occasions, after a practice session at St. Vincent, or in the lobby at Steelers' headquarters or some civic event, that Cowher had his daughters around him. Cowher never looked happier.

"I'm a very family-oriented person," he said. His wife, Kaye, kept a more public profile than Marianne Noll, the wife of Chuck Noll. Kaye and her twin sister Faye had been outstanding basketball players at North Carolina State when Bill was playing football there, and they both played with the New York Stars of the Women's Professional Basketball League. "The jubilant faces of Kaye and her kids and Bill's parents were frequently flashed on the TV screen during home games.

"I would love to spend years and years in Pittsburgh," said Kaye. "Bill's family is here; we have grandparents, uncles and aunts. It's a great situation for our children to have that family influence. It's not something we've had in any other city."

His family was most important to Cowher.

Bill Bellichick, then coach of the Cleveland Browns, came to Pittsburgh on a Monday night during the 1994 season to watch the Steelers play the Oilers. Cowher said he wouldn't be going to any games on the weekend when the Steelers had a bye.

"If I am, it would be the Carlynton Cougars," said Cowher, a 1975 Carlynton grad. "It won't be any professional team. I can guarantee you that. If I do it, it will be with my kids and wherever that takes me, that will be fine. If I was in my bye week and told my wife I was going to go watch the NFL game, she would shoot me."

(For the record, Bellichick and his wife ended up getting divorced later on, when he was coaching the New England Patriots.)

Kaye Cowher's husband had found a home in Pittsburgh once again. He could do no wrong with many of the team's fans. He quickly became a much-admired public figure.

A man with a drinking problem appeared at training camp one day. He came over and talked to Cowher for five minutes. He asked Cowher how he could turn his life around. Cowher conceded that stuff like that had happened before. He said he also got telephone calls from people seeking advice and counseling.

"I guess I look like a man with the answers," said Cowher, with a wide grin on his face.

Cowher could also break up people the way he sometimes expressed himself with some off-the-wall phrases or word choices. The media call them "Cowherisms." But Bill will not be "dee-teered". Or deterred, if you're a fussbudget about such things.

One day at training camp, Cowher was discussing new rules in the NFL permitting offensive linemen to line up a step back of where they were once required to be, better to meet and arrest onrushing linemen.

"They're trying to *circumcise* the rules," Cowher said.

Myron Cope caught that gaffe, and shot up, "What is this, some kind of Jewish plot? You mean 'circumvent,' don't you?"

Another time, Cowher said, "We've got to recapture a new chemistry." Or, after the AFC title game setback by San Diego, he said, "We have a good chemistry, but we may have to work on a new chemistry."

Another Cowherism: "I think it's important now that you step back and, you know, smell the snow."

He has a reputation for being too demanding, or indifferent to the feelings of so-called little people in the Steelers' organization. But he has been quite generous in sharing sports paraphernalia he's been given to those same people. Some say early success had spoiled him, and that he could be impossible to deal with. So who was the real Bill Cowher?

Vic Ketchman covered the Steelers for 20 some years for the *Irwin Standard-Observer* before leaving the area to edit a house weekly newspaper for the expansion Jacksonville Jaguars. The year before he departed, Ketchman wrote a column on how Cowher's antics could wear thin on people.

"Cowher's natural personality is to scream and holler. He often makes his point to the media by raising his voice, and he has been known to raise his voice to even greater heights in other office dealings. His lack of people skills is the only threat to his coaching future.

"As long as he's winning, his forcefulness will be tolerated. However, all coaches experience losing at some point in their careers. That's when a coach needs friends; certainly not enemies."

Ed Bouchette, the beat writer for the *Pittsburgh Post-Gazette*, wrote: "The brick-sized chin juts out, eyes flash, angry words and saliva spew and a finger points sharply. When Wild Bill Cowher becomes upset, diplomacy takes a back seat."

Mike Ciarochi, the sports editor of the *Uniontown Herald-Standard*, had been on the Steelers' beat with Noll and Cowher as the coach. "You must understand," he wrote, "that Cowher is a man whose picture appears next to the definition of 'intense' in the dictionary."

Gerry Dulac of the *Pittsburgh Post-Gazette*, wrote: "The venue doesn't always matter. He'll do it in the locker room or on the playing field. Doesn't matter if it's a player or coach. He gets that mouth all wrinkled and frothy, and he starts delivering a spit-spewing message that very few will ever forget.

"He is a strange mix of yuppie and pure Pittsburgh. He drives a black Saab convertible and wears Tommy Hilfiger sweaters, but he has that Western Pennsylvania tendency to butcher names like Norm Crosby and stumble into malaprops like Yogi Berra."

Tom McMillan, a sports talk show host for the Steelers' flagship station WTAE, wrote in *Steelers Digest*: "Cowher's basic philosophy never wavers, and that allows him to handle each situation forcefully and effectively without 'losing' his team."

Cowher had some opinions about the media at large:

"I think it's too easy to sit here and second-guess and when you're sitting up on the 50-yard line about 100 yards up and you guys can see everything. I'm not going to ever second-guess a player when a player's in the heat of battle and he has to make a decision that's very much a split-second decision. I would never second-guess anyone.

"I think there's a tendency in our society, to be quite honest with you, to accent the negatives. People sometimes think that's what people want to see and read. My point is simply that as we point out the negatives I think it's important that you also point out the positives. That's how I feel. I think that's how you should deal with people. I try to always see the glass as half-full, not half-empty.

"I think there's a tendency, and a very natural one, and the job of the media is to accentuate the highs and to accentuate the lows. My point is in trying to write the balance that says when everything's high, I don't think we should get that high. And when it's low, it's probably not as bad as you think it is. I'm trying to create a consistency and a balance. I'm trying to keep the scales balanced so they don't get tipped too heavily in either direction. And I think that's my job as a head football coach.

"At the lowest point in the (1995) season, we were 3-4 and had just been embarrassed at home by Cincinnati on national TV. But even at 3-4, we were still in first place in our division, and there were nine weeks left in the season. What more can you ask?

"So we had some meetings and changed our outlook. At that time, we started looking at it as a nine-game season and adopted the outlook that the bottle was half-full and not half-empty.

(Cowher and the Steelers took the same approach, it should be noted, in 2005 when the record was 7-5 and playoff prospects looked dim.)

"A lot of players made sacrifices. A lot of unselfish things were done. We made seven changes in our lineup — some due to injury, some to suspension, some due to a lack of consistency.

"You can make all the changes you want, but for it to work the players have to believe in it. The way we did it was to take one game at a time and not look too far ahead. And, before you knew it, we were still playing in January."

As Cowher was coming off the field at Sun Devil Stadium following the Steelers' disappointing setback by the Dallas Cowboys in Super Bowl XXX, he was met by his family. His wife Kaye comforted him with a hug and kiss and some kind words. Then he kissed his daughters. The oldest, Meagan Lyn, left the biggest impression of all.

(She was also the one who hollered as she embraced her dad after the Steelers won Super Bowl XL, "Daddy, we're champions of the world!")

"I looked down at my daughter and what she said to me I'll never forget," Cowher said after that first Super Bowl disappointment. "She looked up and she said, 'Daddy, win or lose, you'll still be my hero.' I remember telling her, 'You win some and you lose some, and the most important thing is that you do your best.' And I can honestly say our football team did that."

George Gojkovich/Getty Images

Bill Cowher in a calm moment on sideline

Joey Porter on his relationship with Bill Cowher:
"He accepts me for who I am. I'm going to go out there and do what I do best. He accepts that, and he accepts how I play. As long as he appreciates what I do, he knows I'll feel the same way about him."

Hines Ward
The complete package

"It's an honor to be in the NFL."

Ines Ward had won the hearts of Steelers' fans long before he was named the Most Valuable Player in Super Bowl XL. Those who follow the fortunes of the Black & Gold simply love the way this handsome and warm-hearted young man plays the game. He gives his all, on every play. He does whatever it takes to get the job done. He's a good guy on a team full of good guys.

Pro football can be a mean game, a difficult game, a hazardous game, and wide receivers are particularly vulnerable. They are easily hit and hurt out there in no man's land, and some, as we were reminded during the two weeks of endless reports prior to the big game in Detroit, were even paralyzed and ended up in wheelchairs. Defensive backs come at ballcarriers like heat-seeking missiles these days, helmets and padded forearms first. Yet Ward and others continued to play with reckless abandon.

Ward was regarded as one of the greatest receivers in the National Football League, and none other than Mike Ditka, the epitome of a tough receiver in his heyday, said Ward was "the best blocker" of all the receivers in the game today.

Ward wasn't sure about such a label. "I don't really like that category," said Ward when that remark was mentioned to him during Super Bowl week. "I want to be the best receiver I can be.

"I know only one way to play the game, and that's to play each play like it's your last." The 6-foot, 215-pound receiver knew his role well.

"I don't try to be Randy Moss. I don't try to be Marvin Harrison or T.O. (Terrell Owens). I just try to be the most complete wideout I can be.

"I just thought I was a perfect fit for the offense we run, for the city of Pittsburgh's blue-collar town. That's kind of how I think of myself — as a blue-collar worker."

He said he gets great satisfaction when opposing coaches such as Bill Parcells of the Dallas Cowboys and Brian Billick of the Baltimore Ravens praise his efforts. He recalls Billick telling him, "I hate you, but I'd love to have you on my team."

Then there's the absolute joy Hines Ward brings to his job. No matter how hard he gets hit, or how hard he hits a defensive back, he always comes up smiling. Like it's just a lark. It has endeared him to Steelers' fans. No matter how difficult the circumstances, or if all hope for a victory seems to be lost, Ward comes away from every clash with a bright smile and his eyes squeezed nearly shut. It's the signature of his game and his attitude. Hines is always hopeful. He seems to be having a good time out there. Some women want to adopt him.

Hines Ward holds son Jared and Super Bowl XL trophy at Ford Field awards ceremony.

When he caught a touchdown pass from Antwaan Randle El in the fourth quarter of Super Bowl XL, he positively skipped through the end zone, looking like a kid in a playground. He didn't do a dance, and that was good, because he'd been blasted by teammates for poor choreography on earlier efforts in the end zone after scoring touchdowns. That play will remain in the minds of Steelers' fans.

Randle El took the ball on a reverse and looked like he was going to run the ball. A quarterback at Indiana University, Randle El disguises his intent like the old-time NFL quarterbacks. Then he threw the ball on the run — like he was tossing a javelin — and he hit Ward in stride to give the Steelers a 21-10 lead with only nine minutes to play. He also was not ashamed to cry in public. He did this, unabashedly, the day after the Steelers lost to the New England Patriots in the AFC Championship game that ended the Steelers' 2004 season. He felt that he and his teammates had let down Jerome Bettis in what might have been Bettis' last game with the Steelers. He loved Bettis and that's why he was shedding tears.

"I took a lot of flack for that from my home boys," said Ward, reflecting on that tearful moment a year later.

Ward and Ben Roethlisberger and others convinced Bettis to come back for one more year, and they promised they'd get him back to his hometown of Detroit for the Super Bowl.

Ward not only helped get Bettis back to Detroit, but he also managed to get Bettis to tag along when Ward went to Disney World as part of his prize for being named the MVP of Super Bowl XL. Ward also won a Cadillac and chose an Escalade model. There are so many Escalades and Hummers in the Steelers' parking lot at their practice facility. Who didn't smile when they saw Ward with his young son, Jaden, in his arms when he was up on the podium to receive the MVP award after the game?

Ward held out for a new contract and more money during the team's summer training camp in 2005, but managed not to offend the fans by his action. He said all the right things in discussing his situation. He never got nasty or disrespectful toward management. He stayed out for the first 15 days of summer camp. Bettis talked to him every day, providing him with support. Ward didn't want his holdout to become a media circus, and he didn't want to ruin his reputation or the way he was perceived by the fans. He didn't want people to think he was greedy. After a telephone call with Bill Cowher, and a promise that the Steelers wouldn't disappoint him, Ward came in to camp. "I like tough people, and he's a tough player," said Cowher. (There was a story in a spring issue of *Sports Illustrated* that suggested Ward was at odds with Cowher, but Ward was quick to correct that impression.)

Shortly after Ward came to camp, he and the Steelers agreed on a 5-year $27.5 million contract. Ward played in 116 consecutive games before missing the fourth game of the season against Jacksonville. Whereas Terrell Owens tore apart the Philadelphia Eagles with his selfish behavior, Ward would help the Steelers get to and win the

Super Bowl. He made five catches for 123 yards and a touchdown to sparkle in the championship game. He dropped another touchdown pass, going high to get his hands on the ball, and was critical of himself. He said he should have caught it. He knew it would have been the kind of catch Lynn Swann made to rate a place in Super Bowl highlight films for the rest of his life and beyond.

"I make that catch in my sleep 100 times a night," said.Ward. "I put such pressure on myself to make all the catches."

It's believed that Ward will retire as a Steeler, and that would suit everyone just fine. "I'd like that," he said. "I think I was supposed to be here. I'm a good fit. I've never seen a city so passionate about its football team. I couldn't imagine going anywhere else. I like the stability of the Steelers, having a coach like Bill Cowher here so long. They're not big on change. I like that. I think myself and the organization are a close-knit fit.

"When you run out of the tunnel and you wave that Terrible Towel the reaction is unreal. You can't describe it. When I see someone wearing my jersey number — 86 — I want to go up and thank them personally. They're supporting me. Early on, I used to see 36 on so many people and, at first, it looked like 86 and I'd have to catch myself. I'd like to line up everybody who wears 86 and shake their hands and thank them. That's why when I score a touchdown I give the ball to somebody wearing 86. They're on my team. I'm giving it all I've got. I'm busting my tail. I want to represent them well."

People like his story, and the way he expresses himself. With his words, with his smile. He has a biracial heritage. He was born to an Asian woman, a South Korean, and an American soldier, a black man who would later go his own way. (An earlier Steelers' hero, Franco Harris, was the son of a black American soldier and an Italian war bride.) Hines Ward admits that there was a time in his foolish youth that he was ashamed of his mother. He talks about how he learned what an important role she had played in his life, raising him the right way, the main reason he is what he is today, the main reason he is how he is today.

He is a four-time Pro Bowl player and he was a co-MVP along with nose tackle Casey Hampton on the 2005 edition of the Steelers. He was one of the main reasons they became the 2005-2006 Steelers, the kind of heading we usually only see on college and pro basketball teams. He finished the season with 69 receptions for 975 yards and 11 touchdowns, which tied him for the third highest total in the NFL. The Steelers didn't pass as much as they had in previous seasons. In fact, the Steelers attempted fewer passes than any other team in the NFL for the second straight season. Ward had strung together four straight 1,000-yard seasons before that. He has led the Steelers in receiving a record seven consecutive seasons.

He was the second of two third-round draft selections the Steelers had in 1998 (a compensation choice), and he had to prove that he could play on the same field as Troy Edwards and Plaxico Burress, the team's top draft picks the following two seasons. He persevered and, before long, he proved that he belonged in the same conversation as Lynn Swann and John Stallworth. Both Swann and Stallworth have been voted into the Pro Football Hall of Fame. After eight seasons, Ward has surpassed Swann and Stallworth in the Steelers' record books. When he was presented with the MVP Award after Super Bowl XL, Ward addressed that situation: "People are always comparing me to Lynn Swann and John Stallworth Those are great comparisons, but something I didn't have they had was a Super Bowl ring. They made a name for themselves in the Super Bowl. Me winning this honor, I kind of feel like I'm in their class now.

"Just to have my name mentioned with them is an honor. There's something about those guys I just don't have. It's more than the rings. They made some acrobatic catches. I want to make some tough catches like that. I've left a few on the field. I want to get better.

"When I went to the Pro Bowl the first time and was out on the field with Jerry Rice and people like that it was a real thrill. Wow. These were guys I used to pretend to be when I was playing in the streets."

Hines Ward was playing for the Pittsburgh Steelers traveling basketball team on a Friday evening, April 26, 2002, against a team of local police officers at Bethel Park High School. Paul Zolak, the athletic director at Bethel Park, assisted me with credentials and was looking after me. Zolak was Joe Montana's backfield coach at Ringgold High School, where he also served a long tenure as athletic director, and he was the father of former NFL quarterback Scott Zolak.

Ward was on the same level as Scott Zolak when it came to being a class act and a personable young man who made you immediately comfortable in his company. I liked Ward because of the way he played football, a clutch receiver who could block with the best of them, and a young man who always seemed to be enjoying himself. There was a sunshine about him.

He and Deshea Townsend kept taking turns attempting three-point shots and they both jumped up and pumped their fists toward the rafters when one of their long shots hit the nets. They had a little bet going on as to who would hit the most three-pointers. Ward was playful with everyone on the court. Ward wanted to win, of course, but he wasn't taking the game or himself too seriously. He joined his teammates in signing autographs for all the young fans at halftime.

He was most cooperative when I introduced myself and mentioned our mutual friend Dick Bestwick as an icebreaker.

I first became aware of Ward when the Steelers drafted him out of the University of Georgia as their third round pick in 1998. Soon after, I received a scouting report from an old friend, Dick Bestwick, who served as an assistant athletic director in support services at Georgia. I first met Bestwick, who was from Grove City, when he was an assistant coach on Dave Hart's first staff at the University of Pittsburgh in 1966. He was later an assistant at Georgia Tech and the head football coach at the University of Virginia. He couldn't say

66

Hines Ward is flanked by good friends Louis Lipps, at left, and Deshea Townsend at golf outing for Highmark's Caring Foundation at Southpointe Golf Club.

Hines Ward on the Good Life:

"When you win the Super Bowl you feel on top of the world the whole off-season. It's hard to describe. I had planned a trip to Korea with my mom before the season started. When I won the MVP Award in the Super Bowl that changed the whole trip. You can't believe how well we were treated by the Korean people. They were intrigued to see us. I can't describe the magnitude of what's been going on since we won the Super Bowl. Good things happen to you. A poor old kid from Forest Park (Ga.) and people giving us all these nice things. My mom and I have to laugh about it."

.26
Steelers!!

enough good about Ward. He predicted that he would be a first-class performer for the Steelers on and off the field.

He said they had created a special award at Georgia to give to Ward to recognize his all-around scholar-athlete qualities. He was the first African-American athlete in the football or basketball programs to graduate with a 3.0 grade point average or better (3.1 GPA, to be exact) at Georgia. He made the All-Academic team in the SEC.

Hines Ward played several positions for the Bulldogs. He played flanker, tailback, quarterback, tailback and quarterback in that order. Finally, the coaches kept him at wide receiver. He finished his career ranked second in school history with 144 receptions and third in receiving yards with 1,965. He also returned punts and kickoffs.

Ward finished his fourth season with the Steelers as the eighth best pass-receiver in the National Football League with 94 catches to his credit good for 1003 yards and a 10.7 yards per catch average. He was an alternate to the Pro Bowl and got to play when injuries forced others out of the game.

One of Ward's qualities is patience. Ward waits his turn. He outperformed two flashier, but seldom as consistent No. 1 draft choices at the wide receiver position in Pittsburgh, namely Troy Edwards and Plaxico Burress. Neither of those individuals performed as well as Ward, and they were problem children whereas Ward was a model citizen. Everybody liked Hines Ward.

People in Pittsburgh were pushing for him to change his name to Heinz Ward, so he would fit in even better at the Steelers' new playpen on Pittsburgh's North Shore. Then again, if he gets any better they might want to change the name of the home facility to Hines Field. Ward led the team in receiving in 2000 and 2001, tying Edwards with 61 catches and then topping Burress as the team's best. He became the starter at the flanker position, and left Burress and Edwards to battle for the starting wide receiver position. "I'm not sure he's looking for the limelight," said Mike Mularkey, the Steelers' offensive coordinator in 2001. "He loves what he's doing and it shows."

Ward understood what his situation was and felt it best not to make waves. That wasn't his style. "They invested so much in Troy and Plaxico, so those guys were going to get all the attention," said Ward. "I'm pretty sure all eyes are going to be on those guys. And that's fine with me."

In truth, though, Steelers' fans felt more enamored with Ward, right from the start, and appreciated his blue collar work ethic, modest manner and marvelous demeanor. He was their kind of guy. He excelled his rookie year primarily as a hard-nosed tackler and blocker on special teams. He came into his own in his second season. Ward couldn't understand why the Steelers kept taking wide receivers with their No. 1 pick. He resented it.

"He just quietly does his job in the run game and pass game," added Mularkey. "He makes plays over and over. Quarterbacks trust that. Your backs trust he's going to be in there blowing somebody up."

This is a guy who had the anterior cruciate ligament removed from his left knee because of a bicycle accident in fourth grade. Ward wants you to know he knows what's behind his success. "It's heart," he said. "You have to fight through it, fight through all that stuff that I've been through and keep producing on the field."

He gives much credit for his success to his mother, Young Ward. Hines Ward Sr. met her when he was stationed with the U.S. Army in Seoul, South Korea. She was then called Kim Young He, and was a clerk in Seoul. They were married, Hines Jr. was born, and the family moved to the United States.

The marriage didn't last, though, and young Hines was sent to live with his father in Monroe, Louisiana. His father had been a good football player there in his youth. His mother worked at several jobs, saved her money and learned the English language. When Hines was 8, his mother was awarded custody of him by the courts. He was able to move in with his mother in Forest Park, just east of Atlanta's Hartsfield International Airport. There was still a language barrier.

He was a latchkey child from a broken biracial home. He knew of no other family. There were no uncles, aunts or cousins. There was no father except for an occasional telephone call. His mother used to tell him, "I live every day of my life for you," and, in time, he realized how fortunate he was to have such a caring mother.

"Here's a lady who comes to this country and nobody gave her anything," Ward says. "She didn't know English. She went out and worked the cashier's job, the produce job, cleaning hotels . . . Everything she got, she earned, and that's how my career is. Nothing was ever given to me."

He spent much of his $150,000 plus rookie salary to improve her position in life. He signed a new $9.5 million contract in September, 2001 and upgraded her car from a Toyota Avalon to a Lexus. He had bought her a new home in suburban Stockbridge that first year as well. "At first, it was kinda hard because I couldn't understand what she was telling me," he recalled. "I was a little kid. I wasn't used to being around her. I was pretty cruel. I deserved a whipping more than once."

The kids in the neighborhood made fun of him for having an Asian mother. "I remember ducking when she took me to school," he said. "I was kind of ashamed." That's all changed as he learned to appreciate his mother and the impact she had on his development. "She is my inspiration," he said.

At Forest Park (Ga.) High School, Ward starred at quarterback as a junior and senior. He was coached by Mike Parris. Ward says Parris was "kind of the father I didn't have." They remain close and often talk on the telephone following games.

Parris told Gary Mihoces of *USA Today* that Ward was a defensive star as well in high school. "Hines was as good at free safety as he was at anything else," said Parris. "He loved to hit people.

"Of course, I'm prejudiced, but to me he's the best all-around receiver in the NFL. He is not the fastest. He might not have the greatest hands, but he's going to do everything for you. He's going to block. He's going to do everything he can to win a football game. He's a complete football player and always has been."

Hines Ward:

My whole career, it's been, "You couldn't do this." My high school teachers said, "You're never going to make the pros." I think about all those things. I think about the players who I played with who said I wouldn't be nothing. And every time I get on national TV, I want to do something spectacular. Then, they can say, "Here's a good football player." My whole career is about proving people wrong. That's the fun part of it.

I still call Lynn Swann Mr. Swann when I see him. I say Mr. Stallworth. It's the respect factor I have for them. They weren't just great on the field, they're great people off of it. And, when I'm done here, that's exactly how I want to be remembered, like Mr. Stallworth and Mr. Swann. When people say, "Hines Ward," I want them to say great things about me, too. Forget about the records. I want to be remembered for more than just my numbers.

My mother raised me to be the way I am now. She never wanted people to look down upon us. Her name is Young Ward and she told me to treat people the way I wanted to be treated. It's that simple; it's the old golden rule. There was just the two of us, her and me. I was an only child. It was more of a team thing. She had to work two or three jobs, and she wasn't around as much as she'd have liked. So she wanted to make sure I didn't get into any trouble.

My mother still treats me like I'm a teenager.

She preached that I should respect everyone. She especially wanted me to respect my teachers. She said you may disagree with what they say, but you should always be respectful.

I was living by myself from an early age, and I had to learn responsibility. She would go to work early in the morning before I was up. She would make me breakfast and leave it out for me. I had to get up myself and fix breakfast, and get on the bus to go to school. My mother wasn't walking me to school.

When I came home at midday my lunch would be on the table. She was off to another job. She'd come home and make me dinner and, more often than not, she was off to another job.

Hines Ward

Photos by George Gojkovich/Getty Images

She usually left my dinner for me in the microwave. She cleaned dishes at a Marriott hotel. She was cashier at a convenience store at night, and sometimes she cleaned hotel rooms. In my rookie season with the Steelers, my whole first paycheck went to her. It wasn't about me. I wanted to be able to repay my mother. I saw my mom sacrifice so much. She's the reason why I go out there and play.

We live in Stockbridge, Georgia and she's been up about three or four times. She didn't like being in the stands at the game. People say stuff about guys on the team, and she didn't like that. People are talking bad about other players she's heard me talk about. She'd rather watch it on TV.

I was a baseball player before I was a football player. I played baseball in eighth and ninth grade. I was drafted in baseball as a high school player and, for awhile, I thought my professional career was going to be in baseball. I was small in high school. I was six feet tall and weighed only about 165 pounds. I built myself up to 200 pounds in college.

My first awareness of my prospects as a pro football player came during my junior year. That's when I first thought I had a chance to make it. In my freshman and sophomore years, I was just glad to be a part of the football program. It was a dream come true just to be playing football for Georgia.

One thing I'm especially proud of at Georgia was that I was the first African-American football player to have a 3.0 or better Grade Point Average. I had a 3.1 GPA, and I completed my requirements for my bachelor's degree in 3½ years. I majored in economics and minored in real estate.

I actually enjoyed going to classes. It was a chance to interact with other students. I didn't want my life to revolve around my teammates all the time.

I enjoy playing pro football. My teammates ask me why I'm always smiling. But I'm also smart enough to know that it's more like a business than any football I played before I signed with the Steelers. I see players come and go. I know teams have to pick up players and get rid of them to stay under the salary cap from year to year. I'm not complaining about that. A lot of guys my age would love to be in the position we're in. Doing what we love to do on the highest level.

We get paid so much more than they used to get paid. I had an opportunity this winter to play basketball with some of the former Steelers, guys like Louis Lipps and Edmund Nelson. It's great to get respect from guys like that who can appreciate what it's all about.

"It's kinda like Forrest Gump.
I just take it as it comes.
— Hines Ward, prior to a return trip
to Seoul, South Korea

I met Lynn Swann a few times when I was in college. He came in with ABC to do some of our games. I had no idea then that I'd be playing the same position he did with the Pittsburgh Steelers.

I hope I have a good reputation on and off the field. My approach to the game is go out and do whatever it takes to get the job done, and to make the best possible contribution. I'll sacrifice my body to block for our backs and other receivers. I hope they'll do the same for me.

I like to put hits on those defensive backs because if I go across the middle for a pass they'll try to take my head off.

I got a lot of attention for the blocking I did on Rod Woodson in the playoff game with the Baltimore Ravens. Hey, a lot was at stake in that game. Rod was a great player around here, and the fans still love Rod. But not when he's going up against the Steelers. I like Rod. I have a lot of respect for him, and I hope I'll earn his respect. I don't take it personally. I wasn't out to get Rod Woodson per se. He was just the man I had to take out.

"I just love playing football."

There's a lot of interest in the Steelers here, and you can see it everywhere you go. I live in Shadyside and I like living in the city. Other guys live in the suburbs. I go to their places, too. I think the guys like playing in Pittsburgh.

They want to play here. We've got great facilities. We've got a grass field. We played in Three Rivers Stadium and we know how hard that surface was. So we know what those great teams had to go through every day at practice, playing on that hard surface.

The Steelers have one of the better fan bases here. They love their Steelers. I go down to Atlanta and they don't care about the Falcons. They don't rally behind the team the way Pittsburgh does. Pro football isn't as important there as it is here.

I know what the Steelers did here in the '70s. They won four Super Bowls in six years. That's a hard act to follow. Every player wants to go to the big dance.

When I first came here they put me on the back burner. I was a third round pick and nobody gave me a chance of getting into the Steelers' starting lineup. But here I am.

When you see No. 86 on the field, he's going to bust his butt every way possible, blocking, catching, just the little things, special teams if I have to. Sometimes, I get frustrated, but when I strap on the pads, I love the excitement of football.

I love playing, and I think it shows on the field. I'm always smiling. I just love playing. There's nothing I would rather do. Troy and Plaxico got all the attention when they came. Nobody talked about me. I went out and was the best ballplayer I could be. When I was drafted, I was just hoping I could stick here.

When I was practicing a few years back for the Pro Bowl in Hawaii, Tim Brown, the great receiver for the Raiders, told me that the best way to get recognized and appreciated is to be consistent.

Just to be out there with people like Troy Brown and Marvin Harrison and Tim Brown was so great. Just to be associated with Tim Brown is a big thing. Those guys tell me the little things and it should help me get better.

I was calling him "Mr. Brown," because that's the kind of respect I have for someone like him. He's been playing this position a lot longer than me. I want to last long in this league, like Jerry Rice.

If I do, I'll still be smiling. Why be sad? Thanks to my mother I had the opportunity to do something special. There are not too many guys my age making the kind of money we get paid. Everyone else would love to be doing what I'm doing.

So I'm going to keep working and try to get better and, of course, more consistent.

I watch what someone like Jerome Bettis does. He's a true professional. He has a great attitude. He knows how to present himself to the public. He's a great people person.

I see Jerome Bettis and I want to be like that. Football is not going to be forever. I have to have people skills. I'll have a nine-to-five job someday, and I have to be able to deal with people.

Judging Miss USA Pageant

Hines Ward was one of the judges for the Miss USA Pageant in late April, 2006, soon after he and his mother had returned from their 10-day trip to their native South Korea. Ward was the second Steelers' receiver to do so. Lynn Swann helped judge the contest in 1991, and Pitt's Heisman Trophy winner Tony Dorsett did the honors in 1984.

Connie Rash with Hines Ward —
a true student-athlete at Georgia

Connie Rash, the assistant director of student services at the University of Georgia, was an academic advisor in the athletic department at the University of Georgia during Hines Ward's student days, and she sent us the following e-mail reflection:

"When Hines Ward came to Georgia, he had an academic plan and a goal. Make good grades and graduate. Hines always followed the plan that would lead to graduation. Dr. Sweeney and I worked with Hines as his academic advisors. He would always thank us for our efforts. He was always polite and took his academics very seriously. He always went to class and always sat in the front row.

"As part of my position, I am in charge of recruitment for the College of Family and Consumer Services. During his junior and senior years, Hines often went with me on numerous high school recruitment trips. Schools were always excited when I said Hines Ward was coming. The speaking engagement would be elevated from a single classroom to having the whole school in the auditorium.

"One day, I received a call from Hart County High School in Hartwell, Ga., saying they wanted to have a "Hines Ward Day." I called Robert Miles, an academic advisor in the athletic department, and asked him to go with us. We drove there in a University of Georgia van. Mr. Miles and I were so impressed with Hines's performance on stage that day. The crowd was so enthusiastic.

"He talked about the importance of getting a good education. He told them to follow their dreams and to never let anybody or anything hold them back from achieving their dreams. He talked about his mother and what she meant to him. He said you had to give it all in football and in the classroom and that you had to work harder than the other guy to get noticed. He was a good guy with a good story for youth.

"I am blessed that in every year I receive a Christmas card from Hines Ward. I treasure these cards because — after all the fame he has gained — he still remembers me."

Bill Cowher
Committed to winning

"I'll let my record speak for itself."

From *Steelers Forever*, 2002

The Steelers and Bill Cowher made quite a comeback during the 2001 season. The Steelers had two sub-par seasons in 1998 and 1999 and failed to make the playoffs again in 2000. Before the start of the 2001 season, not many fans or critics — and we were among them — didn't expect them to do much better in 2001.

Cowher and his Steelers surprised everyone. They didn't look good when they lost their season opener at Jacksonville, bowing by 21-3. The tragic events of September 11, coupled with an NFL-scheduled bye week, gave the Steelers an unusual three-week period to lick their wounds and get whole again.

The Steelers came back to win 13 of their last 15 football games and made it all the way to the AFC Championship game. When they gained the home field advantage late in the schedule, their fans felt they had a good chance of going all the way, certainly making it to the Super Bowl. But they blew it, and got knocked off by the New England Patriots, 24-17. The Patriots stopped the Steelers' running game cold, and took advantage of two special teams touchdowns to deliver the knockout punches. Everybody in Pittsburgh was upset.

No one was more upset than Bill Cowher was. He was determined to get back to work and make sure the Steelers didn't come up short again. He had won his 100th coaching victory during the season, and he recognized it had been a good one. He also knew he was on solid footing with his bosses, Dan Rooney and his son, Art Rooney II. He was just 44 years old, and the Rooneys kept their previous coach for 23 years. Chuck Noll was 60 when he retired from coaching. The Steelers like stability, something they never had until Noll came along.

Before the 2001 season, the Rooneys had extended Cowher's contract, to the chagrin of some, the confusion of others. After all, Cowher was coming off a string of sub-par seasons and he still had two years remaining on his contract. The Steelers hadn't been in the playoffs for three years. Why not wait another year?

"We wanted to show Bill what we thought of him," declared Dan Rooney. "He's one of us. He's a Pittsburgh Steeler."

Cowher had coached the Steelers for ten years, coming into the 2002 season, and he had the longest tenure of any current NFL coach with one team. He and his wife Kaye, whom he met during their respective days at North Carolina State University, had a home in Fox Chapel. They have three beautiful daughters: Meagan Lyn, 16,

Dave Kreider

Marvel Smith

> *When he was putting together his Cleveland Browns football team, Paul Brown searched to find "the high class of people" he was looking for to fill his roster.*

Verron Haynes

Chris Gardocki

Lauren Marie, 14, and Lindsay Morgan, 11 at that time. Cowher shows up at a lot of their school activities, and that always sets off a buzz in the crowd. Everybody in Pittsburgh recognizes Bill Cowher.

He came out of Crafton. His parents, Laird and Dorothy, were still living in the same three-story yellow brick home on Hawthorne Avenue. I had visited them there and their pride in their son, as well as his brothers Doug and Dale, is quite evident. They sit in the family's box at Heinz Field and go through torment and joy at every home game. To them, he'll always be "Billy," and they love it when he comes home, gets a beer out of the refrigerator, and sits down and talks to them.

Bill Cowher covered a lot of ground at a press conference he conducted on January 29, 2002, and interviews since then.

Bill Cowher:

I knew what I was doing. I had a plan. Am I demanding? Sure, I'm demanding. Sometimes you have to show tough love. But I also like to think I'm very fair and compassionate. And I also like to think I demand more of myself than anyone else does. When something goes wrong, I look at me first, "Did I cover that? Did I make the point clear?'

I like to believe one of my strengths is my ability to delegate. I give Mike Mularkey and Tim Lewis a lot of responsibility and let them do their thing. Now, that doesn't mean I won't veto something from time to time. But you need good people around you, and you have to trust them. We've got good people here.

Every person I've hired hasn't been the right fit. Sometimes you don't know about people until you actually start working with them. Through these tough times I've gone through in recent years, I've learned a lot about people. I've learned who my friends really are and who will stick by you in difficult times. You learn a lot about people in tough times.

I don't hold grudges, but I don't forget either.

I still love what I'm doing and I love where I'm doing it. A big motivation for me is to have my kids grow up here and not have to move. That's so rare in this business. But we've got a chance. My youngest, Lindsay, is in fifth grade. That means I've got at least seven more years to sustain this.

In looking at the season as a whole, I think in many ways a very solid foundation has been set. From my perspective personally, it may be the healthiest atmosphere that I have ever experienced on a football team. The organization, the coaching staff, the players, the openness, the unselfishness, the consistency that we played at this year, the way this organization worked as one — like I have said, in many respects is the healthiest that I have ever been involved with since I entered the league in 1980.

I think while we set a solid foundation, there is still going to be an emptiness with how this season ended. But, as I looked at this team, I made an analogy and reference to 1994 where we won a playoff game for the first time in many years. Having lost the first two years upon coming here in 1992 and 1993, and then in 1994 we beat the Cleveland Browns in the playoffs and then we played against San Diego in the AFC title game. We were the favored team, much like we were against New England, and we fell short.

We have the same feeling we felt then and we want to use it to fuel us the next time out. The year after we lost to San Diego we beat the Indianapolis Colts in the AFC championship game and we got to the Super Bowl. We didn't win there, but we got there. We still have to take that last step.

Time will tell, but there is a very solid nucleus here and that is how we are going to approach the coming year.

"The resolve is greater."

It is about us finding a way to win a championship. If you think Sunday's disappointment did anything to this guy, the resolve is greater. I am going to be someone's worst nightmare and keep coming back. If that is how you want to view it, so be it. We are not stopping until we win a championship. That is genuinely how I feel.

I talked to every player and there is not a player that does not understand and does not feel — to a degree — the resolve that I am referring to. When you get that far, is the hurt greater? Yes, it hurts because we threw a lot more into it. We reached emotional highs that some people have never reached before.

Some of the risk involved in doing that is that you end up reaching emotional lows that you have never reached before because the farther you go the more it hurts.

But, that same hurt has to be the same fuel that brings you back next year to say that you are going to the next step.

You look at 22 out of 24 starters coming back and that's a pretty solid foundation from a team that played pretty consistently throughout the season. We'll start soon. We would like to keep this thing intact. This has been a special group of guys; it really has. Not just the free agents, but I look at the group that we brought in last year. Draft choices and free agents. Those are solid, solid people. Jeff Hartings and Mike Logan . . . they're solid people now. That's strong, strong fiber. Casey Hampton, Kendrell Bell, Rodney Bailey . . . that's strong.

It's important to keep what you have and what you do bring in, they have to fit the makeup of the team and it's a team that knows how to work. They've grown tremendously through this year together. In some respects, they can't wait until next year starts.

This is not a bad place to come to and I think people understand that. That in itself will never get things done, but it certainly will help.

Kordell will come back strong. This game meant a lot to him. He wanted an opportunity to go back home (to New Orleans) where he grew up. He had a solid year now. This guy, he was our leader. After talking to the other players through the course of two days, you could see how well he is respected on this football team. He is eager to get back, too. He's not looking back now.

"I think these two guys will get better."

I think Plaxico Burress had a great year. Where is he from where he was? It's light years. I think that he finished up on a high. If you watched us throw the ball against Buffalo and someone would have said that after that game that we were going to have two 1,000-yard receivers I would have said, "What?"

Where we were at the end of the season; the confidence we had throwing the ball; the emergence of Hines Ward and Plaxico, and some of the other guys like Troy Edwards. That's something. I think Plax has a tremendous upside. I think he has a lot going for him as I do Hines Ward. I think these two guys will get nothing but better because I think they're still young receivers. I think as an offensive football team, when you sit there and say that you're not losing one player, it's a pretty good nucleus to begin next year after a year in this system.

Hines Ward is self-made. He's worked so hard to get where he's at today. He's a football player. Some guys you say are so talented, they have this and they have that. Hines Ward, to me, is one of those guys that may not be fast enough, may not be big enough and may not be quick enough but he's a football player. He makes plays. He does all the little things. He studies the game. On gameday is when he thrives. He's a player.

He's one of those guys that when you watched him at Georgia — they didn't even know where to put him because he was one of those guys that do everything well but nothing really great. This guy, we found a place for him at receiver and he's got a chance to be pretty special.

80

"You're not just going to get to January by just showing up."

When you get to the championship and you realize that you're one of four teams and you watch the teams play and you know how you are — you talk about a championship the next year and there's a realistic feeling going in. After finishing strong the year before and not making the playoffs, when you talked about a championship at the beginning of this season I'm sure some people said, "Oh, yeah." But I'm not sure they really felt that way.

When you go and play the way that we were able to play and develop the kind of belief that we developed, you take that into next year. That's not a guarantee that anything is going to happen. You're not just going to get to January by just showing up. You're going to go through minicamps, you're going to go through an off-season program, you're going to have to go through the same commitment, the same approach, the same tough dog days of training camp, the same unfolding of the preseason and probably a different makeup of a squad. The season will take on its own personality again, but there's going to be that belief in knowing that when you just stick together and take that same approach you have to believe that anything is possible. That's what we have to do.

I don't want anybody here that doesn't want to be here. If you don't want to be here then there's the door. There are plenty of other people that want to come in here; there are a lot of good coaches. I like the guys that we have and I don't think any of them don't want to be here.

My feelings are irrelevant. My results speak for themselves and I'll live with that. You guys all have your opinions on me and I'm respectful of that and I understand that you guys have jobs to do. All I can tell you is that the resolve has never been greater and time heals all wounds.

George Gojkovich/Getty Images

Art Rooney II on winning another Super Bowl

Art Rooney II knows the Steelers' history well. He went from ball boy to team president during his lifetime. He remembered sitting in the stands at Tulane Stadium as a child and crying tears of joy after the Steelers won Super Bowl IX.

He knew how much winning another Super Bowl — the team's fifth title — would mean to his father, the oldest owner in the NFL. "It would be great to see," said Art II, "because I think he, like many of us, when we were holding the trophy the last time in January 1980, we probably were a little spoiled at that point. And I don't think any of us thought it would be another 25, 26 years before we got to do it again. So, now that it's been so long, we understand how special it is, and he, in particular, has a special feeling for what it's like to win a championship now."

Dick Hoak knows The Steeler Way

Dick Hoak, at 66, is at an age when most people are retired. But he was looking forward to continuing as the running backs coach of the Steelers. He was one of the few who was actually seeking "one for the thumb" as the Steelers approached Super Bowl XL. He had been an assistant coach for 34 years and played for the Steelers for ten years.

"I don't know if there's a coach in the league who's been with one team as long as Dick has," said Kevin Colbert, director of football operations. "I think it's terrific that he's stayed with the Steelers so long. He understands The Steeler Way, their philosophy of doing things."

Only chairman Dan Rooney, team video coordinator Bob McCartney and player personnel man Joe Greene were current members of the Steelers' organization who had four other Super Bowl rings in their jewelry collection.

"I'm not sure how much longer I'm going to be doing this, so it would be nice to win one more before the end of my career. I know I want to coach at least one more year. After that season, I'll sit down and look at it. Do I still enjoy it? Do I still feel good? Is my health still good? But I've never said I was going to retire at a certain age. I never set a timetable."

New CIA Director
grew up with Steelers

General Michael V. Hayden, the new CIA director, is a protégé of Steelers' chairman Dan Rooney. Gen. Hayden, the former Principal Deputy Director of National Intelligence, grew up on the North Side, played for a St. Peter's Grade School football team that was coached by Dan Rooney, and was an ROTC graduate at Duquesne University. Gen. Hayden was a guest of the Steelers' boss in his box at Ford Field for Super Bowl XL.

Gen. Hayden grew up in a neighborhood that gave way to Three Rivers Stadium. He recalls his early experiences with the Rooneys and Steelers:

"By the time I was in eighth grade, I was his quarterback," said Gen. Hayden. "I kind of hung with the Steelers during my high school years, helping out any way I could. When I was finishing up at Duquesne, Dan's work with the Steelers became so demanding that he could no longer give St. Peter's sufficient time. He asked me to coach the team and I did and I coached them for three years before I went on active duty."

He also worked during training camp and helped out in the press box on game day. He assisted Baldy Regan and Mike Kearns in the press box. "Dan has been wonderful," said Gen. Hayden. "I went to training camp and worked during the summer. I would get a lump sum check for working and that combined with my parents' sacrifice allowed me to pay for my tuition at Duquesne. It was a fundamental gateway to my getting a college education."

He earned a bachelor's degree in history and a master's degree in modern American history in 1969, both from Duquesne. He has always been a great Steelers' fan. "I know I am a little prejudiced knowing the family and growing up with the team and city," he said. "There are very few sports franchises that more clearly reflect the culture of the city in which they are located than this team does. This team just goes to work. It's focused. There is not a lot of glamour. There is not a lot of glitz. There is a reason we don't have cheerleaders. We just go there to watch a football game."

> *"There are those who lose their soul to profit. I want to win the right way."*
> **— Jack Welsh, former CEO**
> **General Electric Company**

Kevin Colbert
The company man

"We have a chance to get the sixth Super Bowl."

Kevin Colbert is one of the best-kept secrets in the Steelers' organization. He keeps a lower profile than the FBI agents who are housed in a building next door to the UPMC Sports Performance Complex on the South Side and often come over to have lunch amid the Steelers in the dining area.

He is never seen in the "Seen" column of the *Pittsburgh Post-Gazette* that keeps track of the city's social scene. Kevin Colbert would offer a thin smile at such an observation.

There's a twinkle in his dark eyes. He doesn't need a spotlight on him to have a gleam in his eyes. He knows what he's doing. He knows his place in the company of the powers-that-be in the Steelers' offices there. Dan Rooney is the chairman of the board. His oldest son, Art Rooney II, is the president. Bill Cowher is the head coach. Kevin Colbert is the director of football operations. Colbert grew up with the Steelers and appreciates their history and style.

On any other NFL team, Colbert would be the general manager. The Steelers have never had a general manager. The Steelers have never been big on titles. Joe Gordon had about four or five different titles during his long stay as publicist for the Pittsburgh pro team when he was recognized as the best at his job in the NFL. None of them captured what he truly meant to the franchise. In truth, he was Dan Rooney's right-hand man.

None of the front office people in the organization get their pictures or their profiles in the Steelers' media guide. It's always been that way. Some owners have pictures of themselves with their prize stallions or political leaders or movie stars, but that's not the Steelers' way, not the Rooneys' approach. Dan Rooney has an ego, mind you, and he keeps a close eye and approves every check that controller Jim Ellenberger sends out, and he is always seeking ways for the Steelers to improve the bottom line in their financial report. The NFL has taken steps to take even more control of its product, and Rooney is running at the head of the pack in that respect. Yet he doesn't look like or behave like most millionaires. He had nine children and it shows. Vito Stellino, a sportswriter, once observed when he was on the Steelers' beat: "Chuck Noll has one child and is always offering advice about how to raise children, and Dan Rooney has nine and never offers any advice."

Dan Rooney lives modestly in Pittsburgh, frequents neighborhood restaurants on the North Side where he grew up. He enjoys more posh surroundings in Palm Beach and Ireland. His father preached that it wasn't smart to play the role of a rich man in

George Gojkovich/Getty Images

Kevin Colbert and Bill Cowher have combined talents to steer Steelers to fifth Super Bowl championship.

Jim O'Brien

Pittsburgh. Don't drive a Cadillac; a loaded Buick is better. Don't let the players think you have a lot of money. It hurts you at contract time. Dan Rooney knows something about good guys and good players. "We interview them," he said, "and we talk about it. We want players who are a good fit for our locker room. And having smart players; that's an important phase of it. We only want to see their names in the sports pages. Kevin Colbert has done a terrific job of selecting players and keeping the team viable." (For the record, he said this before first round pick Santonio Holmes was arrested twice in three weeks.)

Colbert's work hasn't gone unnoticed. He finished fourth in the voting for the NFL Executive of the Year for the 2005 season. His boss, Art Rooney II, won the award.

It's best to keep a low profile in the Steelers' front office. Tom Donahoe was a favorite of the Rooneys. He rose through the ranks from ball boy to director of football operations. But he clashed with Cowher in a battle of strong egos and he was gone. The Rooneys are not reluctant to make tough decisions. Donahoe was the nephew of the late mayor and state governor, David Lawrence, a crony of the late Arthur J. Rooney, founder of the franchise and father of Dan Rooney. It didn't save him. He was exiled to Buffalo where he got the big title and the big money but not the success he had been a part of in Pittsburgh. Donahoe did a great job in Pittsburgh, but he forgot his place. Near the end, he and Cowher were hardly talking. That wouldn't work. Dan is infamous for firing his brother Art as director of player personnel because he had too much to say, enjoyed mixing with the media, and rubbed Coach Chuck Noll the wrong way. "How could he fire his brother?" people still ask.

The Rooneys replaced Donahoe with Colbert. He had the right pedigree. He'd grown up on the North Side, within walking distance of Three Rivers Stadium, and played some sports in an undistinguished career at North Catholic High School. Same as Dan Rooney. The Steelers' early years were mostly unsuccessful because Art Rooney hired so many of his cronies to coach and run the team. Dan Rooney made a mistake in his first hiring, Bill Austin from Vince Lombardi's staff with the great Green Bay Packers teams. Austin tried to be like Lombardi and was a pale imitation. Rooney got it right the next time, hiring Noll away from Don Shula's staff on the Baltimore Colts. Noll was his own man and saved the franchise. Rooney got it right when Noll retired after 23 years when he hired Cowher, a Pittsburgh kid who grew up in nearby Crafton. Cowher is his own man, too. Cowher was looking forward to his 15th year as head coach. No NFL team had the stability that the Steelers enjoyed.

Cowher and Colbert had combined their talents and energies since 2000 to lead the Steelers to a Super Bowl XL title after the 2005 season. They were the toast of the town. They got along well. There was none of the tension or backbiting that went on during the Cowher-Donahoe days.

"I think when you understand and work for the Rooney family, it's very easy to hold your ego in check with the example they set," said Colbert.

I had several opportunities to chat with Colbert during the Steelers' mini-camp and voluntary coaching sessions that stretched from a muggy May through a muggy June at the UPMC Sports Performance Complex.

Colbert doesn't do interviews during the season. He's not one to seek the spotlight. He doesn't crowd Cowher for attention in their hometown.

"Are you hiding in the shade?" Colbert said to me one day as he came off the practice field and found me. I told him that was a wise place for a pale-faced Irishman to hang out. Then I told him a story about Wellington Mara, the late co-owner of the New York Giants.

I was standing with Mara on the sideline at a Giants' practice one summer at Pace University in a place called Pleasantville, New York. Mara had a constant squint. We both had blue eyes. "The Irish were not meant to be out in the sun," said Mara. "They were built for peat bogs, caves and other dark places. That's why they spend so much time in pubs and saloons." Colbert smiled at my reminiscence.

Colbert is good company. He's a pleasant fellow who recognizes his good fortune. He has a dream job in his hometown. He's easy to talk to in the so-called off-season. There's no pretense about him. He's a Pittsburgh guy, and Art Rooney felt that was a title befitting a knight.

Colbert turned 49 on January 29, 2006 and couldn't believe he'd be 50 on his next birthday. Where did the time go?

He had been married for 25 years to Janis and they have three children, Kacie, 23; Jennie, 20; and Dan, 17.

A member of the Steelers' teams of the '70s stopped by to talk to Charlie Batch about getting involved in a community endeavor. When I told him there were a lot of good guys and great personalities on the current club, he said, "It's a different era. There's more money involved and the players are different. Bill Cowher gives them more leeway than Chuck Noll. Cowher doesn't expect them to be robots."

Noll must have done something right. Those robots — and they weren't really robots — managed to win four Super Bowls. Did Terry Bradshaw or Joe Greene or Mel Blount or Mike Wagner or Jack Lambert or Jack Ham or Dwight White or Ernie Holmes or Lynn Swann ever strike you as robots? Noll was fond of saying, "You never start out where you finished the previous year." And that "football takes on a life of its own each year."

"The Irish were not meant to be out in the sun."
— Wellington Mara

"That was class."
— Bob Colbert

Colbert doesn't like to blow his own horn. His brother, Bob, age 59, likes to do that. I have run into Bob Colbert and his wife of 37 years, Christine, a couple of times at Ross Park Mall in the North Hills. He was chosen to be the head football coach at St. Vincent College in Latrobe. That's where the Steelers hold their annual summer training camp. The Colbert connection couldn't have hurt, but Bob has coached a string of championship teams at Bridgewater (Va.) College in NCAA Division III ranks, and held scouting positions with the Baltimore Colts and Washington Redskins in his resume.

"Kevin's got a great mind, a great memory," said brother Bob. "He's studied this game and he amazes me with what he knows. He's a good brother. He provided a pair of tickets for each of his four brothers for the Super Bowl. He got them and paid for them. He didn't have to do that. That was class.

"Success and his position have not changed him at all. He doesn't need a neon sign saying who he is.

"He was an average linebacker and an average punter when he played at North Catholic. He played basketball and hockey. He still plays hockey. Our mom died from cancer when Kevin was just five years old. Our dad died from a stroke when Kevin was 15. Our oldest brother, John or "Bud," as everybody calls him, is 62, and he really raised Kevin. There were five of us boys on 48 Solar Street. There were a lot of good athletes in the neighborhood. You remember Rip Scherer? He coached at Moon Township and rated opposing players for years for the Steelers. He lived nearby. It was a great place to grow up. We had a lot of fun, and I guess we did it under difficult circumstances."

Bud Colbert, the oldest Colbert, said of the early days with his brothers after their parents died: "You do what you have to do. Kevin was a really good kid. If he got tired of my cooking, he'd cook. We were never real fancy. We'd eat fried baloney. Get some ground meat, tomato sauce and noodles and that made a quick supper."

I drove through the Colberts' old neighborhood near St. Boniface Church one Saturday in June of 2006. There are lots of winding steep streets and dead ends. I had to back up just to maneuver one sharp turn. I couldn't find Solar Street on my first tour of the area. But I got some directions from Kevin and went back a second time and found it. It looked a lot like my boyhood neighborhood in Hazelwood. Some houses had been well maintained and others looked like they might fall down if you blew on them. Let's just say Kevin Colbert and his brothers have come a long way in their lives.

St. Vincent once fielded good football teams and even played in the Tangerine Bowl, but discontinued the sport in 1962. Dave Hart, the highly successful college sports administrator, transferred from the University of Georgia to play football at St. Vincent College in the heyday of the Bearcats. Bob Colbert's varsity team would make its debut for the 2007 season. They would play on the same field where the Steelers practiced. The campus has been enhanced by the addition of several dormitories in recent years including Arthur J. Rooney Hall, and the Steelers' association will add to its attractiveness to young prospects.

"Kevin does a fantastic job." — Bill Cowher

Colbert has done a good job of coordinating a scouting effort and player evaluation program. Nineteen of Pittsburgh's 22 starters in Super Bowl XL were acquired in the college draft. His No. 1 picks had panned out well and, more importantly, so had many of the later picks. The Steelers only signed a few free agents, nothing earth-shattering or controversial. They would never go after a Terrell Owens, for instance.

Colbert looks forward to the college draft. "Those two days are like the first game of the year," he said.

You're always hoping you can come up with another Ben Roethlisberger, who was 27-4 as a starting quarterback, or move up in the draft to take a Troy Polamalu, one of the best and most unique safeties in Steelers or NFL history.

Bill Cowher credits Colbert and his staff for making his job easier. "Kevin does a fantastic job of taking everybody's input," said Cowher. "It is an accumulation of a lot of people's viewpoints."

The Steelers have an interesting draft history. Their first-ever draft pick back in 1936 was William Shakespeare of Notre Dame. His name was better than he was. Their first pick in 1936 was Byron "Whizzer" White, one of the most decorated college players ever. He came out of Colorado to lead the league in rushing as a rookie. He was the NFC's highest paid rookie at $15,000. Then he retired because he had other aspirations. He became the youngest member of the Supreme Court when he was sworn in by President John F. Kennedy.

In 1955 the Steelers selected John Unitas, a Pittsburgh-bred quarterback out of the University of Louisville. Walt Kiesling never gave him a fair shot and cut him and he ended up with the Baltimore Colts and became the best quarterback in history. They drafted Lenny Dawson from Purdue and Jack Kemp from Occidental College and let them go and they became star quarterbacks in the American Football League. Buddy Parker traded away most of the draft picks when he was coach in the early '60s. They finally got it right when the Steelers selected Joe Greene of West Texas State ("Joe Who?" ran the headline in the Pittsburgh newspaper the next day) in 1969 and then Terry Bradshaw of Louisiana Tech the following year. That was the beginning of building a dynasty.

Ron Hughes, who was Colbert's boss in Detroit, recalls Kevin coming to see him after the Steelers made him an offer. "He walks in my office when we were still in Detroit," said Hughes, now the college personnel director for the Steelers. "and he says, 'I have to take this other job.' So I said, "Take it. What's the problem?' And he said, "They're offering me a good amount of money.' And I said, 'Take it. It's the Steelers. What's the problem? It's the dream job with the hometown team.'

"That's Kevin for you. He's such a loyal person, and he felt badly about leaving the Lions. He's low maintenance, unpretentious and extremely dedicated."

Cowher recalls when Colbert came to the Steelers. "It was like a breath of fresh air. Kevin is very good with people and I think there is a mutual respect that exists between the two of us. I think our relationship has gotten stronger."

Colbert feels equally blessed. "It's been easy," he said, "because we really believe in a lot of the same things. Obviously, the Steelers had a lot of success before I came on board and, fortunately, I got the opportunity to come in. I think the coach and I agree on what kind of players we want to have to win championships, and we've been able to get those guys."

I thought that Kevin Colbert rated an "A" grade for his interview. The brothers back at North Catholic would be proud of him.

Kevin Colbert:

"It doesn't make your career."

The challenge is not to become complacent. This is the first time I've ever had to follow up on the ultimate success in my profession. The challenge is to push yourself to match it. It was a great accomplishment for a given season. It doesn't make your career.

From my perspective, we have a chance to win the sixth Super Bowl. No one else has done that. That can make you truly successful in this game.

Not a lot of teams have won a Super Bowl. Only 17 teams have won a Super Bowl. I didn't realize that until right before our game with Seattle. Somebody brought it up. To be able to add another Lombardi Trophy to our collection — to get the sixth — that would be special. That's the challenge.

When you come into the organization you know the expectations. Because there is a history of accomplishment here. What they did in the '70s has never been equaled. They won four Super Bowls in six years. Is there a Steelers' way of doing things; does Mr. Rooney want us to do things in a certain way? It's not spoken about, but it's there. It's not something that's etched in stone anywhere. You understand it exists.

To the best of my comprehension, it's to do the right thing in every given circumstance. That's on the field and away from the field. It's even in the marketing of the team, and how we want to do that. We're the only team that doesn't have cheerleaders, for instance. Our fans are our cheerleaders.

We try to find the best people. We look for the ultimate combination. You have to understand that as an organization we want to do it right. In doing our research about players, we sort through every aspect of that person. People with bad character make bad decisions. So much goes into the makeup of a team. Each individual is unique.

We have to adhere to a set of rules. We want everyone to do the right thing in every circumstance. That's not always achievable. You hope you'll select people who'll do that. There's no room for selfish people who put themselves above the best interests of the team and their teammates.

I get along fine with the Rooney family and with Coach Cowher. We just all believe in the same things, and not just because we all work for the same organization. Mr. Rooney, Art, Coach and myself all believe in the same principles.

I don't do interviews during the season because I believe there should only be three voices at that time. That's ownership, the head coach and the players. They're the faces of the organization. They're the ones that catch the heat during the season.

There are times when I have to be accessible, like when we're preparing for the draft. But that's the only time I need to be talking about what we're doing. I worked in Miami for five years with the Dolphins and Chuck Connor was our personnel director, but Coach Shula was the spokesman for the team. I learned this way was the best way early in my career.

I did the same thing when I was with the Detroit Lions for ten years. The Ford family was good to my family and me. I had a great situation there. I wasn't looking for another job. Art Rooney called Chuck Schmidt in the Lions' organization to get permission to talk to me. That was the proper way to do it.

My immediate boss with the Lions was Ron Hughes. He was my coach at North Catholic. When the Lions had a changeover in their front office a few years back, I brought Ron here to be our college scouting director.

I don't know how you could have a better situation professionally when you're working for the best organization, I think, in sports and in my hometown. We have a unique opportunity to work for this family. The more you look around the league and you see other teams and see how they operate, you appreciate it that much more.

"Who can help us win?"

I know what I'm responsible for here. I don't worry about the physical facility, for instance. That's someone else's concern. I'm concerned about making sure I'm not complacent and that I do everything necessary to assure that we have the right players to contend for another championship. You can't rest on your laurels.

I can't worry about how I am perceived by the public. I can't worry about peripheral stuff. I'm out on the field now watching the players and seeing how they practice, how they work. I'm trying to be around them as much as possible to get to know them better. Who can help us win?

Right now they're preparing to get ready for training camp. They're learning what to do, what to put into action. There's a constant evaluation. It's the beginning of an evaluation process. You're watching the players to learn what they're all about now that they're with the Steelers. Can they be Steelers? We want Steelers' guys on this team.

This is the third NFL operation I've been with. I started out scouting for a year for Jack Butler and his Blesto organization. Then I went to the Dolphins for five years, and then ten years with the Lions. I know how NFL teams operate.

You don't know what we have right now. Last year is gone. That team will never exist again. It's a different team. Coach Cowher tells them that all the time. If you take one player off a team it becomes different. We won't have Jerome Bettis, Antwaan Randle El, Kimo von Oelhoffen, Chris Hope, Willie Williams, Tommy Maddox, Russell Stuvaints and some others. There are a lot of quality people on that list. There's a lot of veteran leadership. We'll miss them. Others have an opportunity to take their place and become Steelers. There's no way to know what we've got right now.

You can't think that it will be easy. Each year is totally different. You can't win a Super Bowl because you think we have the best team. Coach Cowher told them we weren't the best team. Nobody expected us to win the Super Bowl last year. And they certainly didn't think so when we lost three games in a row and were 7-5 and not yet in the playoff picture.

We can't just think we'll be back, or that we're set. You're never set. We have some great players like Ben Roethlisberger and Troy Polamalu that enable us to do different things on offense and defense. They set the tone, but I don't know if that changes anything we'll do.

As a personnel guy, you're not just reflecting on what you have, but what you need.

At this stage, we're still trying to get information on the new players, and see how the older players are performing as well. You want to make sure no one is out of place. When we get into training camp, we grade each practice. We don't do that now. This is more of a learning thing.

Every year you're optimistic. You're hopeful that you have good players. But that can come back to haunt you. Other teams in this town have been optimistic but things haven't gone well for them. There was a point last year when we were in the same boat. You're hopeful that they'll be good players. You're always excited at this time.

There are no guarantees. Just because we won it last year doesn't mean we can do it again.

The fans will be expecting us to do that, though. They will have high expectations. I remember the parade they had for us downtown when we returned from winning the Super Bowl. It was fun and it was overwhelming.

We have great support. That so many people were so well behaved was unbelievable. It was good and it was exciting. I never went to any parades as a kid, so I have nothing to compare it to. I was a fan, living on the North Side. I went to their games in the '70s, but I was watching from a distance.

I lived near St. Boniface Church, just off East Street, or now 279. I played tennis at West Park. We could walk there. So I knew all about the Rooneys and St. Peter's Church and Richie McCabe and Baldy Regan and Dan McCann and so many Steelers. I knew the North Side and North Catholic. I've always been a big fan of the Steelers.

That's why being in the organization today is so unique. To be around a guy like Mr. Rooney, one of the most respected owners in the league, is a humbling experience. To have him come by my office three times a day to see how I'm doing is special. He's only two doors away. I have to step back and think about that.

It doesn't overwhelm me. I may pinch myself later on, but I don't do it now. Like any kid, I wanted to be a professional athlete. In my junior year at North Catholic, I had the position of statistician and publicist for the football team. Ron Hughes was my high school coach. I made the team my senior year as a backup linebacker and backup punter. The punter got hurt —he blew his kneecap — and I became the punter.

I played football, baseball and hockey in college. I graduated with a degree in sports management from Robert Morris in 1979. The Steelers won their fourth Super Bowl soon after. I came back to Robert Morris as a graduate assistant basketball coach. I later became the baseball coach there. I also coached football at Ohio Wesleyan for a brief period.

My story is that you can find a place. If you have a passion for sports you have to find something you like and then work at it to show people what you can do, and what you have to offer. There's nothing that's out of reach. You have to be willing to try different things and find out what you do best.

I was with the Lions for ten years and I was happy. I wasn't looking or actively seeking opportunities elsewhere. Art II made the initial contact. I'm glad I came back home.

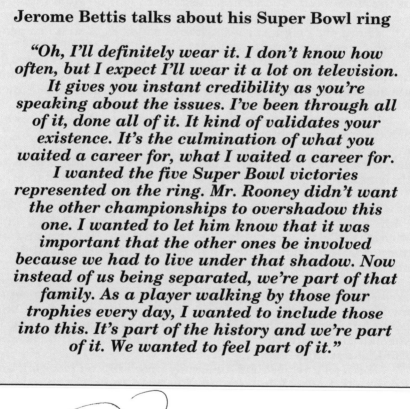

Jerome Bettis talks about his Super Bowl ring

"Oh, I'll definitely wear it. I don't know how often, but I expect I'll wear it a lot on television. It gives you instant credibility as you're speaking about the issues. I've been through all of it, done all of it. It kind of validates your existence. It's the culmination of what you waited a career for, what I waited a career for. I wanted the five Super Bowl victories represented on the ring. Mr. Rooney didn't want the other championships to overshadow this one. I wanted to let him know that it was important that the other ones be involved because we had to live under that shadow. Now instead of us being separated, we're part of that family. As a player walking by those four trophies every day, I wanted to include those into this. It's part of the history and we're part of it. We wanted to feel part of it."

Jerome Bettis
Still a Mama's Boy

"This is my home now."

Jerome Bettis was the best story leading up to Super Bowl XL and the Steelers' gallant and incredible run to the National Football League championship. Bettis was the backbone and spirit that set the Steelers apart from the pack.

Bettis wasn't the best player on the Pittsburgh squad, but he was the heart and soul of the Steelers, the garrulous guy who kept everyone's perspective on the same page, the big picture. Fast Willie Parker had taken his place in the starting backfield, but Bettis made some big runs and scored some key touchdowns and helped steer the Steelers through some challenging times. He definitely made a big contribution to the championship run. He was a mentor and big brother to Fast Willie.

Pittsburgh fans weren't sure this was going to be his last season, but in case it was they wanted Bettis to know how much they cared about him, and how grateful they were that he came their way. He had started out with the Rams in Los Angeles and then St. Louis before the Steelers traded for him on Draft Day in 1995. "It was," said Bettis, "a match made in heaven."

Things were going to hell, or so it seemed, for the Steelers late in the 2005 season. The Steelers lost three straight games and were 7-5 and two games behind the Cincinnati Bengals in the AFC North race, and a game behind the Kansas City Chiefs and San Diego Chargers for the sixth and final wild-card playoff spot. Then, like Silky Sullivan, the come-from-behind horse-racing legend, the Steelers started their stretch run. Like the late John Denver, Bettis sang "Take Me Home." He wasn't interested in touring any country roads, or going off to the wilderness of West Virginia. No, he was always a city boy. He wanted to go back to Detroit. His mother would cook a good home-cooked meal for everyone on the team.

He wanted to play his final football game at Ford Field in downtown Detroit. He wanted to be a part of a positive story about his hometown. After the Steelers had suffered a disappointing loss a year earlier in the AFC championship game to the eventual Super Bowl champion New England Patriots, Ben Roethlisberger, a brash rookie quarterback who hadn't performed up to his own lofty standards in the playoffs and was willing to accept much of the blame for what went wrong, told Bettis if he would come back for one more season that he'd get him home for the Super Bowl. The rest of the Steelers picked up on that and it became everybody's mission.

They embraced Bettis and they showed their love late in the season by wearing his green No. 6 Notre Dame jersey. The defensive unit had done something similar by wearing Dick LeBeau's No. 44. jersey from his days with the Detroit Lions before their final regular season game against the Lions at Heinz Field.

After Roethlisberger had his best game of the season to lead the Steelers to a smashing 34-17 victory over the Denver Broncos in the AFC championship game, the big second-year quarterback said, "Getting Jerome to Detroit has been my driving force all year. I'm so happy for him."

Bettis said it was scary to think that he'd be playing his last game in Pittsburgh at Heinz Field and then his last game ever at Ford Field.

Dan Rooney, the chairman of the board of the Steelers, knew the team's history better than most and he knew where Bettis stood in the record books. "He ranks right up there with all the great running backs," related Rooney. "He and Franco are in a class by themselves."

Bettis was the biggest back in Steelers' history, at 5-feet-11 and 255 or 260 pounds, and with such quick feet and durability. He was always an ambassador for the ballclub. His smile was the team's signature before Hines Ward came along. He was always pleasant and approachable, a super salesman for the Steelers.

It's thought he'll be a natural for the national television gig he picked up as soon as he stepped down from playing for the Steelers. His first regular season assignment was going to be a Sunday night game in Pittsburgh. He'll be able to pick up his Super Bowl ring with the rest of the Steelers.

I was waiting for Jerome Bettis to join me at a corner table in the cafeteria on the Steelers' side of the UPMC Sports Complex on the city's South Side. They share the building, four outside football fields and one indoor field with the University of Pittsburgh football program. It's one of the finest facilities of its kind in the nation.

It had been a hot morning for a voluntary practice session — temperatures would rise to 82 degrees that day — and I knew Bettis would be thirsty.

This was Friday, May 31, 2002 and the Steelers were in the midst of one of the many mini-camps they conduct throughout the year. There is no longer any off-season in the National Football League. It was voluntary, of course, but everybody was there. It didn't count as a real camp, just sweat equity.

Bettis had a bottle of pure spring water in his right hand as he passed the counter in the cafeteria. He stopped to place an order for a sandwich and some fixings, and came over, offering a smile and a warm greeting. Bettis had been pictured on the cover of one of my earlier books, *Keep The Faith*. He was one of my favorites. I liked what he was all about. He knew that. "Thank you for your support," he wrote in a copy I brought with me for him to autograph for my personal library.

As we began to talk, one of the taller rookies I didn't recognize, brought him another bottle of pure spring water. Then Kendrell Bell

brought him a tray with his order on it. Bell thought he wouldn't have to do this sort of thing in his second season — he wasn't a rookie anymore — but he obliged Bettis and offered a smirk of sorts. "At your service," he said, quietly. Bettis smiled back. Bettis smiles back at everything. That's part of his makeup, part of his charm.

The Steelers' training facility is such a spectacular upgrade from anything they had at Three Rivers Stadium, the mini-grass field they had nearby on the North Side, and certainly from their primitive days at the Fair Grounds at South Park. Their meals at Three Rivers were catered affairs, where they'd pick up food and take it back to the locker room and sit on their stools and — it was always a balancing act and awkward — eat their meals. Now they can sit at tables like regular people and enjoy each other's company while they eat. Parkhurst, a division of Eat 'n Park Hospitality Inc., provides the food. I saw owner Jim Broadhurst stop by during one visit, checking to make sure everything was up to his high standards.

Bettis had been getting rave reviews for his running efforts at practice sessions that week, getting "wow" responses from his teammates for one particular move he made to leave linebacker Joey Porter in his wake. It had also been disclosed that week by Ed Bouchette in the *Post-Gazette* that Bettis had reinjured his groin in the AFC title game against the New England Patriots. Bettis had been ineffective in that game, causing some to second-guess Bill Cowher for starting him after Bettis had been sidelined for six games because of a groin injury.

Bettis had gotten off to such a great start in the 2001 schedule. "I'm fine," he said. "I don't have any problems now. My situation has been over-exaggerated by the media. I'm ready to go."

Bettis shared his thoughts on several subjects. I came away from that interview, catching the tail end of the Steelers practice and seeing some old friends, feeling pretty good about everything.

"We have a great opportunity at Heinz Field."

Jerome Bettis is a great running back, but National Football League Commissioner Paul Tagliabue believes he is far more than that. He made that perfectly clear when he introduced Bettis as the 2001 Walter Payton NFL Man of the Year at Super Bowl XXXVI in New Orleans. "Jerome reaches out to help others in so many ways," Tagliabue said, "from assisting troubled children, to giving scholarships, to upgrading facilities in the community for young people, and addressing public health issues."

Since 1970, the NFL has honored one player each season with its Man of the Year Award — renamed the Walter Payton Award in 1999 — to recognize a player's off-the-field community activities as well as his on-the-field playing excellence.

Several players with Pittsburgh area ties have been so honored. They include Len Dawson (1973), George Blanda (1974), Franco Harris (1976), Joe Greene (1979), Lynn Swann (1981), Dan Marino (1998) and Jim Flanigan (2000).

"It's the type of award that you really don't ask for," said Bettis. "You try to do things that are special to you and that mean a lot to you."

Bettis has had a profound effect on the lives of many children through his "Bus Stops Here Foundation," which he founded in 1997 to help troubled and underprivileged children. Since the foundation's inception, youth participants have been provided with scholarships, computer training, mentoring programs, and athletic training. Jerome's commitment to the success of the program is evidenced in his hands-on involvement. He does one-on-one mentoring with children, acts as the football camp director, teaches conflict resolution techniques, and attends as many foundation activities as possible.

"Jerome is the type of player we want to have in the NFL for many years," Tagliabue said.

Bettis embraced a Steelers' long-standing tradition for community service from his first days in Pittsburgh. He remains one of the team's most popular players with the fans because of his exuberant and friendly manner. He just has a way with people. He became even more popular by his exposure on his own weekly TV show hosted by KDKA's Bob Pompeani.

In late April of 2002, Bettis visited Frankfurt, Germany as part of a four-day USO/NFL tour of U.S. military bases. He even got to ride in a tank. He rode in an Abrams MIA12. "I've been interested in that tank," he said over the telephone to writers in Pittsburgh, "because my middle name is Abram."

Who knows? If anyone had made that association earlier, Bettis might be known as "The Tank" instead of "the Bus" by his faithful fans. He said it was exciting to ride in a tank that was traveling 55 miles an hour, and meet the troops. Then again, Bettis gets excited about everything he does. He was looking forward to meeting U.S. soldiers who were recovering from wounds from the fighting in Afghanistan.

"I'm just looking forward to saying thank you," said Bettis. "My goal was just to shake as many hands as I could, say as many thank yous as I could and kinda express the thoughts and minds of all the Americans back home that, hey, we're with you guys, we're living it with you. So many times, you never get the appreciation. I wanted to say thank you, we appreciate you for what you're doing for us."

At the same time, Bettis was eager to get back to Pittsburgh to resume preparations for the 2002 season. He had some ground to make up from the previous season. He had resumed running only a week earlier.

His last game as a Steeler had been a major disappointment for him and his team and for the City of Pittsburgh. He had gained only eight yards in 9 carries in the Steelers' 24-17 AFC title game defeat by the New England Patriots at Heinz Field. Bettis, who had gotten off to such a great start the previous season, had missed the six games before the title game because of a disabling groin injury.

He was leading the NFL with 1,072 yards in the 11th game. He moved up to 12th on the all-time list with 10,876 yards. Missing nearly half a season at this point in his pro career had to be a real disappointment. He could have added another 500 to 600 yards to his totals. He still managed to finish eighth in the league in rushing.

He had started the season looking as good as ever. He seemed swifter and was cutting this way and that more adroitly than he had in years. He had dealt with knee problems the previous three years and seemed to be back in top form once again. "I am a better back than I've ever been," pronounced the bubbly Bettis during his strong streak.

"His ability to dip in and out of cuts, the way his feet move, it is awesome for a big guy," said Russ Grimm, the Steelers' offensive line coach, and a valued associate head coach.

"He is our ride, our rock and we feed off his mind-set," said Steelers' offensive coordinator Mike Mularkey.

"The most exciting thing," said center Jeff Hartings, in his first year with the Steelers, "is to see him run over someone in the secondary. By the fourth quarter, you can tell they aren't so anxious to hit him anymore."

Then the groin injury . . . and the disappointment of the title game outing.

Bettis was aware that he had his doubters as he spoke on the occasion of his 30th birthday on February 16, 2002.

"It'll be 10 years this year," he said. "I don't think I have to prove anything. I just need to be 100 percent healthy, go out there and duplicate what I did last year. Everybody knows what I'm capable of. I'm not really worried about that at all.

"I'm used to that. Going into every season, the questions have always been about me, and I've always proved everybody wrong. I'm not really concerned about it. They just need to check my track record. This is something I've been doing a long time."

One of his biggest fans on the ballclub is Hines Ward. "He's a true professional," said Ward. "When he goes on the field he's all business. The players appreciate that, too."

Steelers director of operations Kevin Colbert is confident Bettis can be the main man in the Steelers' running game once again. The Steelers signed Bettis to a six-year contract before the 2001 season, virtually assuring him of completing his career in Pittsburgh. "We really feel like he wanted to end his career here," said Colbert, "and we wanted him to do that."

Bettis gained more than 1,000 yards in each of his six seasons with the Steelers, and two of his three years with the Rams in Los Angeles and St. Louis. He had missed only three games in his pro career until the 2001 season.

He went into the 2002 season as the NFL's second-leading active rusher behind Emmitt Smith of the Dallas Cowboys. He could reasonably become the NFL's ninth-leading all-time rusher by the end of the season. He needed only 361 yards to pass O.J. Simpson's totals.

Several of the former Steelers felt that Bettis should not have been used in that AFC title game, and they also believe that the Steelers blew a great opportunity to get to the Super Bowl. Dwight White, who was with the Steelers for their four Super Bowl triumphs, has said that the team he played for has cast a long shadow over Steelers' teams ever since and that they can't get out from under it.

Jerome Bettis:

"Let's make our mark as well."

Whenever you've had success, you're always going to live in the shadow of those successful years. But that shouldn't be something that you resent. It should be something that you embrace because it's part of the tradition of the team. If you have a great tradition, that means your fans are supportive, they're loyal, and they're going to be there in good times and bad. That's beneficial.

Now, we want to set the same type of marks as those other guys did in Three Rivers Stadium. We want to win. That's the mark you want to set and we want to be the guys to set it. If you think of Three Rivers, some names come out of your mouth like Lambert and Ham, Swann and Stallworth, Bradshaw and Harris and those guys. But they haven't played in this new stadium. Some other names will have an opportunity to be mentioned.

We have a great opportunity at Heinz Field. We're the first group of guys to go into that new stadium. We have a great opportunity to start a legacy. The guys before us came in and created a tradition at Three Rivers Stadium that we had to uphold. Now, we get the opportunity to start a tradition that players years down the road will get an opportunity to uphold. We need to understand that and not take that lightly. Let's make our mark as well.

We'll see when we get there. You want to make sure you leave a legacy that the players that come after you remember, that you laid the groundwork for the new stadium to be successful.

Sometimes you don't have big games. Sometimes you've just got to pound away and earn your pay. You just have to strap it up and get ready to go the next time.

It took me one training camp to become a Pittsburgh Steeler. I knew what this team meant, what it was all about, what the city was all about. I fit in pretty well. I was from a blue-collar town, Detroit. That's where Joe Louis came from, and look how he took the world by storm. I didn't hear about him when I was growing up, but I know about him now. I like sports history. I knew what it took to be successful. All they want here is a person who works hard. That's what they do every day of their lives.

No doubt about it, you get energized from the fans and, hopefully, you can energize the fans in return.

It makes me feel good that the fans here appreciate me. It spurs me on. It's not flashy; it's not the glitter. It's hard-nosed, the blue-collar work I do between the tackles. I prefer mixing it up in there and pounding away.

I learned a lot about football and about life when I played for Lou Holtz at Notre Dame. He was great for me. He helped me as a person and he helped me as a player. Off the field, he nurtured me. He always wanted me to be gracious and humble. He ran a tight ship.

I followed the rules. I never did anything from the start to go outside the rules. Anything you do, you have to respect rules. Rules are a part of life. It was nothing new for me. I had rules to follow as a kid. I learned quickly to follow rules.

We had basic rules in our home: no fighting with my older brother and sister. I was the youngest of three. There was no turning on the stove after dinner. No company in your room. Visitors were to be in the living room, not your room. Your parents had to know where you were when you left the house. No hats on your head in the house. We had to abide by the rules. You learn to make it part of your everyday behavior.

With the way kids are being raised, they don't have discipline or manners. When these values are highlighted and promoted, the child understandably follows the lead. In our home, we knew and understood the rules. Plus, I've suffered with asthma since I was a kid, and I've had to be careful about that, too, and make sure I had an inhaler with me at all times. I've had to be responsible.

My mom was always big on manners. She made sure I opened doors for her and other adults. We always said, "excuse me" and "pardon me" and "may I" and "please" and "thank you," stuff like that. She always said she wanted us to make her proud. And we tried our best to do just that. My dad was real quiet. He was the disciplinarian. When there were problems, my mother related them to my dad, and he'd get after us.

I was lucky. I was blessed. My dad was the father to all the guys in our neighborhood. He'd teach them things, too. He

Jerome "The Bus" Bettis

didn't want us standing around on the streets. If they were in our house, he didn't want them standing around, either. He wanted them to sit down, and not to sit on the arm rests on chairs or couches. He kept all the guys in line. What they did at their homes might not be acceptable at our home. He was real clear about that. My friends respected my dad. It was always "Mr. Bettis this" and "Mr. Bettis that," and all the guys admired him. Only three families out of the ten or so on our street had two parents at home. I was one of the lucky ones.

One of my mother's rules was that you have to show people you respect your home. If you don't, they won't.

"I knew how to stay out of trouble."

I'm a normal guy, like everybody else. When I first got out to California as a rookie out of college, that was quite an eye-opener for me. Here I was, 21 and in a fast-moving city. Being from the inner city, I knew pitfalls and how to get into trouble. So it was easy to stay away from it. I knew how to stay out of trouble.

As a player, you're going to get approached by a lot of people who want your attention, and some of them are bad people. The wrong people, people I was taught to stay away from at an early age. A ballplayer has to be responsible for his own behavior. The guys who get into trouble allow themselves to be in that situation. They have to live with the decisions they make.

Being a role model is part of the job. That's part of being a professional athlete. Whether you like it or not, you're in the public eye. If you do something wrong, you're going to draw the wrong kind of attention to yourself. Regardless of whether or not I think I'm a role model, I can't help but be a role model.

It comes with the territory. You're a role model because of what you do. Kids look up to you and you have to handle yourself in such a manner that you respect yourself and your family, and you respect the game.

"Family is critical to me."

Pittsburgh is some place special because even the little kids know who I am. It's a good city, definitely a good football town.

It would be nice to have the same football environment in Florida or California. I grew up with weather like this in Detroit, but just because you're from it doesn't mean you have to like it. I know it's a great place to play this game, though. I wouldn't change it for the world.

Last year was the most challenging of my career. I couldn't stand to be on the sideline. I tried to keep my spirits up and be a cheerleader for the rest of the team. I might have looked happy, but I was upset that I couldn't play. As a competitor, I want to be out there playing.

Family is critical to me. In tough times, it's all you have. They're at all my football games, home and away. I get them there because I'm happiest when they're with me. I take the whole crew with me. I'm in constant contact with my family. Sometimes my mom tells me she's going to disown me if I don't call her more often.

I bought a nice home just north of Pittsburgh, in Hampton (The Villas of North Park), just so my family could all stay with me when they come to town. I didn't want to keep putting them up in hotels. Now they can stay with me. Of course, my mom is still asking me if I'm eating my peas, and stuff like that. It never changes. But it's nice to give her a kiss before I go off to battle.

If I go to the Pro Bowl, my family goes with me. My running backs all go with me, too. But I'm gonna have them double up in rooms. I'm crazy, but I'm not stupid. That gets expensive. My home is my prison, too. Sometimes it's hard for me to leave and enjoy myself because of all the attention I draw when I go somewhere. I like the people, and I love my fans, but sometimes I just want to be left alone, to live a more normal life.

When I don't want to talk I don't leave my house. It's my world.

Once I close the door I take a big sigh of relief because I'm home.

It sucks being on the sideline, not being able to be out there mixing it up. I used to be able to play if I was 75 percent all right, but I have to be better than that to go out there now. The difference is my age and the pounding I have taken through the years. I never felt better than I did at the beginning of this year. I was quick and making good cuts, and felt fluid in my motion. That groin has caused me problems in the past.

It's hard to motivate myself when I am rehabbing. I have to think of the prize. That's the goal.

At some point I will have to call it quits. I wouldn't want to leave this team worse off that it is now. Some people don't like their job, usually because of the boss or job conditions.

Mr. Rooney is the best owner in the NFL. Bill Cowher is a coach you want to play for. He's got a lot of bark. He does have some bite, too. But he's a good guy in his heart.

I'm doing a TV show of my own with Bob Pompeani and some of the other players are guests. I want to see what that's all about in case I want to get into that later on. I want to have options when the game is over.

When all is said and done, and when I'm finished playing, I want people to say Jerome was a great person. Not only was he a great football player, but he was a great person.

When I see people wearing my No. 36 jersey, it's like an honor to me. After all, the people have their pick of a lot of jerseys. And they can take mine off. They chose to wear my jersey. So it's important that you do all the things to make sure they keep that jersey on.

Kordell is the No. 1 man here, and I'm right behind him. I won the team MVP twice and that puts me in some pretty good company. Bradshaw won four Super Bowls, and I would like to get one of those rings. We're that close to the Super Bowl.

I'm on a championship team that is only a win away from the Super Bowl. And that's where I want to go. And I like our chances. We have a solid defense. When you have a solid defense and your special teams play well, you create the opportunity to win a lot of football games. That's what we've got to do, get everything going good at the same time.

"I have to be skinny through a hole."

Eric Dickerson and Tony Dorsett and O.J. Simpson and Jim Brown, guys like that, had a pedigree when they came into the NFL. They had been star runners probably from the first time they played organized football. They were stars in high school and college, and it was no shock when they continued in the NFL. I didn't even expect me to gain this kind of yardage in the pros. I had to teach myself how to run in this league, really.

I have to be skinny through a hole. I am contorting myself because if I run square through the hole, I am too big. So I turn my shoulder or twist my body, whatever it takes to make myself thinner. It's funny when you see it on tape.

Maybe I am past my prime as far as age goes. But I am a better runner now. It took more of the down years to learn, and now this is the best I have ever done it. I can't ever remember being as shifty and as quick.

My improvement is shown on my long runs. Because, on most of those, I make people miss. Before, I didn't get myself in position to do that. Didn't know how. But now I do.

106

"It's an honor."

On the field, my stay with the Steelers has been a dream come true in a sense. Having watched the Steelers over the years, I knew the franchise had a history of running the ball. They liked big backs. It's been incredible; it's been everything I expected and more.

The team has stuck to running the ball. They play a style of football that fits my character and me more than most teams.

Off the field, no other city has embraced a player as quickly as they embraced me when I got here. It's an honor.

The community has been behind me — win, lose or draw. It's been so good I've decided this is where I want to live when I'm finished playing football.

I've heard about Byron "Whizzer" White — he became a Supreme Court Justice, right — and I've heard about John Henry Johnson. He also played for the Detroit Lions. So did "Bullet Bill" Dudley. So did Bobby Layne. The Lions were great in those days, too. Buddy Parker coached there before he came to the Steelers. I like history and I have heard about those guys. No, I didn't know about Sam Francis and Joe Geri, the guys you mentioned. I'll have to check on them.

The Steelers back I know best, of course, is Franco Harris. I heard about him when I was growing up. I've met him many times; he comes into our clubhouse on occasion, especially when we were at Three Rivers Stadium. I know he lives in that neighborhood.

I have the ultimate respect for him. He's the one who paved the way for me. From the big running back perspective, he was one of the first guys to glamorize the big running back. I owe him a lot.

I learned from him, too. Look how gracious he has been. That really trickled down to myself. He opened a lot of doors off the field so they could see that we're good people. We're not a bad thing to be a fan of; we're upstanding people. That's the way I want to be. When I see him, I give him the utmost respect.

I try to be at my best behavior at all times. People make bad decisions. I made bad decisions in my day. What I try to do is to use those mistakes and hope not to make those same mistakes again. So you won't repeat it.

My family has been a tremendous support system for me. My family has been the biggest part of my success. Regardless of my situation, they've been there for me.

As far as the Steelers' success in the '70s goes, I see it as a plus and a minus. This organization is geared to winning. If you've never won before, how do you know how to win? We understand what winning is all about, and what's needed to succeed. That's the hardest thing to do — to learn how to win.

The hardest part of the job is living up to those expectations. The expectations are high. There are four Super Bowl trophies upstairs and I see them from time to time. They are reminders of the standards the Steelers are held up to. It's a hard accomplishment to match. The bar is raised high. That's fine. Our job is to give it our best effort, every time out. The fans expect you to win. Sometimes we disappoint them.

I've been in situations where the bar is raised high. Why do you think I went to Notre Dame? If I were afraid of ghosts of the past, or great players to be compared to, do you think I would have gone to Notre Dame? Hey, that was part of the appeal for me. I wanted to be part of a great tradition, a great football program. That should be one of the reasons you want to go there.

I'm pretty familiar with the history of the game. I like to know about those who had been there before. The game itself needs to be respected. The guys before us laid down the road for us. They broke their backs to give us this great opportunity.

I was sad when I got hurt last year. I was having such a great season. It was heart-breaking. Some things like that happen for a reason.

I'm happy here. Bill Cowher is a good guy. He's always treated me with respect and as a man. That's all you want in a football coach. And for him to be honest with you. I give Coach Cowher a lot of credit. Those are three difficult things to do, and he does a good job of it.

I respect what Kordell Stewart did last season. I saw it as a success story. I probably would have become hardened by the treatment, or lack of communication, that went on with Kordell. I probably would have had resentment. But he hung in there and he worked his butt off. I don't know if I could have had that much diplomacy.

We want to get everyone on the same page here. That's the goal of every team in sports. Everybody has to buy into it. Everyone has to be responsible and reliable. They have to realize they represent the Steelers at all times. I try to explain two things to the young players: what's expected of them, and what they should expect of themselves. That's the name of the game.

It's nice that I've gotten some great honors for some of the things I've done off the field. But you don't do it to get recognition or awards. My rewards are the faces of the kids.

That brings a lot of gratification. Being a pro football player allows me to get out and do special things in the community, to make a difference. In that regard, I am thankful. You want to help.

I knew that the Steelers like to run the ball when I came here, but I didn't know they wanted their ballplayers to be so involved in the community, to do things that show the Steelers in a positive light. Once I got a chance to meet Mr. Rooney and found out the type of person he was, I knew I wanted to carry the ball in that respect, too. I don't think Mr. Rooney would ever turn down anybody. There's a wisdom here. He can clear things up. There is more of a family atmosphere here than you had at Notre Dame, or the other teams I played for.

It makes going to work easy. The facilities here and at Heinz Field are fantastic. It's so beautiful. It makes everything a lot easier. It allows us to do what we do best. If it's cold or snowing, we can go inside. We're never going to have bad conditions in which to practice.

Life is great. I can't complain. I've been fortunate. All I can say as far as the fans are concerned is "Thank you." I thank them for believing in me, for believing what I stood for and supporting me through good and bad times.

Letter to New York Times

To the sports editor:

The rise of the Pittsburgh Steelers to the Super Bowl drives home a good point. Bill Cowher, arguably the best coach in the game, has the longest current tenure of any coach in the N.F.L. These days, N.F.L. coaches are given three years, many times less, to produce a playoff team.
Perhaps more N.F.L. teams should invest more time and resources when they hire a new coach to give him the opportunity to take his team to the Super Bowl.

Steven M. Clayton
Ocean, N.J.
Jan. 29, 2006

A phone call pays off

Bill Cowher called Lou Holtz on the telephone to find out what Holtz thought of Jerome Bettis, whose effort and attitude were being questioned as a young member of the St. Louis Rams. "We're thinking about making a trade for him," Cowher told Holtz.

Holtz had coached Bettis during his days at Notre Dame and years earlier he was the coach at North Carolina State when Cowher accepted a scholarship to play football at the university in Raleigh. Holtz had called Bettis on the telephone a few months earlier and left him a message, chastising him for being a pale imitation of the Jerome Bettis that Holtz had known at Notre Dame. Holtz hung up and never identified himself.

In the interim, Bettis had come back to Notre Dame in an attempt to complete his schoolwork and get his degree. Bettis had departed Notre Dame after his junior season to sign with the Rams, then located in Los Angeles. He is still shy of having enough credits to earn a degree, but takes pride in being a Notre Dame man.

Holtz had an opportunity to talk to Bettis when they were reunited on the South Bend campus, and he was able to convince Cowher that Bettis was changing. During his stay, Bettis was reminded of the outstanding player and person he'd been at Notre Dame.

Tom Donahoe, then the director of football operations, and Cowher made a trade to get Bettis on draft day in 1996. It might have been Donahoe's best move in his tenure with the Steelers.

When the Steelers traveled to Detroit for Super Bowl XL, making good on a promise to get Bettis back home for the big one, several of them wore green Notre Dame jerseys with Jerome's No. 6 on them. It had been Joey Porter's idea to get the jerseys to pay tribute to the team's beloved leader. Bettis had worn No. 6 in high school and college, and No. 36 in the NFL.

Cowher's call to Holtz brings to mind another phone call that paid off for a pro football team. Pitt's Dan Marino was bypassed by most NFL teams in the 1993 draft, including the hometown Steelers. A rumor was making the rounds that Marino had fooled around with drugs during his days on the Oakland campus. "The only pro coach who called me and asked me about that issue was Don Shula of the Dolphins," said Foge Fazio, then the head football coach at Pitt. "I assured him that Danny was a good kid, and that he'd be no problem."

Marino and Bettis were both honored as NFL Man of the Year during their pro careers, cited as role models for their distinguished play and community efforts. The moral of the story is that it pays to call to get first-hand reports when you are thinking of hiring someone to work for you.

The Bettis Family
Lots of discipline

*"I knew how to stay
out of trouble."*

Adapted from Keep The Faith

The Steelers were in the playoffs in 2001 when I sat down with Jerome Bettis in the players' lounge, just off the clubhouse at Three Rivers Stadium. This area was normally off-limits to the media, but I had been given permission by the p.r. department to sit in the Steelers' inner sanctum where Bettis might be more relaxed. He had just beaten Darren Perry in a chess match at the same table where we sat. Bettis was known for his bowling prowess. He was, indeed, a man for all seasons.

"My father taught me how to play chess when I was little," said Bettis. "When I was with the Rams, there were several guys who liked to play chess. So I got back to playing again. Darren's just learning to play. I hadn't played in a while, but I'm more experienced. I like to play video games, everything competitive. Darren wants a rematch. He's competitive, too. That's what it's all about."

In his youth, Bettis was often told by his parents that sports and games were a good way to keep busy, to stay out of trouble, and he hadn't forgotten that lesson. "Stay out of trouble" could have been his schoolboy mantra. It had a familiar ring to it. One of his teammates in 1996, Jonathan Hayes, heard the same directive from his dad and mom when he was growing up in South Fayette.

Bettis grew up on Aurora Street on the West Side of Detroit. The Bettis family had its own free-standing home.

His father, Johnnie, was an electrical inspector for the city and he taught electrical wiring in adult education classes at night. Jerome's mother, Gladys, worked at a bank, processing checks when he was growing up.

"Before my junior year in college, she got laid off," said Jerome. "That helped me make my decision to turn pro a year early to help my family.

"I still need two semesters. I've gone back to take some classes since I've been playing pro ball. I enjoyed the Notre Dame experience. They stayed after me pretty good. It was a followup to what my family had stressed. The work was hard. There was no way you could get through it unless you worked hard."

Lou Holtz was his coach at Notre Dame. "I've been back to see Coach Holtz," said Bettis. "He still gets on my case.

Bettis had visited Holtz at Notre Dame in January, 1996, just before winter classes started. The coach greeted him with a challenge.

"He came in," Holtz recalled to Shelly Anderson of the *Post-Gazette*, "and before he could say anything, I said, 'Jerome, I want to tell you something. There's a guy wearing your jersey that is not doing you any favors. It's not the Jerome Bettis I know, and I know you wouldn't play like that. So it's obviously not you.'"

Jerome replied, "Coach, I came back for two reasons. One, I promised you I'd work on my degree. No. 2, I came back to get my attitude right. When I was at Notre Dame, I left here with a tremendous attitude. Right now, I just want to get my attitude right."

Holtz added, "He worked out with our players. I visited with him from time to time, and when that trade came through (in April), I was really happy for him."

One of the Steelers' assistant coaches, John Mitchell, had been an assistant coach under Holtz for several years at Arkansas, and liked to share stories about Holtz. Mitchell and Bettis also share a similar enthusiasm and near-reverence when referring to their parents' influence on their lives. "Yeah, he gave me some stories," Bettis said of Coach Mitchell. "We both share a high regard for Coach Holtz. He was great for me. He helped me as a person and he helped me as a player. Off the field, he nurtured me. He always wanted me to be gracious and humble. He ran a tight ship."

Did Holtz ever come down hard on Bettis?

"I never crossed that line," Bettis said. "I never saw the disciplinarian side. I followed the rules. I never did anything from the start to go outside the rules. Anything you do, you have to respect rules. Rules are a part of life. It was nothing new for me. I had rules to follow as a kid. I learned quickly to follow rules.

Tough Guys Finish First

"There are good tough bosses and there are bad ones, and which is which is often in the eye of the beholder. Again, we're not talking about the egregious cases of jerk bosses who berate and belittle their people. Everyone hates them, and they deserve universal loathing. We're talking about bosses who operate in the middle ground — bosses who are tough but fair, push hard but reward in equal measure, and who give it to you straight. Weak performers usually wish these bosses would go away. People who want to win seek them out."

— Suzi and Jack Welch
Co-authors of best-seller
Winning (Harper Collins), 2005

"I'm comfortable in Detroit."

To hear Jerome Bettis talk about Detroit you would think he grew up not far from the Land of Oz. Wasn't Detroit one of the toughest towns in America? Didn't Detroit's mean streets rival those of New York, Chicago, Philadelphia, Miami and LA?

"It's where I'm from," said Bettis. "It's a city that's greatly misunderstood. A lot of people assume it's the murder capital of this country. Like it has to be a terrible place to live. I see it as home. It's a place where if you give it an opportunity it will surprise you. I can see myself raising a family there.

"I'm comfortable in Detroit. That's home. The city is more receptive to me now. They do things to celebrate me. I'm invited there with PAL (Police Athletic League). I go and see them and give them money. I was involved in PAL as a kid and now they point to me as one of their success stories, a role model. I like to show the kids it's cool to go to school and play sports and to stay out of trouble."

When he signed his new contract with the Steelers, Bettis spoke of buying a bowling alley in Detroit. As a child, Bettis became a bowler because his mother thought it would be a good way to spend his free time on Saturday. "She made us go bowling in the beginning," he recalled, "but I was good at it, right away, and I looked forward to going."

So his older brother and sister and Jerome, in turn, all trudged off crosstown to the Central City Lanes, all 60 lanes.

"My mom would take us every Saturday," recalled Bettis. "I was in a youth league called Coke & Bowl. You got a Coke and a hot dog in addition to bowling as part of the program. I was seven years old when I started. But I was big for my age. I was always a big kid. And I was good at it.

"Nobody else in the neighborhood went bowling, but none of them made fun of me about it. They all understood that was something we did. My parents both bowled."

I shared some stories with Bettis about my own boyhood bowling experiences. As a grade school student, I competed in the Hit & Miss League at St. Anthony's Club Bowling Lanes on Elizabeth Street in Hazelwood. As a freshman at Central Catholic High School, I

Dick Hoak on his 44 years with Steelers

"Why go someplace else? The Rooneys always treated me very well. I couldn't leave Mr. Rooney. I couldn't leave Pittsburgh. My family is from Pittsburgh. My wife's family is from Pittsburgh. I was raised to do things for family."

competed in intramural bowling for Class 1F. My parents weren't bowlers, but both of my in-laws, Barbara and Harvey Churchman, bowled in leagues.

Bettis went to a private school, Detroit Urban Lutheran, during his elementary school years, and that was important to his parents.

"They did everything they could to give us an edge," he said. "They made sure I didn't have pitfalls that caused a lot of other kids to stumble and fall. My father paid for us to go to private school. I hated it for a long time. It was so restrictive and we always had homework.

"Every day I wanted to go to the public school. I didn't want to do homework. The public school kids never seemed to have homework. They said they did it in school, which was kind of confusing. How can you do homework in school? That makes it schoolwork, not homework. They'd be playing another hour every day after school while I was home doing my homework. I always wanted to be in public school because they never had homework.

"Now I'm thankful they did what they did. When I got to public school for high school I was so far advanced. I graduated with honors from McKenzie High School. I played football the whole time and basketball for one year."

Did he get into any trouble as a kid?

"Not real trouble. I've never been in a situation where that came up. I always thought my actions through before I did them. If I had an irrational thought about doing something I shouldn't do, that we cleared up quickly. If I misbehaved in any manner, my mother always told me why I was getting a whipping. It holds true now. I know right from wrong and watch myself."

"That's part of the job," said Bettis. "That's part of being a professional athlete. Whether you like it or not, you're in the public eye. If you do something wrong, you're going to draw the wrong kind of attention to yourself.

"Regardless of whether or not I think I'm a role model, I can't help but be a role model."

Who were his own sports idols as he was growing up in Detroit?

"Walter Ray Williams and Norm Duke," said Bettis.

I must have looked like I didn't recognize those names. "They're bowlers," Bettis said. "They're big on the pro tour. They're in a profession I love and I'd love to be in. They'd love to be in football. I chat with them. I watched bowling on TV as a kid, guys like Marshall Holman, Earl Anthony, Mark Roth and Johnny Petraglia. Chris Schenkel was the announcer. I watched that show religiously.

"I also like Michael Jordan, because of his competitiveness. If he's pitching pennies, he likes to pitch them farther and closer to the wall than anyone else. He's working hard all the time, in every game. You have to respect that.

"Jerry Rice has that same reputation. He doesn't take a play off, even in practice. Emmett Smith is the same way. All your great competitors are that way.

114

"One guy in football I idolized was Walter Payton. 'Sweetness' . . . that's what they called him. I wasn't a big baseball fan, so I don't have any heroes there. I'm getting into the Red Wings more now. I admire anyone who can play on a pro level, those who are willing to pay the price.

"It's important to work out and be ready. You don't want to be in any way, shape or form not at your best because of your own negligence."

"I want to make my family proud of me."

When Steelers' games were on national TV, the cameras often caught the Bettis family in the stands. They stand out because they're obvious in their rooting for Jerome and the Steelers. The Bettis family got more airtime during the weeks that led up to Super Bowl XL than most of the participants in the big game. It was the feel-good story of Super Bowl Week. It probably intrigues fans that Jerome brings his entire family to games, which has to be an expensive undertaking.

In addition to his parents, Jerome's brother, Johnnie, 37, and sister, Kimberly, 40, were usually there.

"I want to be capable of taking care of my family," said Bettis, as if bankrolling them on such trips was no big deal. "If you take away my family I wouldn't be the same ballplayer or person. That's why I take them to road games. They've always been there for me; it's the least thing I can do.

"They believed in me when no one else believed in me. They were there when I was a freshman in high school. I was a star in their eyes. Back in high school, when I was a knucklehead nobody for two years, they thought I was the greatest.

"When I was at Notre Dame, they came to South Bend. They drove there for every game, and it was a three-hour drive. They went to nearly all the road games, like Michigan State, Purdue, Penn State and Pitt. They'd make those games. They didn't go to our game at USC. But they went to all the home games. They were always there.

"This season they drove to Pittsburgh, and sometimes, in the past, they took the train. They would fly to away games. When I was with the Rams, they flew out every week. That's the least thing I can do. They were there when they had to pick up the tab. It meant a lot to see them. It still does.

"I look for them at the beginning of every game. When they see me, they always wave. I know they're watching. I want to make them proud. Me and my family . . . it means a lot to everybody. They suffer with me. Going to games . . . that's a reward. It means that we all made it. I think about it."

"We were always there
to cheer him on."

Kim Bettis, 40, and six years older than her brother Jerome, was attending Wayne County Community College when we spoke in the spring of 1997. She was one of the family members who attended most of Jerome's games and had been to Hawaii at the outset of the year to see her brother perform in the Pro Bowl.

I told Kim I thought most pro football players who were nursing serious injuries the way her brother had at the end of the 1996 season would have begged off playing in the Pro Bowl. I felt Jerome struggled to rehabilitate himself in time to play so that he wouldn't disappoint his family and the Steelers' teammates he had promised he would take to Hawaii.

"We didn't expect him to play," said Kim. "But he told us he was sending us to Hawaii whether or not he was able to play. He said that was our reward for coming to his games."

Some football fans might think that getting to go to all the Steelers' games, home and away, at the expense of your brother would be a bonus to begin with.

"It's the way we were raised," said Kim. "When we were kids and we went bowling, if one was in a tournament the other was expected to go to cheer. Everyone went. It was an all-for-one and one-for-all sort of thing. It's always been that way. We went to all his high school football games. It's a supportive thing. It's just the way it was. We were always there to cheer him on."

She and Jerome and his older brother, Johnnie, grew up in a disciplined home in the inner-city of Detroit.

"Both my parents were working," recalled Kim. "We had to do our housework or homework, and we weren't supposed to have friends in the house when our parents weren't home. Sometimes we'd sneak out, but we knew we were in trouble if we broke the rules. We realized later it was for our benefit. Some of the kids we grew up with are not doing as well. A lot of them are in jail, some are dead."

I mentioned that Jerome had said friends were permitted in the home if his parents were there, but they better not sit on the arms of the chairs or couches, or be caught standing on the stairway, or something like that. They were expected to sit down, and to sit properly.

"One of my mother's rules was that you have to show people you respect your home. If you don't, they won't."

Like Jerome, Kim loves to go bowling. "All three of us, Johnnie, myself and Jerome, were all brought up as bowlers. My mother wanted to keep us all busy. Jerome was the baby. When my brother and I were away in school, Jerome caught it even worse at home.

"One of his best friends, Rick, was shot and wounded walking home from school. It was a drive-by shooting and the shot wasn't meant for his friend. If Jerome wasn't at practice he could have been with him. Jerome could have been shot. My parents would take Jerome to and from practice. Rick's OK now, but he could have been killed.

"My mother still worries about Jerome all the time. That never changes. She calls him when he's injured to find out how he's doing. When he gets hit hard, she'll worry.

"We would drive to Pittsburgh, or take the train. It took five hours either way. Jerome always takes good care of us. He's a nice guy, really a nice guy. We're proud of him. He has remained the same. When he comes home, he's the same Jerome I grew up with. None of it's gone to his head."

"Pittsburgh is someplace special."

No one was happier when Bettis signed a five-year contract to stay with the Steelers — just one day after his 25th birthday — than his family.

"My family was overjoyed, elated," said Bettis. "When I told my parents the situation had arisen and the other team, there was a lot of negative feedback. My mother was adamant about the fact that she liked Pittsburgh and didn't want me to go. She said if I did, it was OK, but there were reservations in her voice. My father was definitely dead-set against me leaving, and my brother was heart-broken about the thought of me leaving the Steelers. I think he would have suffered the most."

When did it dawn on Bettis just how popular he is in Pittsburgh?

"It's really starting to dawn on me," admitted Bettis. "I was in Detroit and went out to play laser tag. There were about 100 kids there, and nobody said anything to me. I thought to myself, if I was in Pittsburgh I wouldn't have been able to escape one kid without an autograph. I realized Pittsburgh is someplace special in that even the little kids know who I am. That doesn't happen in too many other places."

> *"Super Bowl XL included some entries in the record book — Fast Willie Parker, 75-yard touchdown, the longest run in Super Bowl history. Looking sharp, too. Your quarterback was the youngest quarterback in history to win an NFL title. But the most amazing thing about the victory, it seemed like to me, and for a lot of other fans, was you had a fine man, a man you call 'The Bus,' retire in his home city of Detroit, with the Lombardi Trophy in his arms. It was a touching moment for football fans."*
> **— President George Bush at White House reception for champion Steelers, June 2, 2006**

"The Bus" is her baby
By Gladys Bettis

His name is Jerome Bettis, but they've been calling him "The Bus" because he's so big and tough and he runs over people. He's become quite the football player, and we're so proud of him.

I'd never call him "The Bus," though. To me, he'll always be my baby. That's something the fans don't understand. They see him in a completely different light.

I remember him growing up. And he was such a crybaby. But he's so tough now.

Till the time he got to be 12, he just cried about everything. It didn't take much to start him crying. He was so sensitive about everything. He was the baby and I tried to spoil him. He was funny.

When he was in grade school, Jerome used to carry a briefcase with him to and from school. It had been his dad's briefcase before, one of those Samsonite numbers. He always wanted to be like his dad, and do things like his dad did. It was an old briefcase and it wouldn't stay closed. That's why his dad discarded it.

Jerome would take it and he'd leave the house and as soon as he got out of the house he'd drop the briefcase, and it would pop open and his papers would spill out all over the sidewalk. He'd start to cry. It was like a morning ritual at our house. He and my niece would pick up the papers. Her name was Gloria and they went to school together. My sister and I married brothers, so our families were close.

Jerome wore glasses back then, just like his dad. He wore dress shirts to school, shirts like his dad wore, because it was a private school. He'd always have one of those protective shields for ballpoint pens in the breast pocket of his shirt, just like his dad did. He'd leave his lunch at home. I'd take him and my niece to school before I went to work. He'd end up going to one of our neighbors for lunch. Maybe he liked their lunches better.

Me and Johnnie have been married for (40 years). I come from a large family. I had eight brothers and four sisters, and my mom and dad were there for us. My dad was strict. We grew up in Detroit. I played a lot of baseball myself and I was a big Tigers fan. Back then, I liked Willie Horton. We went to the same school, Northwestern High. I liked Gates Brown and Alan Trammell. I thought my older son, Johnnie III — my husband is Johnnie Jr. — would play baseball. He was quite good at it when he was young. My husband was an electrician for the City of Detroit and I worked at a local bank.

Jerome was a pleasant young child. He was just one of the sweetest young men you'd ever want to meet. He has my niceness about him. That comes from my mom. His dad can be gruff, and he gets a little of that from him, too.

118

I taught my children how to be gentlemen and a young lady. I also gave them some of the street knowledge I felt they needed. I gave them what I had. I'm a stickler for good manners. I taught them to treat people the way they wanted to be treated. (Art Rooney Sr., by the way, preached the same sermon to his five sons). I taught them to hold the door open for someone, to say "thank you" and "please" and "pardon me," and things like that. You can't use these words enough.

I told them that rules are there for a reason. A lot of people in our area don't take the time to talk to and do with their children what my husband and I thought was necessary. We have three fantastic children.

The biggest problem I feel today is that parents don't have any time for their children.

Jerome is my pride and joy. That's my baby. We back him now the way we did when he was a child. I told his older brother, Johnnie, that he had to set a good example for Jerome. "Everything you do, Johnnie, Jerome is going to do. So you have to be a good boy, Johnnie, you are your brother's keeper." Jerome was always there at his heels. They shared a bedroom and they continue to be the best of friends.

I'm glad we're all able to go to the games to see him play. I can't do anything but go to his games. If he ever got hurt and I wasn't there, I couldn't forgive myself. As soon as we get to the stadium, I start looking around and find the closest way I can get down on the field if I had to be there. I know he'll be looking for his mom.

Before the game starts, he'll start walking behind the bench, and he starts looking for us up in the stands. He has an idea where we are, but sometimes we're not all together. We usually have about five of us there, sometimes as many as eight.

I'm glad he stayed with the Steelers. I told him to be sure to give the Steelers the last chance to sign him. I wanted him to stay there. They treated him so well. They gave him a chance after they criticized him in St. Louis. They gave him a chance to show what he's all about. Jerome wanted to stay there, too.

As soon as I sit down in the stands I start praying. I say, "Lord, it's me again. You know what I'm here for. Please look after him." I pray every day, at different times during the day. I've been doing it since he was in Little League. I know Jerome is giving his life to this. It's in his heart and soul. I've got to help him. I'm there for him.

You must have faith. It if weren't for faith, I wouldn't be where I am today. God is good. I didn't let Jerome play football when he was young because I wanted him to concentrate more on school and academics. I let him go bowling for exercise and fun.

You do the best you can in raising kids, but have to have faith in a higher power to make it all work. I love the Steelers. I have faith in them, too. They've been good for Jerome. We're so happy he's stayed in Pittsburgh.

Detroit
Some memories of Motor City

"This town makes Pompeii
look alive at night."
— Jimmy Cannon

Super Bowl XL put the spotlight on Detroit. Mitch Albom, a columnist for *The Detroit Free Press*, said that Detroit was rooting for the Steelers. He said Lions' fans could identify better with fans from Pittsburgh than they could fans from Seattle. Detroit and Pittsburgh were both cities that were attempting comebacks from the loss of their industrial base. Both were hurting financially.

Detroit brings images to mind. Motor City. Motown. That's where they make many of America's automobiles. Diana Ross and the Supremes came out of this city's projects. I was all set to move there and work there in 1970, after I received an offer from the *Detroit Free Press*. I remember my wife, Kathie, and I staying at the Book-Cadillac Hotel when we were there to check out the city. It reminded us of a larger version of Pittsburgh.

I had been recommended by *The Miami Herald*, a sister newspaper in the Knight-Ridder chain. I changed my mind after initially accepting the offer to go to Detroit, and ended up instead going to *The New York Post* that year.

I had worked the previous year for *The Miami News*, covering the Miami Dolphins. The Dolphins were 3-10-1 in George Wilson's last season as head coach. Wilson had previously coached the Detroit Lions, and shared stories of his days with the Lions.

Don Shula came to Miami in 1970 and turned the Dolphins completely around. The Dolphins finished 10-4 in Shula's first season. The following year they would play in the Super Bowl in the first of three consecutive appearances, the only team ever to do that. In 1972, the Dolphins would become the only undefeated team in National Football League history with a 17-0 record. Hard to believe that was 34 years ago.

Most of the players I had known from the 1979 team that went 3-10-1 were key contributors to the Dolphins' fantastic success. Hall of Famers such as Larry Csonka, Bob Griese, Larry Little and Nick Buoniconti formed the core of that club, along with Dick Anderson, Manny Fernandez, Mercury Morris, Jim Kiick, Howard Twilley, Larry Seiple, Norm Evans, Bill Stanfel and Lloyd Mumphord.

I missed that successful run, though, because in 1970 I moved to New York, where the Mets and Jets had just won championships, and where the Knicks, Nets and Islanders were about to become champions as well. I also got to meet Muhammad Ali and cover several of his championship fights, which helped me not to feel too badly about missing out on the Dolphins' Super Bowl days.

When I was talking to Bettis about Detroit and his boyhood memories it made me think about what it might have been like to have worked in Detroit during the '70s.

"I heard you're going to Detroit," Larry Merchant of *The New York Post*, told me one night at Madison Square Garden where I'd gone to cover a basketball game while completing my stay at *The Miami News*. "You're going to be out of the mainstream in the Midwest. Why don't you come here?"

Merchant, now an HBO boxing analyst and wordsmith, introduced me to Ike Gellis, the sports editor of *The Post* that same night, and Gellis offered me a job on the spot. So I went to New York instead of Detroit.

Detroit was the city of Joe Falls and Jerry Green, two of the best sports writers in the business. Mitch Albom, the gifted author of *Tuesdays With Morrie* and a national sports commentator, had yet to come on the scene. I was offered different mixes of teams to cover, but it could have included the Pistons, the Lions and the University of Michigan. I could have filled in on occasion with the Tigers and Red Wings as well.

I visited Tiger Stadium in downtown Detroit a few times with the New York Yankees. Every press box in baseball boasted of something special — it was the crab cakes in Baltimore — and I recall they had great ice cream in the press box at Tiger Stadium. No one liked it more or boasted about it more than Joe Falls. He had grown up in New York, but he came to be an ambassador for Detroit. When I think of the Tigers, I think about Al Kaline, Norm Cash, Willie Horton, Rocky Colavito, Denny McLain, Mickey Lolich and Billy Martin. I had a chance to interview all of them.

The Tigers also boasted some Hall of Fame ballplayers earlier such as Ty Cobb, Mickey Cochrane, Charley Gehringer and Hank Greenberg, who would finish his career playing for the Pirates in Pittsburgh. Greenberg became a mentor for a young Pirate slugger named Ralph Kiner. Greenberg Gardens became Kiner's Korner.

Detroit is where the Lions played. The Lions of the '50s, as well as the Browns, the two best teams at the time, are a team from my youth that won't go away. The Lions of that era won five division crowns and three league titles. Buddy Parker,who later came to the Steelers, was their coach. They had such magic names on those teams, beginning with Dick "Night Train" Lane.

Then, too, there was Bobby Layne, Doak Walker, Bob "Hunchy" Hoernschemeyer, Tom "The Bomb" Tracy, Dick Stanfel, Marty Wendell, John Henry Johnson, Les Bingaman, Howard "Hopalong" Cassady and Jug Girard. The names run through my mind and it's fun just to say those names aloud again, to remember them as their bubble gum cards they were for a kid growing up in Pittsburgh, about four to five miles from the ballparks and stadiums of the Pirates and Steelers. The cards were as close as I came to big league sports in those days.

The Lions had Cloyce Box, Jim Doran, Jim David, Dorne Dibble, Jack Christiansen, Lou Creekmur, LaVern Torgeson, Thurman McGraw, Joe Schmidt from Brentwood, Pa., Harley Sewell, Charlie Ane, Gene Gedman from Duquesne, Pa., Pat Harder and Yale Lary. Dick LeBeau and Mike Lucci of Ambridge came along later. All magic names that roll off the tongue. Like Lem Barney and Mal Farr, they just sounded like Lions. This was the team that George Plimpton played with for his wonderful book *Paper Lion*.

Detroit has had more than its share of sports stars. I think of Gordy Howe, Alex Delvecchio, Ted Lindsay and Terry Sawchuck of the Red Wings, legendary boxers Joe Louis and Sugar Ray Robinson, and Pistons such as Dave Bing, Bob Lanier and Ray "Chink" Scott. Detroit was a good sports town. Bettis reminds you that it's been a great bowling town, too.

I remember going there to cover a heavyweight boxing championship bout between Joe Frazier and Bob Foster. Frazier caught Foster flush on the forehead and opened a cut which bled profusely. Some of the blood spurted on the canvas and some of it caught a woman who was working for Western Union at ringside. It was her first ringside assignment. When the blood flew her way, she fainted dead away on top of her machine.

One night before the fight, I was walking through the dark streets of downtown Detroit with two of my favorite sports writers, Jimmy Cannon, a nationally-syndicated columnist from New York who used to delight me with his stories of his days in Paris during the War with Ernest Hemingway, and Roy McHugh, a sports columnist from *The Pittsburgh Press*. They wrote boxing, and most other sports, as well as anybody ever did it. I thought I was in heaven just to be with two little guys who were giants in the business.

The streets of Detroit were empty this particular evening. There was no one to be seen. Maybe everybody was smarter than the three sportswriters who stood on a corner, trying to decide where they might go to catch a bite to eat.

"This town makes Pittsburgh look alive at night," I observed.

"This town," came back Cannon as only he could, "makes Pompeii look alive at night."

* * *

In late June of 2002, my wife Kathie and her best friend, Sharon Pociask, went with some other women on a "gals-only" vacation. So I went on a week-long sports odyssey with Alex Pociask, our second such adventure that coincided with our wives' trip.

Alex and I combined our ideas to develop the trip, most of the stops at his urging, but it worked out beautifully. We went to the College Football Hall of Fame and the campus of Notre Dame University in South Bend, for starters. Then we went to see the

Chicago Cubs play the White Sox in an inter-league game at Wrigley Field and had great seats right behind home plate.

We had dinner at Mike Ditka's Restaurant in midtown Chicago, and Ditka paid a personal visit to our table to talk with us. We also checked out Soldiers Field, where the Bears play.

We toured Milwaukee and had lunch at Miller Park, which would be the site of the 2002 Baseball All-Star Game. We went to Appleton, Wisconsin and had a beer at the bar and restaurant previously owned by the parents of Rocky Bleier. Rocky lived upstairs in his youth, and you could see his boyhood school and church (St. Joseph's). Appleton boasts of being the hometown of Bleier, the writer Edna Ferber, the magician and escape artist Harry Houdini and the infamous political figure Joe McCarthy. Movie actor Willem Dafoe was also from Appleton. We had dinner at a restaurant called Lombardi's that had hundreds of framed photos of the Green Bay Packers.

We visited Lambeau Field in Green Bay and checked out the Packers' Hall of Fame. While touring Michigan's Upper Peninsula, where my pal Alex was an outstanding football player and student at Michigan Tech (he's in their Sports Hall of Fame), we visited a memorial park dedicated to George Gipp, Notre Dame's first All-American football player, in Laurium, Michigan. My middle name is Pat and I got it because Pat O'Brien was playing the part of Notre Dame coach Knute Rockne in a movie about his life. Ronald Reagan played the part of George Gipp. When Gipp was dying during his playing days, he asked Rockne to invoke his name someday when the Irish were up against it, and ask the players "to win one for the Gipper." Great stuff.

We then drove to Detroit. We stopped along the way to tour Mackinac Island and we went on four boat rides on various lakes. We stopped at Comerica Park and the abandoned Tiger Stadium in Detroit, and saw the Ford Field that was under construction at the time. We visited Hockey Town, a restaurant that had photos on the walls of all the greats of the Red Wings. I asked our host, Jim Grimes and his wife, Mary Ann, if they knew of the Lindell A.C., and they drove us there. It was just two blocks down Michigan Avenue from Tiger Stadium. The Lindell A.C. was a legendary bar-restaurant where Bobby Layne used to hold court when he was leading the Lions to championships in the National Football League, prior to his coming to Pittsburgh with his coach, Buddy Parker.

There were pictures of Layne and the Lions of his day, and Detroit greats such as Joe Louis and Hank Greenberg pictured on the walls of what was now a dingy, dimly-lit restaurant. It was like taking a step back in time to another era. I closed my eyes and I could envision Layne entertaining his buddies there after practice. Like he would later on at Dante's Restaurant in Whitehall when he played for the Steelers.

Dick LeBeau
The Renaissance Man

"Never give up on your dream."

Dick LeBeau looked back over his shoulder and stole one more glance at the glass-encased room that is a duplication of the late Art Rooney's office. What caught the eye were the five silver football trophies, four in one cluster, and one standing alone. Each was a Lombardi Trophy, named in honor of the great coach of the Green Bay Packers and Washington Redskins.

"I used to look at those four trophies when I first joined the Steelers (in 1992) when we were over at Three Rivers Stadium," allowed LeBeau. "They were in a glass case in the lobby back then. You had to pass them every day you went to work.

"The new one is special to me. I'm glad Dan Rooney decided it should stand alone. That's ours."

The display that points up the Steelers' achievements is on the second floor of the team's headquarters and training complex at the UPMC Sports Performance Complex on the city's South Side. The University of Pittsburgh football team shares the facility with the Steelers. There are four full football fields outside and an indoor football field nearby. It is quite a contrast to their surroundings at Three Rivers Stadium. This is as good as it gets.

This was Wednesday, February 8, 2006 and it was my second visit with LeBeau in as many weeks to talk about the Steelers' championship season. LeBeau was in his second go-round as defensive coordinator of the Steelers, best known for his "Blitzburgh" defensive schemes. He and Bill Cowher both believed in "attacking" defenses.

LeBeau is credited with creating the "Fire Zone" or "Zone Blitz" defense, with sound pass coverage accompanying blitzes from unpredictable angles. His defense typically employs 3-4 sets, with any of the four linebackers and frequently a defensive back among the blitzers, so the opposition is unsure how many people and just who will rush the passer.

LeBeau was about to take me into a conference room across the way from Mr. Rooney's office when he placed a hand on my shoulder and turned me around. He wanted me to see something.

He took me over closer to the glass partition and pointed out the lone Lombardi Trophy. "See it doesn't have the names of the coaches and players down the sides of it like the four other trophies in there. But my name will be engraved on it soon. That might not mean much to anyone else — except maybe my mother — but it will mean a great deal to me."

Then he pointed out some record books at the bottom of one of the bookshelves. "I like to go in there and pull those out," he said.

Dick LeBeau and Dick Hoak have strong staying power in National Football League. They are two of Bill Cowher's most trusted assistant coaches, and highly regarded throughout the league.

"They have the records from every season. I like to go through them and check them out. It brings back good memories."

I spotted several of my books about the Steelers, bunched together in the center of the top shelf. I felt good about that. I was honored to have my books in Mr. Rooney's library. It was my Lombardi Trophy.

Seeing that room brought back memories for me as well. I used to visit Mr. Rooney — the one who founded the franchise in 1933 and was its grand patriarch when I covered the team for *The Pittsburgh Press* from 1979 to 1983 — and sit in a chair and just talk to him. I did it as often as I could, not just for interviews for stories, because I knew he was special. I learned so much from that man.

After he died, and his office was turned into a memorial library, I had sat in his chair at his desk and did research for a book I wrote about him called *The Chief — Art Rooney and His Pittsburgh Steelers*. Pat Hanlon, who was the assistant public relations director at the time and had been my assistant when I served as the assistant athletic director for sports information at the University of Pittsburgh from 1984 through 1987, had suggested I use that office while I was working on the book.

I could sit there and pick off passersby, ballplayers and coaches, and interview them. I remembered Chuck Noll coming into the office one day and talking to me. As he spoke, I could see a reflection of an oil painting of Mr. Rooney on the glass behind him. Mr. Rooney was smiling over his shoulder. It was like a ghost was in the room.

"You see the way you're sitting here talking to me," Mr. Rooney told me one day. "Chuck Noll never comes in here and just sits and talks to me. Dan is his man. He goes to see Dan when he wants something or needs to talk about something concerning the club. He just says hello to me when he sees me. That's okay."

The Steelers weren't a very good football team for the first 40 or so years that Mr. Rooney ran the franchise. They got better when Dan took over the direction of the ballclub and, most of all, when he hired Chuck Noll to coach the team in 1969. The Steelers won four of those Lombardi Trophies in the '70s when they were the NFL's Team of the Decade, when Pittsburgh was hailed as the "City of Champions."

"I don't go by that I don't look at those trophies."

This was LeBeau's second stint as defensive coordinator with the Steelers. When he first came to the Steelers he served as a defensive backfield coach with Dom Capers as defensive coordinator.

LeBeau, age 68, had been in the National Football League longer than any other coach in the league. He had been involved in some capacity for 47 years, 14 as a player and the previous 33 seasons as a coach. As we were talking, two other recognizable figures in Steelers' history walked by on their way to lunch. Dick Hoak, the running backs coach, said hello and stopped for a moment. Hoak had been with the Steelers for 44 years, 10 as a player and 34 as an assistant coach. He was the only coach Bill Cowher kept from the previous staff that served under Chuck Noll. No current coach has been with one team longer than Hoak.

Then came Joe Greene, the first building block for Noll's championship team, now working in the team's player personnel department. Greene shook my hand, and his hand is so large that mine was lost in it. Greene still had the great grin. I noticed that he took the elevator down to the first floor cafeteria, a concession, no doubt, to balky knees. Former team publicist Ed Kiely came by, on his way to his daily workout session. The Steelers' training facility is his health club. You can't beat the dues.

LeBeau walks with a bounce in his step. He's in great shape for any man, no matter his age. Like Mel Blount, a Hall of Fame cornerback who comes by on occasion to visit old friends, LeBeau looks like he could still play ball. There is a natural wave in his gray-specked brown hair, a wink in his brown eyes and an easy smile. Sometimes it sounds like he's singing softly instead of speaking when you're talking to him. He was wearing a casual white shirt, beige slacks and white sneakers. He looked ready for a stroll on a boardwalk at the beach. He's a pretty fair golfer. During the summer of 2005, he had a hole-in-one in consecutive weeks, one in Ohio and one in Pennsylvania. "It had been about 20 years since I had hit a hole in one," said LeBeau, who said he began playing golf at age seven when he caddied for his father. "I was on quite a streak during that period when I had those holes-in-one. I also had three eagles in a month's span. I was feeling pretty hot."

In his heyday with the Detroit Lions, LeBeau was one of the best defensive backs in the NFL. He played on good teams with the Lions, but he missed out on their championship seasons. One of his teammates was Joe Schmidt of Pitt and Mt. Oliver, a middle linebacker and coach with the Lions who is a member of the Pro Football Hall of Fame. Schmidt's number has been retired at Pitt. LeBeau has the highest regard for Schmidt, and the sentiment, no doubt, is shared by Schmidt. Many believe LeBeau belongs in the Pro Football Hall of Fame. He is one of those players such as the Steelers' Jack Butler and Andy Russell who have a Hall of Fame resume but were somehow overlooked in the voting for such honors.

LeBeau still held the record of playing 171 consecutive games as a cornerback, and going into the 2006 season, he was tied for seventh all-time in the NFL with 62 career interceptions. His nine interceptions in 1970 led the NFC. His 62 career interceptions ranked third in the NFL when he retired. LeBeau appeared in three Pro Bowls, the same as Lynn Swann, for instance. Butler played in four Pro Bowls and Russell represented the Steelers in seven Pro Bowls.

"I don't walk by here," LeBeau said with that "life is good" signature smile of his, "that I don't take a peek at those trophies. I love to look at those trophies. I don't go by that I don't look at those trophies.

"This was the first time I have been part of a championship team in the NFL. There's a lesson to be learned from that. Don't ever give up on your dream. You're never too old to realize your dreams. That's my story. Look how long it took me to be a part of something like this. It's been a month since we won that game, and it still hasn't sunk in completely.

"When that game was over, I looked at the scoreboard and it said Steelers 21 and Seahawks 10, and I couldn't believe it was over. I thought there was another down to play. I kept staring at the scoreboard. I thought there had to be another play." When Seattle's last-ditch effort on fourth-and-7 failed, he said he thought it was only third down. "The guys said, 'No, Coach, that was fourth down.' I was getting ready for another play. I couldn't believe it was over. They put a championship hat on my head, so it must be real.

"I kept saying 'We did it! We did it!' And I must have said it 50 times. I said it to everyone who came near me. 'We did it! We did it!' It's still hard to believe that we did it.

"And we held them to 10 points, don't forget that. That was the No. 1 scoring offense in the league this year."

"And sometimes the bear gets you."

Dick LeBeau is a beautiful man with a beautiful mind. He is different from most coaches I've met. It's easy to be comfortable in his company. Like Chuck Noll, he likes to talk about things other than football. In fact, he prefers to talk about things other than football. He has been referred to as "a renaissance man" on many occasions. Writer Gene Collier referred to him as a "romantic" as well because of his far flung interests and his optimistic approach to life.

He says things different from most people. He says "Adios" when it's time to say goodbye. Sometimes, there's a musical lilt to his voice. He likes to pick up a guitar and sing to amuse himself.

He likes to relate the story of "The Night Before Christmas" to the players during the holiday season, and he does it from memory. He has the rapt attention of everyone in the room. It's a surreal scene.

The players love him. Talk to Troy Polamalu or Kimo von Oelhoffen about him, and they sound his praises. For the last game of the regular season, against the Detroit Lions at Heinz Field, at the urging of linebacker Joey Porter, the defensive players all wore throwback jerseys bearing LeBeau's No. 44 from his days with the Lions. "That really touched my heart," said LeBeau. "They don't know how much I appreciated their gesture. There was a lot of love in the room."

128

"I think he deserves to be in the Hall of Fame," said Steelers' safety Troy Polamalu. "He had 62 interceptions as a player, and he's one of the greatest defensive innovators the league has seen. The Fire Zone blitz has confused a lot of teams." LeBeau knows something about a lot of things, is a music and movie and history buff, likes to sketch and even learned how to crochet. He says he's not that good at crocheting, not as good as his aunt, but he says he likes to try to learn things he doesn't know how to do. I'm just the opposite. I avoid things I don't know how to do. It's a wide field. Later in the summer, after the Steelers concluded their coaching sessions, LeBeau and his buddy Bill Priatko paid a visit to Fort Necessity in Fayette County. LeBeau is interested in the French and Indian War.

LeBeau asked me if he could get me something to drink before we began the first of our two extensive interviews. You have no idea how that makes him different. Most coaches must think it's sissy stuff to need any refreshment when you're just talking. I thought coaches had changed their minds about water breaks and how they are beneficial. Most never offer a drink.

He likes to talk about Clark Gable, who was born in Cadiz, Ohio — "I go by there on the way home," he said — and Humphrey Bogart, John Wayne, Steve McQueen, Charles Bronson and Michael Caine. LeBeau can be seen in the 1970 movie *Too Late the Hero*, where he played Michael Caine's double in a scene.

Two days after my first visit with LeBeau, I watched the Academy Awards Show on TV. Reese Witherspoon won an Oscar as the best actress for her performance as June Carter, the second wife of Johnny Carter, in the movie *Walk The Line*. In her acceptance speech, she said that when people used to ask June Carter how she was doing, she'd reply, "Just trying to be someone who matters."

That phrase fits LeBeau well. He understands there is life beyond the football field. No one has enjoyed the game more, and being part of a team that won the Super Bowl is the realization of a dream from his early adult years.

He has another saying, when someone suggests he always has the answer to another team's attack. "Sometimes you get the bear," he says with a smile, "and sometimes the bear gets you."

He talked about his mother, Beulah Katherine LeBeau, who was 92 at the time of Super Bowl XL. "I didn't know if she was going to survive that game with the Colts," recalled LeBeau. "She's still my biggest fan, so she's the Steelers' biggest fan. I was lucky to have the best mother in the world. My father was an influence on me as well. His name was Robert Emerson LeBeau. He was an auditor for the state of Ohio for 40 years. He liked to see things balance out, as auditors do. He didn't like loose ends. He was a highly principled man and he thought it was important to be honest. He taught me that your name was your most important possession, and you had to protect your reputation. He said you had to protect your name and show respect for your family and upbringing by the way you behaved.

He said your word had to mean something. That a contract wasn't necessary. If you told somebody something they could take it to the bank. I think the Rooneys are like that. You don't need a contract with these people, either."

"We had a lot of good people."

LeBeau was born September 9, 1937 in London, Ohio. It was football country. He went to Ohio State and played for Woody Hayes. He was a member of the Buckeyes when they shared a national football title with Auburn. He played both ways, and he scored two touchdowns as Ohio State came back to beat Michigan, 31-14.

Before the Steelers beat the Seahawks in Super Bowl XL, the last time LeBeau won a title of any kind he was a 19-year-old junior on the 1957 Ohio State team. "I still have the ring, too," said LeBeau. "And now I finally got another one. And I can't imagine it getting any better than this."

He worked for Paul Brown later in life when he became a coach with the Cincinnati Bengals. He worked for the Bengals on two occasions, and was their head coach for 2½ seasons starting in 2000.

He's played and coached with the best in his long career in the NFL. He's the kind of guy who could come back to the Bengals and come back to the Steelers. He never burned any bridges behind him. He's a forgiving guy. He's been popular wherever he played or coached. He considers himself a lucky man to have met all the wonderful people he's known through the years.

"Paul Brown was so far ahead of his time as a coach in pro football," said LeBeau. "He was the first to have a full-time coaching staff. He was so organized. He knew how to judge personnel. That was his gift."

I reminded LeBeau that Brown had cut him as a rookie when he reported to training camp with the Cleveland Browns, LeBeau had to go to Detroit to find a place to play in the NFL.

LeBeau had a comeback story about that. "One time Paul Brown came to my country club to speak at a sports dinner," related LeBeau. "Some of my friends were there. During the question and answer session, one of them asked Brown how he could have cut such a terrific ballplayer as their friend Dick LeBeau.

"Brown came right back. 'I've cut a lot better ballplayers than Dick LeBeau in my time,' said Brown. He was a master of the parry; he was never caught off guard.

"They had some great defensive backs when I was in the Browns' camp. They kept only five defensive backs then. When I got to Detroit they had some great defensive backs, too. They had Dick 'Night Train' Lane, Yale Lary, and Jim David. I played later with Lem Barney for about seven years. When I first played at Cleveland and Detroit they

130

had 30-man squads then, and each team had two quarterbacks. So there were only 12 teams and 24 quarterbacks. Now there are 32 teams. So the No. 2 quarterback on most ballclubs was pretty good then. You had to be special to stick with an NFL team in those days."

Yet the 2005 edition of the Steelers was something special. "I was never around a closer-knit group of guys," he said. "I can't remember any altercation of any kind at St. Vincent or here on the South Side last season. Your job as a coach is to take young men from all kinds of backgrounds, every ethnic group you can think of, every economic situation, and mold them into a team.

"That's not easy. Sometimes you have two kids in a family from the very same environment and they're totally different. It's tough to figure out sometimes. But we had a lot of good people who were all pointed in the same direction.

"It starts on top with the Rooneys and the way they run this franchise. They really want us to do it a certain way. They want us to do it right, with the right people. People pick up on that. Maybe some of our guys would be different in a different environment, but here they blend in and recognize that team goals are more important than personal goals.

"It starts with Bill Cowher. He's the one who sets the standards for our team. He sets the standards high. He is a great coach. He's a very competitive person and he does a good job of conveying that to the team. We've always worked well together. We've been a great combination. When we've worked together we've always made the playoffs. I think he knows that I have something to offer, too. I think he's confident in my calls, and the schemes I come up with. But he sets the tone.

"Winning this Super Bowl will put him in the Pro Football Hall of Fame. It's the only thing that was missing from his resume. No one can ever say again that Bill can't win the big game. He's won a lot of big games in his career. It gives me a great deal of satisfaction to know that I, as an assistant coach, helped him achieve this. It's a good feeling for an assistant coach to be a part of this."

LeBeau has been married twice. His first wife died. His wife Nancy resides in Cincinnati. He has four children from his first marriage — Linda, 43; Rick, 42; Lori, 40; and Phyllis, 38 — and he and Nancy are the parents of Brandon, 27.

LeBeau came up with some ideas on how to defend the Seahawks on the eve of the game. He had the players walk through it at the hotel. One of the changes resulted in an interception by Ike Taylor. Another resulted in Deshea Townsend sacking Matt Hasselbeck. After the game, Hasselbeck said he saw some sets he hadn't seen on tape, and that it confused him. LeBeau blew off any attempt on my part to praise him about that. "Sometimes you get credit when you don't deserve it," he said. "Then, too, sometimes you get blamed when you don't deserve it, either." LeBeau believed that the Steelers had a lot of great players, but pointed to Troy Polamalu and Ben Roethlisberger as rare individuals who set the tone for their teammates on both sides of the ball.

He said they were creative individuals who found a way to get things accomplished on a football field. They were confident athletes who could do special things. "Ben is so big, and he has a strong arm, and he finds a way to advance the ball and come up with big plays.

"Troy is our Roethlisberger on the defensive side. He enables me to make calls that I couldn't make unless I had someone who was so versatile and such a demon out there. People say it looks like Troy is everywhere on the field. Well, that's the way we employ him. He's not just running around out there. He's responding to what he sees and he recognizes what's going on out there better than most.

"Troy is already one of my all-time favorite players that I've been privileged to work with. He's intelligent and he's very introspective, and has interests beyond the ballfield. He's a wonderful football player and an even better human being. He's a unique individual, different from most football players. But he sure knows how to play football. He's not afraid to stick his head in there, no matter the situation.

"Ben Roethlisberger is pretty special, too. We were fortunate to get him when we did. When I was at Cincinnati, I had a chance to catch Roethlisberger in a lot of games that were televised out there. During his junior year, the year before he came out for the NFL draft, I saw him in a game late in the season where the wind was blowing so hard. It was so cold, and yet he was throwing into that wind as if it were a beautiful August day. You could see he was special.

"When he got to training camp, it didn't take long to see he had something special going for him. He can do things you're not used to seeing. I remember that Don Shula said he knew Dan Marino was special the first time he watched him throwing a ball at the Dolphins' training camp. He said the first time he saw him throw the 'out' pass at the combine in Detroit he knew Marino was special."

That brought another Pittsburgh-area quarterback product to mind, namely Joe Montana. LeBeau believed the great ones had something special going for them in the big games.

The Steelers practiced for Super Bowl XL at the Pontiac Silverdome, where the Lions used to play before they built Ford Field in downtown Detroit. I covered Super Bowl XVI when it was played in the Pontiac Silverdome in January of 1982.

Joe Montana of Monongahela was the MVP in that game when he led the San Francisco 49ers to a 26-21 victory over the Cincinnati Bengals. LeBeau was a defensive backfield coach for the Bengals that day. "I thought about that game when we were practicing in the Silverdome," said LeBeau. "We should've won that game that day, but Montana wouldn't let us. That's what sets the great ones apart from the pack."

LeBeau believes that ballplayers have always had strong egos. "That's one of the qualities that makes them stand out from the pack," he said. "They want to be up on the stage. They want to be in the spotlight. It brings out the best in them. They weren't satisfied to play football in their backyard. They wanted to play in a stadium. They wanted to play under the lights."

He says the Steelers have more than their share of strong, confident ballplayers who want to be the best.

"Danny Marino had exceptional arm strength and he was so quick at getting rid of the ball. I think the final answer to your question is that those guys have such great field presence. They see and react better than most quarterbacks. They have the ability to make order out of chaos. They see things other people don't. They have the physical skills to take advantage of the things they see.

"Montana had it. Bobby Layne had it. He falls into that category, too. Toward the end of his playing days, Bobby couldn't throw a ball across this room, but he could take a team down the field and get it into the end zone."

"I want to see their eyes."

"I'll never forget the last few minutes of our game in Indianapolis. So much happened in such a short time, as everyone knows. We made some big defensive plays at the end and we sacked Peyton Manning at his own two-yard line.

"It looked like we had won the game. My guys were strung out along the sideline, and they were shouting and screaming. I try to make sure we don't celebrate too soon because I've seen too much go wrong in my long career in the NFL. So I couldn't control them this time.

"Then we give the ball up the middle to Jerome Bettis. I can't think of anyone I'd feel more confident about running the ball in that situation. He never fumbles. But they got a helmet on the ball and it comes loose. It's a wonder they didn't go all the way with it. But Ben makes the big tackle. See, Ben doesn't think of himself as a quarterback in that situation. He's just a football player. He didn't think twice about making that stop.

"I like coaching from the sideline because I like to see the way my guys look. I want to see their eyes. It might be easier to work from the booth up high, but I want to be able to talk to them and see the look in their eyes.

"That was impossible in this situation. Our guys were strung out everywhere along the sideline. I couldn't get them in a huddle. They were running out on the field. I started running out on the field with them. I was about 15 yards on the field and they're looking back at me like they're wondering, 'Coach, what are you doing out here? Just give us the call. What set do you want us in?' I could see the look in their eyes, and it wasn't a worried look.

"They looked, to a man, like just give us the call and we'll keep them from scoring. They weren't going to lose this game. We might give up a field goal, but we could beat them in overtime if we had to. The Colts had a big gainer, about 15 yards on the first play, and that got them to midfield. But we held and they missed the field goal wide right.

"Then we could celebrate."

"In my mind, no one was better."

"I missed playing with Bobby Layne in Detroit, but I saw him play and I played against him when he came to the Steelers. Bobby didn't have a strong arm. He was no Roethlisberger. Bobby probably came up to Ben's chest. But he was a great competitor and he could put that ball out there where his receivers could catch it. They talk about how great Johnny Unitas was in the two-minute drill, but Bobby Layne was pretty good when the game was on the line. In my mind, no one was better.

"Ben has some Bobby Layne in him, but I hope he trains better. Bobby kept some late hours on the night before ballgames. Ben is bigger and a better athlete, and he has that fire in his belly like Bobby Layne.

"Our players in Detroit used to hang out after practice at a place called the Lindell A.C."

I mentioned to LeBeau that I had been there three years earlier when I was touring the area with my buddy Alex Pociask, and we were taking in ballparks and sports shrines in Chicago, Milwaukee, Green Bay, Appleton (Rocky Bleier's hometown), Laurium (George Gipp's hometown) and Detroit. I remember all the old sports photos filling up the walls of the Lindell A.C.

"I was there once having a cheeseburger and Coke when the owner, Jimmy Butschikarris, introduced me to Bronko Nagurski. I'll never forget that. I've always been a big history guy, and I've always had great respect for guys who showed us the way. I love to read books about historical figures and learn why they were successful.

"George Washington and Abraham Lincoln both had a lot more setbacks than successes, but they never gave in. They kept moving on. You have to have the same attitude and persistence and perseverance in sports. And, more important, in life."

LeBeau believes he connects with the players because he understands their situations.

"I've lived their life," he told Gene Collier in a wonderful piece in *Pittsburgh Quarterly*. "I'm blessed because we have this common denominator in that the essence of the game hasn't changed. Knute Rockne, with a few adjustments, could be a successful coach today as he was at Notre Dame. I'm a bridge for these guys to those times.

"I'm seeing the same things. I've lived their life. Athletes haven't changed that much. They're proud of themselves and proud of their families."

Dan Rooney believes that LeBeau belongs in the Hall of Fame. 'He's been successful at everything," Rooney remarked.

LeBeau might believe that, but he doesn't boast of his personal achievements. LeBeau lets others talk about him. We share a good friend in Bill Priatko. They were roommates in that training camp with the Cleveland Browns, and they have remained close through the years.

Priatko and his daughter Debbie visited with LeBeau after every home game at Heinz Field, and LeBeau saw to it that they had an opportunity to attend many V.I.P. events at Super Bowl XL in Detroit.

Priatko was at the team's final practice. The only other sideline observers were Tony Quatrini, the team's marketing director; Bill Hillgrove, the team's radio voice, Mel Blount, a Hall of Fame member, and Bill Nunn, the old Steelers' scout. At that practice, they saw the maneuver in which Antwaan Randle El took a handoff and rolled right and threw a touchdown pass to Hines Ward. Bill and Debbie were at the Steelers' post-game victory party, which lasted until 4 a.m.

"Bill gives me credit for things I don't deserve," said LeBeau. "I'm lucky to have a friend like him. He's such a good man and he has such a good family. He's a genuine good person. America used to have a lot of men like Bill Priatko, but there aren't many like him anymore. He loves America. He's a true patriot. The majority of Americans used to be like that."

LeBeau left me a message on my telephone answering machine one day. He mentioned my wife Kathie by name, though he never met her. He closed by saying, "God loves you both."

It had a familiar ring to it. When Bill Priatko sends me greeting cards on special occasions, he always closes his hand-written message with the line: "God loves you both." I wondered whether these friends were aware of how much they were alike.

Priatko is always telling people his friend Dick LeBeau belongs in the Pro Football Hall of Fame.

"I'm a Midwestern guy who thinks that if there is a guy walking around saying, 'I should be in the Hall of Fame,' you know, there's something wrong with that person," LeBeau told Collier in their interview. "To me the Hall of Fame is my little town (New London.) They put my name on the corporate sign at the edge of town, 'Home of Dick LeBeau.' To me, that's the supreme compliment. I have a picture of me and my mom by that sign."

I reminded LeBeau of his remark. "Yeah, that's good enough for me," he said.

"The team was surrounded by a lot of doubt when they were 7-and-5, but there was no doubt in the locker room."
— Bill Hillgrove Voice of the Steelers

LeBeau's late change catches Seahawks by surprise . . .

On the eve of Super Bowl XL, Dick LeBeau called his defensive unit together at a meeting and put in a few changes that contributed to the Steelers' 21-10 victory over the Seattle Seahawks. Seahawks' quarterback Matt Hasselbeck conceded in the post-game press conference that he was confused by some "new looks" the Steelers' secondary showed him. One of those led to an interception by Ike Taylor.

LeBeau, credited as the father of the zone-blitz concept, installed a new coverage package at the final team meeting at 8 p.m. the night before the big game. "And you know what?" asked LeBeau after the ballgame, "Even though we just put the thing in on Saturday night, it was probably one of the most successful packages we used the entire game. We just walked through it in the hotel ballroom."

It was a bogus pressure alignment designed to nullify some of the Seahawks' strong-side formations. It gave the Hawks some headaches.

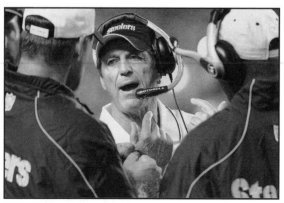

Dick LeBeau likes working from the sideline so he can look into everyone's eyes when he's communicating with them.

Bill Cowher
Super Bowl XL
Post-Game Press Conference

"What a great way to go out."

Bill Cowher couldn't stop smiling. His smile is an ear-to-ear grin. Steelers' fans love to see it. He was seated behind microphones and taping devices after his Steelers had beaten the Seattle Seahawks, 21-10, in Super Bowl XL at Ford Field in Detroit.

As the father of two daughters, I was touched by the post-game scene when Cowher was rushed by his wife and three daughters and they all hugged him and kissed him. One of them, I think it was Lauren, the oldest daughter, who shouted, "Daddy, we're world champions!" That grabbed my heart and squeezed it real good. Then to see Bill Cowher with tears in his eyes. Here are excerpts from his post-game press conference:

Q: You said you wanted nothing more than to give Dan Rooney the trophy. What did it feel like to give him the trophy?

Bill Cowher: Very special. Just for the whole organization, for the City of Pittsburgh. And to give it to him; he's what's great about the NFL. I'm very fortunate and blessed to work for an organization and a man like that.

Q: Talk about Jerome right now.

Bill Cowher: Well, this means so much to the game because — this is a blessing. Jerome is a great guy. The way he played off the field, he brings so much class and professionalism to our team. If it is his last game, what a great way to go out. He's a Hall of Fame running back.

Q: How did you get this team turned around? This couldn't have seemed possible when the team lost three games in a row and was 7-5.

Bill Cowher: We talked about that eight weeks ago. We wiped the slate clean and we kind of took a little of that old saying — one game at a time. But each week was a unique set of circumstances. But with that approach we gained some confidence and we started to have a pretty good team and the last win at Indy, I thought that probably helped us more than anything else, because it allowed us to prepare for the noise we had to deal with on the road in the playoffs.

Q: What does this mean for Dan Rooney?

Bill Cowher: I'm just happy for him. It was for him. He's a special guy and I'm happy for him. He's a very inspired individual. He looks at you and he makes you want to work as hard as you can to succeed.

Q: The Christopher Columbus speech . . . what was that all about?

Bill Cowher: Yeah, the old Christopher Columbus speech. The guys kind of like that. We talked about it the other day and I said we're going to get the periscopes instead of the telescopes because we don't know if we're on a submarine or a ship. So I did a little twist to it every now and then. But you know what, I think the purpose or meaning of it is that Columbus got on that boat and a lot of people told him not to go out there because they said the world was flat. And he just kept going and he found the new world. And that's what I told them. There's a lot of people telling you that you can't do it, but you know what, that doesn't mean you don't go try. And like I said, history is not going to determine our fate, but our effort today made history. And that's what's special to me.

Q: What was the difference in the end?

Bill Cowher: You know what, we really didn't run the ball very good this post-season. I was just talking about that. The running game got going for the second half and it really kind of took care of that on the second play. But our quarterback played well, we had a great team balance in the post-season. Defense stepped up. We were getting great plays made. We were playing the best football at the end of the season.

Q: Do you think owners should be more patient with their coaches?

Bill Cowher: I certainly think that in this business it's hard to sustain it. I think if you have good people and people who you can trust, people who you can communicate with. And you got to just trust. We still have to win. We work in a performance-based business. I don't think I'm in a position to tell an owner what to do. They know the situation. I think patience is a virtue if you have the right person.

Q: It wasn't necessarily the Steelers' best all-around game they were saying and, in fact, you guys have played many better games than you did tonight. Ben said that; he said that this wasn't necessarily your best overall performance, but obviously it's the most important win. Can you talk about how sometimes you don't have to play your best game to do it?

Bill Cowher: There's no question. Like I said, we never go off track on offense. I thought defensively we played our tail off. But we made the plays on offense when we had to. Ben made plays on offense

138

James Farrior

Deshea Townsend

Defensive standouts

Joey Porter

Ike Taylor

when he had to. I just think it's a sign of a good football team when you come out and not play your best football and still win the games. And we were able to top it off like this, and that's very special.

Q: In your heart, can you talk about what you're feeling right now?

Bill Cowher: I'm just really happy for the players and coaches. I'm happy for everybody else. Honestly, because when you see what the sacrifices they made and they have done everything I've asked them to do, and to see it pay off, that's special. And I'm happy for Mr. Rooney. I'm happy for the support and, you talk about a class guy. He's a very inspiring individual. And he's inspired me. It's a very humbling experience with him.

Q: What was your impression of Detroit?

Bill Cowher: Detroit was great. It's such a sports city. You get a chance to see the Pistons play. The Red Wings were playing the same night. You've got Swin Cash (of McKeesport), my favorite WNBA player. I got basketball in my family, so that's big. And then obviously the Lions and the Tigers and Jim (Leyland) coming up here to coach the Tigers; he's a good friend of mine. I love Detroit. I think Detroit's a sports city. And they did a fantastic job of playing host to us.

Q: Why do you think the Steelers stayed with you through the lean years?

Bill Cowher: You win early and you buy yourself maybe a couple down years. You got to have support. People like Kevin Colbert coming in; he's added a lot of years to my career. And Mr. Rooney, and the assistant coaching staff. I can't say enough about them. And the players. It's an unselfish group of coaches and players, the best I've ever been around.

Q: Has this hit you yet?

Bill Cowher: I don't know. Like I said, I don't know; this may not hit me for a couple of days. Probably when I'm sitting home some time with my family and away from all this. That's when it will hit me.

Q: When you huddled up with your girls and your wife, what were you saying to them?

Bill Cowher: Those four women are very important to me. They're the ones that . . . they mean the most. I'm the head coach today, but I tell you what. Tomorrow I go back to being an assistant coach. Because the head coach will be telling me what to do. I got a basketball game to go to tomorrow. Because the girls got to be back in school by one o'clock. So I'm going to watch my kids play ball and that's the way it should be and that's where I want to be.

Q: Do you remember what you said to them exactly?

Bill Cowher: I don't know. I really don't. It's been so much…my kids were talking to me. I know one said, "Daddy, we're world champions." And I thought like, well, yeah, I guess we are. It's just, I don't know. It was special to have them there though.

Q: A lot of people are now going to say that this validates your career. What, to you, what does this mean?

Bill Cowher: This is not about me. It's about this team. It's about this ownership. It's about the coaches and players. I don't worry about what people say. I can't control that. I'm not in it for my validation. I'm in it because I really enjoy the group of players and the challenges that you get in trying to bring people together to see them experience this and they have been working so hard. That is very gratifying to me.

Q: You called Hines Ward when he was holding out and convinced him that ownership would take care of him contractwise and that you thought it was in everyone's best interest if he reported to camp. How'd you do that?

Bill Cowher: We talked. Those are very sensitive issues. And I understood where everyone was at and I just try to keep talking through it with them. And I know how much he's meant to this organization and what he does. And he's out there every week. Yeah, there may be faster receivers. There may be guys with better hands, but I tell you what, I wouldn't want another receiver than Hines Ward. The way he plays the game, the passion, he's so competitive, he's smart. I love the guy.

Q: You say Ben tests your patience. What do you mean by that?

Bill Cowher: Well, I don't know if he tests your patience; that's probably not the right word. You got to let him go. Sometimes you look at him and you know he's fighting through it, but he'll come out of it. He's extremely mature for a guy in the second year. Sometimes you got to just keep that in mind. Yeah, he will make plays. The play that he bootlegged on, he did that by himself. No one else did that. And he got the first down.

Q: How much will he improve?

Bill Cowher: I think he's going to get better. He'll get more comfortable in the offense. We'll start to give him more leeway to do things and best is way ahead of him.

"It doesn't hurt to say hello to people.
They appreciate it."
— Sugar Ray Robinson

Troy Polamalu
A different breed of cat

"He seems too nice
to be a pro football player."

Let me tell you my story about Troy Polamalu. You already know what kind of a ballplayer he is, a defensive demon, something of a Tazmanian Devil on the football field, racing here, there and everywhere. Torpedoing people left and right. That long black hair flowing out from under his helmet and draping his shoulder pads like a black cape. He's a Polynesian version of Darth Vader. There were times you wanted him to cut that hair — you hated that look on opposing players — but you got used to it, and it became part of Polamalu's persona. He was from another world, or so it seemed.

Polamalu is a deeply private man, yet he commands your attention. He does so in the best way, not the way Terrel Owens and Chad Johnson do, not with a big mouth and look-at-me theatrics. He's no jerk, just the opposite. It would be nice if the National Football League had more like him. Opposing quarterbacks can't keep their eyes off Troy Polamalu, and Pittsburgh football fans have learned that he is the catalyst for much of what happens in a positive way when the other team has the ball. He is the Steelers' strong safety, but there are times you'd think he was a linebacker, an end, and a nose tackle. There are times when he appears to be a running back in the other team's backfield. He seems to know just when the ball will be snapped. And boy can he run whenever he gets his hands on the football. Polamalu has become one of the most popular sports figures in Pittsburgh, and his jersey one of the best selling ones around the country.

He was the Steelers' No. 1 draft choice out of Southern Cal in 2003. He didn't do much for the Steelers in his rookie season, playing mostly as a nickel-back in obvious passing situations, Long-time fans might have suspected the Steelers had selected another stiff from USC, recalling an offensive tackle named Mike Taylor they took on the first round back in 1968, in Bill Austin's last season as head coach. Austin, a Vince Lombardi protégé in Green Bay, gave way the next year to Chuck Noll, and long-suffering fans were finally rewarded with a coach who knew what he was doing, and would, in time, deliver solid contenders and, eventually, championship teams.

It was difficult to assess Polamalu at his first Steelers' training camp at St. Vincent College that summer of 2003. The following summer, there were stories coming out of the camp that Polamalu was impressive in drills, and looked like the real deal. Polamalu was a promising prospect after all. I paid a visit toward the end of that summer session, and I traveled to Latrobe hoping I might be able to interview Troy Polamalu. He sounded like an intriguing individual.

Troy Polamalu

Troy Polamalu performs his own conditioning workout.

When I covered the Steelers for *The Pittsburgh Press* from 1979 through 1983 it was easy to interview whomever you wanted to talk to at the Steelers' training camp. You'd catch a player coming off the practice field and ask him if you could come up to his dorm room at Bonaventure Hall during the break. You could sit at his bedside while he relaxed and stretched his legs, and talk to him for a half-hour or so, just a casual conversation. You could get a better read on a guy, checking out his simple surroundings, maybe spotting a book or two, or some music tapes, a clue to his interests, something to start a conversation. No rush.

The rules had changed, however, during the days after Chuck Noll gave way to Bill Cowher, and now it is like moving around a concentration camp. You had to have a media badge. You were constantly checked for your credentials by an army of security guards, and there were barriers wherever you went. You had to check with the team's public relations staff to see if it was all right to see one of the Steelers, and you might get ten minutes of his time, stopping him on a sidewalk as he was going to lunch in one of the campus cafeterias. Sound bites don't work when you're writing a book.

Let's just say it was different. The same can be said for Troy Polamalu. He's just different, that's all, different from most football players you've met through the years, different from the Dolphins, the Jets and the Giants you'd met and interviewed while covering teams in Miami, New York and then back home in Pittsburgh through the years. I was used to traveling on airplanes and buses with the ballclubs I covered. You could get to know the guys better, and you could sort out what to write and what not to write. You didn't want to rock the boat or the bus — though I did at times — and kill off news sources or willing subjects.

It was Tuesday, August 10, 2004, two days before my 37th wedding anniversary, when I was walking across the campus at St. Vincent College, heading for lunch with the Steelers. As I was walking by myself, I was suddenly aware of someone at my left side. I glanced over, and lo and behold, it was Troy Polamalu. Was this a chance meeting, or had my prayers been answered? We'd never met, so I introduced myself, told him I was working on a book, and wanted to do an interview. Perhaps after lunch.

"Let's do it now," said Polamalu. He pointed to a bench where we might sit and talk. It was perfect. It was off the beaten path. There was lots of shrubbery and it was like a grotto. We sat on a wooden bench where I'd seen the Benedictine priests who teach and work at St. Vincent sit and relax, and perhaps say some prayers. I liked the privacy. I didn't want any of the other writers to see me talking to Troy Polamalu. I didn't want to share him. I prefer one-on-one interviews to the gang bang that is usually the scene at St. Vincent and at the Steelers' training facility on the South Side or after a game at Heinz Field on the North Side. Besides, I hadn't cleared the interview with the p.r. staff. Shame on me.

Jason Gildon, a veteran linebacker, drove by on his bicycle and waved to Troy. Squirrels scurried under the surrounding shrubbery and raced up tree trunks. We were in the shade on a warm, sunny day.

Polamalu was so pleasant. At one point, trying not to keep him from eating, I asked him if he wanted to continue our interview after lunch. He said it was okay to continue. He had time. He even met me after lunch and accompanied me to a site where I thought I could take some good photographs of him. Polamalu posed for me. He couldn't have been more obliging. Yet he seemed shy, and not one seeking the spotlight. I'd watched him doing television interviews and he had seemed uncomfortable with a camera pointed his way, and microphone pushed toward his handsome face. At one point, when we were talking about the Rooney family that owned and operated the Steelers, I explained that Dan Rooney, the team's president at the time, was the oldest of five sons of team founder Art Rooney. That's how the leadership baton had been passed on to him.

"That's how they do it in Samoa," said Polamalu, who was born to Samoan parents in Garden Grove, California on August 19, 1981. I celebrated my 39th birthday the next day, more than likely when I was covering the Steelers' training camp at St. Vincent College. I had one other meeting with Polamalu at the camp a few days later. I gave him a copy of the new University of Southern California football guide I had received in the mail. Polamalu was pictured in the thick guide, and mentioned in several places. He seemed pleased to get this gift.

I watched him during warm-up drills, when the assistant coaches were leading the players through their exercises, to limber them up. Polamalu never seemed to be doing what everyone else was doing. He had his own routine. Normally, this wouldn't be permitted. Jock Sutherland, who coached at Pitt in the '30s and then with the Steelers, must have been spinning in his grave. With Jock Sutherland, a stern, dour disciplinarian, there was only one way, and it was his way. Bill Cowher made concessions for Polamalu. It took him awhile to get with it, but Cowher came to the same conclusion about Polamalu as most people who've met him. He's just different, that's all.

Polamalu was so pleasant and soft-spoken, and deeper in his ideas and reflections than most players. There was a strong spiritual side to him. He seemed almost too sweet. I remember coming home that night and sharing my day with my wife Kathie. I told her about Troy Polamalu. I said he didn't seem tough enough to be a pro football player. "He seems too nice to be a pro football player," I said. I was wrong. He was a different breed of cat.

John Stallworth was that way, deeply spiritual, such a pleasant fellow, but offering his thoughts with a squeaky voice. You should hear Terry Bradshaw imitate Stallworth's speech. Stallworth was certainly tough enough to play pro ball. He stayed 14 seasons (1974-

---

Kimo von Oelhoffen on Troy Polamalu:
"I love to watch him. He smiles between plays.
Then it's Bing! Bing! Bing!
He's all over the place."

1987). I'd gone to Canton in the summer of 2002 to see Stallworth inducted into the Pro Football Hall of Fame.

Sometime in December 2004, at the height of the Christmas season, I was doing a book signing at Waldenbooks in the center of the first floor at Monroeville Mall when Troy Polamalu approached me with a big smile and said hello. There was a beautiful woman at his side, and he introduced her. Her name was Isadora, and she was his fiancée. She looked like one of those native beauties from the South Seas you've seen in movies, or an animated Disney production.

Troy Polamalu had met me twice. I wasn't a regular on the Steelers' beat. It was so surprising that he remembered me and more surprising that he stopped to say hello. Then he introduced his girl friend. Polamalu seemed proud to do so. This seems like common social behavior, but it's not, not for football players, not for professional athletes.

About ten minutes later, I looked up and caught sight of Polamalu across the way, and he waved to me. About a half-hour later, Polamalu approached my table once more and placed a steaming hot Cinnabun on my table. He didn't say a word this time. He just put the treat there, an early Christmas gift, and smiled and walked away. Polamalu was a real prince in my eyes, a handsome Samoan prince.

Troy Polamalu

"I'm a sunshine kind of guy."

Who am I? I'm still hoping to figure that out. What do I want to be known as? There have been a lot of great players here, like Terry Bradshaw. I hear a lot about Carnell Lake, and what a class guy he was. I hear about those big names. I would love to be known along with those great people.

The spiritual side of me is important too. My own Christian beliefs. Some people are good at sports. Like Frank Thomas is good. M.J. or Michael Jordan is good. And Terry Bradshaw. I'm aware of their personal lives and they all had struggles of different sorts. They made a commitment to be great. I want to be great like that. But I don't want to sacrifice my personal life. I want to be able to move around and enjoy myself without attracting a crowd. I want to have my own life. It doesn't matter whether you're a baseball player, a basketball player or a football player . . . you lose some of your own life. Sometimes you lose your way, like what happened to O.J. Simpson. He went to Southern Cal and he was so great, and so many people loved him. He had it all. And he lost it just as fast. What happened to O.J. Simpson? No one can make any sense of that.

146

For me, when I was growing up, I gave up plenty of things. I had hard discipline rules. I grew up with my own family till age 8. I lived in a Samoan community. There are more Samoans in Southern California than there are in Samoa. Some families have lost the Samoan culture. I moved from Southern California to Oregon. I was there from 9 till I graduated from high school. I lived with my aunt and uncle all that time. He was very hard on me. The head of a Samoan family has a title. He is the head of all the siblings. There is a Samoan word for it. He is the *Matai* of our family. I am the son of Suila Polamalu. I was the next oldest of her 12 children.

Religion was important. Jesus Christ is my savior. I'm very family-oriented.

I looked up to Junior Seau when I was coming along as a ballplayer. He had played at UCLA and he was outstanding with the San Diego Chargers. He said some things that were pretty much true about his strict upbringing, and people in Samoa didn't like him for it. You have to be careful about what you say. I really look up to him for what he's done and what he's accomplished. Another famous Samoan in pro football was Jack Thompson — the 'Throwin' Samoan' — who came out of Washington State to play in the NFL.

I got into trouble when I was real young. I was hanging out with the wrong guys in Santa Ana. That's when I was sent to Oregon to live with relatives. My father's name was Troy Aumua. He's still alive, but he's not a part of my life. That was a struggle for me also. I tried to reestablish that relationship. My Christian values are such that I would like to forgive and forget.

You mentioned Carnell Lake. He went to UCLA, too. I never heard of him when I was a kid. I never paid much attention to college or pro football. I never liked football. The last thing I'm going to do is sit down and watch ESPN sports highlights. So I have a lack of knowledge in that respect. Some people say I have the opportunities and abilities and attitude to be the next Carnell Lake. From what I know, that's pretty good.

I had a hard time making the adjustment from college to the pros. The longer schedule is tough on your body. It's no secret that NFL players make a lot of money. I never had as much money as I have now. The problem now is I want to do something for God, but I don't know what. I'm not advertising it, but I am sure I will find the right way to do something.

I grew up in a ghetto and was fine with that. God has completely taken me away from my comfort zone. Pittsburgh is not like where I grew up. It's raining here, it's snowing here. I'm a sunshine kind of guy. Football is important here, though, and we have great support.

I am getting a lot of attention but I want to stay humble. I want to sit like an animal alone out in the field. When I am with people I want to be polite and maintain my principles. You want to please God and show him you are grateful for what he has given you. He made so many sacrifices for us, even sacrificing his life.

People say I am like two different people, the nice guy off the field and a hard-hitting guy on the field. I'm a little ill at ease about that. I don't see two different people when I see myself in the mirror. I'm going to be fully committed to something.

USC was my favorite school growing up. My uncle played football there and I grew up as a USC fan. I'm trying to learn to be a Pittsburgh Steeler fan, and what that's all about.

I'm a guy who goes in the back door up here. I'm not seeking attention. I've walked through some of these buildings. They're very spiritual. I'm very comfortable here. It usually takes me a while to get comfortable. By nature, I'm a loner. I'm not the type who is comfortable in most social settings. I sit back and watch. I have fun watching people have fun. I'm a stay-at-home-and-watch-TV kind of guy. I don't have a dark side.

The Pittsburgh Steelers are not going to put any more pressure on me to succeed than I'm going to put on myself. Most of the reading I do is Scripture. I like to read my Bible. It's hard to be away from home. So I read, and lose myself, trying to learn. Jesus preaches peace. I don't understand why there is so much killing in the name of religion. People think they have to kill somebody to defend their own beliefs. If you really know the Bible you'll know that's not right. That's not God's plan.

The Eucharist is the symbol of Jesus. I believe that. I'm just worshiping Jesus. I went to a Catholic school and I've gone to Mass. I've been around Mormons much of my life. Many Samoans are Mormons. I'm learning slowly who I am and what I want to be, God willing. I know I'm a Christian. It was good talking to you. God bless you.

"When there is no hope one must invent hope."
— Albert Camus

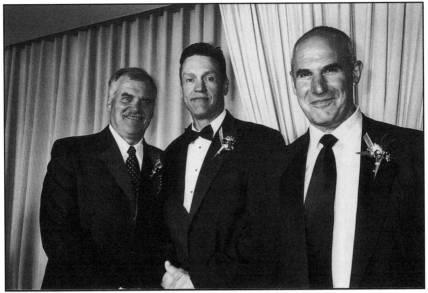

Former Steelers who attended Mel Blount's black tie 2006 Celebrity Dinner to raise funds for his youth home in Washington County include, left to right, Gerry "Moon" Mullins, Ted Petersen and Randy Grossman.

Polamalu Picks Up The Tab

Here's a story about Troy Polamalu that was offered by Bob Milie, who was the assistant trainer for the Steelers during the glory days of the '70s.

"My cousin was out to dinner at an Italian restaurant in Sarver, up beyond New Kensington. Troy Polamalu and his wife were eating there that same evening. Everyone was discreet enough not to disturb them during dinner. After finishing his meal, Polamalu rose and asked for everyone's attention. He thanked everyone for not disturbing him and his wife while they were dining. He then announced, in appreciation, that he was picking up the tab for everyone, and that he'd sign autographs for a few minutes before he left. How about that? Can't you just see Barry Bonds doing something like this? I don't think so."

Ben Roethlisberger
The real deal

"I want to be the best quarterback to ever play the game."

There has never been an athlete that captured Pittsburgh quite like Big Ben Roethlisberger. He was an instant sports star. Big Ben was bigger than the U.S. Steel Building in the mind of Pittsburgh sports fans. Unlike Halley's Comet, we didn't see him coming. The Steelers had their eyes set on David Rivers, a quarterback at North Carolina State, but he was the second player picked in the 2004 college draft, right after Eli Manning of Mississippi. The Steelers had to settle for Ben Roethlisberger the way the Miami Dolphins had to settle for Dan Marino in 1983. The Steelers selected Roethlisberger as the eleventh pick in the first round of the draft.

Sometimes you get lucky. "I'd rather be lucky than good," Art Rooney, the original owner and patriarch of the Pittsburgh Steelers, was fond of saying.

Big Ben had the size and stature and magic of Mario Lemieux and the pride and combativeness of Roberto Clemente. He had the nerve and brashness of Bobby Layne and Terry Bradshaw. Big Ben combined the best of Pittsburgh's two best all-time athletes and the Steelers' two previous Hall of Fame quarterbacks.

He did it right away and that separated him from the pack. The Steelers were 15-1 in his rookie season. Roethlisberger was 13-0 as a starter, the first NFL rookie quarterback who could make such a claim. He was 27-4 as a starter in his first two seasons, and that includes a 4-1 playoff record. Like Marino, he made it to the Super Bowl in his second pro season. And he came away a winner, the only thing missing from Marino's unreal resume. Bradshaw directed the Steelers to four Super Bowl championships in four seasons in the '70s, and — with free agency and player movement — it's much more difficult to do that these days. It's harder to keep a championship team intact.

Roethlisberger wasn't at his best in Super Bowl XL, but he came up with enough big plays to pull out a victory. Steelers' fans hoped the best was yet to come. Marino has become a mentor for Big Ben and Bradshaw has become a booster on national TV. Both have embraced this young man because they like what he's about, they like his style and potential, and they are still Steelers' fans and want to continue to help the cause. Bradshaw said Roethlisberger was irresponsible for riding a motorcycle — especially without a helmet — but he had a high regard for his football ability.

Big Ben not only has a strong arm, but also, like a kid playing touch football in the street, he is resourceful and finds ways to make good things happen. Much of it was not in the Steelers' playbook. He

Ben Roethlisberger

Ben Roethlisberger (7) has loved playing basketball with Steelers' teammates like Brett Keisel. "It's something I enjoy doing," he said.

just knows how to win. Whatever it takes. The Pirates never had a Hall of Fame pitcher and they never had a pitcher with Roethlisberger's record as a starter.

He was different, something special. His public relations efforts were outstanding as well, even if a bit forced at times. Big Ben seemed eager to please, and to develop the kind of image that would attract fans and endorsements. Sometimes he tried too hard, and forced things. He did the same thing in football games, but so did Bradshaw and Marino. Big Ben used his celebrity to embrace good causes and to come to the aid of ailing and hurting individuals. That's what sports stars should do. He had a strong spiritual side. Pittsburgh and the Steelers Nation embraced Big Ben from the beginning. He was a savior of sorts. The same people who couldn't stomach the likes of Terrell Owens and other showboating individuals in sports loved this kid from Findlay, Ohio.

Soon after Hines Ward announced that he was planning a trip back to South Korea with his mother to visit places where they lived — he was born there and came to America when he was a year old — Roethlisberger announced that he was going to Switzerland to trace his roots. Who knew he was Swiss? The only Swiss connection I was aware of was when Swiss cheese was the choice for topping off that high-cholesterol concoction known as a "Roethlisburger." More than likely Ben and his managerial team saw another opportunity to cash in on his star status. Turns out that Big Ben was the first quarterback of Swiss heritage to lead a team to victory in the Super Bowl. Some saw holes in his Swiss cheese story.

He gained national fame and fortune, appearing on late night television shows with the likes of David Letterman. And anything signed by Big Ben carried a high price.

Art Rooney, the founder of the Steelers, liked to say, "We know something about quarterbacks. We've given away some of the best in the business."

The Steelers, indeed, allowed Sid Luckman and Johnny Unitas to get away, in different manners, and both ended up in the Pro Football Hall of Fame. So did Lenny Dawson. They didn't use Dawson or Jack Kemp, who both went on to become two of the best quarterbacks in the American Football League. They gave up on Bill Nelsen and he became a star with the Cleveland Browns. They gave up on Earl Morrall and he starred for the Baltimore Colts and Miami Dolphins and lasted forever in the National Football League. They were smart enough to get Bobby Layne late in his career, after he had directed the Detroit Lions to NFL titles, and he and Buddy Parker improved the Steelers to a degree not previously known.

They learned their lessons the hard way. Dan Rooney knew the history — he and his brothers had caught passes from Johnny Unitas at training camp and thought he was pretty good — and Dan and his oldest son, Art II, weren't going to let that happen again. They have signed Big Ben to a long-term contract. They want to keep him in Pittsburgh.

"Ben's what you want in today's game."
— Ken Whisenhunt,
Steelers' offensive coordinator

In the midst of the 2004-2005 NFL playoffs, Gerry Dulac of the *Pittsburgh Post-Gazette*, wrote: "He has been a little of everything and everybody in the six victories that have led the Steelers to their third AFC championship game in five years, orchestrating an offense that has suddenly become the most potent and diverse in the NFL.

"In Cleveland, in a 41-0 shutout victory on Christmas Eve, he looked like Dan Marino, throwing passes so deft, so accurate that a defensive back couldn't afford to turn his shoulder, let alone his back.

"In Indianapolis, he was the best quarterback on a field that included Peyton Manning — NFL passing leader, single-season touchdown record-holder, future Hall of Famer — setting a tone from the very first series that his teammates followed as if he were the Pied Piper."

Bill Cowher, his coach, said, "We are going to go as far as he's going to take us. I'm not going to put any pressure on him. That's the facts, and he likes that, he knows that."

Antwaan Randle El dropped a so-catchable pass on the first play at Indianapolis. That didn't rattle Roethlisberger. He completed the next seven passes and led the Steelers to a 14-0 lead.

"I have no problem with that," Roethlisberger said of the role Cowher had chosen for him. "I want to come out and make sure I take care of the things I have to do. As a quarterback, naturally, if you do that, if you don't turn the ball over and do the things you're supposed to do at the quarterback position, you give yourself and your team a better chance of winning the game."

Ken Whisenhunt, the offensive coordinator, wanted to bring Roethlisberger along slowly, but Ben was begging to go deeper into the playbook so they could go deeper into the playoffs. He had thrown five interceptions in the playoffs as a rookie, and wanted to redeem himself.

"He's been saying for a year he wanted to do more of that, and he's getting better at it," Whisenhunt said of a more complex offense. "He's a very good one to have that (responsibility) on his shoulders."

A year earlier, some of his teammates weren't sure he was quite ready for that responsibility, and they weren't being critical, just honest. When Alan Faneca, the Pro Bowl offensive tackle, was asked if it was exciting to have the team's top draft pick playing quarterback.

"Exciting?" offered Faneca. "No, it's not exciting. Do you want to go to work with some little kid who's just out of college?" Later, Faneca wanted everyone to make sure he wasn't coming down on the rookie.

No one knew quite what to expect.

Cowher said he was more confident about Roethlisberger's ability the second time around. "To me, he has earned that trust," said Cowher.

"Roethlisberger has that magic it."
— USA Today

The 6-5, 240-pound Roethlisberger drew rave reviews from his coaches as the Steelers approached Super Bowl XL at Detroit's Ford Field. *USA Today* trumped that "Big Ben's Got Big Game" in a headline. He was only 23 years old, second only to Marino as the youngest quarterback to lead a team in a Super Bowl game, but he had matured in a hurry. Ben didn't blanch at the idea of directing the Steelers to a Super Bowl victory.

Cowher called him "a young quarterback who doesn't play young."

"Ben's what you want at quarterback in today's game," said Ken Whisenhunt. "He's big, tough, mobile, a real confident guy who has vision, poise, makes smart decisions and is real accurate with his throws in and out of the pocket. The guys really believe in him."

On another occasion, Cowher said, "I've got a lot of respect for Ben. He's a competitive guy; he's a tough guy."

Hines Ward was one of those guys. "I don't know if it would have happened last year because we were trying to take more pressure off him," said Ward the week before the big game. "In the playoffs, you can't sit there and be conservative. You got to be aggressive. You can't try to not lose the game; you got to try to win the game.

"It's night and day from last year to this year the way Ben's playing with so much confidence. Ben's maturation, watching him become a rising star at the quarterback position, makes my job easier. He comes up and asks me about certain coverages and what he should do against this or that defense. We're working hard to get on the same page the way Marvin Harrison and Peyton Manning are."

Cowher could see a great work in progress. "He's much more mature than his age would indicate," said the Steelers' coach. "He's very much in control. He's got a great feel for the game and a lot of self-confidence. I don't think he knows what not having success is."

Jim Corbett of *USA Today* wrote: "Roethlisberger has that magic 'it' — whatever that intangible 'it' is that sets apart the great ones. He's the new breed counter-puncher to today's suffocating zone blitzes — a bigger, more mobile Tom Brady who can shuck off pass rushers with the rugged ease of his idol, John Elway."

Nobody was better than Marino at moving a step or two to avoid a rush and was seldom sacked, and nobody was better than Marino at withstanding would-be tacklers and taking off and running the ball. Bradshaw had a strong arm and a strong body.

Phil Simms, a former standout NFL quarterback and now a CBS analyst, rates Roethlisberger highly. "Ben Roethlisberger is on an offense that runs the ball," said Simms. "They're in a lot of third-down situations, and he is the perfect quarterback for a team that likes to run it because he's big enough to stand in there and shake off some tacklers and get 5- and 6-yard passes off. And he's just elusive enough to move around and make first downs running every once in a while."

The Steelers selected Bradshaw with the first overall pick in the 1970 draft. The last time they had taken a quarterback with their first pick they took Mark Malone of Arizona State in 1980. Malone was good, but he was no Marino or Bradshaw. It's tough to know how they will do in the pro ranks.

Roethlisberger had no doubt he was the real deal. His coach at Miami of Ohio, Terry Hoeppner, had no doubt, either. "I tried to tell people before the (2005) draft Ben's the prototype," said Hoeppner, who is now coaching at Indiana. "I made a tape for scouts during his last year at Miami called *The Great Escapes*. It was 30 minutes of that escape and throw he made against Denver (a 17-yard scramble touchdown to Hines Ward in the AFC Championship game) over and over in various forms. It was an 18-yard scramble play against Colorado State, the one against Louisville and on and on.

"Receivers get excited, because when the protection breaks down, it's good for them. Ben has that God-given ability to escape. He's bigger and more athletic than you think. Right now, Ben is the straw that stirs the drink."

Hoeppner had no idea he was also setting the scene for Big Ben's out-of-the-pocket pass to Hines Ward at the one-yard line to set up one of the Steelers' touchdowns in the Super Bowl victory over the Seattle Seahawks.

"A lot of people can scramble around," Hoeppner went on to say. "But there aren't many quarterbacks who can keep their cool and are able to accurately throw the football for huge plays that are demoralizing to teams like the escapes and throws Ben made against the Broncos. That's what separates Ben."

"It was a near-virtuoso performance."
— Bob Smizik's rating on Roethlisberger's Super Bowl Media Day outing

Bill Cowher chose to keep Ben Roethlisberger back at the team's hotel and not attend the first day's press conference for Super Bowl XL. Bob Smizik, the columnist for the *Pittsburgh Post-Gazette* who has attended his share of press conferences in all sports through the years, thought Cowher didn't need to protect his second-passer from the press and media spotlight.

Reflecting on the scene on Media Day, Smizik wrote with a Detroit dateline: "The questions come fast and from many different perspectives. What takes place over the next 55 minutes is what has come to be expected of Roethlisberger. He's cool under the pressure of the questioning. He's charming when the questions are stupid or tough. He's thoughtful, friendly, happy, funny. He gave every indication he was pleased to be here. It was a near-virtuoso performance. "Many of the great quarterbacks of the recent past have been mediocre in dealing with the media and the public. Dan Marino, for all the presence he brings to his TV job today, wasn't much good in such situations. Joe Montana was worse. Troy Aikman, who excels in front of the camera today, was ordinary."

Smizik also liked what he had seen of Roethlisberger behind center. "Roethlisberger appears to be a quarterback on the verge of greatness," wrote Smizik in another column.

Pat Hanlon, the vice-president for communications of the New York Giants, was in Detroit for Super Bowl XL and he was kind enough to send me all the interviews the NFL public relations staff provides for all in the media room at the headquarters hotel.

Here's what Roethlisberger had to say on some subjects:

He was asked about the death of his grandfather the previous summer and how that might have motivated him.

"There are quite a few things that you put into this game and the season," replied Roethlisberger. "My grandfather passed this summer, and it is something that is motivating to me. Jerome (Bettis) obviously is a motivator. Another thing is we still have troops overseas. I think people forget that there is a bigger picture than this football game.

"We are playing a game, and they are serving our country. And people forget about them a lot. I think people need to remember that there are thousands of troops over there. This game is dedicated to a lot of those guys who are over there waving their Terrible Towels, and just fans in general. A lot of love, thanks and respect go out from me and the rest of my teammates for them."

Roethlisberger was asked what he thought Jerome Bettis would say to the team before the big game.

"I'm going to tell him not to say too much because I don't want to start getting teary-eyed. When Jerome starts talking you start getting teary-eyed because of how much he means to you. We don't want to have a bunch of guys crying coming out of the locker room."

Simms says Big Ben is for real

Phil Simms, a former Super Bowl MVP and CBS analyst, rates Ben Roethlisberger among the best quarterbacks in the NFL. "He's a leader of men. He's got a good touch of everything in him. He's got the physical ability to get it done. He's got just enough humility and absolutely enough arrogance blended together. The Steelers have done a tremendous job of molding their quarterback from Bill Cowher on down. He handles this guy perfectly. I watch them all, and they are massaging this man and getting a lot out of him."

"I love our quarterback."
— Bill Cowher

Back in November, the day after Roethlisberger had directed the Steelers to a 20-19 victory over the Baltimore Ravens in a nationally televised Monday night contest, Bill Cowher offered some high praise. Roethlisberger had played through some pain to pull this one out. One of the writers asked if Big Ben was like Brett Favre, the Green Bay Packers quarterback, in regard to his toughness.

"I think it's too early to make those kinds of comparisons," Cowher came back. "I think they're different quarterbacks. Brett, he's done it year in and year out.

"He's won a Super Bowl. And he's done it through a period of time. That's not to say Ben won't over a period of time, but certainly, I think it would be unfair to make those comparisons now.

"I love our quarterback and his demeanor and his competitiveness and his toughness. I think Ben's got a great future ahead of him. And I think it's hard not to respect what Brett Favre brings to the game, the toughness, the passion, the pride, the competitiveness he has week in and week out."

Reflecting on Roethlisberger, Cowher continued, "He's a very competitive, confident individual . . . You never sense the guy is overreacting. You can equate it to a lot of things, but he's like the guy in basketball who wants the ball in his hands with the game on the line."

Roethlisberger wanted to make big plays, but toward the end of his second season he admitted he was trying to be more careful, and not trying to force passes into double coverage as much as he might have his first year.

"It's coming down to crunch time when you know you can't afford to make mistakes," he told Ed Bouchette of the *Pittsburgh Post-Gazette* during the Christmas holiday season. "I'm taking that playoff mentality now. There are probably a couple of times where maybe I could have tried to sneak one in, but you never know what can happen. I'd rather take the high road right now and play it smart.

"That competitor, that quarterback in me wants to make plays every play, wants to fire the ball in and give my guys opportunities. I'll still do that, but I also have to be able to use my head and be smart and make sure I don't hurt this team."

"I'm getting an opportunity to live a dream."

Ben Roethlisberger felt honored to have Dan Marino call him on the telephone from time to time. They had first met when Marino came to Pittsburgh to do an interview with Big Ben for HBO's "Inside the NFL" show.

Following Roethlisberger's rookie season, Marino was inducted into the Pro Football Hall of Fame. "Dan and I have spent a lot of time together," Roethlisberger revealed after reporting to the Steelers' summer training camp at St. Vincent. "We've been talking about two, three times in the month, hanging out, spending time picking his brain." A few weeks before Super Bowl XL, Roethlisberger said he'd gotten another call. "We talked the other day," said Big Ben. "He said, listen, enjoy this. You're young; you're doing the same thing I did. You think no matter what happens you're going to get back, but it doesn't necessarily happen like that. He said on one hand enjoy it, have a good time, but take it seriously enough that you want to win it because you never know when it's going to happen again."

Marino's Dolphins were defeated by the San Francisco 49ers in Super Bowl XIX. He never made it back to the big game in 17 years in the NFL. "I do know what he did" in 1984, remarked Roethlisberger. "But I also know how his career ended."

Roethlisberger reminds one at times of one of those young, strong-armed baseball pitchers who think they are the second coming of Nolan Ryan. They just have a certain air about them, like they are superior. He has the swagger that is the hubris of youth, taking his invincibility for granted when nobody ever should, receiving too much early attention and slathering in it. Ben has never blinked when there are bright lights. He loves to be on stage, any stage. That's also one of the reasons he's so damn good at what he does. He has to be careful about how he handles his stardom, but he is, indeed, a star performer.

Roethlisberger also heard from a college buddy who kept asking Ben if he realized he was going to be playing in the Super Bowl. "I said, 'I know.' It was bizarre because he said when you're a kid you don't talk about playing in the national championship game or playing in the AFC championship game, you talk about playing in the Super Bowl. That's when it started sinking in, when I talked to him. Every kid dreams of doing this and I'm getting an opportunity to live a dream. This year I understand where I'm at and where we're at as a team and the situation. So I think that I'm better prepared than I was last year in that situation."

Cowher shared Big Ben's confident approach. "He's a very confident, competitive person," Cowher said of his prize recruit. "I think when you take guys who have those characteristics, they don't like not to have success. I've never had any issues with Ben. I certainly have talked to him sometimes about choices and consequences, the same thing you do with any other player. But I have never had any problems with him in terms of our communications and what his responses are, and that's all I can ask."

Cowher recalled what Roethlisberger was like in his rookie season, and how far he'd come. "A year ago he was calling the plays, and I don't even know if he looked up in the huddle," said Cowher. "I'm not sure he even knew who was in the huddle a year ago because he was down there reading his wrist band the whole time. He's at a comfort level now. He knows what he's doing. That's evident now."

Charlie Batch

James Harrison

Casey Hampton

Heath Miller

George Gojkovich/Getty Images

Brett Keisel
A big smile from Big Sky country

"He's a perfect Steelers player."
— Pete Prisco, CBSsportsline.com

Brett Keisel couldn't stop smiling during our interview. It's no wonder. Life was good for the Steelers' rising young defensive end. A week earlier, Keisel signed a four-year contract to stay with the Steelers for $13.1 million. Imagine what that must have been like. He got a $3.29 million signing bonus.

Keisel had not been a starter in his first four seasons with the Steelers. He played behind veteran Kimo von Oelhoffen, but when he played he had been productive. Keisel had spectacular sacks and he forced fumbles and he made things happen, especially in the playoffs.

His timing couldn't have been better. He was a valued reserve and special teams demon on a team that had just won Super Bowl XL. He had shown he was ready to assume more responsibilities, play more ball and push von Oelhoffen for that starting post position on the Steelers' highly respected defensive unit.

He was listed as one of the Top 30 free agents available in the market by CBSsportsline.com in the Internet world. His evaluation report by columnist Pete Prisco went like this: "Doesn't start, but is a heck of a reserve. An effort player. Gets by with toughness rather than athletic ability. In other words, he's a perfect Steelers player."

It was a perfect time for all the free agents on the Steelers' roster. Antwaan Randle El, Chris Hope and von Oelhoffen left the team for big money elsewhere. Randle El signed for over $26 million with the Washington Redskins, Hope signed with the Tennessee Titans and von Oelhoffen with the New York Jets. The Jets signed Kimo for a three-year deal worth $9.2 million. He couldn't turn that down to remain in Pittsburgh at a reduced salary.

Von Oelhoffen was 35 and the Steelers had hoped to restructure his contract, and pay him less than he had been paid in recent seasons. They were able to do that with center Jeff Hartings. With Keisel available, there was no way the Steelers could up the ante to keep von Oelhoffen, one of the team's most popular players and a positive force in the clubhouse. Von Oelhoffen had played six seasons with the Steelers and twelve years altogether in the NFL. He had started every game but one during his stay with the Steelers.

They expected Keisel to step up and fill the void. Aaron Smith was still on the other wing, with Pro Bowl nose tackle Casey Hampton in between. Keisel, at 6-5, 285 pounds appeared ready for a starting assignment. Anyone who saw him in action against the Denver Broncos in the AFC Championship game on January 22, 2006 had to

Photo by George Gojkovich/Getty Images ⟶

160

believe he was equal to the task. In that game, Keisel recorded four solo tackles, including two sacks and forced one fumble. His sacks totaled ten yards in losses.

"We don't see a lot of sun around here."

Brett Cameron Keisel was good company and a good interview. We had a late lunch courtesy of Gary Rutter's Steak Escape in the food court at Ross Park Mall on Thursday, April 20, 2006. Keisel had a 12-inch steak hoagie with large fries and a large Coke. "Gotta put some weight on," he said, almost apologetically, as he bit into his hoagie. "Excuse me if I eat while we're talking."

He wore a beige ballcap that had a Jackson Hole, Wyoming logo in the center. "One of my favorite places in the world to visit," claimed Keisel. He wore an olive green T-shirt with a Pink Floyd portrait across the chest. "I like Pink Floyd but Pearl Jam is my favorite," he volunteered. The T-shirt fit him snugly. He wore olive green slacks. He wore a constant smile. His dark brown eyes were gleaming. He offered good stories. He talks in a laidback manner and makes you feel comfortable. When I later saw him at the Steelers' training complex he always offered a hello and a handshake.

We were sitting at a table that was off the beaten path, so we'd have some privacy, but we were interrupted three times by passersby. One woman touched him on the shoulder and said, "Forgive me, but are you a Steeler? My son says you are, but my daughter doesn't believe him."

Keisel offered a smile and a nod and some pleasantries to the woman and three children. Everyone seemed pleased. A man came by and said, "I just wanted to say congratulations on what you did." Another said, "I just wanted to say hello and shake your hand."

Unlike his teammate Ben Roethlisberger, Keisel can still go shopping in a place like Ross Park Mall and not get mauled by Steelers' fans. Only the most ardent fans would recognize Keisel. His size draws attention, though, and provides the first clue that he just might be a football player.

The 27-year-old Keisel never started in four years with the Steelers, but he saw increased playing time the previous two seasons. He missed the entire 2003 season following shoulder surgery.

Keisel is a surprising success story with the Steelers. He was their final draft pick with the second of their two seventh-round draft choices in 2002. That was a good draft class for Kevin Colbert, the director of football operations, and his scouting staff. The Steelers' selections in order that spring were Kendall Simmons of Auburn, Randle El of Indiana, Hope of Florida State, Larry Foote of Michigan, Verron Haynes of Georgia and Lee Mays of Texas-El Paso. The first seventh-round pick, LaVar Glover, a defensive back from Cincinnati, was the only one who failed to stick from that group.

Keisel came from Brigham Young University. The Steelers had signed Chris Hoke from BYU as a free agent the year before. Both proved to be valuable reserves on the Steelers' squad and both performed well when given opportunities to play. Both were good guys.

I'm sitting across from him, knowing what I know at 63 and after nearly 50 years as a professional sports writer, and wondering what it must be like to be Brett Keisel, 27 years of age and an instant millionaire. I didn't envy him; I just wondered if he was pinching himself, or thinking about how far he'd come in such a short time. Heck, he was younger than both of my daughters. I'd interviewed some great ones, such as Muhammad Ali, Joe Namath, Joe Greene, Terry Bradshaw, Ted Williams, Joe DiMaggio and Joe Louis, and they never made as much money in their sports careers as Keisel was going to make. Only Michael Jordan of the great athletes I'd interviewed had made that kind of money.

Keisel had to postpone a scheduled interview with me two days earlier because he had a "meeting with some entrepreneurs." I told him he'd have been better off meeting with me. I wasn't after his money, just his stories.

He had spoken in February about how people "were coming out of the woodwork" to ask him for tickets for the Super Bowl, people he hadn't seen or heard of since grade school in some cases. I warned him that he'd have "entrepreneurs" coming out of the woodwork now that he had signed a four-year deal for $13.1 million.

"You don't have to do anything exciting or risky to assure your financial future," I advised him. "If you are conservative you'll never have to worry about money again."

I asked him if he thought he could get by on $100,000 a year for the rest of his life, with annual boosts to keep up with inflation, and he offered a positive nod. "If you had $2 million in your investment portfolio," I told him, "and you tapped into it at just 4% a year you could do that."

Keisel smiled when he heard that. Maybe he wasn't looking for or counting on financial advice, but I couldn't help myself. Sportswriters never sign million dollar deals, unless they are John Feinstein, Tony Kornheiser and Mitch Albom, but that doesn't mean you can't be smart and save your money.

Then again, the good agents, reputable guys like Leigh Steinberg and Ralph Cindrich, steer their clients toward sound, trustworthy investment opportunities. It's always difficult to understand stories about sports stars going broke or into debt, however, after they've made millions in their careers.

Keisel comes from Big Sky Country. He was raised on a ranch in Greybull, Wyoming. His birthplace was Provo, Utah. He is used to big blue skies so Pittsburgh is a bit of a change for him. "We don't see a lot of sun around here," he said, "but it's a great place to play football."

He and his wife, Sarah, who is from the same small town (1400 or so residents) near the border of Montana, have a home in

Treesdale, an upscale community north of Pittsburgh. "I took a chance and bought a home here, hoping things would turn out okay for me," he said. It was a good investment.

He said he and Sarah would be married two years come July. They didn't have any children yet, but they had a six-month-old male dog, a black Labrador named Deegan. "Life is good," proclaimed Keisel.

I had seen Keisel playing for the Steelers' basketball team several times during the past three winters and was impressed with his ability. He had certainly demonstrated his athletic skills on the hardwood, which made me wonder about that CBSsportsline.com scouting report on him.

After playing in a game against a team of all-stars at Canon McMillan High School in Canonsburg, Keisel drew high praise from one of the opposing players. Doug West said, "That Keisel could play in the NBA."

West might have been overly generous in his appraisal of Keisel's basketball skills, but he knew a good basketball player when he saw one. West had been a star at Altoona High School and Villanova University and with the Minnesota Timberwolves of the National Basketball Association.

Keisel can shoot free throws a lot better than Shaquille O'Neal, that's for sure. He runs the court pretty well for a guy his size, barrels his way to the basket, banks in close-in shots and draws a lot of fouls. His form at the free throw line is perfect and swift. He has confidence in his shot. He seemed pleased to hear me offer praise, especially when I told him I was the founding editor of *Street & Smith's Basketball Magazine*, and had been associated with the highly-respected annual for 36 years. Like West, I know a basketball player when I see one.

Keisel had been a star basketball player as a high school student back in Wyoming. His name appeared in a McDonald's All-American basketball listing. "I represented Wyoming," he said. He played in a basketball all-star game while passing on a football all-star game. "Basketball was my first love," he said, "but I figured I had a better future in football."

He was a fan of the Utah Jazz, and loved John Stockton and Karl Malone, the team's all-star performers. He loved Michael Jordan and Magic Johnson and Larry Bird.

He had some scholarship offers from smaller schools to play basketball or both sports, but he wanted to concentrate on football.

I told him about Dick Groat. I had just seen Groat two days earlier at a sports banquet, and had just read about him in a book about Red Auerbach — *Let Me Tell You A Story* — by John Feinstein. Groat was the National League batting champion and MVP in 1960 when the Pirates won the World Series. But he had also been an All-American basketball player at Duke and played one season (1952-53) with the Fort Wayne Pistons of the NBA. Groat still says he was a better basketball player than a baseball player.

What he was, like Keisel perhaps, was a great competitor, a fierce competitor.

I told him I'd met only two sports people from Wyoming. One was Curt Gowdy, the sports broadcaster who had died a few months earlier. The other was Kenny Sailors, an All-American basketball player on Wyoming's 1943 national championship basketball team. I met Sailors and interviewed him when he was coaching a high school basketball team in Alaska when I was stationed there in the U.S. Army in 1965.

Keisel simply smiled when I told him this ancient sports history. He should know, I thought, about Curt Gowdy and Kenny Sailors if he was from Wyoming.

Keisel was happy that the Steelers were able to sign another of their free agents, veteran cornerback Deshea Townsend, and that Rodney Bailey was coming back to the ballclub after stints at New England and Seattle. I had mentioned to Keisel that I really liked Bailey and had gotten to know him well when he played for the Steelers several years earlier. I had shared the spotlight with Bailey speaking before a Pittsburgh Club in Columbus. Bailey had graduated with a degree in 3½ years at Ohio State University. I had met his beautiful wife there when they were dating. I had spent time at the apartment Bailey shared with Kendrell Bell. I thought Bell was going to be a Pro Bowl performer for the Steelers, and still couldn't figure out what happened to him and why his play had fallen off. Bell had signed as a free agent three years earlier with the Kansas City Chiefs. "Bailey was one of my best friends on the team," said Keisel. "He'll fit right in and he'll help us."

Keisel was confident that he could play up to the expectations the Steelers had for him. He wouldn't be a disappointment. Eric Metz, his agent, says, "He's looking forward to showing the Steelers they made the right decision."

Brett Keisel:

"Something special was going on here."

The strangest phone call we got in the weeks leading up to the Super Bowl was a call to my father in Utah. He got a call from someone that he knew in high school. The guy said, "Hey, we live close to Detroit and we're expecting tickets and whatever else you can do. My dad laughed at him. He said, "I haven't seen you in 40 years and you're expecting me to get you Super Bowl tickets. We have enough for our immediate family and that's it."

165

You asked me about the entrepreneur I had a meeting with this week. He created a business in California and he's a multi-millionaire and he's got some good ideas. They sounded good to me. You don't have to worry about me, though.

I'm very conservative. I've worked too hard to get what I've got to just give it away. I would never get involved in anything I didn't believe in. I come from a hard-working family. I lived on a ranch in the northern end of Wyoming.

When I got the call from my agent telling me about the deal he had worked out with the Steelers and what they were offering, I just kinda sat there in my house. I was home alone out in Treesdale with my dog. I just sat there and thought about what he'd just told me. It didn't seem real.

I was pleased, of course. I gambled and bought a nice home up there. I hope I'd be able to stay. My wife Sarah is like me. We grew up together.

"I thought I was moving up there to be John Wayne."

I was born in Provo, Utah and our family used to go and visit my grandparents' place in Greybull, Wyoming. These were my mom's parents. They had a thousand-acre ranch up there. I was up there once when I was seven years old when I witnessed a terrible accident. I'll never forget it.

My grandfather and my mother were both on horses and I was standing nearby. My grandfather had just brought all the cows down from the hills. It was in the spring and they were branding them. It was a beautiful day. But it turned into a crazy day. My grandfather took off after a calf and his horse went out from under him. The horse slipped on shale and my grandfather fell and hit his head hard. It crushed his head. It was weird. My mother was following him, and I heard her screaming, "Dad!" I have a brother named Chad and I thought she was calling him. My father was the chief of the fire department in Orem, Utah, and he gave first aid to my grandfather. He ended up in a coma for about a year before he finally came out of it. I had just been getting to know my grandfather. I loved playing cowboys when I was young.

My grandfather was never the same after that. He was like a vegetable from that head injury. I remember my folks had to help him in and out of bed when he came home to be with my grandmother. It was difficult for everyone. He lived for a few years after that before he died.

After my grandfather got hurt, we moved to Wyoming and took over the ranch. I started playing sports while we were in Wyoming. I love that part of the country. From the time I was a kid I loved the outdoors. I love those wide-open spaces. I thought I was moving up there to be John Wayne.

I loved riding horses. It was a great feeling. You had the best childhood you can have up there in that wide-open country. I can appreciate that landscape even more now, as an adult, than I could then. It's great looking at those big blue skies, or going up on top of a mountain in the night and seeing the stars. Sitting on top of those mountains is like sitting on top of the world. I like to get out there in the off-season and get my mind right and get ready to rock.

I think the stars were aligned right for me in Pittsburgh these past few months. Winning the Super Bowl with the kind of finish we had. It being Kimo's last year so there's an opportunity for me to start and really show what I can do. I was fortunate enough to make some significant plays in big games. For me, being a role player, I wasn't out there much. So doing what I did is reassuring for me and, I guess, for our coaches. I know I can do it and, hopefully, now they know I can do it, too.

For four years I've been watching and waiting. I tried to make an impact on special teams and when I'd spell Kimo I was fortunate to be able to do that.

We have had great guys on our defensive line. The coaches have to find out whether you can play or not play. I have had a chance to show my speed, to show my toughness. Everyone has to start somewhere. I was a seventh round pick, the last pick by the Steelers that year (2002). You want to know the pick number? I was the 242nd pick in the draft that year.

I was at my parents' house that weekend. They live in Fairview, Utah. They have a little house there. The draft is a tough thing. According to everything I had read or heard I was supposed to go early on the second day. I was going to be a fourth or fifth round pick. All of a sudden some guys are getting picked that I feel I might be better than they are. Who knows? I couldn't believe it. I ended up here and thank God I did. I got a Super Bowl ring; I got a great contract. Life is good.

I'm with a great group of guys. This is truly a close team. I have been fortunate throughout my football career to be with teams that were close. To me, that's the key to success.

Everyone laid it all out there on the line. We believe in each other. We trust in each other. That's the key to a championship team. Toward the end of the season when we had to win every game I could see and feel that something special was happening here.

After that Chicago game, the first of the games we absolutely had to win to get to the playoffs, I thought, "Here we go. We're gonna run and nobody is going to stop us." Everyone believed it; everyone made it happen.

"You are expected to be a professional."

The Steelers have a special environment and tradition. There definitely is an expectation level. You are expected to be a professional — not only on the field but also in the Pittsburgh community. We hear about the great ones of the '70s. We see the four Super Bowls in the front office. We hear about The Chief. All of us are very aware of these things.

I'm involved with the Homeless Children Education Fund — we had a big auction at the Rivers Club recently — and it's really a worthwhile venture. I hope to do more of that sort of thing.

When the Steelers look at players to bring in they want to know about your character and what your values are. They don't want any troublemaker in here. You could be a great player, but if you're a problem they're not interested. There might be a few guys who could go the other way, but they follow the leaders here, and we have lots of leaders.

They want you to carry yourself with dignity. They definitely want to mold you into what they consider a Steeler player.

Kimo was great for me in that regard. If I could say I had a mentor on the defensive line it would be Kimo. And Aaron helped me, too, at my outside position. I always had Casey's back when I was in there. Or Hoke. He showed he could play, too.

From the second I was drafted those guys have shown me nothing but love. Sometimes hard love. But you want them to be honest and help you if you're not doing something right. They have to tell you that and maybe you don't like criticism. Kimo and I got to be good buds. Throughout my four years, Kimo was always there for me and if there's a guy I'm going to miss it's him. He's everyone's friend in the locker room. In four years, I never saw him come in to the locker room without a smile on his face. He was happy to be at work. He's a good guy. He cares about people. If there's one guy I would like to be like someday it's him.

When he hurt Carson Palmer in our game with the Bengals I know he felt horrible. You knew it was bad the way Palmer laid there. That's why Kimo stood there. He was talking to him, hoping he'd be all right. Kimo has a heart as big as this mall and there was no way he was trying to hurt that guy. No one felt more sorry than he did.

You know, you want to hit the opposing players with all you've got, but you're not out to hurt them. It's a physical game, but you never want to hurt anyone intentionally.

"It's hard to believe he was a cornerback."

I saw Mel Blount come to one of our practices last year, and I saw him again at the Super Bowl. He came up to me and told me what a great job I was doing. He said some nice things to me. It was a tremendous honor just to talk to him. I hunt out by his place (The Mel Blount Youth Home in Claysville, Washington County), and he's invited me to come to his ranch and ride his horses. I'd like to do that.

It's hard to believe he was a cornerback. He's huge. He looks more like a guy who'd play defensive end or linebacker. I've seen him on film and he could hit and cover with the best of them. They say they had to change the rules because of him and the way that he held up receivers.

I hear about the kind of guys Blount and Joe Greene and them were when they played for the Steelers and we want to be held in the same high regard. We've got to earn it.

I was lucky to have a lot of good people around me in my four years here, and I hope to pass on what I learned from them. Take Jerome Bettis. My man J.B. His was the first locker I looked for when I first reported to our practice facility on the South Side. "Where's Jerome's locker?" I asked when I went in there. I grew up idolizing this guy. I loved his style: tough, smash-mouth Pittsburgh football.

To be around him a little bit, to joke with him a little bit, you learn that he's just one of the guys. If you were a first-year free agent or a practice squad player or Ben Roethlisberger, Jerome would treat you the same way. That's not true of a lot of guys. That's why Jerome is so loved by his teammates. He shows the way. He's a warm guy.

The veteran guys know you're trying to take their job. But most of them are pretty good about mentoring the new guys, showing them how it's done. Jerome always has a smile on his face. He's a person the entire team could look up to and try to emulate. I feel blessed to call him a friend and, hopefully, he won't say too many bad things about me now that he's in the (broadcast) booth. I love the guy.

Rodney Bailey and I hit it off right away. He's a silly guy. I don't know if I've met a sillier guy. Rodney was at my wedding in Wyoming. He and Lee Mays both came. They stood out among our little country folk, two handsome black guys coming out to my wedding.

Ben Roethlisberger is so big in terms of popularity in Pittsburgh that he can't lead a normal life. When we're out somewhere, like playing for the Steelers basketball team, everyone wants a piece of him. They want him to sign something, they want him to call their sister. "Hey, I'm your greatest fan. Will you sign this?"

Ben is a great guy. You can't please everyone, but he honestly tries. That's why he has bodyguards. He doesn't want to say no, or have people thinking he's a bad guy, so the guards keep the people at bay. Guys like Hoke and me can come to a mall like this and it's not bad. It isn't a big deal. We're not the Berger. He has a great responsibility. I'm glad I'm me and he's him.

I can't say enough about him. I played golf with him yesterday. His life is different than all of ours. He's kind of on top of the mountain. We're the villagers down below. He's great, though. You can joke around with him. You can tell him things. He doesn't let all this stuff mess him up. He doesn't hide. He plays basketball because he enjoys being with the guys, and it's a game he can play and enjoy without any pressure on him. He's still very grounded and humble. He wants more. He wants to get better.

I think Hines Ward is special. Hines is everything a receiver should be. He catches the ball when it's thrown to him. He's with such an elite group of players who ever played the game.

I love Hines to death. He works so hard at everything he does. He's definitely one of our leaders.

I think Bill Cowher is great. I'm very lucky to have such a good coach. He's a player's coach. He's someone who's been on the field. I love how he coaches, I love how he gets us ready. We don't win through finesse; we beat people down. That's Steeler football. He has a great staff. We have real support, from the top to the bottom of the organization. I can't say enough for the organization. There's no place I'd rather be. This is something I dreamed about. I think I have a good future. The Good Lord above gave me a great body and a great mind to get me to the point where I am right now. I am so excited to be in this situation.

My family comes first. My wife and my family are the most important people in my world. I want to live the good life. I want to be a good person and respect others. I'm just a normal dude and that's good enough for me.

I had a great upbringing. My parents kept me well grounded. I was always involved in something, playing some kind of sport. I never had a job because my father felt I had the rest of my life to work. He wanted me to enjoy my youth.

I think my story points up that you don't have to be the best at something in order to have a satisfying life. You can have a goal in life, as I did, and it can be realized.

When I was in seventh grade our teacher asked us what we wanted to be when we grew up. I said I wanted to be a professional athlete. The teacher said that was impossible. There were 37 kids in my entire class. But I insisted I wanted to do that. There's no question in my mind I'm ready to be a starter for the Steelers. I'm ready for this role. I'm ready to be on the field. I know what I'm capable of. I'm ready to rock and roll. I want another run at a championship.

I think we have guys on our team who are ready to step up, like Lee Mays, Verron Haynes, Duce Staley, and we all know what Hoke can do. They will be geared up for the challenge. No one is satisfied with one Super Bowl victory. If you're not getting better you're getting worse. You always want to get better.

Jim O'Brien

Steelers basketball line-up at Canon-McMillan is, left to right, Manager Tom O'Malley Jr., Rod Rutherford, Louis Lipps, Ricardo Colclough, Lee Mays, Brett Keisel, Ben Roethlisberger and Chris Hoke.

Big Ben on Big Ben
He was raised right

"It's been crazy."

Big Ben Roethlisberger seemed to be everywhere following the Steelers' triumph in Super Bowl XL. He was even in Pittsburgh from time to time, and was present for most of the important events in the so-called off-season. There is no such thing as an off-season in pro football anymore.

There is something going on all the time, one mini-camp after another mini-camp, one golf outing after another golf outing, one basketball game after another basketball game, one sports talk show after another. The newly established National Football League Network was going to make sure we could watch something about the Steelers and Giants and Titans on TV every day of the week. Indeed, there is no off-season in the NFL.

Willie Parker threw out the first pitch for the Pirates' second game at PNC Park. He said, "My life's been unreal since the Super Bowl. Everybody knows you now."

The Steelers were in demand everywhere. Guys on the practice squad were getting paid for their signature at Pittsburgh's suburban shopping malls. Even Lee Mays, the lowest man on the Steelers' totem pole, told me, "I am very busy every day," when I asked when we could get together for an interview.

ESPN had a new "survivor" show of sorts called "Bonds on Bonds," a weekly offering in which the troubled Barry Bonds — once the best baseball player in Pittsburgh as well as America — tried to explain why Barry Bonds wasn't such a bad person and didn't deserve to be called a jerk. He was closing in on Babe Ruth and Henry Aaron in the all-time home run record department, but his heroic feat was tainted by allegations that he had beefed up his body by taking steroids. Now he had his own soap opera.

Big Ben was on late-night talk shows with the likes of David Letterman and national sports shows and local sports shows. Big Ben enjoyed a better reputation than Barry Bonds, to be sure, and he seemed to be doing whatever he could do to make his image even more appealing. Sometimes Big Ben seemed to be working overtime at doing the right thing and saying the right thing.

From the beginning, Big Ben seemed too good to be true, but so far he was keeping his squeaky-clean image intact. It was great for the game, and more reason for Steelers' fans to celebrate their good fortune that this fine young man from Findlay, Ohio had come their way.

One day in early April I was watching television as the Pirates were playing the Reds in Cincinnati, hoping they might win a game

There's still a lot of little kid in Ben Roethlisberger.

Ben Roethlisberger

Fans who put up this banner had no idea how accurate it would prove to be.

after dropping their first six games of the 2006 season. I may have dozed or just moved and I must have pressed my body on the remote control gizmo. It changed the channel from Fox Sports to ESPN and there was Big Ben. He was about to be interviewed in a half-hour segment by Chris Myers. It was meant to be. I was eager to hear Big Ben on Big Ben. I had no plans to watch Bonds on Bonds.

It was a shame. I thought Barry Bonds could have been just like Big Ben. He was handsome and he was such a skilled baseball player. But he had bad mentors just as Ben had good influences in his family life. Barry was brought along by his father, Bobby Bonds, and his godfather, Willie Mays. Both were great all-around baseball players. Both were constant whiners who thought the world was out to get them.

Here's what Big Ben had to say for himself that day:

Ben Roethlisberger:

"I've just been myself."

It's been crazy. I have been on the go ever since we won the Super Bowl. It's been plenty of fun. Have things changed in my life? I'm sure, but I've just been myself. I just try to be thankful for what's happened.

I was lucky to have an opportunity to play as much as I did my rookie season. I didn't think Tommy Maddox was going to be out as long as he was. He was a good friend, and I didn't want to take anything away from him.

I had a good first season, but then I had difficulties during the playoffs, and we lost that AFC championship game to the Patriots. That humbled me. I didn't play well. I used it for motivation for my next season. I had something to prove. I always have something to prove.

Toward the end of that game, I sat on the bench next to Jerome Bettis and I talked to him. I wanted to thank him for what he had done to help me through my rookie season. He had given me great encouragement and showed me the way. He had hinted that this was going to be his last season. He wasn't sure what he was going to do.

I remember telling him to give me one more chance. If you come back, I'll get you to the Super Bowl. I didn't say we'll win the Super Bowl. But the Super Bowl was going to be played in Jerome's hometown of Detroit. I thought that would be a great place for him to close out his career. It became a rallying cry for our ballclub.

So when they talk about "The Tackle" in Indianapolis, it was something I just had to do. When I gave the ball to Jerome at their one-yard line I didn't carry out my fake the way I should. I turned to watch Jerome score a touchdown. I wanted to watch it. To me, with Jerome having the ball at the one, it was an automatic touchdown.

Then the ball came loose and Nick Harper had it and he's running the other way. I had to do what I could do to stop him. Jerome couldn't end his career with a fumble that cost us the game. There was no way I could let that happen. I guessed right and caught Harper by his shoetops.

When I hurt my thumb during the season I didn't know how that was going to turn out. It hurt so bad. I couldn't grip the ball. I did a lot of praying. It looked like I was going to need surgery. The Steelers let me make that call. It's a great organization in that respect. I didn't want to stop playing. I wanted to be out there with my teammates. If there was any way I could do it, I was going to be out there.

I was disappointed when I didn't get taken higher in the draft because I had a strong belief in my ability. Maybe those guys who went ahead of me were better quarterbacks. I got with a great team. I fit in well with the veterans. I didn't have to do too much, or that's the way it looked anyhow. Guys who knew the game, quarterbacks like Dan Marino and Phil Simms and Boomer Esiason, knew how difficult my assignment was.

There were times when I wanted to pass more, sure. It would be great to have the freedom of a Peyton Manning. I think I could have 300-yard passing games, too. I want to make something else clear, too, while I'm here. I know there have been stories that I was going on the Internet looking for a date or a wife, and that's just not so.

It's nice to hear my name in the same sentence as Terry Bradshaw, or someone like Dan Marino. It's always an honor when someone compares me to a great quarterback. But I have a long way to go.

I want to be my own guy. I want people to compare young quarterbacks to me. I want to be the best quarterback who's ever played the game. There's a lot of responsibility on my shoulders. When you have a running team, sometimes you have third-and-long and you're expected to get that first down.

I know I said on one of the television shows that I didn't think I was in the end zone when I scored that touchdown against Seattle in the Super Bowl. When I came down I knew I was short of the goal line. But, later, I saw it in slow motion on film and I clearly crossed the plane of the goal line. That was a good touchdown. I had to clear that up.

Now they've made some new rules to cut down on the celebrations in the end zone. I kind of look forward to what they're gonna do. I get a kick out of guys like Chad Johnson.

I'm glad to see they've made some new rules regarding hitting quarterbacks low. It's nice to be protected. I know that Kimo wasn't trying to hurt Carson Palmer, and I don't think guys are out to hurt me, either. I've been hit low and hurt, but I don't think it was intentional.

I've been to some non-sports celebrity outings and what's surprised me the most is that some of these movie stars and music artists are coming up to me and congratulating me on my season and the Steelers' success. These are people I've watched and listened to, and looked up to. Now they're making a fuss over me. That's special.

I didn't get to play quarterback in high school until my senior season. So I played wide receiver. That turned out to be a good thing. The coach's son was a good quarterback and he was a year ahead of me in school. The first game I played at quarterback I threw six touchdown passes. I had 54 touchdown passes my senior year.

I was upset at first when I didn't get to play quarterback earlier, because I believed I had the ability to start. It was probably better for me in the long run. I might have been recruited more and I might have gone to a bigger football program that Miami of Ohio. I might not have played as much as I did there. Ohio State had shown some interest, but I heard I wasn't going to be a quarterback there.

I got in trouble with the league for having a religious message on my shoes. They made me get rid of that. They have a uniform code. That message might be somewhere else now. I probably shouldn't say that. I'll get in trouble again. But I'm not afraid to show my faith. I may be more famous now, but I don't want to forget where I come from, or what I'm all about.

Big Ben uses all the space on his broad back.

Willie Parker
A real find from Carolina

"I always gave it my all."

T he Willie Parker Story is a real success story and an unlikely one at that. Not too many players saw so little action in college as Parker did and then went on to play pro ball. The Steelers have had a few. Carlton Haselrig was an NCAA champion wrestler at Pitt-Johnstown and didn't play college football. Myron Cope pushed the Steelers to draft him and they did with their last pick in 1989. Haselrig became a Pro Bowl guard before his life unraveled off the field. Ray Seals was another who didn't play college football yet made the grade in the NFL.

Parker started only five games in four seasons at the University of North Carolina. He was not picked in the NFL draft. Neither were the two running backs he played behind at Chapel Hill, Jacque Lewis and Chad Scott. Parker signed with the Steelers as a free agent. How did Willie Parker manage to get lost in the shuffle at North Carolina?

"I don't know what happened," his father, Willie Sr., told Gerry Dulac of the *Pittsburgh Post-Gazette*. "For all I know, it could have been Willie's fault."

Dan Rooney Jr., a team scout and the son of the Steelers' chairman, lived in Gastonia, North Carolina, and his wife, Allison, was a family physician in Clinton. The young Rooney had seen Parker help Clinton High School win the state AA football title as a junior and lead them to the state quarterfinals as a senior. A few years later, Rooney and another NFL scout went to North Carolina to work out some of the Tar Heels' players. They wanted to see Parker and they were impressed by what they saw. Rooney recommended Parker to the Pittsburgh Steelers.

Parker was the only free agent to stick with the Steelers in 2004. He made the 53-man roster and he dressed for the final nine games of the regular season because of an injury to Duce Staley. Parker finished the season on a high note when he had a 58-yard run and rushed for 102 yards on 19 carries in the season finale in Buffalo.

"The first thing you saw with him," said Coach Bill Cowher, "was the speed. But he was raw. I think being around Jerome, watching how to use blockers and how to set up blocks, helped him a lot. He is more patient now. He's stronger now (at 209 pounds) than he was. He'll take the ball inside now and jam it up in there."

In 2005, Parker became a starter in training camp when Staley had to undergo surgery to repair a torn meniscus and Bettis hurt his calf in the third pre-season game. Parker put up some significant numbers in a hurry— why do you think they call him Fast Willie? — with 161 yards against the Tennessee Titans and 111 yards against the Houston Texans. He had the starting position to himself after that.

He ran for 1,202 yards during the 2005 season, and tacked on another 225 yards in four playoff games.

"I'm thankful for the opportunity and I'm thankful for taking advantage of the opportunity," Parker said. "It's a blessing, man. A lot of guys don't get opportunities like I did, and I just feel fortunate to be in the situation I am. I'm on a good football team and I'm getting a chance to play."

The Steelers have a history of finding some wonderful football players that they didn't draft.

They include three players who were starters for four Super Bowl teams in the '70s, namely guard Sam Davis, tight end Randy Grossman and defensive back Donnie Shell. Jeff Reed, the reliable place-kicker for the current Steelers, was signed as a free agent in 2002. They signed Tommy Maddox as a free agent in 2001, but that was different. He had been a No. 1 draft choice by the Denver Broncos after his junior season at UCLA.

The mention of Maddox brings something else to mind. When I interviewed Parker on Tuesday, June 6, 2006 at the Steelers' practice facility, I came upon Maddox in the lobby. He had stopped by to pick up his Super Bowl ring. Maddox had been released after the Super Bowl and he did not accompany the team to The White House for the recognition ceremony and he did not attend the team dinner where the rings were presented. Maddox was all smiles when anyone stopped him to shake his hand, but he had to feel a bit awkward considering the circumstances.

He'd been a hero for the Steelers, indeed the NFL's Comeback Player of the Year in 2002, but he was often booed in his final two seasons with the Steelers. He deserved better.

Willie Parker gained international attention when he raced 75 yards for a touchdown in the third quarter of the Steelers' 21-10 victory over the Seattle Seahawks in Super Bowl XL. It was the longest touchdown run in the 40-year history of the NFL's championship game.

Bill Cowher is a big fan of Willie Parker. "Willie has the one thing that we never had, and that's speed," commented Cowher during the 2005 season. "For a team that runs the football like we would like to run the football, to be able to have a big-play player back there is a bonus. He shows that ability to do that."

Hines Ward, a playmaker himself, echoes Cowher's sentiments. "He brings that home-run threat every time," Hines told Dulac a month before Super Bowl XL. "You have that threat like that, teams have to scheme for that. People keep saying that they put eight or nine men in the box, but what happens if we block all eight or nine? He's going to get out and break a long one.

"That threat right there really changes coverage. A lot of teams won't go out and play certain coverages when you have a guy who can

---

*Prior to the 2005 season, I asked Dick Hoak,
the running backs coach,
for a personal insight.
"Don't be surprised," said Hoak, "if Willie Parker
has a breakout season."*

Willie
Parker

Dan and John Rooney, sons of Steelers' Chairman Dan Rooney, appear at team's summer camp. Dan discovered Willie Parker.

Jim O'Brien

go deep like that. When you don't have a guy who goes deep, a lot of teams continue to play a lot of different coverages because they know a guy is not going to take it to the house. When you got a guy who can take it to the house, the opposing teams don't tend to be as risky."

To hear his coaches and teammates talk about him, Willie Parker looks like a kid who's gonna make it.

Maybe he's made it already. He had to postpone one of his interviews for this book because, as he put it, "I have to meet with my financial advisor." I did get a chance to speak to Parker on several occasions during mini-camp and voluntary coaching sessions at the team's South Side facility.

Parker lives in the nearby Waterfront complex, as do several other Steelers. So he's living and practicing where steel mills once stood. He's practicing on fields where Jones & Laughlin Steel Co. once stood, and he's living where the U.S. Steel Homestead Works once stood. It's a new day in Pittsburgh, with a changing skyline, and Willie Parker is part of the change.

Willie Parker:

"Never give up."

What can anyone learn from Willie Parker's story? Never give up. I always kept striving to be the best; I always tried to be better. I'm a real competitor. When things went bad I didn't quit.

I've always been goal-oriented. You try to keep your parents happy. Staying out of trouble was a big part of that. I always gave it my all. My father told me I didn't have to be the best, I just had to do my best. Even if it wasn't good enough. There was nothing else I could do. He told me never to get complacent.

My parents kept after me pretty good. "Do your homework," they'd say. "Do your bed."

My friends came to my home. They'd be in my room playing games; I had some video games. Some of them didn't have two parents like I have. They called my parents "mother" and "father." Maybe they wanted to connect like that. They respected my parents.

I had one main friend. His name was Jamar Smith. He's dead now. He got killed my sophomore year in college. He was my closest friend; he was like a brother. It was hard on my family when he died. He got shot in my hometown. No, I never thought that could have happened to me if I hadn't gone to school.

We led two different lifestyles. I loved talking to him, and he loved watching me play football. If I had been home I'd have been a passenger in his car, riding next to him, when he was shot. Sometimes you get lucky in life.

Much has been made of the fact that I didn't even get to play on Senior Day, my final game at North Carolina. My family and friends came to the game, and I was glad they were there. I wanted them to see the whole environment, to appreciate the atmosphere when I went to school. It was my last game and I wanted to make the best of it. I'm the only running back from that North Carolina team who is playing pro football.

I felt really bad that things hadn't gone better for me at North Carolina. With about one minute left in that last game I was so happy that it would soon be over. The frustration and pain was over. A lot of players were crying because it was the end of our days together, but I was happy.

This past season makes it all worthwhile. It was a dream season for all of us, and especially for me. I came here as a free agent (in 2004) and I know I'm the only free agent from the group that came in with me who is still with the Steelers. I take pride in making the most of my opportunity. I've always tried to make the most of my opportunities.

Going to The White House and meeting President Bush was very special. I learned a lot during our visit to The White House. We had a tour of the different rooms and you learn a lot of history. It was very impressive. Getting all that history was a highlight for me.

I talked to my parents about our visit to The White House. I told them how everything was. I told them how much security they have there to protect our leaders. President Bush asked where Fast Willie was. He told me I was sharp. He knew where Joey Porter was. He knew that Joey had some fun at his expense prior to our visit, with some of the stuff he said he was going to tell President Bush when he saw him. He knew where everybody was. It was a big deal for a kid from Clinton, North Carolina, but it was a big deal for a lot of other people in our party as well. It meant a lot to the coaches and the players.

Now that I've tasted what it can be like to be a champion in the National Football League I want more of it. You want to continue to play at a championship level. Being with great guys like I am is a great thing. You want to go for more. Why can't we get another championship and have another great run?

I want more. It's in me. I have that fire in my belly. It's burning in me.

181

"I wanted to be like Mike."

Jerome Bettis taught me a lot about playing in the NFL. He told me the average playing expectancy for running backs in the league was three or four years. Everything after that is a plus. Jerome managed to stay 13 seasons, ten with the Steelers. I'd love to have that kind of career.

He told me it's a tough game, and you've got to have a tough body to stay in it. I'm trying to do that, to make sure I'm ready, to make sure I can survive the hard knocks.

I think I'm a good athlete. I played two years of basketball in high school, and I played with the Steelers' basketball team my first year here. I was on the track & field team for two years in high school.

My sports idols when I was growing up were Michael Jordan, Emmitt Smith and Barry Sanders. I loved Michael Jordan for the way he carried himself on and off the court. I loved the guy. I saw those "Be Like Mike" ads on TV. And I wanted to be like Mike. I was a football player, but I wanted to be like Mike. He was from Wilmington, North Carolina and, of course, he played his college ball at North Carolina. So he was a homeboy. And he always talked about "The Carolina Way," the way Dean Smith wanted his players to behave on and off the court.

I came in the same year as Big Ben and we could be a winning combination. We're still young and, hopefully, we'll stay together. Big Ben is special. He can make something out of nothing. He can turn a broken play into something positive.

I'm pretty proud of my record 75-yard touchdown run in the Super Bowl. I knew as soon as I broke through the line — running right behind that great block by Alan Faneca — that I could go all the way. Hines Ward also threw a key block on that run. I saw one of their cornerbacks, but I didn't think he could catch me. I knew there was no way that he was going to catch me. I knew this was a Super Bowl moment. I've been playing that run back in my mind a few times since then.

I want to build on that. I'm going to try my hardest as I always have. You can't do more than that.

There are about 8,000 people in my hometown of Clinton and they love their football. I was a big deal in high school. Since we won the Super Bowl, there were signs with my name around town. They are pretty proud of me.

Dan Rooney, the son of our owner, lives in North Carolina and he saw me play high school football. He worked me out after I finished college and he recommended me to the Steelers. I'm grateful to him for that and I have told him so on more than one occasion. We keep in touch by telephone, and he keeps track of what I'm doing. I'm his guy.

I tell people my story. You have to believe in yourself. I always thought I could play this game, but I didn't always get a chance to show what I could do.

When I escorted my parents onto the field for that final game at North Carolina, I showed my father what I had written on my wristband. It said, "I'm Gonna Make It." My mother called me "June," and that was short for Junior. She was always the first to greet me when I came off the field after a game. She gave me a long hug that day. She was still proud of me. I didn't get into a single play against Duke that day, but it didn't matter to my mother. If she was hurting it was because I might have been hurting.

I got that chance here and, best of all, the guy who had the job — Jerome Bettis — couldn't have treated me any better than he did. He was my mentor from my first day in training camp. He taught me all he knew. He taught me to be patient, about getting to play and about allowing things to open up on the field and not forcing things. He taught me that it wasn't a track meet, that I might have to wait for an opening, to allow my blockers to stay ahead of me, stuff like that.

For a big guy like him to do what he did was special. He taught a speedy guy how to run with a football. I give him a lot of credit for what I achieved. I'm going to miss him. We are going to miss him as a team. I'm going to miss him personally. He passed the ball on to me. I saw what he did on and off the field. He told me to be more responsible off the field. I plan to make him proud of me in every way.

Jerome Bettis was not my savior. The Lord is my savior. God presented him to me. I think he had something in mind for me. I pray that I play up to everyone's expectations, especially mine.

"I'm still learning."

My life has changed. I've signed so many 75-yard autograph inscriptions my hand's about to fall off. They always want me to write something like "longest run in Super Bowl history" and all that above my signature.

I'm still a young guy. I'm still learning. I'm still in the playbook every day, trying to get more knowledge of the offense. I know the playbook now, but I want to stay sharp.

I lost the football momentarily when I leaped into the end zone in the Super Bowl, but I retrieved it in a hurry. I wanted it for my parents, or they would have gotten on me a little bit. That football is now on a shelf in our home in Clinton. I want to get some work done on it to capture what happened.

They presented me with a key to my hometown (on Feb. 9, 2006) and they had a day in my honor.

I don't care about those records. The only record that mattered is that we won the Super Bowl and we shocked the world.

I had gained only 11 yards on six carries in the first half and we were struggling. That touchdown gave us the momentum in the early part of the third quarter to get the victory.

Alan Faneca deserves a lot of credit for my run. He winked at me when they called that play. He led me to daylight. He's the one who gave me my nickname early in my first season with the Steelers. He said to me after one of my runs, "Boy, you're kind of fast."

During the week that led up to the big game, one of my friends told me over the telephone, "Do you know you're playing in the Super Bowl?" I hadn't really thought about that, but it was a great feeling to think about it.

I wouldn't have thought in a million years I'd be where I was, and where I am today. Don't let anybody tell you that you can't do something. If they tell you that, you've got to work harder. That's what I did. I kept with it, and that's why I'm where I'm at today.

George Gojkovich/Getty Images

Willie Parker is off to the races against Tennessee Titans.

Alan Faneca
He overcame epilepsy

"I was going to do everything normally."

Alan Faneca stood firm, his beefy arms at his sides, his bright hazel eyes focused on the activity nearby. He was standing behind his offensive line coach, Russ Grimm, listening as Grimm directed the offensive linemen through a blocking sequence.

It looked like tedious work. They were walking through different blocking schemes, like dancers working on their footwork. Grimm had them do it over and over again, growling at them the way Joe Bugel growled at him and "the Hogs" when he was with the Washington Redskins when they were winning Super Bowls.

Grimm, also a former Pitt standout and one of Bill Cowher's most valued coaches, was working with the new candidates for the most part. The regulars were given different roles. Marvel Smith was on the opposing side of the line, playing defensive end. Max Starks was the middle linebacker. Jeff Hartings was a safety, blitzing now and then to confuse the newcomers on their blocking assignments.

"Sixty-two, down, hup," hollored Grimm. He called that number out at least six times until he was satisfied with what he was seeing. "Sixty-two, down, hup."

Grimm would go over the blocking assignments, the keys, how you knew whom to block, depending on the other team's set. "Blue, fifty, set, hup." Or "Seventy-five quick." Or "Jab, thirty-three, bubble, set, hup."

How do these guys remember all this stuff?

Grimm told them they had to go through "all the different scenarios." When someone made the wrong move, he admonished him, but in an instructional tone. "It has to click in that fast," said Grimm to one of the dozen linemen in his midst.

Faneca had heard it all before. He could do those footsteps in his sleep, but his dark eyes didn't blink. He was paying attention. He didn't want to miss anything. He wanted the Steelers to succeed again, and he needed to set a proper example. He wanted more of what he and his teammates had experienced over the past few months. This had been the best winter of his pro career.

This was Wednesday, May 17, 2006 and the Steelers were conducting what they call "coaching sessions." They had completed a three-day mini-camp two days earlier, with Mother's Day in the middle. They had a day off and they were back at the Steelers' training complex on the South Side, part of the UPMC Sports Performance Complex that is shared by the University of Pittsburgh.

There is no off-season for the Steelers or anyone else in the National Football League these days. That's fine with Faneca. He makes millions a year for his efforts. He's been with the Steelers for nine seasons and he had been selected to play in the Pro Bowl five consecutive years. He was especially happy to be back with his teammates because they had won Super Bowl XL together. This was a "voluntary" session, but everyone knew that Coach Bill Cowher expected him to be there.

"We weren't the best football team in the league," Cowher had told them at a team meeting that started this reunion. "We have a lot of work to do. It starts now."

Cowher had a lot of respect for Faneca. "He's a battler, a tough guy; he is so dependable," Cowher had commented before Super Bowl XL. "I think he gets better every year at his position."

Faneca, the team's No. 1 pick out of LSU in 1998, may be the best guard in Steelers' history. No other Steelers' guard made the Pro Bowl more than once in 43 seasons and none ever made it more than twice since 1950. He didn't plan to rest on his laurels, so he was eager to get going. He had been working out on his own, at a health club near his home in the North Hills, prior to reporting for these special sessions.

The Steelers really didn't get a chance to celebrate their Super Bowl victory properly, according to Faneca. They didn't get to share their stories, their experiences, their embraces. They departed Detroit and went home. They came back to Pittsburgh for The Parade. That was great, but Faneca said there were players he hadn't seen or spoken to since February. He hadn't seen Kevin Colbert, the director of football operations, for instance, and he wanted to compliment him on a job well done, a Lombardi Trophy well earned. He wanted to relive the big victory with one of his bosses.

In fact, Faneca had forgotten to take another look at the Lombardi Trophy that was on display in the Steelers' library, a re-creation of the office once occupied by the team's founder, the late Art Rooney. "Yeah, I wanted to take a peek at that," offered Faneca.

It had been raining in Pittsburgh the past week or so, and there was a light drizzle outside as the Steelers worked out from 11:45 a.m. till 1 p.m. It was dreary for most Pittsburghers, but it didn't dampen the spirit of the Steelers. These are light workouts, just enough to get them started on another long journey, as Cowher calls the season, just enough to get the newcomers acquainted with the Steelers' system. Everyone is expected to study and memorize his playbook.

The offensive players, such as Faneca, were wearing white jerseys with black numbers, and the defensive players were wearing gold jerseys with black numbers. The linemen were all wearing protective gloves. Faneca was wearing his familiar No. 66. They weren't wearing pads — they're not allowed to at that time of the year — though some of them looked like they were. Faneca, for instance, is 6-5, 307 or so pounds. He doesn't need much padding. The players were wearing black helmets.

Alan Faneca

Alan Faneca (66) has become fixture as Pro Bowl guard.

George Gojkovich/Getty Images

Faneca wasn't wearing a helmet because he was not in the fray during this time frame. There were over 80 players working out in the indoor practice facility. It is something to behold. The UPMC Indoor Training Center includes a full 100-yard football field with plenty of room on the sidelines. It is like an airplane hangar at Pittsburgh International Airport. has an artificial turf and a high ceiling. You can practice punting and kicking field goals there. It is well lit. Pitt practices there, too. There are four grass football fields nearby on grounds once occupied by Jones & Laughlin Steel Company. That's when there were steel mills in Pittsburgh.

The Steelers were inside because it was raining outside. The skies had been steel gray ever since they reported to practice; the sun would peek out later in the day. It was worse in the Northeast section of the country. There had been record rainfalls in New England and disastrous flooding.

There were at least 30 members of the media, counting cameramen, at most of the workouts. Back in the '70s, there might have been ten for similar off-season activity. Many of them remarked that there was a special excitement in the air, a buzz in the building, more so than they recalled in the past. Of course, similar sentiments had been expressed the past spring at the Pirates' workouts in Bradenton, and there had been much anticipation for the Pitt football team and the Penguins the previous year and they all failed to play up to expectations.

Cowher didn't want to see the Steelers fail. He started every season with one goal in mind: winning the Super Bowl. The Steelers set high standards. There was a cluster of four Lombardi Trophies near the one Cowher and his crew had earned.

The media coverage of the Steelers was unreal. The news side at the local television stations had gotten into the act, and they were seeking feature stories, sending reporters over for "live" reports to the South Side facility at 5 a.m., stuff like that.

Hines Ward was busy explaining why he was going back to South Korea to help kids with mixed racial backgrounds like him to enjoy a better and fairer experience. He was also explaining that he had no problems with Coach Cowher, as a recent *Sports Illustrated* story seemed to indicate, and that he was only kidding when he said he was going to have something Payton Manning didn't have — a Super Bowl ring — when he competed with Manning and some other NFL stars at one of those made-for-TV sports competitions. "He's the best quarterback in football," Ward allowed. "I wouldn't put him down. I was just having fun."

The Steelers had to watch what they said because of the attention they were drawing because of their Super Bowl success. They were headed for The White House the following month and a special recognition ceremony with President Bush. Joey Porter spouted off some stupid remarks, as he is prone to do, saying he was going to say something to the President about the high taxes he was

#55

paying and what the President was doing with that money. He took exception to some of the things President Bush was doing. Porter was only kidding, of course, performing for the press, but his remarks upset the Steelers' brass as well, and they put out a press release quoting Joey Porter apologizing. It didn't sound like Joey Porter. "There was no malice aforethought," wrote Gene Collier, "because, with Porter, there is never any aforethought." The remarks sounded more like club president Art Rooney II, an attorney.

Alan Joseph Faneca could just smile at all the fuss. He could empathize with Ward and Porter. He knew what that was like. Two years earlier, when his roommate Tommy Maddox got hurt and Ben Roethlisberger, the rookie, had to be rushed in to take over the quarterback duties, Faneca had offered a comment that he was concerned about the team having to go with such a young leader. That got twisted to mean he had no faith in Big Ben. Faneca had to talk his way out of that one. Faneca isn't featured too much in local television or newspaper reports even though he is one of the Steelers' best players. He's the one who was most responsible for springing Willie Parker on his record 75-yard touchdown run in the third quarter of Super Bowl XL. He's solid and steady. He prefers to keep a low profile. He doesn't seek the spotlight.

Frankly, I didn't know much about him until I interviewed him when he had lunch following practice that first day of the "coaching sessions." He wore a faded burgundy jersey and black sweatpants and ate a cold cut sandwich and sipped a soda as we spoke. We had an hour-and-a-half session. He was pleasant and earnest company.

Faneca is different from the rest of the Steelers in more ways than being the only redhead on the roster. He's the only one of French and Spanish descent. He's also the only one with epilepsy. He takes six pills every day to fend off its debilitating effects. The Epilepsy Foundation saluted Alan Faneca on Super Bowl Sunday for being an inspiration to almost 3 million Americans living with epilepsy. Faneca was diagnosed with epilepsy at age 14. Now, almost 30, he is recognized as one of the finest offensive guards in the NFL.

Epilepsy is the third most common neurological disorder in the United States after Alzheimer's disease and stroke. It is equal in prevalence to cerebral palsy, multiple sclerosis, Parkinson's disease and Tourette's Syndrome combined.

Epilepsy is marked by recurring seizures, according to an Epilepsy Foundation information sheet. "Seizures are caused by brief, spontaneous disturbances in the brain's electrical activity. The episodes can be traced to genetic abnormalities, head trauma, infectious diseases that spread to the brain, and other conditions. In the majority of cases, the cause is unknown."

"I honestly didn't let it affect me," Faneca said. "I wasn't going to let it. I was going to do everything normally."

He said he went public with his problem to help others. "My parents instilled in me the importance of telling people," he explained. "If you have a seizure and your family's not around, people need to know what's going on with you. By being open, you don't have to feel like you're hiding something. You don't have to feel inferior to your friends if that's how you're feeling. You can be yourself and be open about it and move on and do what you're able to do."

I learned in a television special that Hercules was thought to have epilepsy, so Faneca is not the first strongman so affected.

One of Faneca's biggest fans is Tony Coelho, chair of the Epilepsy Foundation. "He has the courage to speak candidly about his own experience with epilepsy," said Coelho. "It's very difficult for many people — especially celebrities — to admit to living with this unfairly stigmatized condition, let alone a five-time Pro Bowl football player. Thanks to Faneca, people living with epilepsy are finally seeing why epilepsy isn't a barrier to success."

Faneca and his wife Julie are also active in raising funds for breast cancer treatment. His family has a history of that ailment as well. He thinks it's important to help wherever you can and to put your celebrity status to good use. It's better than flexing your muscles in front of a mirror.

Alan and Julie have one child, Anaebelle, who would be a year old in June. Alan also has a sister, Cheryl, who is 18.

He also grew up in New Orleans, went to school in Baton Rouge, and later shared a home with his high school sweetheart in Metarie, Louisiana. So Faneca felt the pain and dismay of the many people who suffered losses in the Hurricane Katrina episode.

He would be turning 30 on December 7 — the anniversary of Pearl Harbor — and he wanted to make sure he was ready to play at the same Pro Bowl and Super Bowl level as the year before.

"I'm not going to let this stop me."

Alan Faneca:

I had my first seizure in 1990, my freshman year in high school. I was diagnosed with epilepsy at age 14. It was more frightening for everybody else than it was for me. As a kid, you just wonder what's going on. It took a while to figure that out, and find the proper medicine to combat it. I had to go through a lot of tests. Once it became evident that something was going on in my head. I was a young kid and I was active in sports. I was wondering how this was going to affect my life. I found out what it was from my doctor. I was lucky in that respect. A lot of kids, unfortunately, are told by doctors to take it easy. Right out of the gate, I was told it was okay for me to continue to play sports. My doctor told me it was all right for me to play football even though we knew I'd be hitting people with my head.

I took the attitude that I'm not going to let this stop me.

I've become more active with the Epilepsy Foundation the last two years. I had been quite busy with the breast cancer issues. That really took a lot of my time and my wife's time. But it was something I wanted to get into. There have been breast cancer cases on my mom's side of the family. That's how we got involved with "A Glimmer of Hope."

Diana Napper got us into it. She was a friend and neighbor of Brendan Stai when he played here. He and his wife Jackie got involved with "A Glimmer of Hope," and they recruited us to help her out. Brendan had hosted some golf outings to raise funds for that.

The new guys in the locker room will learn about why they should get involved in community activities while they are playing here. I definitely think we need to be involved. Once you see what you can do, and what you can get accomplished, it's very rewarding. When you put your name on something you can help that cause attract people and needed funds.

You gotta do it. You have to use your name for a good cause. Everybody in this organization advocates that. I think the Steelers like to be associated with stuff like that. The Steelers hired Michelle Rosenthal to coordinate charity-related activity by the players. She does a great job. When you go inside many of the NFL stadiums you see signs about the various community projects with which they are associated. The NFL promotes the idea of giving back to the community.

"The turnout was absolutely crazy."

Super Bowl XL was very special. That feeling when you looked at the clock and saw zero, zero, zero (0.00). It was finally over and we won the game. What a rush. That feeling is addictive. It only happened once for us. You want to do it again and again.

I was one of the last guys out of the locker room. I didn't want to miss anything. I just wanted to take it all in. There were thousands of people out on the field so it was hard to find guys you wanted to see and share the moment with.

I remember growing up and watching the Super Bowl games on television with my dad, first in New Orleans and then in Houston.

I lived in New Orleans up until my freshman year in high school. Then we moved to the Houston suburb of Richmond. That's when I learned I had epilepsy.

I went to school in Baton Rouge, up the road from New Orleans, and later had a home in Metarie, just outside of New Orleans. So I watched a lot of TV during Hurricane Katrina. The images hit home with Julie and me. We had sold our house there three months before Katrina hit. I've been told our home was damaged in the storm. We moved from there to Thibodaux, where Nicholls State University is located. My dad's side of the family still lives around New Orleans. I had second cousins that lost everything in the storm. I couldn't contact my dad for four days after Katrina hit. I didn't know if he was okay. My parents are divorced, and my mother still lives in Richmond. We had friends live in our home in Thibodaux after Katrina while we were up here in Pittsburgh. They stayed there until December.

So it all hit home. We were glued to the TV every day. We saw glimpses of places we knew. That was difficult for everybody.

We were down in the dumps about what was going on. So winning the Super Bowl, and finishing the way we did, was a real pick-me-up experience, at least for everyone associated with the Steelers.

Just to see everybody again is great. Everything happened so fast in Detroit, and then that parade in downtown Pittsburgh. We were in the first vehicle in the parade. We were riding with Kendall Simmons and his wife Celesta. Chukky Akobi was with us, too. We knew something about parades, having been to Mardi Gras in New Orleans a few times. My wife and I thought right away that we needed some beads to throw to the crowd. Some guy gave us a bunch of beads midway through the parade and we passed them on to the fans.

The turnout was absolutely crazy. It was truly reliving what it felt like to win the Super Bowl all over again.

"I take pride in what people think of me."

What we're doing here now is basically to get everybody back on the same page again.

I think the Steelers do a pretty good job of drafting the right kind of players and the right kind of people. If you bring in the right people you don't need to have a policeman around. They bring in good guys for the most part. They may bring in one or two guys who could be bad guys, but they have to conform to the 50 other people in the locker room.

I think the Rooneys want people who'll take pride in being Pittsburgh Steelers. They look for guys who are a good fit. You're expected to be a solid citizen. If you're not you won't be here long.

I like to think I'm a good guy. That comes from my parents and my grandparents. I take pride in what people think of me. People look up to us. Whether you want to be a role model or not doesn't matter. People are going to look up to you. If they see you hold a door for an elderly couple it sends a message. It's the right thing to do.

Jerome Bettis did more than set the tone for our team. He kept the atmosphere upbeat all the time. He was always telling some joke, always laughing. That's how he set the tone. He kept it light-hearted, always ribbing on somebody. He's irreplaceable.

Other guys will help fill the void. No one can be Jerome Bettis. That can't happen.

A lot of people will be watching Ben. The rest of the world is watching him. He can't go anywhere in Pittsburgh without being recognized. He might as well be Michael Jordan in Chicago.

"Everybody's face on our team is familiar to some of the fans. I can't go shopping without being overwhelmed. I hear the chitter-chatter, people saying "There goes so-and-so. . ." as I pass. If you move quickly enough you can avoid getting swarmed. I sign autographs when I can.

It is impossible to please everybody. You always have to say "no" to someone. I try as much as possible to please the fans.

We have to put the Super Bowl behind us now. I've been working out by myself to get prepared for this next season. I'm focusing on the coming season. Coach Cowher did tell us that we weren't the best team in the league. He said you don't start where you finished. He said everyone starts at zero.

We're the champs right now and it feels so good. You want to relive that experience again. Russ Grimm thanked us at a meeting for the offensive line for getting him another size 13 Super Bowl ring. He talked about how hard it will be to do it twice. He knows something about that.

We've had respect for Coach Grimm before he even got here, just from his reputation, and what he had accomplished as a player. Then we saw how he coaches, how smart he is. He gets us well prepared for every challenge.

I've been here for nine years, and most of what we're doing are the same plays we've been using since I came here. Coach Grimm does a good job. These walk-through exercises are part of our continuing education. You have to picture things. It's better for your body because you're not taking a beating in scrimmage sessions.

193

I hope to stay healthy, and I want to be out there and be the best guard I can be, the best Alan Faneca I can be. I've trained all during the off-season to sustain that effort. I'm glad I'll be lining up again next to Jeff Hartings, our center. I'm thankful to have a guy like that next to me. He has to make a lot of calls, as to who has to block whom, and he knows what he's doing. As a center, you can either do your job or you can do your job and also help others. He does a great job in both respects.

We feel better about our offensive line right now. Last year, at this time, Kendall was coming off surgery on his knee. You're never sure about that. Max had seen a little playing time, but you didn't know if he could be a starter. Now we've seen what people have done, so you have to feel better about our group. Hopefully, we'll improve our depth. You need help during the long season. Trai Essex, Chukky Okobi and Chris Kemoeatu and Barrett Brooks have all gotten more work under their belts. It takes more than five guys.

I couldn't watch the end of the Super Bowl. I was sitting on the bench, and I saw reporters gathering behind us. I'm thinking, "Not now. Don't jinx this thing." Everybody had the look like we'd already won it.

Doing it the way we did it made it even more special. We came back to get to the top. We did it like it's never been done before. It was the first time in 40 years anyone traveled the route we did to get there.

When we had one of our team meetings before Super Bowl XL, Dan Rooney and his son Art spoke to us for a few minutes. Mr. Rooney told us, "This isn't one for the thumb...this is one for you." I thought that was good of him to say that. After all, none of us had anything to do with winning those other four Super Bowls.

As a player, I look at myself as a hustle guy. Even as a kid, playing intramural sports, I learned that hustle makes up for a lot of what you might lack as an athlete. A lot of times I'm able to do what I can because of hustle.

"Tommy Maddox was a great leader."

It's a shame what happened to my roommate Tommy Maddox. He went from being a hero here to an outcast. He didn't deserve that; no one deserves that. Without Tommy, we don't beat the Browns (36-33) in that playoff game in 2002.

He was the guy who rallied us. Tommy Maddox was a great leader. He spoke to us on the sideline before the start of the second half. He said, "If you don't believe it's going to happen then just turn around get take your bleeping bleep into the locker room." Tommy never swore off the field. He did it to get everyone's attention. They knew he meant it.

He was an older guy, and everyone recognized what he'd been through to get back to the NFL. He did a good job for us and had a good run. He finally got a chance to start in the NFL. He wanted that badly and he kept working to achieve it. He was the Comeback Player of the Year.

Alan Faneca felt his roommate Tommy Maddox was mistreated and left out in the cold by fans who forgot his contribution to Steelers' success.

George Gojkovich/Getty Images

A Super Weekend for Fanecas

Alan Faneca insists he hasn't changed since the Steelers won Super Bowl XL, but he says life has been full of exciting events. He says the weekend of June 2-4 will be difficult to top. "Our team went to The White House on Friday, we celebrated the first birthday of our only child Annabelle at our home on Saturday, and on Sunday my wife Julie and I joined my teammates and their families at a special dinner at Heinz Field where we received our Super Bowl rings. That was a great weekend."

Kendall Simmons
A diabetic dynamo

"I want to help others deal with problems."

Kendall Simmons was sweating profusely as he walked off the practice fields at the Steelers' South Side training facility. Beads of sweat glistened on his shaven skull and slithered down the sides. Sweat shone on his massive shoulders and biceps and stained the Auburn XXL sleeveless gray jersey he was wearing. He had removed his white Steelers' practice jersey, the ones the offensive players wear at workouts, and was carrying it in his right hand, along with his black helmet.

He looked like a field hand coming in from picking beets or potatoes. The Steelers' practice fields form a green valley in what was once a dirty industrial site. Jones & Laughlin Steel Company once occupied that space. One of Kendall's teammates, Mike Logan of McKeesport, was running dashes where his grandfather once worked at J&L. It's amazing how they turned this land into a green space that rivals the Laurel Highlands where the Steelers practice each summer.

It's surrounded by high hills —they'd be called mountains in Ohio — and, to the left, just over the Monongahela River, I could see the boyhood neighborhoods of Pirates' slugger Frank Thomas, pro wrestling champion Bruno Sammartino, and Pro Football Hall of Fame quarterback Dan Marino. As an amateur artist, Simmons said he appreciated the picture, and said it would make a nice painting.

It was 12:45 p.m., quitting time for the Steelers' so-called voluntary coaching session, on Wednesday, June 7, 2006. The workout was timed at an hour and 45 minutes. Chet Fuhrman, the team's conditioning coach, keeps the clock and sounds an air-horn at different time intervals. It was nearly 90 degrees on a bright sunny day in Pittsburgh.

When I said something about how hot it was, Simmons smiled and said, "This is fine. This isn't hot. I'm from Mississippi and I played my college ball in Alabama. This is nothing compared to how hot and humid it gets in those places. Trust me."

Kendall Simmons is a large man with a large and long head. He has no sideburns. His mustache and beard are black and shaven precisely, giving him a theatrical mask. He smiles a lot because he considers himself a lucky man.

He has often said no one is ever going to hear him complain about practicing. He missed the entire 2004 season with a knee injury he suffered at summer training camp in Latrobe. A year earlier, just prior to the opening of the 2003 training camp, he was diagnosed as having adult diabetes. He lost nearly 40 pounds and was never at full strength that season. At top form, Simmons is a robust 6-3, 320 pounds.

Photo by George Gojkovich/Getty Images →

"I have a lot of respect for that guy," said Russ Grimm, the associate head coach and offensive line coach of the Steelers. "He played through it. He knew he wasn't as strong, as big, and as durable as he was the year before, but he had to go because we needed him. He can still get better, and he's working hard to do just that."

Simmons, age 27 as he prepared for his fifth season with the Steelers, has to keep a close eye on his diabetes.

The weather plays tricks with his system. Either extreme heat or cold can send his blood sugar count dipping or soaring, and affect how he feels. He said team trainer John Norwig is great about monitoring his health condition. Simmons also gets regular checkups from Dr. Hersha Rao, an endocrinologist at UPMC.

"I have to watch it," said Simmons, "but I try not to worry about it. It's just a part of my life I had to get used to. It can be a real chess game. No matter what I do, there are just some days I don't feel so hot. It's hard to play football when you don't feel right."

Simmons is the starting right guard for a highly respected offensive line, and one of the reasons Bill Cowher likes to emphasize running the ball. Simmons gained some All-American attention at Auburn and was the first draft choice of the Steelers in 2002, the 30th player picked in the draft. His teammates named him rookie of the year and he was given the Joe Greene Great Performance Award. He's been a solid performer ever since, when he's been healthy.

He was born in Ripley, Mississippi — believe it or not — the same hometown as best-selling author John Grisham. His full handle is Henry Alexander Kendall Simmons. He is the son of Henry and Glenda Simmons. He's married to Celesta Henry, whom he met in his first month at Auburn. They have a daughter, Celesta Kensley, who would celebrate her second birthday in August, 2006.

Kendall says his parents have a successful marriage and he is determined to do the same. When he has some spare time, and he says he has less since his daughter was born, he likes to paint. "It's a little release," he said, "and I enjoy doing it." He graduated from Auburn with a degree in visual communication/graphic arts.

In the aftermath of Hurricane Katrina, he painted a picture of a man riding a bike down Bourbon Street in New Orleans on a nice day. "I wanted a piece with a lot of meaning behind it," he told Joe Bendel, the Steelers' beat writer for the *Pittsburgh Tribune-Review.*

"You could see it was a quiet day, unlike the way Bourbon Street normally is; it's usually packed with people. I wanted to do more than a sports picture. I wanted something that really had impact."

The person on the bike is shown with a shirt with the words ALL GOOD on his back.

"To me," Simmons told Bendel, "It's saying that things will get back to the point where everything's good again. It gives hope. That's what I was looking for."

Simmons always tries to see the best in all situations. He's involved with the Pittsburgh chapter of the Juvenile Diabetes Association and often speaks to children about dealing with diabetes.

Kendall Simmons:

"I felt like I was part of something again."

It was strange when I injured my knee at training camp before the 2004 season. As a result, I was able to be with my wife Celesta at the hospital when she gave birth to our daughter, Celesta Kensley.

My wife was due to deliver our daughter on August 28. I blew out my knee on August 18, and my wife delivered our daughter on August 21. As pro athletes, sometimes we don't get to be home when our kids are born, or when they are small. So I got to see my daughter change through different phases. Football was taken away from me. I got to be with my wife and baby. It was almost as if my injury was supposed to happen at that time.

The negative part of it was that our team went 15-1 and I didn't feel like I was part of it.

It was good to get back on the field this past season. I felt like I was part of something again. I'm happy to be back in action again.

I think God has put this diabetes in my life so that I could help others to deal with it. I've had time to reflect on all of this, and I don't feel sorry for myself, or feel like it shouldn't have happened to me.

Diabetes is in my family. It's in my wife's family. It's in the blood. We're hoping it will pass by our child. That's something we have to keep an eye on.

I have to check my blood sugar several times a day and make sure I take all my medications. I feel like I should be a role model to show kids that you can overcome something like this and still pursue your dreams. When they see professional athletes who are ailing in some respect but are still successful it can inspire them. Attitude is so important in dealing with any kind of adversity.

It's important that I have been able to talk to Dan Rooney and Art Rooney about my condition. You know if you have any problems and want to talk or whatever, they're going to be there. That makes it so much easier to come to work every day. It's kind of like a family atmosphere. The Rooneys try their best to take care of the guys and make it where everybody's comfortable. It makes the whole thing run a lot smoother. You want to play harder for them because they believe in you.

People in their family have diabetes, so they knew what I was going through, and they talked to me about it. On other teams, when they find out you have it, it's like you have a handicap and you become a liability. They don't even give you a chance. They always ask me how I'm doing every time they see me. They tell me to take care of myself because they know what I'm going through. That makes you feel a lot better right there.

"My wife gave me a lot of leeway."

Going to The White House was one of the best things that have happened to us. I've been to the state capitol in Alabama, but I had never been in The White House. To be there with guys you call your friends made it really special. To be with them again and get the ring really capped the whole year. I wish my wife could have been with us at The White House.

I owe her for the way she put up with me when I was miserable about not being able to play, and feeling so frustrated by the whole thing. I was walking around the house and pouting. My wife gave me a lot of leeway.

It was tough on both of us. We were first-time parents and learning as we went along how best to take care of our daughter. Having kids will change your life. A lot of people need kids to slow them down, so they can appreciate what life is all about and what it really means to be married.

I want us to be together until we pass on into eternity.

I have nieces and nephews, but being a parent gives you a totally new outlook about children. Now you're an adult. You have to become a team with your wife. It's a learning experience. Raising a child requires a team effort. You might not always agree on how to raise a child, but you have to make compromises. In any case, you may make mistakes. It can put a strain on a relationship. You have to make sure you pay attention to your spouse as well during this demanding time.

I had good parents and I benefited from having two parents at home. My mother is Glinda and my father is Henry Simmons. It makes a difference when your parents remain together and they both are active in raising you. I had a stable father at home. From a manly side, there's only so much a mother can do in showing a son what to do.

There's been a big difference in my life to have both parents. There was a lot of stuff my dad preached to me that I didn't agree with. My dad got smarter as I got older. I'm trying to live now by the stuff he told me. I used to say, 'You crazy.' But now I know he wasn't so crazy after all.

He has seen ten times more than I've seen. He's seen a hundred times what I've seen, especially him being in Vietnam as a soldier in the U.S. Army. He got shot there four times. I have two older sisters, Lynn and Mia, and a younger brother Thomas. I'm the third child and both sisters looked after me pretty good. I was lucky to have them all.

I grew up in Ripley, Mississippi. It's about 35 minutes north of Tupelo. My dad is quite the mechanic and handyman. He taught me a lot. I can change my own brakes and change the transmission fluid.

With my knee, some times I am reminded of that injury with every step I have to take. With the diabetes, I have to take six shots of insulin a day, stabbing myself in the stomach, and I hate needles. I have to prick my fingers and check my blood sugar. My fingers have calluses. I think it's important for me to be a role model for people who have diabetes. It's important to see that I can live a normal life and be successful. I like to teach people how important having a good attitude is when you are so challenged.

The Steelers like for us to be involved in the community. I enjoy being on the team, and I think that if there's a way you can help people in the community you ought to do it.

I care about how people view me. I care to a certain degree. I always try to do the right thing. I try to please everybody. Sometimes that gets me in trouble. I'm not going to say "no" to anyone. If you try to keep everybody happy you can get into a situation where you don't have time for yourself and your family.

You can only spread yourself so thin. I think Ben Roethlisberger, for instance, tries to please everyone, but it's impossible. There are so many demands and requests for his time. I don't want anybody to get mad at him. I'm sure that sometimes he just wants to go home and sit down and be like everybody else.

Now that these spring sessions are over, we'll get a chance to relax and rest. We have to work hard to try and repeat. It won't happen without an all-out effort. The hunger is still there. A lot of people didn't think we should have won it. People think we lucked out. We have to prove them wrong.

"To fully appreciate the vanity license plate (IHOP) of Steelers guard Kendall Simmons, it helps to know what a pancake block is."
— Steve Rushin, *Sports Illustrated*

A fun night in Mt. Lebanon
Hines Ward wows 'em

*"He must have been born
with a smile on his face.'*

An Irishman with a microphone at his mouth can be a dangerous thing. Tom O'Malley Jr. is always on his best behavior when he serves as the manager for the Steelers' basketball team and he is an old hand at this stuff. He inherited a gift of gab from his late father, an ace advertising sales executive for *The Pittsburgh Press* who moonlighted for over 20 years as the mayor of Castle Shannon. His dad talked like the comic George Gobel and was just as funny.

One of Gobel's best lines went like this: "My uncle was the town drunk and we lived in Chicago."

One of Tom Jr.'s mentors was the late great Bernard "Baldy" Regan, known as the "mayor of the North Side," a Rooney favorite who founded the Steelers' basketball team and had a little Abe Saperstein in him.

Saperstein, a Chicago-based sportsman and promoter, started the Harlem Globetrotters and developed them into an international attraction.

Tom Sr. once told a story about Baldy Regan asking a cabbie for directions from a club in Carrick. "How do I get to the North Side?" Regan asked the cabbie. "Drink wine, man, lots of wine," came back the cabbie.

Beads of sweat were visible on Tom O'Malley Jr.'s balding head as the gym, and especially the locker room downstairs, were uncomfortably warm. By day, he manages the Bob Purkey Insurance Agency in Bethel Park, and has taken over the business from the former Pirates pitcher.

The Steelers barnstorm throughout the tri-state area in April and May, playing in high school gyms. It's O'Malley's job to book the games, get out the p.r. materials, and to round up seven or eight Steelers on any given night for the next game and lead them to the site. They usually appear on the court a few minutes before the scheduled starting time. The Steelers were selling out gyms wherever they played because of increased popularity from winning Super Bowl XL. The players and O'Malley were making extra moola.

This was Thursday night, April 27, 2006 and O'Malley was standing at mid-court of the Mt. Lebanon High School gymnasium. He looked splendid in a cream-colored suit, with a brown-gold paisley pocket-handkerchief fluffed just so, a real Dapper Dan.

His job was to announce the seven Steelers he had brought to the gym for a game with staff and faculty and a few local policemen. Part of the proceeds were going for Amy's Army, a community effort to find

Hines Ward and Brett Keisel were crowd favorites when Steelers' basketball team played at Mt. Lebanon High School.

Photos by Mike Longo

Tom O'Malley Jr. and author Jim O'Brien share bench with left to right, Hines Ward, Deshea Townsend and Tyrone Carter during Steelers' basketball game. O'Malley is the Red Auerbach of Steelers' basketball.

a blood stem cell donor for 11-year-old Amy Katz who has a rare type of leukemia for a child her age. The only known cure for her cancer is a bone marrow transplant. A search on her behalf has turned up over 40 matches for others similarly challenged, but to date no match for Amy.

She was in the sellout crowd, a beautiful blonde who was accompanied by classmates. She seemed to be having a good time and looked as healthy as any of the students in the stands. The game sponsors would turn over a check for $1,000 to Amy's Army, with the rest of the profits going to the school's intramural sports program.

The Steelers help raise funds wherever they go. They were involved in the first fund-raiser for Amy Katz two years earlier.

O'Malley saved the best for last in announcing the Steelers' lineup. That was Hines Ward, the MVP of Super Bowl XL and recently returned from taking his Korean mother back to Seoul for a much-publicized tour of the city where Ward was born — his father was a black American soldier — and where he lived until he was a year old.

Ward got the biggest cheer from the crowd and he flashed that brilliant signature smile in response. "He must have been born with that smile on his face," observed Frankie Paladino, a Mt. Lebanon resident I had met a year earlier at the Pirates' 2005 Fantasy Camp in Bradenton, Florida. "He never stops smiling."

That's one of the reasons Ward is such a popular guy with Pittsburgh Steelers' fans.

Most of the Steelers were playing for the paycheck. They get about $200 or $300 a night for these outings. That's spending money for some of the lower-paid players

Hines Ward and his pal Deshea Townsend don't need the money, but they still retain a child-like enthusiasm for sports. Both love to launch three-point bombs and sometimes get into a competition of their own. Deshea was more deadly on this particular night because this was Ward's first basketball outing of the off-season. He was a bit rusty.

He smiled when he threw up an air-ball and took a clown's fall onto the steps in the end zone after chasing a fleet-footed member of the Mt. Lebanon team down the court. He lay on the steps for awhile, feigning exhaustion, but smiling all the while to the delight of the crowd.

Ward and Townsend's teammates for this game included Ricardo Colclough, Lee Mays, Bryant McFadden and Nate Washington. Louis Lipps, a former Steeler receiver, helped fill out the lineup. Tyrone Carter, a cornerback on the ballclub, came along to lend vocal support from the bench. Lipps was second in career catches for the Steelers until Ward came along and surpassed him and John Stallworth in the record books. He lives in Mt. Washington these days and works for a mortgage lender in Aspinwall. He's one of the basketball team's most reliable performers.

Mt. Lebanon had a good team, with several former college varsity performers in their lineup, from Duke and Duquesne, and they gave the Steelers a stern test. But they lost; the score never matters, because the Steelers, like the Harlem Globetrotters, almost always win. The real winner is always the benefit the game is being played for.

O'Malley told me that they had played to a sellout crowd the night before at Steel Valley High School in Munhall. Quarterback Charley Batch showed up to play for the Steelers at his alma mater. The host team included Carl Krauser, the former Pitt guard. "He's a good kid," said O'Malley. "We had a good night there."

One never knows — and that includes Tom O'Malley Jr. — just who's going to show up for the Steelers at one of their basketball outings.

So I was surprised and delighted to see Hines Ward walking down a hallway outside the basement a floor below the basketball court. They were assigned to the girls' locker room. Townsend has always treated me with enthusiastic greetings, and it was no different as he entered the locker room.

Ward and Lipps went to the far end of the locker room to change into their uniforms and lace up their sneakers. Ward was wearing No. 86, of course.

I went over to say hello and talk to him. He was as friendly as ever. There is no pretense about Hines Ward. He has never gotten a big head.

I had attended a press conference a month earlier at Steelers' headquarters on the South Side where Ward outlined his plans to take his mother to South Korea. He said he was having this press conference to get it out of the way before they traveled to their native hometown.

He said he was hoping he and his mother would not create a fuss when they got there. I remember thinking at the time that Ward was crazy to think he and his mother would be left to tour on their own. I thought the media frenzy would be far greater than he had experienced on Media Day at Super Bowl XL in Detroit back in February.

"You were right about that," said Ward. "It was crazy. Everywhere we went crowds followed us. This one day we were walking through town and I felt like Tiger Woods walking up the fairway on the final hole at Augusta for the Masters."

Ward knows something about that. He grew up in Georgia and starred for the football team and in the classroom at the University of Georgia. Woods had an Asian mother and a black father who had served in the military, so they had something in common heritage-wise. I had mentioned Tiger Woods, in fact, in a story I had written after attending Ward's press conference. He, too, had a chance to become big on the international sports scene, if not quite in the same league as Woods.

Ward was getting a lot of attention since he won the MVP award with his heroics in the victory over the Seattle Seahawks. He told me he had a deal to do a book about his life. I told him it was a good story.

I asked him if his wondrous season had sunk in yet. "Maybe in some respects," he said. "It's still surreal. Like it didn't happen. You work hard all your life to get to this point. So it was a very emotional experience. There are so many aspects to it that it's hard to keep track of them.

"There was the stretch run to the playoffs, the playoffs and, of course, the Super Bowl. Going to Disney World with Jerome. The Bettis family and all they experienced. Jerome's story is certainly surreal. The way it all came to a fitting end. We were all so happy for him.

"Getting mentioned in the same breath as John Stallworth and Lynn Swann. And Louie Lipps. Don't forget Louie. These guys made the plays. They made the big plays every time. You can't compare stats. The Steelers have sometimes rushed the ball more and sometimes thrown the ball more. I just want to make big plays like they did.

"We're still so run-oriented. So I find other ways to make myself useful. It's all football and I take pride in being a complete football player. Making big plays is, I think, the M.O. for Steeler wideouts. We've had some great playmakers on this team through the years.

"It was a great experience to go to South Korea with my mother. The trip was a tribute to her. Seoul is like New York City, a city that never sleeps, a city with lights on all the time. My mom was telling me stories wherever we went.

"She left Korea in bad times. A woman with a racially mixed child was shunned, and so were any children like that. I plan to go back to Korea in the future. I want to help change that culture in that regard. There was much conversation in that respect when I was there, and stories in the newspapers and on television about an increased sensitivity to that kind of situation.

"You shouldn't have to be an MVP in the Super Bowl to be accepted. They couldn't have treated us better. We got to see the president of South Korea and we became honorary citizens of Seoul. We received some great gifts and kindness. The elderly Korean people stood and applauded us whenever they saw us in a restaurant or public place. They didn't have to do that. As I said, it was surreal.

"My mother had a negative view of what she had experienced as a young woman in South Korea. She was not certain she wanted to go back. But she knew how much it meant to me. Now she's happy we went. It put a closure on a lot of things.

"I had planned this trip a year earlier. I had no idea we were going to be in a Super Bowl, or that I would get so much attention. That's not what we planned on. It was just going to be a trip home to learn more about my mother and where we came from. I wanted to know about the tradition and my heritage."

"He makes things happen."
— Louis Lipps

I asked Louis Lipps to rate Hines Ward. "He's just tough, man. He plays hard. He makes things happen. If they're not throwing to him he's knocking someone on their ass. If they throw it to him he catches the ball and makes the other team pay. He just plays the game the way it's meant to be played. He's a 110 per cent all the time."

When I was talking to Hines Ward I told him about something I had read in a book called *America's Game* that same day. It's a book by author Michael MacCambridge about the evolution of the National Football League. It should be must reading — a required primer — for every professional football player. They should all learn more about their tradition and heritage as NFL players, and learn more about the individuals who paved the way for them.

I was telling Ward a story about how Raymond Berry, a great receiver in the '50s and '60s, used to carry a football with him wherever he went. He wanted to touch the ball, get the feel of it, so it would be natural to hold onto it.

Ward shrugged his shoulders when I mentioned Raymond Berry. The name didn't mean anything to him. "He was the favorite receiver of Johnny Unitas," I said. Ward nodded. That was a name he recognized.

"I'm like that at training camp," said Ward. "I carry a football with me wherever I go."

There was a tall gentleman with dark wavy hair and dark eyeglasses standing at the other end of the locker room. He was talking to some of the players, getting some stuff signed, and taking pictures with a digital camera.

I recognized him. It was Zeb Jansante, the principal of Mt. Lebanon High School. He was the principal at Quaker Valley High School when I first met him a few years earlier. He had helped me line up an interview with his father, Val Jansante. He said his father would be 86 in September and was still living in Bentleyville.

Val Jansante was one of my favorite Steelers when I was a kid and first became aware of Pittsburgh's pro team. I had Val Jansante's bubble gum card.

Later, just before the game began, I saw Hines Ward shaking hands with Zeb Jansante at mid-court. When Ward sat next to me on the bench, I told him, "That fellow you just shook hands with is the son of one of the Steelers' all-time greatest receivers."

Ward had never heard of Val Jansante. "He led the Steelers in receiving five straight years back in the '40s," I told Ward.

Lynn Swann led the Steelers in receiving five out of six years in the mid-to-late '70s. Ward had just led the Steelers in receiving for the sixth straight season to set a team record in that regard.

"Sometimes people have a misconception about people with the bling-bling and the cars. Those are material things. They don't have a thing to do with who I am."
— Hines Ward

I think Ward and everyone associated with the Steelers should know something about Val Jansante. He was the Steelers' tenth round draft choice in 1944, but didn't report to the team until 1946 after a two-year stint in the Navy during World War II. He was with the Steelers from 1946 through 1951, leading the team in receptions all but his final season.

I got to know him for another reason. He was the head football coach at Central Catholic High School in Oakland when I was a freshman there in 1957. I tried out for the team and he cut me after the first day's tryout. He knew a good sportswriter when he saw one. I'd forgiven him in the interim. I had some nerve trying out for the Central Catholic football team. I had to be one of the six smallest kids in the freshman class.

I landed a spot on the school newspaper, *The Viking*, and enjoyed that immensely. Midway through my sophomore year, I asked the newspaper's sponsor, one Brother Francis Emery, a question about why my byline had been left off a long story I'd written in that month's issue. His response was to slap me in the face for insubordination. That was the end of my Central Catholic career. I called my mother and told her I wanted to transfer to Allderdice High School, where I wanted to go in the first place. Three days later, I was attending school in Squirrel Hill.

It worked out fine. Looking back on it, I enjoyed the best of both worlds and benefited from both experiences. During the 2005 holiday season I had classmates from each school stop at my table when I was signing books in the malls. Each of them recalled a day in class when our teacher asked us what we wanted to be when we grew up. "You said you wanted to be a sportswriter," each of them said, "and that's exactly what you did. You always knew what you wanted to do."

When I spoke to Zeb Jansante, I told him I figured he was glad to have a night of fun at Mt. Lebanon High School. A scandal had struck the school that same month. Male students had put together a "Top 25" sex ranking list of the female students. They named names and rated faces, buttocks, breasts and desirability, and made some crude comments in some cases. Jansante and school officials found themselves in the middle of a stormy protest from parents of the girls as well as the boys.

It seemed like the suburban communities in the South Hills of Pittsburgh were playing a "Can You Top This?" game. Mt. Lebanon had a controversial story a year earlier, followed by one in Peters Township, then Bethel Park, then Upper St. Clair before Mt. Lebanon regained the spotlight in the local news reports.

These are all fairly affluent suburban communities and they didn't want anyone thinking that only the city schools and the ones in financially fragile communities were having all the problems.

So having the Steelers playing basketball against the principal, some of the school's teachers and local policemen was a good way to bring some balance and some smiles — and not just Hines Ward's — to the community for one blessed night.

Former Steelers' star pass-catcher Val Jansante joins son Zeb at Galleria.

Hines Ward holds young fan Adam Lumish of South Park during game at Mt. Lebanon High School.

Chris Hoke
Hanging in there

"It keeps my heart beating."

C hris Hoke is a cliffhanger. I checked his fingernails and they're no longer than mine are. I thought they'd be longer, since Hoke has been hanging on for his dear life ever since the Steelers signed him as a free agent back in the spring of 2001.

"I got the smallest signing bonus of anybody in years," he recalled with a thin smile. "How much? How about $2,500?"

Every NFL team signs a slew of free agents following the annual college draft, hoping they'll get lucky with one or two of them, but knowing they need bodies for summer camp drills. Hoke was a blocking sled who could move. He was a hard worker. That was in the slim scouting report.

He came cheap.

Back in 1967 the Steelers signed a free agent named Sam Davis out of Allen University in South Carolina. He started at guard for four Super Bowl teams. In 1974, they signed a free agent from Temple named Randy Grossman. He started at tight end for four Super Bowl teams. That same summer, when there was a players' strike and veterans reported late to camp, they also signed a free agent from South Carolina State named Donnie Shell. He was a strong safety and he also picked up four Super Bowl rings. And he has drawn voting support, but not nearly enough, to be inducted into the Pro Football Hall of Fame.

Sometimes you get lucky. The Steelers got lucky with Chris Hoke. In 2004, for instance, the Steelers signed a free agent from North Carolina named Willie Parker. He hardly played for the Tar Heels, and he never left the sideline for Senior Day to close the home schedule. That's the same Willie Parker — now known as "Fast Willie" Parker — who set a Super Bowl record in February, 2006 when he raced 75 yards for a touchdown to spark the Steelers' victory over the Seattle Seahawks. Hoke saw some action in that game, as a backup to Casey Hampton at nose tackle. He'd be getting his own Super Bowl ring.

Hampton got hurt early in the previous campaign, and Hoke started most of the 2004 season in the middle of the Steelers' defensive line. Hoke performed admirably and assured the Steelers that they were truly two-deep at nose tackle. They had a Pro Bowl caliber ballplayer in Hampton, their No. 1 draft choice out of Texas in 2001. They had a reliable reserve in Chris Hoke, the pride of Brigham Young University and Foothill High School in Santa Ana, California. He could fill in, if needed, on some special teams.

Chris Hoke of Steelers embraces three outstanding members of the 2004 Upper St. Clair High School football team at Coaches Corner luncheon. The Panthers, from left to right, are Sean Lee, Danny Cafaro and Josh Helmrich.

No one enjoys playing basketball for Steelers any more than Chris Hoke. "I play for the money," says reliable reserve nose tackle.

Hoke hadn't played in a regular season game his first three seasons with the Steelers. He was on the roster except for two weeks when he was cut and put on the practice squad in late December of his rookie season to make room for running back R.J. Bowers of Grove City College. Hoke dressed for two games in his second season, and that's all he had to show for his first three seasons. He was in twice — two plays — when the other team was attempting a field goal.

"They must have seen something they liked at camp or in our practice sessions," said Hoke. "I was a nervous wreck every Tuesday, though. If someone was hurt and had to be put on injured reserve they would have to activate or sign someone else and they'd have to drop someone from the roster to make room. I was worried that I'd be cut."

The public is more aware of the stars of the Steelers' team, of course, but there are many like Hoke who are hanging in there, hoping they'll stick, hoping the Turk won't come calling on them in their dorm room and telling them to bring their playbook along. Hoke was just happy to have survived with the Steelers. He was more confident than ever that there was a spot on the Steelers' roster for him, and that he'd help get their offensive line ready for the real stuff each week.

Playing for the Steelers is a boyhood dream come true.

I think Chris Hoke smiled through most of our hour-and-a-half interview over coffee (my drink at 10 a.m.) and lemonade and fried chicken sandwich from Chick-filet (his idea of a balanced breakfast) on Saturday, April 8, 2006. We sat at a table in the food court at Ross Park Mall, near the Steak Escape outlet. I introduced him to Brittany and Rachel who were working the counter on the opening shift.

They'd never heard of Chris Hoke, but he looked like he could be a Steeler. He was wearing a bright red T-shirt with a Hurley insignia in the center of his chest — that's a California surfing outlet — and an orange-red crewcut and a warm smile that could melt the cheese on a Philly steak. He stood 6-foot-3 and weighed about 300 pounds, a few pounds over his playing weight. His chest and biceps bulged and were squeezed tight by that red T-shirt. He has that Pittsburgh pale look, the sort that makes the sun smile when it sees him. He is a dermatologist's dream come true.

He'd been taking it easy for the most part, coming down off the high of having played for the Super Bowl XL champions. He was happy to spend more time with his wife, Jaimee, and their two sons, Cade, 5; Nathan, nearly 3; and a daughter, Chloee, 8 months. "I don't get the time to play with them during the season," he said.

I'd seen him playing for the Steelers' basketball team for four years, and as recently as the previous week. Tom O'Malley, Jr., who managed the team and coordinated the schedule, said he was one of the reliable ones who showed up fairly often. When I asked Hoke why he played on the Steelers' basketball team, he actually blushed.

After a pause, he replied, "For the money."

"That's your spending money, right?" I said. "Your wife Jaimee lets you have that."

"You got that right," he said. "Plus, I enjoy playing. It's good to be out with the guys. And I get some exercise. It keeps my heart beating."

I had seen Chris Hoke at Ross Park Mall many times before when I was doing a signing at the nearby Waldenbooks outlet. Hoke can shop there without too many fans recognizing him. He can still go out in public, unlike Jerome Bettis or Ben Roethlisberger, without creating a stir and drawing a crowd.

"Some people come up to me and say something," said Hoke. "I'm not like Jerome, of course, or Big Ben, but real fans know me. They holler, 'Hey, Hokey, how ya doin'? What's up, man?"

His name was often confused with Chris Hope, a starting safety on the Steelers' highly respected defensive unit. Hope had taken advantage of his free agent status after Super Bowl XL to sign with the Tennessee Titans. It might help Chris Hoke establish a clearer identity in Pittsburgh. In truth, considering the tenuous nature of his stay with the Steelers, it would be more fitting if, indeed, his name were Chris Hope.

He said he also bought homes in Florida, Arizona and California — "the hot spots" — and rented them out or sold them. He was making an investment in his future. He said he was going to be turning 30 the following Wednesday.

"I missed two years when I went on a Mormon mission when I was at BYU, and I didn't play much my first three years here," said Hoke. "I may be 30, but football-wise I have a 25-year-old body. I'm still young."

Chris Hoke:

"People always counted me out."

I'll tell you what my story is. I was a player in high school and in college that people looked at and said I couldn't make it. It was always kind of like that. People always counted me out.

When I came out of BYU the Steelers were the only NFL team that was interested in signing me. My agent called me and said the Steelers wanted me. I signed for the smallest signing bonus that year.

Ever since I was a kid, I wanted to play in the National Football League someday. When I talk to kids in schools I always tell them that future belongs to those who dream. I tell kids they have to work hard to realize their dreams, whatever they may be.

I come from a big sports family and every Sunday we watched the NFL games. I was a big fan of the 49ers. When I was in college, I liked Steve Young. He played at BYU.

So I was excited the first time I stepped on a field with NFL players. I remember coming to Pittsburgh for my first mini-camp. I remember I went up against Tom Myslinski. You remember him? I rushed and got too close to the quarterback to suit Mylo. He tackled me and shoved my helmet into the turf. He said, "Don't get close to the quarterback, rook." I thought, wow, this is the NFL. I'll be fighting a lot. I'm not sure if the quarterback was Kordell Stewart or not. But I knew I'd be getting close to any quarterback I could get close to. That's what I was supposed to do. I had to show them what I was made of.

I do that every practice. A lot of the offensive linemen don't like me at practice. I try to play at a high level every play. I take pride in being on the No. 1 defense in the National Football League. Even though I didn't play much my first three years I always felt I could do it. I have to do it every snap so I stay here.

That's why they kept me around. I think they saw something. I try hard. I gave it everything I could. I was always prepared to play and prepared to practice. I wanted to be ready when my opportunity came.

The offensive linemen come in to practice on Wednesday and they're still sore from the last game. I worked hard every day. Some of the guys were scolding me, telling me to cool it.

Wayne Gandy, Jeff Hartings, Alan Faneca, Keydrick Vincent and Oliver Ross were always complaining about me coming at them too hard at practice. Kendall Simmons likes it when you come hard. Marvel Smith never complains either. I probably fought Keydrick Vincent more in two years than I fought anybody else in my life.

Coach (John) Mitchell is on my side. He knows I work hard and he encourages me to continue to do that. He knew how hard I worked to make this team in the first place. Mitchell praised my efforts. For me, it was very satisfying.

Of all the veterans, the one who helped me the most was Kimo (von Oelhoffen). He helped all the young guys. I learned a lot from watching Casey Hampton, too. When he was hurt, and I was in there for him he talked to me on the sideline constantly and told me what I needed to do. His technique is so good. It seems to come naturally to Casey. It's like a gift to him. The whole defensive line, like Aaron Smith, they're all good friends and they help whenever they can.

You gotta love Dick LeBeau, our defensive coordinator. He's very supportive. Of all the coaches I've ever played for, he's the easiest to work with. You have a lot of coaches who are ruthless and screaming all the time. They think that's the way to motivate you. I don't care for that. It doesn't work for me.

During my first few years here Tim Lewis was our defensive coordinator. He was always yelling and screaming at me. I don't respond well to that. I remember in my first few practices after Coach LeBeau came here that I did something that I wasn't supposed to do. Coach LeBeau said something to me about it. "Just sit in there, Hoke," he said. The next day that play came up on film, and Coach Mitchell started to get on me a little bit. Coach LeBeau interrupted him and said, "I already got on him about that." Coach LeBeau treats you and talks to you like a man. That's why the guys all want to play for him.

"You're not sure of your future."

There's a lot of insecurity for guys like me in this business. It changes you as a person. You can't be who you are. I was a different person at our practice facility than I was at home. You're not sure of your future. There's a lot of pressure.

A lot of the guys on our team know they're going to be there the next day. It's hard to be comfortable when you're on the borderline all the time. The NFL is a business. They're always looking for someone better. You don't want to see them draft another nose tackle. Or sign a free agent at your position. You hope they feel that they're solid at your position. You hope they're counting on you.

I know I'm going to be Casey's backup at best. But I want to get in better shape and be faster. I want to be better. I want to do everything I can to be ready. I will be running and lifting. I will be playing basketball. I'll work on my conditioning and my footwork.

I want to be a Steeler. Playing in that Super Bowl was the highlight of my playing career so far. The whole season was an amazing experience. Lots of ups and downs. We were 7-and-2 and feeling on top of the world. Then we hit that three-game skid. We lost to the Bengals and we're 7-and-5.

I remember coming to work that week and there was just a dead feeling in the facility. Coach Cowher came in and he got on us, but he wasn't ripping us apart. He did a great job of turning us around. He told us just to worry about the next game, a game with the Bears. We went game to game from then on. The whole ride was exciting.

In the Indy game, I got the call to go in on our kickoff return team when Dan Kreider got hurt. Someone hollered, "Hoke, get in there!" You got to be ready at all times.

215

In the Super Bowl, I played a few plays as backup to Casey. I was in with our field-goal-block team. I usually am on that unit. I played about 12 or 15 plays in the Super Bowl. It was very surreal. The whole playoffs were surreal. After you beat Indy you wanted to celebrate, but you couldn't. There was another game to be played. We had to stay under control. Nobody thought it could be done, but we did it.

We wanted to complete the mission. Nothing would be accomplished until we won the Super Bowl. The way it went down was unreal. No sixth seed had ever won the Super Bowl before.

"That made me a better person."

Now they have put in some rules to curtail the celebrations in the end zone when a touchdown is scored. I don't know what to make of some of those guys. I'm sure some of them are different when they are with family and friends. That's their game. It makes them money. It draws attention to them.

That's not me. There's a song about celebrations by Brad Paisley. About how to celebrate when you do something special. I don't get to do too many special things where I play. It's mostly grunt work. So I've had little occasion to carry on out there on a football field.

You're not going to catch me dancing out there, even if we'd win another Super Bowl.

A lot of what I am came from the way I grew up. My parents made me work. My dad owned a general contracting firm. I worked on construction sites. One summer he got me a job with a plumbing company. I carried 16 pipe on my shoulders up about four flights of stairs. That was hard work. I didn't think I'd finish my work shift. I'd be carrying that pipe for six or seven hours each day.

That made me a better person.

My dad used to say there are three types of people in the world. There are people who make things happen. There are people who watch things happen. There are people who ask, "What happened?"

There was an NFL player who lived in our neighborhood when I was a little kid, maybe between five and eight years old. His name was Carl Ekern, and he was a linebacker for the Los Angeles Rams. He lived on my street in Fountain Valley, near Huntington Beach. My brother and I would go down and visit with this man and he spent time with us, and was so nice to us. He helped foster my interest in playing in the NFL some day.

216

My parents Ed and Cathy Hoke got divorced when I was about three. They both remarried. My mom married again when I was five, and my dad when I was eight. So I had four parents, Ed and Kim Hoke and Frank and Cathy Winger. I'm close to all four of them. Some of my teammates come from single parent homes. I had four parents and they all loved us. There were some challenges. You had to split time between the two families. But you got more gifts at Christmas time and for your birthday and such.

I saw some of the tough situations that came out from divorced families and that's why I want my marriage to succeed. I've told my wife that we'll work our way through any difficulties we happen to encounter. No matter what happens we'll stick together. I learned from my experience; it can be tough. It can be hard on the kids.

It's not hard to be a good husband and father. They just want to be loved and taken care of. You have to let them know every day that you love them, and I do. I don't think I could have made it through my early years in the NFL without my wife.

She caught me crying a few times. I'd come away from a tough practice and I'd come home and she didn't care what had happened out on the football field. She loves me unconditionally. Hey, make sure you don't make me look bad about this. (Hey, Hines Ward and Jerome Bettis have been known to shed some tears in public. So has Bill Cowher. It's okay for men to cry.)

After I made the team the first time, I was just so drained. I just didn't know what was going to happen. I was so emotionally drained that when I got home I just went to bed. I just wanted to sleep.

I'm glad I had the year I had two years ago when Casey Hampton was hurt. I had to have a year like that to show them something, so they knew I could play. I had to have a great camp. I was playing in the first six games before Casey got hurt and that was good. I was ready. I think that year prolonged my career.

Coach Cowher knows how to motivate us. He does a great job of getting us prepared. There's not much messing around in practice. He's a player's coach. And that's not bad. He has the best interest of the players at heart.

He's played the game and he knows what we go through. He wasn't a star, either, so he appreciates guys like me. He knows what we're going through. He suffered the same aches and bruises and disappointments.

The Steelers are special. There's only a few teams that have the kind of history we have. There's so much pride. You had the Steel Curtain. All those Super Bowl trophies. It's consistent. We work so hard for a city that appreciates hard work. You learn in this organization that you have to give back. They don't want a guy all stuck on himself. They love players that are out with the public. The victory parade in Pittsburgh will always stay in my mind. I had two of my boys riding in the parade with me. It was the single-most-exciting experience I've had in Pittsburgh since I came here. Everyone was celebrating in the proper spirit. I didn't see one scuffle in the streets or sidewalks. We celebrated as a city.

You get a lot of confidence from being part of a Super Bowl champion team. Now we want to make another run at it. And I want to be a part of it. I take great pride in being a Pittsburgh Steeler. I'm going to work hard so I can stay here.

Chris Hoke poses at Ross Park Mall during interview.

Bill Hillgrove
On Draft Day 2006

"It's been a good run."

B ill Hillgrove grew up in Garfield in Pittsburgh's East End, playing sports in the streets and playgrounds, and paying attention to what was going on in nearby Oakland where the Steelers, Pirates and Pitt all played in those days. There were times, yes, just like Marv Albert and Lanny Frattare did as kids, that he pretended to be announcing sports contests.

Garfield was famous as the hometown of Harry Greb, "The Pittsburgh Windmill," a world championship fighter who is regarded as the greatest boxer in Pittsburgh history. Hillgrove graduated from Central Catholic High School in 1958 and Duquesne University in 1962. One of his contemporaries was Phil Musick, who also grew up in Garfield and graduated from Peabody High School and Duquesne University, and became one of the finest sportswriters to come out of Pittsburgh, right up there with Myron Cope and George Kiseda.

To get to Garfield from downtown Pittsburgh you travel out Penn Avenue through, in order, The Strip, Lawrenceville and Bloomfield. East Liberty comes after Garfield. My wife Kathie and I lived in an apartment on the border of Garfield and East Liberty for nearly two years after we were married in 1967, and our neighbors in the Pennley Park Apartments included Roberto Clemente and Maury Wills of the Pirates and Moe Becker, the legendary basketball coach at Braddock High School.

Hillgrove got into broadcasting during his student days at Duquesne. He is old enough to remember when Duquesne vs. Dayton in basketball was a big deal in collegiate circles. He can swap first-hand inside stories about Tony Dorsett, Dan Marino, Bill Fralic and Curtis Martin at Pitt.

Hillgrove is a great guy, with the ability to get along with everybody. He's been a popular presence on the Pittsburgh sports scene for nearly 40 years. His rosy face is a familiar one, as he was the sports director at WTAE-TV for many years.

At 65, he was looking forward to his 11th year as the radio voice of the Steelers, and his 33rd year as the radio voice of the Pitt Panthers football team. He has been doing Pitt's basketball broadcasts since 1969, and Steelers' broadcasts since 1995.

This was Saturday, April 29, 2006, Draft Day in the National Football League, and Hillgrove was swapping stories with young sportswriters at a table in the dining facility at the Steelers' training complex on the city's South Side. The first day of the two-day draft would begin in about an hour. Hillgrove had to file some radio reports during the draft.

"It's been a good run," said Hillgrove. "I've had highs and lows with the teams I've followed, but there have been a lot more highs than lows."

That's more than his friend Lanny Frattare, "The Voice of the Pirates" the past 30 years, could say.

Hillgrove replaced Ed Conway as the Pitt broadcaster and Jack Fleming on the Steelers' assignment. Fleming had also been "The Voice of the Mountaineers" for West Virginia football and basketball broadcasts. Joe Tucker had once doubled as the Voice of the Steelers and Duquesne basketball. So Hillgrove respects and is grateful for the position he's in.

Hillgrove and I shared several bonds. We were both Irish and had grown up in similar inner-city neighborhoods and we shared a passion for Pittsburgh sports teams. Our mothers both lived at St. Augustine Plaza, a senior residence in Lawrenceville, in their latter years. I often took my mother to lunch in Lawrenceville, Bloomfield and Garfield, so I am familiar with those neighborhoods.

Hillgrove has lived in Murrysville for many years, but he has never forgotten where he came from. He's still a "Pittsburgh guy." He remains one of the positive voices on the sports scene and, indeed, one of the most popular personalities in his field.

"They've got a great chemistry."

Asked to assess the character of the current Steelers, Hillgrove offered a thoughtful pause and proceeded to say, "I spend enough time with these guys, traveling with them to and from games on most of the charters, to get a feel for their character. I see how they act going through security checks and such, and in the hotel lobby. There are a lot of polite people on the Steelers' squad. I see the way they interact with each other, and with other people. They have fun with each other."

Sitting in the Steelers' dining area, one can see the parking lot outside where Joey Porter usually parks his black Hummer, and the trees that line the shore of the Monongahela River. Looking out that way, Hillgrove was reminded of an incident during the 2005 season. He related that Kimo von Oelhoffen and Aaron Smith dared Chris Hoke to dive in the river in pads after practice one day. They told Hoke they'd each give him $500 if he'd accept their challenge. "Hoke walked out and jumped in the river," said Hillgrove. "He looked like some kind of swamp monster when he emerged from the water, and swam to shore. He was covered with all kind of slimy stuff. Everyone had a big laugh.

"Everyone got a big laugh except Bill Cowher. He read the riot act to Hoke. 'If you get so much as a sniffle the fine is $1,000,' Cowher told him. So Hoke would have to give back the $1,000 he got for going in the drink. He was lucky that he never caught a cold."

Chris Hoke added to this epic tale in a later interview: "That was on Thanksgiving morning. It was 20 degrees out and it was snowing. It was really cold and miserable. Coach Cowher told me that if I so much as sniffled I'd have to pay him $100 more than I made from going in."

Almost as if on cue, Cowher appeared in the parking lot and we watched him approaching the front door of the Steelers' facility. It was 12:20 p.m., about 40 minutes before the draft would begin with the Houston Texans making the first selection. Cowher was dressed casually. It was going to be a long day.

"The head coach sets the tone," said Hillgrove. "He's the guy who draws the line in the sand. He's going to tell everyone where they're supposed to be."

I asked Hillgrove if he'd gotten close to Cowher during his stay with the Steelers. "He won't let you know him," said Hillgrove. "He keeps you at arm's length. I'm sure he has some close friends he's more at ease with. He's more apt to be relaxed around me at a golf tournament. He'll chat with me a little there. Here it's all business. We tape a pre-game show each week. I go over some things before we do the taping to see what he wants to talk about, and what he doesn't want to talk about. I talk to him about sensitive issues beforehand so I know how to handle it.

"When Ben had the bad thumb I asked Bill, 'What do we do about the quarterback position?' He said, 'We don't discuss the quarterback position.' And that's it. It's his show. He'll give me background so I know what's going on, but there's only so much he personally wants to talk about on the air. I tape the show on Friday, so we don't want to do anything that will be dated by Sunday.

"I think Bill's gotten a little more comfortable with some of the media through the years. He's become a little more engaging with the media."

Cowher came by me later on, when I was sitting with Craig Wolfley and Tunch Ilkin, watching the draft proceedings. He nodded at each of us, but didn't pause for any small talk.

Hillgrove felt there were a few players who helped Cowher set the standards for what the team needs to do to remain successful.

"It takes guys like Jerome Bettis and Jeff Hartings and Joey Porter and James Farrior to step forward," continued Hillgrove. "These are the guys who took it upon themselves to show the way for everyone else. From my view, they've got a great chemistry.

"Like the way Duce Staley handled his situation. Here's a guy whose ego had to be beaten badly. He's not a pup. He didn't dress for most of the games, even when he was healthy enough to play, yet he never balked about it. It had to pain him. He could have been disruptive, but he wasn't. Little things like that add up. He was supportive of the people who were playing at this position.

"They have a lottery when they're on the planes going to games. Each one of them puts a $20 bill in the pot. They write their names on the bill. They draw a bill and whose ever name is on it wins the pot. And guess who collected the money? It was Jerome Bettis. You might think they'd get a rookie to collect the money.

"Players of eight years or more in the NFL get to sit in front class. Cowher and Dan Rooney aren't up there. They ride coach with the rest of the team. When I see Jerome Bettis walking through the plane picking up the money, and having a light word for everybody, it tells me a lot about him and them."

Jack Butler

"Sundays became almost a redeeming day for me."

Pitt had a losing season in 2005 in Dave Wannstedt's first season as head coach, but the Steelers had a sensational run, rallying in the stretch run to win Super Bowl XL.

"Saturdays were disappointing to me," said Hillgrove, "so Sundays became almost a redeeming day for me. I love 2-and-0 weekends. It puts a spring in your step."

Hillgrove says the first Steeler he was aware of, when he was a kid back in the early '50s, was Joe Geri, the tailback when the Steelers still employed the single-wing offense. "He was the do-all back," recalled Hillgrove, "and he was one of the guys my uncles talked about at family get-togethers. They'd talk about Jimmy Finks, Fran Rogel, Lynn Chandnois, Johnny Lattner, Ernie Stautner, Jack Butler and Dale Dodrill. Those guys often physically beat up the opposing team, but we usually came up on the short end of the score.

"I rode the 77/54 trolley from Garfield to Lawrenceville in those days," added Hillgrove. "One time I was on one of those streetcars and I saw Murry Dickson, the Pirates' best pitcher, sitting in the back and he had a ballglove on his hand. It's unlikely you'd ever see a ballplayer riding a bus around the city these days, not even Jerome."

Hillgrove likes to tell stories about some of the Pitt guys he got to know well, such as Marino and Dorsett and Curtis Martin. "I know Chuck Noll brought Danny in for a workout," said Hillgrove. "He had him throwing the ball to someone like John Stallworth, but I'm not sure it was Stallworth. Noll told Marino 'We love you. You're going to be a great quarterback, but we don't need another quarterback right now as much as we need some help defensively.' I was with Danny on the day of the draft (in 1983) and I saw him get sick after the Jets drafted Ken O'Brien. Danny finally got a phone call and I heard him say 'yes' and 'yes' and it was Don Shula on the other end of the phone. He had asked him, I later learned, if he was in good health and he asked him if he wanted to play for the Miami Dolphins."

I told Hillgrove a good story I had heard from Danny's dad. "People were always telling me I must've been so disappointed when Danny didn't get drafted by the Steelers and I'd tell them, 'Yeah, I really miss all those vacations on the North Side," said Mr. Marino. "I told Danny the later he was drafted the better team he'd be playing for. It turned out that way for sure."

Hillgrove recalled talking to Danny's dad that draft day. "He told me that was the best thing that could've happened to Danny," said Hillgrove. "He knew he'd get to play right away. That never would have happened here.

"Dallas made a multi-player swap with Seattle to get the draft pick to get Dorsett and the Steelers never had a crack at him. The rap on Curtis Martin when he was at Pitt was that he never paid attention to lifting weights. And he couldn't finish a college season. I remember Tom Donohoe telling me that when he was the head of the Steelers' player personnel department. Martin got with Bill Parcells in New England and he got on the weights and he got endurance."

Hillgrove didn't know what to think when the Steelers lost three straight games and were 7-5 and had to win every game just to get a wildcard berth in the playoffs. "In that stretch," pointed out Hillgrove, "the Steelers ended the Bears' winning streak, the Vikings' winning streak and kicked the Browns' butts royally. They made the Lions look good in the final game of the regular season for a half before they got their act together and won the game. They had made Harrington look like an all-pro quarterback. We had been taking them one game at a time, and Cowher got them to think that way.

"That was so obvious. I think they'd have beaten Cincinnati in the playoffs even if their quarterback (Carson Palmer) hadn't gotten hurt. The big game was beating the Colts in Indianapolis. Then they played great when they won at Denver. They didn't play their best against the Seahawks in the Super Bowl, but they made the big plays when they had to to win the game."

Jim O'Brien

Bill Hillgrove and Foge Fazio appear at annual Thompson Club Sports Dinner in West Mifflin.

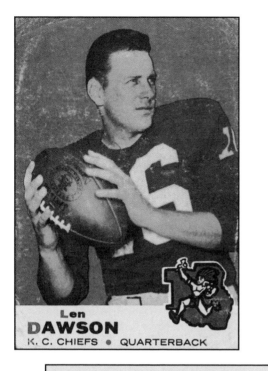

Len
DAWSON
K. C. CHIEFS • QUARTERBACK

EARL MORRALL
QUARTERBACK   PITTSBURGH STEELERS

"If I knew I was going to live this long,
I'd have taken better care of myself."
— **Ray Mathews**

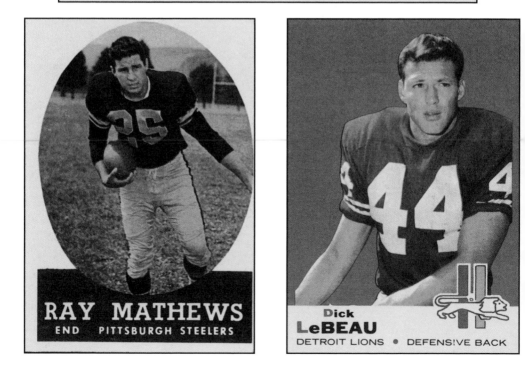

RAY MATHEWS
END   PITTSBURGH STEELERS

Dick
LeBEAU
DETROIT LIONS • DEFENSIVE BACK

Jeff Reed
He wouldn't quit kicking

"He's got a good mind-set."
— Kevin Colbert

Kickers are often real characters. They are just a different breed, cut from a different cloth than the rest of the players on a football team. Jeff Reed is definitely a different breed. His dark hair, for instance, stands straight up with the help of some sticky stuff. It looks like he uses TNT instead of a comb. He wears diamond earrings. He has a mischievous smile.

When Jeffrey Montgomery Reed was a rookie with the Steelers in 2002, the team's punter, Josh Miller, reflected on Reed's appearance: "He'll grow out of it someday." Some of his teammates call him "Skippy."

As he was preparing for his fourth season with the Steelers and the National Football League wars, Reed remained the same. He was 27, but he still looked like a college kid. Now he was keeping company with Chris Gardocki, who had replaced Miller as the Steelers' punter prior to the 2004 season, signed as a free agent from the Cleveland Browns.

Punters and place-kickers always hang out together at training camp, whether it's at the UPMC Sports Performance Complex on the South Side or at St. Vincent College in Latrobe. They work out together, off to themselves with special teams coach Kevin Spencer. They think differently and act differently than the rest of the cast.

"He can wear the earrings and the flashy haircut," said Spencer, "but you'd better be a tough son-of-a-gun on game day, and he's all that."

Reed is one of the most reliable kickers in the NFL and the Steelers are lucky to have him. He won a kicking contest with three other job applicants on a cold and windy day at Heinz Field late in the 2002 season. Kevin Colbert, the football operations director of the Steelers, remembers that day well. He and Bill Cowher checked out the place-kicking candidates that blustery afternoon.

It was Reed's eighth pro tryout. Reed refused to give up in his quest to find a job in the NFL.

"The conditions couldn't have been worse," recalled Colbert, "but Bill and I wanted to see them kicking under conditions they might have to kick under in Pittsburgh. Heinz Field had gotten a reputation already as a kicker's nightmare. Kris Brown had signed as a free agent with Houston after his first year here when he had problems kicking at Heinz Field. His replacement Todd Peterson had injured his ribs and we needed a kicker. None of the kickers were that consistent that day, but Jeff was definitely the best of the bunch.

There was no doubt in our minds he was the best. But Bill and I didn't come away convinced we had the kicker for our future."

Reed responded to the challenge and he's been a good one. "He's solid and he's got a good mind-set," said Colbert. "He's tough-minded. He wants to kick under pressure. So far, he's met the challenge quite nicely. We're happy we have Jeff Reed."

"He always comes through," said teammate Joey Porter.

"Kicking is a lonely job," said Hines Ward. "But we're all behind Jeff. He's come through for us in some big games. We know Jeff is vital to us."

"Think positive thoughts and make the kick."

I don't think Jeff Reed missed a meal during the Steelers' May and June mini-camp and coaches sessions at their South Side facility. He's 5-11, 232 pounds and requires three meals a day to maintain his solid stature. He's ready to make a tackle on kick-offs if necessary. He had hip surgery early in 2004, but it never hindered him.

I noticed that Reed took the time to bow his head and say a silent prayer before each meal. That tells you something about Reed. It was usually the only time Jeff Reed was silent during the meal. He's a talker. He majored in journalism with a minor in communications at the University of North Carolina.

He was a good student as well as an ace kicker at the Chapel Hill campus. He set a school record with 66 consecutive extra points. He connected on 28 of 36 field goal attempts. He had never kicked in a college game until the 2000 season, but he was one of the most consistent kickers in the country over his last two seasons at school. He was among the finalists for the Lou Groza Award given to the best college place-kicker. Reed was a walk-on candidate but he won a scholarship with his efforts. He was a first-team Academic All-America. So he's smart, too. He's also a bit of a cutup.

He was pictured with his left hand on the shoulder of President Bush during the team's visit to The White House as Super Bowl winners in early June. His right hand flashed a V for Victory sign. A picture of that appeared in the Pittsburgh newspapers and in other publications around the country. He heard from some of his old classmates about that one. President Bush was flanked by Reed and Steelers' nose tackle Casey Hampton. President Bush had met Hampton when he was the governor of Texas and Hampton was an All-American on the state's favorite college football team.

Reed's resume at North Carolina was an impressive one, yet he was not taken in the college draft. Soon after the Steelers signed him on November 19, 2002, he set a Steelers' record with six field goals in a game at Jacksonville on December 1.

Jeff Reed

Photos by George Gojkovich/Getty Images

He was a star soccer player in high school at East Mecklenburg in Charlotte. He wanted to be a pro soccer player. "But even when I was playing soccer, I dreamed of kicking a game-winning field goal in the Super Bowl someday."

He didn't get a chance to kick a field goal in Super Bowl XL, but he was three-for-three on extra-point attempts. He's kicked some game-winning field goals in the closing seconds for the Steelers on several occasions. He hit on 24 of 29 field goal attempts during the 2005 season. He made 28 of 33 kicks the previous season, and was 92 for 113 in his four seasons with the Steelers. He broke Gary Anderson's team record of 19 field goals without a miss when he made 22 straight, stretching from the 2004 season to the start of the 2005 season.

Reed has a simple philosophy about his role with the Steelers: "Think positive thoughts and make the kick."

He remembers how he felt when Mike Vanderjagt of the Indianapolis Colts missed wide right on a 46-yard field goal attempt to allow the Steelers to preserve a 21-18 win in the playoffs in January of 2006.

"At the time, I was so happy he missed it, of course," recalled Reed. "I don't want it to happen to anybody. I felt bad for him later. Kickers are part of a fraternity; that's why. Normally, we root for each other."

His hero is Adam Vinatieri, who has replaced Vanderjagt with the Indianapolis Colts. "Adam is a great role model for me," said Reed. "I want to be like he is someday."

When he was younger, Reed's hero was pro kicker John Carney. That's why he wears No. 3, which is Carney's number.

Reed was three-for-three as far as field goals went in the playoffs and 14-for-14 in extra-point kicks. He hit a 47-yarder to start the scoring against Denver in the AFC championship game. That set a good tone for the visiting team.

"I'm not out to prove anything," remarked Reed going into the Super Bowl. "I'm out to do my job and help the team win."

There's a good reason Reed smiles so much. He signed a five-year contract before the 2005 season for $7.5 million, including a $1.5 million signing bonus.

He comes from a sports-minded family. His father, Morris, played basketball at Wichita State University, and his mother, Pam, was a cheerleader at Wichita State University. His sister, Kristen, played soccer at UNC-Charlotte and one year professionally for the Carolina Speed. Jeff was born in Kansas City on April 9, 1979.

WDVE personality Jim Krenn admits to having a "man crush" on Steelers quarterback Ben Roethlisberger. "He's a great guy," says Krenn. "He's a guy you want to hang out with or live vicariously through."

Jeff Reed:

"I had to find something in sports."

If I were to write a headline on the story of my life it would be Nothing Comes Easy. That's pretty routine, I realize, but it would sum up my story. My No. 1 dream was to play professional soccer. I didn't even think about playing football until my junior year in high school.

I kicked a football in a game for the first time in my senior year in high school. I walked on as a freshman at the University of North Carolina and didn't become the No. 1 kicker until my junior and senior seasons.

I lived my life for sports. And I used to wonder what I would do without a sport. I'd be nothing. I had to find something in sports. I watch sports all the time on television. I watch the Women's College Baseball World Series. I'll be watching the World Cup; I'm still a big soccer fan. I have a Super Bowl ring on my finger now. It reminds me of the influence of my father and my coaches. They were after me when I was in middle school to try kicking a field goal and I resisted. I was a soccer player. I was trying to be a good soccer player.

I didn't want to mess up my form. They were saying to me, "Just give it a shot."

I went to an NKS (National Kicking Service) camp. A fellow named Gene Muriarty helped me learn how to kick a football. He was a real blessing in my life. I went out for my high school football team my senior year. I had the foot for it and the leg for it. I was given this talent by God.

I made the all-conference team and all-county. I kicked a 54-yard field goal in high school. That was my longest. I was kicking for East Mecklenburg High School in Southeast Charlotte. I got the chance to make the team at the University of North Carolina and I made the most of it. John Bunting was the coach and I'm grateful for the opportunity he gave me. I'm close to him and his wife. They were great to me.

I wasn't taken in the NFL college draft, but I signed as a free agent with the New Orleans Saints. John Carney was there and he's been around a long, long time. I looked up to that guy. Jim Haslett was the head coach at the time, and he really liked me. He told me I impressed him during the time I was with the Saints. I kicked two field goals in the pre-season.

Now it's my livelihood. Nobody is going to take it away from me. It's in my court. I want to get better, become one of the most reliable kickers in the league. Adam Vinatieri has been the best one with the New England Patriots, and now he's been signed to play for the Indianapolis Colts. I know how much he's respected. He's replacing Mike Vanderjagt. I don't know if the Colts cut Vanderjagt because he missed that field goal against us that would have tied the game and sent it into overtime. He'd been so sure-footed there for so long, but I think he gave them other reasons to release him.

I know I had a tryout with the New York Giants, Jacksonville, Detroit, Tampa Bay, Seattle twice and all of those were in 2002. I may have left a team or two out.

My tryout for the Steelers might have been my last opportunity to play pro football. I'd been to about seven pro tryouts when I came to Pittsburgh. I was one of four kickers at Heinz Field. It was a terrible day. Heinz Field had a reputation for being a tough place to kick. Kris Brown got out of here after one year when he had the chance.

Todd Peterson took his place, but then he suffered a broken rib and the Steelers were desperate for a kicker. It was before Week Ten of the 2002 season.

It was about 30 degrees that day. It was very windy. The field was horrible. There was sand all over the place. And it was sleeting. I was in shorts, and had short sleeves on my jersey. All the guys had the wrong cleats; we were all slipping. We all missed about four kicks, but I didn't do that badly.

We were all in the same boat. Coach Cowher was there. After we did the kicking we went back to the Steelers' facility on the South Side. Coach Cowher and Kevin Colbert spoke to me. Cowher said, "We picked you to play on Sunday." I was so excited. If you knew how crazy I am about football you could appreciate how I felt.

And now I'm with the Steelers and we just visited The White House to see President Bush. It was great seeing the President of our country. I had my hand on the President's shoulder and they showed it on television. Now I'm famous. There's the guy who runs the country and he's next to the place-kicker of the Pittsburgh Steelers.

No one cracks more jokes than I do, but this was no joking situation. I was serious. I thought it was really cool. You couldn't pay me enough money to be the President. People think my job has pressure. By comparison, my job is a walk in the park. It was great to tour all the rooms and learn about the history of The White House. To see how secure he is. You could see riflemen on the roof. I was in the front row for the actual ceremony because I'm one of the shorter guys. The man who runs our country is an arm's length away from me. He looked me in the eyes. I always have a comeback line, but I didn't even say "Thank you." I didn't want to say anything stupid.

He told us that he knew something about comebacks. Then we came back to Pittsburgh and we got our Super Bowl rings.

It's still hard to believe what we've experienced over the past six or seven months. You don't know if it's reality. One in a million people, probably less than that, get to do what I've done. Every time I put the ring on my finger I get goosebumps. I've been out to a few public events already, like a wrestling show at the Mellon Arena with a bunch of the guys. They showed us on TV. We got a standing ovation there. We were introduced at a Pitt basketball game and we got a standing ovation. Everyone wants to see the ring. It's great. This is something I can't afford to misplace.

I've had a lot of phone calls from family and friends. They said they couldn't believe I was right there before the President, and that I'd been to The White House.

My parents were present for the ring ceremony at Heinz Field and my parents had never met Bill Cowher before, so they were excited about that. I introduced him to my parents and my sister. Coach Cowher told my father, "I don't think we'd have done it without him." That was nice of him to say that to my parents. It meant a lot to us.

"You've got to come through for them."

My goal now is to be the best I can be. I want to be more successful. I want to be the best. I want to have the kind of reputation and respect as Adam Vinatieri. I want people to know I'm going to kick that field goal, that they can count on me to do it. That's my role here.

I tell Kevin Colbert all the time how much I appreciate the opportunity he gave me. I don't take these things for granted. Sometimes you forget where you come from, but I hope I never do. Coach Cowher told us it's hard to get where we are, but that it's even harder to stay there.

Coach Cowher puts pressure on you, but it's a positive pressure. If you can kick in front of him in practice, you can kick for him in a game.

When the pressure is on you, and your team gets you in position, you've got to come through for them. I'm here to make kicks.

> *"It's always fun to play football.*
> *No matter what it is; to throw the football*
> *around is always fun."*
> — **Dan Marino**

Tunch Ilkin
On a mission

"Nice guys can finish first."

Steelers' fans sometimes forget that Tunch Ilkin was cut from the squad near the end of his first training camp with the team at St. Vincent College in 1980. He went home to Chicago and worked at a health club, looking after the locker room. He cleaned toilets among other things — he can't forget that — and he worked out and he stayed in shape.

He might never have been heard from again.

But we hear Tunch Ilkin and his closest friend, Craig Wolfley, another former offensive lineman with the Steelers, on a non-stop basis, or so it seems, on the television and radio throughout the year in Pittsburgh. Tunch Ilkin counts his blessings every day and says "thank you" to the Lord with his prayers and actions. Ilkin and Wolfley form a formidable team.

Their thoughts and opinions about the Steelers and sports in general in Pittsburgh, as they have the scope of their interests, are sought everywhere. They not only served as analysts and reporters on the Steelers' radio network (WDVE-FM, 102.5), but they had a morning show on WGBB-AM (970). They have pre-game shows and post-game shows and they are frequent guests on the other sports talk shows in Pittsburgh. They are called upon to offer their views on the Steelers to radio stations throughout the National Football League world. Ilkin left "In the Locker Room with Tunch Ilkin and Wolf" at mid-summer to devote more time to his church ministry.

They can talk. They keep it clean, and they have great enthusiasm and spirit. They laugh at each other. I liked to start my workday listening to their Monday-through-Friday talk show. It was like an extra cup of coffee and orange juice to get you going. It started at 7 a.m. and ran to 10 a.m. Then I usually turned to ESPN Radio (1250 AM) and caught Guy Junker and Eddy Crow.

My wife Kathie leaves the house to go to work just before 7 a.m. She has to be at Allegheny General Hospital on the North Side by 7:30. She is a social worker in the Cancer Center there. She's now in her 15th year in that role. So I am home alone. I don't like to be alone. So I listened to "In The Locker Room With Tunch and Wolf" most mornings. They are good company. They're fun to listen to. You feel like you're in the locker room with them and their guests. They enjoy each other's company and they have great guests. During the season, they get Steelers to call their show for interviews early in the morning. So the Steelers must love and trust these guys.

Tunch and Wolf have been best of friends ever since they came to the Steelers in the summer of 1980. Their love for one another

Tunch Ilkin and Craig Wolfley get dressed up for 2006 Mel Blount Youth Home Celebrity Dinner at Hilton. Ilkin, below, visits author Jim O'Brien at his home in Upper St. Clair for interview for this book.

Photos by Jim O'Brien

comes across clearly on the air. They are like brothers fussing with each other at the breakfast table before going off to school. They are never lost for words. They don't always choose the right words — and they poke fun at one another for such gaffes — but they keep on talkin'. When Wolfley can't find the right word he just makes one up. "Mojo" and "Mojination" are among Wolfley's favorites. "He's created a Mojo Monster," complains Ilkin. You never hear too many "ing" sounds at the end of words when they go at it, but who cares?

Their callers don't always choose the right words, either. It's a Pittsburgh characteristic. But they get their points across. Ilkin and Wolfley are at their best, and most comfortable, talking football and Steeler stuff. But, to their credit, they have made the effort and do their homework to catch up on other sports and interests as well.

A voice-over on the show says: "And you thought Seinfeld was a show about nothing. . ." Ilkin closes each show by saying, "As my father used to say, 'that's all what it is.'"

Sometimes Ilkin comes up with a gem such as "There's an old Turkish proverb: If you hang out with a blind person you'll go cross-eyed."

Consider that bit of wisdom for a while.

"I listen to those guys every morning, and sometimes my son is in the car, and I don't have to worry about what they're going to say," said Paul Dunn, the offensive line coach of the Pitt Panthers, and a former Pitt player. "They're a riot. They could make you pee your pants."

When a caller makes an off-color remark, Ilkin is quick to admonish them. "Hey, this is a family show!" he'll shout. "Let's keep it clean, huh?"

When Wolfley seems headed into anything that Ilkin isn't comfortable with, he'll rein him in. "Wolf, let's not go there."

They do their shows from a variety of sites, in addition to the radio studio in Green Tree. They often do shows from sites such as the Light of Life Mission on the North Side, one of their pet non-profit projects. Ilkin has served on the board there for many years, and they both help in fund-raising drives. Ilkin finds time to hang out with the guys, mostly down-on-their-luck men who are looking for a warm meal and a safe place to hang out. Some women come in on occasion and are taken care of as well. It's on the same street, East North Avenue, as Allegheny General Hospital. A passerby can catch lines forming outside, even on the coldest winter days, at meal times.

Ilkin and Wolfley are big guys with big hearts. Ilkin was a 6-3, 265-pound tackle and he played tight end in short-yardage situations. He weighs a lot less now. With his Marine crewcut and well-chiseled features he is absolutely buff these days. He was wearing a casual blue and gray sweatshirt, dark sweatpants and white sneakers when he appeared at my door. He and Wolfley have a strong spiritual side, and take pride in doing good wherever they are wanted. They speak at schools and churches and spread the gospel of the Steelers and spiritual causes. They are missionaries of sorts. They have other business interests. They take pride in their respective families. They have learned to sleep fast.

They came to the team a year after the Steelers had won their fourth Super Bowl in six years. They thought they'd be a part of more championship teams. It didn't work out that way. That's why 2005 and 2006 were so special to them as well as the Steelers and the Steeler Nation. They finally were associated with a Steelers team that won a Super Bowl.

When one of the Steelers' linemen got hurt midway through the 1980 season, Chuck Noll had his personnel people call Ilkin in Chicago and get him back in the fold. Ilkin never looked back. He had one of the longest playing tours with the team, putting in 13 seasons with the Steelers and one more with the Green Bay Packers before he packed it in. He made some big money in Green Bay, and it was like a bonus.

"And to think it almost didn't happen, yeah. That's the grace of God. But I never thought of 'What if?' I always felt I would play pro football," said Ilkin.

Bill Cowher has offered Ilkin a job on his coaching staff, but Ilkin, after wrestling with his decision, turned it down. He has helped out on occasion with different drills.

He had always been a popular player and always got along with the media. So he was asked to do interviews and then offer commentaries and before long his face was a familiar one on Pittsburgh television, and his voice on Pittsburgh radio stations.

One of his teammates who joined the Steelers in 1980 was Mark Malone, a quarterback who was the team's top draft choice. Malone was interested in a career in television, and he encouraged Ilkin to do the same. Ilkin got after his buddy Craig Wolfley to join him in that regard. He knew Wolfley was funny, and smarter than he lets on, and kept after him to pursue similar opportunities in the Pittsburgh market.

He paid a visit on Wednesday, March 22, 2006 to my home in Upper St. Clair, about four miles from his own home at the other end of the community. He stayed for two hours and shared his thoughts on many subjects relating to the Steelers.

"Let's talk Turkey."
— Myron Cope

His full name is Tunch Ali Ilkin. He was born in Istanbul, Turkey on September 25, 1957. He was 48 at the time of his visit. According to the Steelers' 1987 press guide, his name is pronounced Toonch Ill-kin.

Nowadays, it's pronounced Tunch as in Punch. For one thing, he offers clinics on Power Punch blocking techniques. For another, it plays better on all the commercials he does on radio and TV. And Myron Cope could pronounce it better and in less time that way.

No matter how you say it, Tunch Ilkin is one former Steelers' player who is doing quite well, thank you. He proves that it pays to be a nice guy. Everybody who loves Raymond also loves Tunch. He was always a media favorite and he made the switch to the other side nicely. He managed to remain friendly with all the fellows in the locker room as well.

He was a nice guy to begin with, when he first reported to the Steelers in 1980 as a sixth round draft choice from Indiana State University in Terre Haute, Indiana. His wife Sharon was a cheerleader at Indiana State. She once appeared on the cover of *Sports Illustrated* with one of the Sycamores' basketball players, a blond fellow from French Lick, Indiana named Larry Bird.

Ilkin's kids have since asked their dad why he never made the cover of *SI* since Mom did. The best Ilkin could do was to have his shoe or helmet show up on the edges of an *SI* cover featuring one of his teammates. At least, he claims it was his shoe or helmet.

Ilkin, for the record, actually graduated from Indiana State with a degree in radio broadcasting, so he knew what he wanted to be when he was a young man.

"I was a center when I came to the Steelers," recalled Ilkin. "I saw Mike Webster and how great he was and I thought I'd never get on the field. So I learned to play tackle. You have to find a place to play."

Ilkin played in 26 games his first two seasons, but didn't start until the final game of his third season, 1982, when he opened against the Cleveland Browns. He managed to play 13 seasons with the Steelers. There are only seven Steelers who've seen more service time with the Black and Gold and five of them — Mike Webster, John Stallworth, Mel Blount, Terry Bradshaw and Ernie Stautner — are in the Pro Football Hall of Fame.

There were a lot of nice guys in that Steelers' draft class of 1980, back when I was covering the club for *The Pittsburgh Press*. So I can vouch for their outstanding virtues. The class included Mark Malone, Bob Kohrs, Bill Hurley, Craig Wolfley, Frank Pollard and Tyrone McGriff.

In review, Ilkin turned out to be the most productive player from that class, with Wolfley a close second. Ilkin is the only one who ever played in the Pro Bowl, and he did it twice, in 1989 and 1990. McGriff died in 2001, which was a blow to everybody in the class. He had been the last player taken in the entire draft year and he made the team. They figured they, too, would be playing in Super Bowls. But it never happened.

The kid from Turkey is doing just fine. His mother, who was Miss Turkey in 1950 and a contestant in Miss World, was so proud of him.

He was so impressed and influenced by some of the Steelers he met at St. Vincent, and their strong religious acumen, that he converted from being a Muslim, then an agnostic, to a Christian. He was so fearful of what his father would say that he never told him. His dad learned of the decision two years later, and didn't make a big deal about it. Soon after, both his father and mother became Christians as well.

Ilkin and Wolfley— they're like Dean Martin and Jerry Lewis, or Bud Abbott and Lou Costello — do a lot of Christian inspirational talks. They attract crowds because they're still Steelers, but they hold them because they have something genuine and good to offer.

Tunch and Sharon have three children. They are Tanner, now 20 and living in an apartment in Carnegie, and Natalie, 17, a junior at Upper St. Clair High School, and Clay, 15, a freshman. "They all came to Detroit for the Super Bowl, and they said it was the best time of their lives. We went to the post-game party and had a great time."

Tunch Ilkin:

"We wanted to do something different."

Wolf and I came up with this idea to do a show together and we said we'd sell the ad time ourselves. We wanted to do something different. We wanted a show that everybody could listen to, including children. We're family guys. We're both happily married and we wanted to celebrate those things. We wanted to share our ideas and values. If we could make a dollar doing that that would be good, too.

We wanted to recreate what it was like in the locker room. Guys getting on one another, throwing jabs at their respective schools, getting on each other's cases.

I don't know if the two of us could make it in any other city. Pittsburgh is different. It embraced Myron Cope and he often said his voice wasn't a radio voice. We thought we could make it here.

Our timing couldn't have been better. We have been at it for about 18 or 19 months now. The first Steelers' season was a 15-1 season, and then they win the Super Bowl. It doesn't get any better. It's still tough to sell ad time, but it's gotten a little easier. We have found an audience.

We're going to work hard, not taking anything for granted, to make sure we do our best to keep it. Football is what we know best, but we're working hard to get up to snuff with other stuff as well.

The Steelers have become a year-round story, but we like to talk about the Pirates and the Penguins, Pitt and the other colleges, and we know a little bit about boxing and some other sports.

We're showing people that you can still have standards and be on the air without compromising your values. We're happily married men and we celebrate the Lord.

I was fortunate to come here and be surrounded by the kind of people I was surrounded by. So many of the Pittsburgh Steelers had such strong faith. In giving my life to Christ — I can remember it so vividly — I changed my life.

Someone like Jon Kolb had such an impact on my life. My roomie, Craig Wolfley, impressed me so much the way he dealt with his father's illness and death while we were at camp. He had such inner strength, a sense of acceptance. I wanted to know more about how he was able to be that way. We've had a great friendship for 26 years. There's a chemistry there, and that's why we work so well together when we've teamed on TV or the radio.

"I have come a long way."

I was a free agent the first year there was free agency. The Steelers didn't need me anymore. They felt they had a young player in Leon Searcy who was ready to take over the position. Bill was up front with me, and he told me he wanted me to stay around as insurance. Green Bay signed me as a starter for starter's money and it was more than I'd made to play for the Steelers. Mike Holmgren was looking for some veterans to show the way in Green Bay, and they came after me. It was a no-brainer.

Then I came back to Pittsburgh a year later. I hadn't moved. This was going to be my home. And I have had one opportunity after another here. I was lucky that Mark Malone left WPXI to go to ESPN. They had an opening, and they invited me to take his place. I learned a lot from the way Mark approached it. He had really worked at learning the TV business. He did everything behind the scenes as well as on camera. He was a good role model.

It was great to work with Bill Hillgrove and Myron Cope. We had a great time doing the games. It was a lot of fun. I've heard so many of Myron's old stories. We poked fun at each other during the games. I missed him this past year. Bill is a solid pro. He sets the table and gets us back on track when we wander.

I just thank God for all he's given my family and me. I've had my lovely wife Sharon (Senefeld) for 24 years this April. I have come a long way since I came to this country from

Turkey when I was 2½ years old. I was probably shy in school in the beginning because I was an immigrant and I had a strange name. I used to tell people my name was Tom when I was in high school, but I had a girlfriend named Carol who convinced me that Tunch was really a special name. So I went back to being Tunch Ilkin. I've been comfortable with being Tunch Ilkin ever since.

"They truly love one another."

I think this current Steelers' team has proven something. You want me to capture it in one sentence, right? Nice guys can finish first. Good guys can be winners. The first thing that comes to my mind about this team is that they truly love one another.

You saw how Hines Ward broke down and cried after the Steelers lost to the Patriots in the AFC championship game the year before because he thought the team had let down its veteran leader Jerome Bettis.

Everyone had a desire to win for some one else. They wanted to win for Jerome; they wanted to win for Bill (Cowher). They wanted to win for (Dick) LeBeau. They wanted to win for the veteran guys.

I watch practice every day. There's a real playfulness about it. There are footraces to get to the ball. There's a lot of fun in the locker room. They play a lot of games with one another. There's a lot of banter.

I think people see that. I think the fans feel that. They look at the character of the players. They are real stand-up guys. They are the kind of guys you'd like your kids to bring home as friends.

How'd it come about? That's a good question. The leadership is critical. It is huge. You have to look at Dan Rooney, the owner, and his son, Art III, who's now the president of the team, and Bill Cowher, the head coach, and Kevin Colbert, the director of football operations.

They want the Steelers to be special. They talk about the Steelers wanting to do it right, caring about character. Most teams pay lip service to that sort of thing. But I think these guys here are serious and genuine about it. One bad person can tear down a team. We saw that with Terrell Owens with the Philadelphia Eagles. You see it elsewhere in sports today. That's too bad. I don't think it was a shock to a lot of people that T.O. could do that. He's got a bad track record.

I'm a good friend of Greg Napp. He was an assistant coach with the San Francisco 49ers. He's probably the last guy who anybody should go off on, and I'll never forget seeing T.O. hollering at him on the sideline during a televised game. I worked with Greg on some NFL training films. He's a good person and he knows his stuff. I saw him during a Monday Night game during the pre-season and I asked him how his boy T.O. was doing, and he didn't say anything negative about him. He just said, "To know T.O. is to love T.O." He always takes the high road. I've heard T.O. didn't have a dad at home when he was growing up, and that his upbringing was difficult. But other guys have similar stories and they don't behave the way he does. You should always respect your teammates and your opponents.

"I don't know Bill Cowher very well."

I think Bill Cowher has changed a bit in the way he directs the Steelers. I think he delegates more to his assistant coaches. I think that's part of the maturation process. He's got a great staff of assistants. He has great coaches and he allows them to do their jobs. When you're in a leadership position, you learn you can trust people to do what they're supposed to do.

I look at Russ Grimm and Ken Whisenhunt, Dick LeBeau and Dick Hoak, John Mitchell and the rest of those guys, and it's just a great group of coaches. They know what they're doing. It's a professional staff. Bill Cowher has always had good assistants. Several of them have moved on to become head coaches and coordinators at other teams, and Bill just goes out and brings in other good coaches.

I don't know Bill Cowher very well. He's always been a good guy to me, but we don't talk about anything that's revealing.

I wasn't close to Chuck Noll when he was my coach. Because he was the coach. We feared him. But I love Chuck. I go up and hug Chuck when I see him now. To see Chuck now is different. He's my old coach. It's great to visit with him. In my playing days, he was such an intimidating person. You were never sure when the conversation should end. You were awkward around him.

Everybody who played for him is an admirer. You talk to Joe Greene or anyone who was on our football team and they'll tell you. We all find ourselves saying things he said, repeating his philosophy about so many things. If you do any coaching you can't help but repeat things he said. Like: "Understand what we're trying to do here."

I got to see Tony Dungy during the playoffs. He'd lost his son late in the season. He committed suicide and it was a true

tragedy. I just hugged him. Tony was a coach during nine or ten years that I was on the team. He and his wife Lauren — she's from Sewickley — were good friends of ours. Tony was in our Bible study. Guys like John Stallworth and Donnie Shell loved Tony when he was playing for the Steelers. He was always the best kind of person and teammate.

I have talked to people who were at the breakfast where Tony spoke the weekend of the Super Bowl in Detroit and they told me he had a powerful message.

I learned a little from everybody when I played for the Steelers. Jon Kolb had a great impact on my life. He loves the Lord. He had a sense of purpose and humility, and a true sense of servanthood. It was just the way he lives his life. The way he works with kids.

Jon pointed the way for me, sharing his gospel message. I looked at him and I said, "This is what a man of God looks like." He led the Bible study classes at his home. First, his home was in Peters Township, and then he moved to the North Hills and then to Grove City. But he remained a powerful influence on all of us.

Hollis Haff, who's now a pastor at the New Community Church in Wexford, was the Steelers' chaplain when I was playing, and he really challenged me to grow in my faith. He, too, helped me a lot. John Stallworth and Donnie Shell were two guys I looked up to. "These are what men of God look like," I said at the time. They were both humble men. It makes you do a double take. Like John Stallworth, so soft-spoken. So bright. He runs an aeronautics company in Alabama. He was the Alabama Businessman of the Year. But the most important thing in his life was not the Pittsburgh Steelers or the Super Bowls, but Jesus Christ. Donnie Shell . . . he was like a human torpedo. He'd just blast guys when he played strong safety or on special teams. Yet he was such a great guy. So intense. So was his passion for God. They were never guys who said, "Boy, am I great! " They were more inclined to say, "Boy, do I serve a great God!"

The Steelers had so many guys who were in tune with mentorship. They welcomed you to the team and embraced you. When you got here you didn't feel like you weren't part of it. The guys were eager to share with you. People like John Stallworth, Donnie Shell, Mike Webster, Jon Kolb, Sam Davis and Larry Brown talked to and told you how they did things and what worked for them. They taught you what had helped them.

Webby was the same way. Webby loved his children. When we were playing together, Webby gave his life to his family. I remember how tender he was with children, the way he held those spina bifida children he helped raise money for.

There was a strong spiritual side to Webby. That's why it was so difficult to deal with how he lost it all, how he became brain-damaged and didn't know what he was doing. And, finally, when he died so young. He loved Jesus. He was very excited about his faith and about sharing his faith.

Mel Blount has been a favorite of mine. There's something about Mel that's regal. He is a genuine guy. He loves all his old teammates. I see his love for the kids at the Mel Blount Youth Home. What a stewardship he has.

He came to practice on the South Side last season, and he had his kids with him. When he appeared on the sideline, I'm telling you that practice just stopped. For a few seconds, everyone turned and looked. "There's Mel Blount." That's what they seemed to be saying. He was wearing his white cowboy hat, his boots and his blue jeans, as he often does. I'm telling you practice just came to a stop for a second or two.

"You don't expect an offensive lineman to be an artist."

Having been an offensive lineman, I pay attention to the offensive linemen. They're often taken for granted. I think the Steelers have some terrific offensive linemen in Alan Faneca, Kendall Simmons, Jeff Hartings, Marvel Smith and Max Starks. I love Kendall Simmons. He comes on our show every Tuesday. He's an artist, and he has a very unique personality. You don't expect an offensive lineman to be an artist. His wife, Celesta, is such an Auburn fan. They have such a loyalty to their alma mater.

My son Clay is a huge fan of Pitt, for instance, but nobody loves their team like Kendall Simmons and his wife.

Alan Faneca is just a natural. He's big and strong and fast on his feet, great in space. He and his wife Julie have done so much with their "Glimmer of Hope" program to raise funds for breast cancer research.

Max Starks is so big and so bright. He's only going to get better. Marvel Smith plays his position well. He was more appreciated when he was hurt and unable to play.

The team is full of good guys.

"Giving back is the ultimate talent in life."
— Ozzie Smith
Baseball Hall of Fame

"Something special is happening here."
— Brett Keisel

I was impressed with the resolve of this group. The way they did it, winning their last four games of the regular season, winning three playoff games on the road. It's about as impressive a feat that I've seen in the National Football League. It's not that they weren't capable of winning all those games, but they did it. They did what they had to do. They believed they could do it. And Bill Cowher took the right approach, focusing only on the next game.

I remember Brett Keisel was on our show late in the season, and he said, "Something special is happening here. There's something special with this team."

They never got caught up in the celebration of each victory along the way. There was unfinished business. They had to get ready for the next game.

It was great to be a part of it. I finally got to go to a Super Bowl. It was so far removed from my time as a player that I didn't feel like I just lost out on something, or that I missed it. It was a lot easier. If they had gone when I first got out of the game I might be doing the gnashing of the teeth. But it's been eleven or twelve years since I've been out of the game. I didn't feel any sense of loss. I was happy for everybody. I played on a team with so many Super Bowl greats. I didn't want to retire until I won a Super Bowl. It was something I never experienced as a player. I see what these guys are getting paid these days. The Minnesota Vikings just signed a guard, Steve Hutchinson, for $49 million. For a guard! Look at what Randall El got ($27 million or more) from the Redskins. I'd never begrudge anybody a dollar. I tell these guys that we paved the way for them. Hines Ward cannot believe what we were paid. I made $25,000 my first season with the Steelers. I went through two player strikes to get better contracts from the owners, to get free agency in the first place. They all benefit from our efforts. I kid them about that.

When I was a kid at Highland Park High School in Chicago trying to figure out what I wanted to do with myself I couldn't have conceived that I'd play 14 years in the NFL. If you told me I was going to play that long in the NFL, and still be a part of it today, I wouldn't have believed you.

"I played on a team with great people."
— Lynn Swann

244

"It was the beginning of a beautiful relationship."

Wolf is my brother. We've been tight for so long. He was the first person I met when I got off the plane when I reported to Pittsburgh after the 1980 draft. Our planes landed at the same time. I forget who came out from the Steelers to pick us up, but we rode in to the stadium together. It was the beginning of a beautiful relationship.

I remember when I came back a few weeks later for my physical. I was sitting in the lobby with Nate Johnson and Ted Walton. We were all rookies. This is my favorite story about Art Rooney. Mr. Rooney came out and said hello to us. He was wearing a blue button-down sweater and he was putting some things in order in the lobby. He asked us our names and wanted to know where we came from.

"Are you the janitor?" Walton asked him.

Mr. Rooney just smiled and said, "Sort of. I do a lot of things around here."

In the years that followed, whenever I'd see Mr. Rooney he'd always say the same thing. "Tunch, my boy, how are your people doing over in Turkey? Are they still killing each other like the Irish?"

I think Mr. Rooney set the tone for the Steelers. You've got the tradition and the history. There's something about The Chief that stays with the Steelers. His family still runs the team.

I'm still tight with Craig Wolfley, Ted Petersen, Edmund Nelson, Gary Dunn, Jon Kolb, Mark Malone, Bill Hurley and so many other guys.

I took Wolf into the business. I hoped he would get involved. I wanted to work with my buddy. I knew he was funny. I thought he'd be a natural. I thought it would be cool for us to work together. Steve Wayhart has helped us market the show. I played football with his brother John at Indiana State. They both played at Canevin High here. Steve knows what he's doing and he's kept us going.

We get up at 4:15 each morning, so you gotta love it.

I don't have a complaint in the world. I enjoy what I do. I love the city. Pittsburgh has been great for us. I've gotten to be a part of it. I was shocked when I saw how many people turned out for the parade to celebrate the team's Super Bowl victory.

I was drinking a lot of coffee that day and during the parade I had to go to the bathroom, but there was no place to run. The crowds were so deep and you couldn't get through them. When we got near the platform at the end I ran into a bank, but a woman intercepted me and told me I couldn't use their bathroom. I was desperate.

When I was on the show the next day I apologized to anybody I might have run through to get to the bathroom. People wanted me to sign things, but I had to find a bathroom and I finally did. I didn't think I was going to make it. I thought I was going to wet my pants.

They said they expected about 30 thousand people. But soon after the parade started it was evident to me that this was a much bigger turnout. I hadn't seen this many people in one place since I saw the Indy 500 in Indianapolis.

Being in that parade just makes you proud to be a Pittsburgh guy. Art Rooney used to think that was a special honor.

Dan Ranker

Hines Ward wanted his own video tape of parade in downtown Pittsburgh to celebrate returning Super Bowl XL champions.

"I don't think anything can beat driving down Fifth Avenue after a Super Bowl win as mayor."
— Mayor Bob O'Connor

McKeesport's Mike Logan liked all his teams having great seasons. His grandfather worked at Jones & Laughlin Steel Co., on the same site where Steelers now practice.

McKeesport kid gets to Super Bowl

Mike Logan, a veteran defensive back for the Steelers, had a good feeling about his team's chances as they approached Super Bowl XL.

The former West Virginia University standout pointed out how his beloved Mountaineer basketball team had reached the Elite Eight in the NCAA Tournament the previous season, his McKeesport High School team won the Class AAAA state football championship, and WVU's football team, for which Logan starred from the early- to mid-1990s, won the Sugar Bowl.

Playing in the Super Bowl was a boyhood dream come true. Growing up in McKeesport, he used to pretend that he was one of the Steelers' star players that he watched on television.

"I got a call from a friend the other day," allowed Logan, following a team practice in Detroit, "and he said, 'Think about your story. Think about those days we were out posing in the yard — pretending to be Lynn Swann and Franco Harris. Now you're on that stage, accomplishing all the dreams you've had. Did you ever think about that?'

"And I hadn't . . . up until that point. Then I started to think about the road I traveled to get here, and it's pretty special. If we win the Super Bowl then I'll know it's my year."

Jim Clack
He inspired people

"I love being alive."

I called Jim Clack on Saturday, February 4 — the day before Super
Bowl XL — at his home in Rocky Mount, North Carolina. Clack
had played on the offensive line for the Steelers in their first two
Super Bowl triumphs, at the end of the 1974 and 1975 seasons.

I'm not sure what prompted me to call him that day. I had heard
that his cancer was back, that this hideous disease was again
threatening him. Clack was grateful for the call. I could hardly make
out what he was saying from time to time. There was noise in the
background and his voice was weak and raspy-sounding.

"I'm happy to be alive," he said. "I'm happy to be able to talk to
you, or anyone else. I love being called. I love hearing from old friends."

He sent me some stuff in the mail and I made a note to call him
back. In the meantime, I received some e-mail messages from Andy
Russell, a teammate of Clack on those two Super Bowl champion
teams, in which Russell was addressing former teammates, telling
them about Clack's condition. Even so, I had no idea his time was so
limited. I didn't realize just how sick Jim Clack was.

Russell mentioned that Clack was unable to work as a
motivational speaker, and that he needed funds to help him with his
health care and just to pay the bills at home. Russell had suggested
that teammates send Clack one of the checks they might get for a
signing or for a speaking engagement.

Calling Clack this time reminded me of an earlier conversation I
had with him back in mid-May, 2003. I had to check my files to come
up with that date. Those files contained information about Clack's
career. He had played center and guard for the Steelers for eight
seasons (1970-1977) and four years with the New York Giants (1978-
1981). He was a popular player with his teammates. He was the
offensive captain of the Giants for three seasons and was nominated
for the NFL Man of the Year Award.

"Do you know I have cancer?" Clack asked me when I made that
call three years earlier. He knew that I had to know something was
wrong when he had to pause several times just to catch his breath.

"Yes, I know," I said then. "I was sorry to hear that."

He told me he had lost a lot of weight because of his illness, going
from 245 to 195 pounds. He said he was starting to put some weight
back on, and was hopeful he'd be back to normal soon. Clack told me
he had throat cancer.

Jim Clack had forged a successful career as a motivational
speaker, telling his own comeback story in the same way that Rocky
Bleier has been making his living after he retired as a running back
for the Steelers.

Clack told me he received encouraging cards on a regular basis from Art Rooney Jr., who had discovered Clack at Wake Forest University when Rooney was responsible for the Steelers' scouting operation. He also said he heard from Joe Gordon, the Steelers' publicist in those days, inquiring about his well being.

"Jim Clack, I'm happy to say," he related, "has had time to reflect on how good we were and what a great bunch of guys we assembled in Pittsburgh. No matter how long it's been since we were together and playing football, we're going to take care of each other."

Hearing how Clack was having such a difficult time carrying on a conversation with me on the telephone reminded me of the cruel manner in which legendary Pirates' broadcaster Bob Prince was stricken with and died from head and neck cancer, mostly in his mouth of all places. Myron Cope was challenged by throat cancer and other health issues. In June of 2006, Cope moved into an assisted-care residence — The Covenant of South Hills — in Scott Township.

Like Merril Hoge, another former Steeler who learned he had cancer in February of 2003, Clack was doing his best to be positive about his situation. He'd been telling people for years about the importance of a positive attitude, and he had to once again heed his own words. It wasn't easy.

"Career-wise, it's set me back as far as speaking," commented Clack. "It's been tough on my family, especially my wife, but we're working our way through it. I'm doing my best to battle it."

Clack overcame that first bout with cancer. Then, after being cancer-free for several years, Clack was revisited by his cancer.

He was cheerful when we spoke the day before Super Bowl XL. He told me he'd be watching the game and rooting for the Steelers. I had no idea he was in such a perilous state. So I was stunned when I learned that he had died on April 7, 2006. I was signing books in front of Waldenbooks in Ross Park Mall when someone informed me of his death. I had called Clack from that same outpost back in February. The news of his death came on the heels of hearing that Maggie Dixon, the women's basketball coach at Army and the kid sister of the Pitt men's basketball coach, Jamie Dixon, had died of an enlarged heart at the tender age of 28. Clack was 58. Pitt's immortal All-American running back Marshall Goldberg had died the week before at 88. They say these things happen in threes.

Clack had died, according to an *Associated Press* report, of heart failure. He had fought neck and throat cancer for about four years before his death at Moses Cone Memorial Hospital in Greensboro, said his wife, Susan Clack. He was also survived by his stepchildren, Joseph and Linzi Curtis, both of Wilmington. Clack, who helped the Steelers win Super Bowls following the 1974 and 1975 seasons, played in 146 NFL games between 1971 and 1981.

Born in Rocky Mount, North Carolina, Clack attended Wake Forest and was inducted into the school's Hall of Fame in 1991. He was inducted into the North Carolina Sports Hall of Fame in 2004.

He returned to North Carolina after his football career, developing commercial and residential real estate and owning a restaurant. He started a sales training business and worked as a motivational speaker. Some of the charitable organizations he worked with were Hospice, American Lung Association, American Cancer Society, Multiple Sclerosis, the Boys' and Girls' Club, YMCA and American Heart Association.

His story touched thousands of people and encouraged them to achieve and continue to strive in spite of their own personal obstacles. His inspirational and heart-warming messages were celebrated in the motivational speaking world. Jim Clack was considered one of the best in the business, someone that could get an audience's attention in a hurry. He could touch their hearts and their minds.

Clack sent me one of his inspirational messages the week after Super Bowl XL and excepts are reprinted here:

Jim Clack:

"Never hesitate to ask someone for help."

Have you ever asked yourself why some people have all the luck rebounding from adversity and obstacles, no matter whether personal relationships, health conditions, athletic challenges, or business difficulties?

In May 2004 I was sitting on stage at Raleigh, North Carolina Hilton Hotel, anxiously awaiting my name to be called as an inductee in the North Carolina Sports Hall of Fame, when my wife, Susan, looked at me and said, "Relax! Relax!" I was so nervous that my short acceptance speech had pretty much disappeared in my head.

I slowly walked to the podium as my name was announced. My head was spinning. By the time I reached the podium, I had completely discarded my notes for the 20 minutes we were allowed and gave a 45-minute "Thank You" to everyone who had put me on that stage, present or not. It was a speech straight from the heart.

Mentoring was a concept I had never spoken about in my presentations in fifteen years, but that night and forever more will be included. That evening, I realized why I am still alive and kicking at 57. One of the characteristics that separate high achievers from everyone else is the drive and willingness to succeed. They also have a navigator, better known as a mentor.

I have discovered over years of training and developing 15-to-20 thousand individuals in sales, management, and customer service that one can have the greatest resiliencies but cannot succeed without a mentor: someone who can give you answers, support, and continuous positive reinforcement. They come in all positions, ages, relationships, and connections. Never hesitate to ask someone for help when you are in need. A mentor may supply you with a map, provide you with the guidance to maintain the discipline needed for the journey, or share good old, plain experience. People who are successful or have come back from obstacles, are deceiving you if they say they did not have a mentor, they did not come back or succeed. Mentors are essential to success.

If a person maintains the inner belief that he or she can succeed, there is a mysterious, almost magnetic power that somehow attracts significant others to assist them in the journey.

Enough of the philosophy and review. Let's get down to the basics, as Chuck Noll would say to us in Pittsburgh during the '70s. Many of my close friends and associates say I am a real person, not a cat with nine lives. Well, folks, I am here to tell you that I am a cat. Six or seven lives have already been used. God has left me here for a purpose.

Please let me share with you my setbacks and comebacks for 57 years, with the hope they will give you a plan and encourage you to use mentors when you face similar obstacles. My first setback occurred in 1963. My father, Linwood Clack, passed away at the young age of 47. This was particularly shocking for a high school sophomore who had grown to love, admire, and respect his father's balance of harsh discipline and fair judgment. My father's expectations for me were high and his support unparalleled. His belief in his son was unmatched.

The week before his untimely death, my father was able to see me score the winning basket in the final game of the North Carolina State Basketball Championship. He made the 260-mile round trip in one day, despite a serious illness that he had kept a secret from my mom, two sisters and me.

Anytime I mention the word mentor, everyone I come into contact with knows that my father and mother were my first and best mentors.

Our team arrived back in Rocky Mount, North Carolina, my hometown, from the game on the following day. Upon my return to my house, I spotted my dad on our front porch, proudly cutting up fifty copies of our local paper bearing the bold headline, "Sophomore Jim Clack Wins State Championship" and sending all fifty to friends and relatives. Dad said, "I am not crazy, I just want all my friends to know how proud I am of my son." Unfortunately, he passed away a few days later. To this day, forty-two years later, I still picture him surrounded with those articles that he so lovingly and proudly clipped and sent in the mail.

My mother and my high school football and track coach, Henry Trevathan, kept my spirits up and made sure I held my head high and did what I needed to do to realize my dreams of getting an athletic scholarship so I could go to college. I was lucky to get a lot of offers for both football and basketball and to make the right choice, Wake Forest University.

I learned some things along the way. For one thing, no one can motivate you but you. Your mentor can create a plan and environment that encourages you to motivate yourself. Leadership by power and forces is the worst possible method. A great mentor always raises the bar to assist you in succeeding. I was signed by the Pittsburgh Steelers in 1969 as a free agent. Art Rooney Jr. recommended me. My next encounter with mentoring was in the Steel City. I was a 217-pound string bean when I signed with the Steelers. The Rooney family and several coaches, especially the line coach, Dan Radakovich, and the strength coach, Lou Riecke, became my new mentors.

These gentlemen turned what seemed an impossible dream into a reality. Even at their lowest point in 1969, I was not able to make the team. The next year, 1970, was a repeat. I was put on waivers the last day of the exhibition season. Yet, thanks to the Rooneys' and Coach Noll's patience, I made the team in 1971. The mentors then sat back and watched their return. Seven great years, starting two Super Bowls and playing four years with the New York Giants, where I made All-Pro and was captain, were the rewards. You can see a pattern. You have to face reality. You must establish a plan and set goals. You have to correct your course when necessary. You have to stay focused and meet all your commitments to become successful.

On July 17, 1985 this pattern took on greater significance as I faced the biggest comeback of my life. My previous wife and I were involved in a horrendous automobile accident that evening. An eighteen-wheeler broadsided us on my side of the car. Fortunately, my wife sustained injuries that were treatable and she was released seven days later.

I wasn't nearly as lucky. I was pinned in the car nearly two hours. I had a broken back, hip, ribs, nerves torn throughout, and a spleen had to be removed, just to name a few of my injuries. I will always be thankful to the great teams of doctors for putting me back together. I spent seventeen days in intensive care and about two weeks of additional hospitalization were followed by six months of home care.

My family, friends and fans were all encouraging, but one gentleman stood out among the crowd. Randy Stuart was my main rehabilitation specialist. He had to convince me, a man who could bench press the side of a barn, to lift five pounds with my leg. A long struggle followed but with his assistance as a mentor, we succeeded together. He brought me back to reality. We set goals and worked to the point that you would have no idea that I had ever been so badly injured.

Even so, my restaurant business tanked and I found myself wondering what I was going to do with the rest of my life. At the time, I was selling life insurance, and doing well at it, but decided it wasn't my cup of tea. I heard a speaker who addressed a group of former NFL players. His name was Bill Brooks, and he became my next mentor. We teamed up together and we became a winning combination.

The fall of 2002 changed my life again. I had already had a heart attack, a ruptured blood vessel and some other close calls, but no obstacle was greater than when I learned I had neck cancer at the Stage 4 level. My cancer specialist had a plan to fight it. My battle is still a day-to-day struggle, but I am sure I will survive. With the help of some great mentors and great friends I have been able to meet the challenge.

You can believe me when I tell you that times have been bad. They have really been bad.

The past has taught me about overcoming setbacks. I will follow the same process as I did in the other adversities I have encountered. Coming back to reality has been hard but not impossible. You never know what to expect with Mr. C.

Former Steelers' offensive lineman Jim Clack poses for family portrait with wife Susan and her children by a previous marriage, Joseph, and Linzi.

Tony Dungy
He'll always be close to Steelers

Hardly a perfect season.

Tony Dungy, Curtis Martin and Bart Starr would seem to be an unlikely trifecta, but they share common bonds. These three distinguished National Football League figures were all on the same program at the 19th annual Athletes in Action Super Bowl breakfast held the morning before the big game at the Renaissance Hotel in Detroit. They are all good company.

I have spent quality time with all of them, and think I know they are special. They have all been tested, more than men should be tested perhaps, but they have survived, and showed the way for the rest of us. We can learn from their lives.

The hotel was headquarters for Super Bowl XL, matching the AFC champion Pittsburgh Steelers against the NFC champion Seattle Seahawks. Everybody who's anybody in pro football was there.

Dungy and Martin both had a strong Pittsburgh connection. Dungy had played for and coached the Pittsburgh Steelers. He had been a member of three Super Bowl championship teams in the '70s and returned in the '80s to serve as a defensive backfield coach and defensive coordinator to Coach Chuck Noll.

During his days with the Steelers, he was one of their more popular and spiritual members of the team. He was especially close to Donnie Shell, Mel Blount and John Stallworth. They were among the 28 to 30 players who met for Bible study sessions on a weekly basis. Jon Kolb was one of the leaders of those gatherings. The Steelers of the '70s were men of the highest character, for the most part.

Martin had grown up in Pittsburgh, and starred at Taylor Allderdice High School and the University of Pittsburgh. His mother was from my hometown of Hazelwood. We'd gone to the same schools, so I have been a big fan of Martin. He had shared stories of narrow scrapes, getting caught in the middle of gunfire involving gangs in the city's Hill District.

Martin received the Bart Starr Award at the breakfast. This award is given annually to an NFL player on the basis of character and service. Bart Starr was also among the former Super Bowl MVPs who had been invited to participate in a recognition ceremony that preceded the kickoff in Super Bowl XL. Starr was the MVP of the first two Super Bowls, leading Vince Lombardi's Green Bay Packers to consecutive NFL championships.

Starr had a different kind of connection. Starr shared a tragic setback with Dungy, though no one mentioned this publicly during the program. It was something that came to my mind when I saw the speakers' lineup for the Athletes in Action program. One of my

Photos by George Gojkovich/Getty Images

Tony Dungy had a season of highs and lows as coach of the Indianapolis Colts. He was a former defensive back and coach with the Steelers.

friends, Bill Priatko, played briefly with the Green Bay Packers and has kept in touch with Starr because he admires him so much. Priatko has prized letters sent to him by Starr, always with kind words and encouragement. Priatko and his daughter, Debbie, were both present at the breakfast.

"What beautiful speeches," reported Priatko when he came back home to North Huntingdon. "I had a chance to talk briefly with Bart. He's always so accommodating."

I had an opportunity to play tennis with Bart Starr and his wife, Cherry, at an NFL Owners' Meeting once in Rancho Mirage, California. They are a classy couple. In talking to the Starrs afterward, I learned that they had a son who had committed suicide. No one ever gets over that completely. Priatko told me when Starr was speaking, he told the crowd, "Every day . . . hug your children and tell them that you love them."

Anyone who paid attention to pro football during the 2005 season knows that Dungy suffered the setback of his life when his 18-year-old son James committed suicide during the 2005 season. Dungy was the head coach of the Indianapolis Colts in 2005. When the Colts came rushing out of the gate and won their first 13 games, there was talk of a perfect season.

Then Dungy got the telephone call informing him that his son, a 6-7 athletic-looking young man who was often mistaken for a ballplayer when he was with his dad, had used a belt to hang himself from a ceiling fan. His girl friend discovered him when she came to his apartment in Lutz, Florida.

The Colts lost their next game, with Dungy missing from the sideline, and they would get upset by the Steelers in the first game of the AFC playoffs in Indianapolis. The Colts became the first NFL team to start the season 13-0 and not reach the Super Bowl. No matter what happened in those games, for Tony Dungy it could never have been a perfect season.

I am all too familiar with suicide and what it can do to tear apart a family. Whose fault was it? Why did he kill himself? Who's to blame? What went wrong? Why did he feel so bad? How could he hurt everyone like this? Did he give any hints that he was hurting so badly? Did I miss something? How could I have helped him save himself?

I remember a movie — but I can't think of the name of it — in which the daughters of a woman who had committed suicide were reflecting on what happened. "Mom was just having a bad day," said one of them. That's often the case.

Dungy was such a respected and popular man throughout the league that the death of his son caused widespread loss. It was loss suffered by many beyond Tony and his wife, Lauren, their two other sons, Eric and Jordan, and their two daughters, Tiara and Jade. Dan Rooney, the chairman of the board of the Steelers, expressed sorrow for him, his family and the Steelers' family. "Tony has always been special to us," related Rooney.

Rooney had lost one of his own nine children to Lupus disease many years earlier, and the loss had left a hole in his heart.

Dungy was always different. There was a time when he considered leaving as a coach in the NFL to assume a prison ministry. There were some that thought he was too soft and sensitive to be a head coach in the NFL, but he proved them wrong at Tampa and Indianapolis.

During his days as coach in both places, he was involved in many community service organizations. He worked as a public speaker for the Fellowship of Christian Athletes and Athletes in Action. He began a mentoring program for young people called Mentors for Life. He was also involved in Big Brothers/Big Sisters, Boys and Girls Club, the Prison Crusade Ministry, foster parenting organizations, and Family First. He helped launch a Basket of Hope program, which aids children at Riley Hospital for Children.

With such a resume, having a son commit suicide had to hurt even more. Tony had reached out to so many young people with problems. What happened to his son James? Suicide in the family always leaves more questions than answers.

Friends felt Dungy's faith in God would get him through this difficult time in his life. In his first public speaking engagement since the death of his son, Dungy told of the pain and lessons learned from what happened.

Speaking of James, who was near his 19th birthday, Dungy said, "He was a Christian and is today in heaven. He was struggling with things of the world and took his own life. People ask how I could come back to work so soon.

"I'm not totally recovered. I don't know if I ever will be. It's still ever-painful." He wiped back tears as he said this. "But some good things have come of it."

He mentioned that two people had been given the gift of eyesight from his son's donated corneas. He spoke of troubled youth he has spoken to who were dealing with some of the same kind of difficulties as his son.

"If God had talked to me before James' death and said his death would have helped all these people, it would have saved them and healed their sins, but I would have to take your son. I would have said no. I can't do that.

"But God had the same choice 2,000 years ago with his Son, Jesus Christ, and it paved the way for you and me to have eternal life. That's the benefit I got, that's the benefit James got and that's the benefit you can get if you accept Jesus into your heart today as your Savior."

Dungy told the audience of NFL officials, coaches and fans that one of his biggest regrets was that when he saw his son during the Thanksgiving holidays he didn't give him a hug when they departed. He said he just gave him a casual goodbye.

Dungy told the gathering that he had attended his breakfast eight or nine times previously, and had always dreamed that someday he'd be there the day before he led his team into the Super Bowl. "My goal," he said, "is to fill a couple of tables with my players the day before the game. It hasn't happened yet. I'll sure be happy when it does."

In his acceptance speech for the Bart Starr Award, Curtis Martin said his faith in God helped him overcome a bad start in his teens. He mentioned family and friends being killed when he was young. He told of an abusive home environment where his father often beat his mother. "I always thought I would die before I was 21, but I appreciate life now," said Martin, "and I do realize we have a God who forgives whatever we can do."

I have met and spoken with Martin's mother, Rochella Martin, at shopping malls in the Pittsburgh suburbs. I know how proud she is of her son. Their relationship is a special one. Her mother and sister were killed — one in a robbery and the other in an auto accident — when Curtis was a kid. Her husband, Curtis Sr., had walked away soon after their only child was born. Rochella and her son remained close. They made the best of their lives in Homewood. Anybody who grows up in Homewood is familiar with heartache. John Wideman, the great writer who grew up there, has written books about it.

"Athletes have a great influence," said Curtis Martin, whose boyhood hero was Michael Jordan, in an interview for one of my earlier books, *Hometown Heroes*. "I believe he had the greatest influence on kids. If someone, one of my sports heroes, would have come to me as a youngster and could have helped me and steered me, I could have saved myself a lot of heartache and my parents' heartache. I could have lived a safer life and a more focused life. I may have done better in school or in a lot of different areas. When I go back to Homewood now, it's fulfilling to know that you can actually impact the future of a child. We have that power."

Curtis #28
Martin

> *"He came here as a skinny athlete who they knew could play, but they couldn't decide where. He played out of position his first two years, at running back and quarterback. Of course, that wouldn't bother Hines, just like playing in a run-oriented pro offense that keeps him from putting up the numbers he would with a team that threw more. He is all about the team and winning rather than personal glory."*
> — **Dick Bestwick, former college football coach and academic advisor**

A Seoul-searching trip to Korea
Hines has a gift for his Mom

"America is a great country."

M ove over, Tiger Woods. Here comes Hines Ward. When Ward was named the Most Valuable Player in Super Bowl XL, suddenly South Korea discovered a new homegrown sports star. Ward has done much since then to strengthen the link.

Like Woods, Ward was the son of an Asian woman and a black American soldier. Ward's father was stationed in the military service in South Korea. Those who follow the Steelers closely were aware of Ward's heritage for several years, or ever since he became one of Pittsburgh's most popular athletes. Now the world will know.

The Steelers have had a similar story with Hall of Famer Franco Harris. He was the son of a black American soldier and an Italian war bride. They suffered indignities as well because of the mixed heritage. "I remember my mother went to look for a house for us," offered Harris, "She went alone, and she didn't speak English that well, because they were afraid my father would get turned away."

It wasn't until Ward worked his magic in the Super Bowl in February 2006 that the rest of the world learned of his story. The journey of Jerome Bettis back to his hometown of Detroit had been the feel-good story that set the stage for Super Bowl XL. Now Ward's journey to America as a one-year-old child and a planned return to South Korea with his mother was gaining the attention of the international press.

Woods is well spoken, but somewhat shy and reserved. He is a pleasant personality, and golf is an international game. So Ward will not ever be as big a deal as Tiger Woods. But, like Bettis, he has a smile that lights up a room. And such a smile breaks down a lot of language barriers. There's no mistaking that Hines Ward is having a good time and that life is good. His happy nature is infectious.

He placed his hands atop his head at one point, and offered some Korean words. He said it was a gesture that meant "I love you." He said he had a Korean language book and was trying to learn some key Korean phrases before he departed on the trip to South Korea.

Before the Steelers knew they would be playing in the Super Bowl, Ward had made plans to take a week-long sojourn to South Korea with his mother because he was eager to learn more about his heritage. He and his Mom had talked about doing this for years. He wanted to see the home where he was born, learn some of the language and customs, and embrace his newest fans. The possibilities were beyond his wildest dreams.

I attended one of the strangest press conferences in Steelers' history when Hines Ward met with the media to discuss his plans to go to his hometown. It was held on Friday, March 3 in the Steelers' headquarters and practice complex on the South Side.

It was held in the room where Bill Cowher conducts his weekly press conferences each Tuesday during the regular season. It was a different crowd than Cowher usually attracts. Ed Bouchette of the *Pittsburgh Post-Gazette* and Joe Bendel of the *Pittsburgh Tribune-Review*, the two main beat writers, were there.

But Bob Pompeani, Stan Savran, Ellis Cannon, Alby Oxenreiter and Bob Smizik, the local sports media stars, and Steelers' insiders such as Bob Labriola and Jim Wexell were not in the room. Brenda Waters, the "good news" reporter, came for KDKA-TV, and Sally Wiggin of WTAE was there instead for the Steelers' latest "feel-good" story. I was sitting behind eight men from media outlets in South Korea, with a woman TV reporter from South Korea sitting behind me. When they spoke to each other, I had no idea what they were saying. There were several cameramen from South Korea stationed around the room.

In recent years, I have been in the press box at PNC Park where there were representatives of newspapers from Asia to report on the doings of visiting ballplayers who hail from Japan. They are there to report on their homegrown greats.

"It's overwhelming to see what's happened to me in this regard," said Ward. "I can't believe the support of my mother and I from Korea. It has been overwhelming. I'm very proud of my mom. I'm proud of my Korean heritage. Not only am I African-American, but I'm Korean as well. Coming from where I came from, none of this seemed possible. It's a great story. America is a great country."

Baldy Regan would agree. Hines Ward came on the Steelers' scene too late to know the late Baldy Regan, a friend of the Rooney family who was known as "the mayor of the North Side." Regan organized and coached the Steelers' basketball team, which he turned over to Tom O'Malley Jr. Ward was one of the regulars on the Steelers' basketball team that played games to raise money for various endeavors at high schools throughout the tri-state area surrounding Pittsburgh.

Regan had a pet phrase whenever he'd come across someone he knew to be a rags-to-riches story. "Only in America," Regan would say, borrowing a phrase from Harry Golden, a Jewish writer-philosopher who wrote and published *The Carolina Israelite*.

"I used to be ashamed."

Hines Ward was scheduled to meet South Korea President Roh Moo-hyun. After he returned to the U.S., Ward and the Steelers were scheduled to have lunch with President Bush in Washington, D.C.

"Having lunch with the President," Ward exclaimed, shaking his head at the thought. "I never would have thought that in my wildest imagination. I'm speechless for what is happening for me."

Ward said he was holding this press conference, as well as one in South Korea when he and his Mom arrived there in April, to get such demands out of the way so that he and his mother could have a relaxing stay in South Korea. He asked the South Korean media to get the word out that he and his mother hoped the people would respect their privacy and allow them to tour the town without much attention.

As I sat there, and listened to his request, I had to smile. There was no way, I thought, this was going to happen. Judging by the excitement of the South Korean reporters in the room, I had to believe that Ward's visit to Seoul was going to be like Media Day at the Super Bowl. It was going to be crazy.

Ward, who would turn 30 the following week, was wearing a black warm-up suit and a black tassel cap on a cold day in Pittsburgh. Ballplayers never give much thought to how they might look at such public appearances. I could see his legs under the table where he sat, and he was nervously rubbing his knees as he spoke to the assembled media. He smiled a lot, as he always does — that's his signature — but he also appeared more nervous, not sure what to say, or how to handle his increased celebrity status.

It was obvious his management team had told him there was a great opportunity for him to cash in on his newfound celebrity in South Korea, or Asia at large. Ward was genuinely interested in learning more about where he came from, but he was smart enough to recognize that this was another window of financial opportunity for a professional athlete. He promised that this would be the first of several visits to South Korea, that he would keep in touch with the people there, that he planned on doing some things to help change the culture there. He knew that mixed children like him had a difficult time in South Korea, that they had traditionally been shunned, even abandoned. It's one of the reasons his parents left Korea to come to America.

When he was at Georgia, he received a scholarship established for a Korean-American student, and Ward wants to do the same, in honor of his mother. "I used to be ashamed of being Korean when I was a kid," he said. "I had trouble with that when I was a kid. I was looked down upon when I was growing up in a predominantly African-American community."

I recalled that when I was stationed at Fort Greely, Alaska in the mid-'60s, there were soldiers, some of them black, who had married women they met in Korea or other Asian countries. They tended to stick together, and had a community within a community on the military post.

"Looking back on it now, I can understand that we left for a reason," Ward said at his press conference. "My father was probably coming back because his tour was coming to an end. For my mother to leave at that time, it wasn't cool to have a mixed kid (in Korea). I think she left the country to seek a new life with my father."

Things did not go as planned. His parents broke up, and his dad was given custody of Hines because his mother, Young-hee, could not speak English and was unable to hold down a steady job. She wanted to get her son back, however, and she ended up working three jobs — at an airport, a convenience store and a school cafeteria — to prove her worthiness. When Ward was six years old, the courts awarded his mother custody of her son.

"I've been with her ever since," said Ward. "There is no way I can ever pay her back for what she sacrificed to bring me up. In a way, this trip to Korea is my gift to my mother, my way of saying thank you for what she did. My mother taught me to be humble, and to treat other people the way you want to be treated."

It's the Golden Rule, and Art Rooney related this to his five sons on many occasions. He always thought the family should live in a modest manner, and not make a show of wealth.

I asked Ward if, since he was born and lived in Seoul for a year, he had a Korean name. "That's a great question," he said. "I don't know. I'll have to ask my mother about that."

When Ward was presented with the MVP at Super Bowl XL, he held his son Jared in his arms. It's a picture that turned up on the front page of newspapers around the world, and magazine covers.

"My son's first birthday is a big birthday in Korea," explained Ward. "My mom bought a Korean outfit and dressed my son. There's a tradition in Korea where you put a ring, money, a pencil and whatever the kid picks out is the path he's supposed to take. My son picked out the pencil and dollar bill, so whatever that means."

I couldn't help myself. "Hines," I hollered out from the back of the press pack, "it means your son is going to be a sportswriter."

Ward smiled in response.

He had many interesting observations during his press conference.

Hines Ward:

"Maybe I can change some views over there."

My mother and I have talked about making this trip a long time ago, but there was never the right time to do it. I'm excited about going over there to see where it all happened. I want to find out where it all began, where I was born and where my mother grew up. I want to spend some quality time with my mother, do some sightseeing, some relaxing. I want to catch up on my heritage.

I'm having this press conference to talk about it now. I don't want to make it a media-fest. My mother is really shy, and she's not comfortable in the spotlight. I don't want it to be

262

a media circus. My mother has been back about three times. I'm really excited about going there with her.

My whole life has been teaching her about football. She still doesn't understand it. She can't understand why you get only one point for a kick after a touchdown and three points for a field goal. She says they look the same. Now it's her turn to teach me about something I don't know.

I really want to get caught up on my traditions and my heritage of where it all happened for me. I want to see where my mom grew up. I want to see where she played hooky or took a drink or took a smoke. I am going to ask her all those questions. That is really what this trip is all about.

I want my mom to teach me everything about the Korean heritage that I missed out on . . . I will learn a lot more about my mother and what she had to overcome growing up as a child.

Back in the day, interracial dating really wasn't accepted and, for the Korean community to finally come together and not really look at race, but claim me as Korean, because that is who I am, is a great feeling to have that Korean community support. It is still something that looms over. Mixing races together really isn't accepted.

I kid some of the Koreans I meet here that I am more Korean than they are because I was born there.

Now she's going to be able to teach me about her customs. It's exciting because I have no knowledge of my background or my heritage. All I know of Koreans is that we take our shoes off when we enter the house.

It's a great feeling and, hopefully, by me winning the Super Bowl MVP and having the Korean community support me and rally around me, maybe I can change some views over there on how they look at things and how roles have changed over there. Don't just look at color; look at who I am as a person.

I know they still look down upon kids who are of other races over there. They are treated very badly. It is sad that happens. If there is anything I can do to help us out of that mentality, to accept it that it is not the kids' faults. Just accept them for who they are.

My story is a great story. It's inspiring. All my trials and tribulations . . . and I'm here now. Living my dream. We won the Super Bowl. You have to keep working hard. All my career people are telling me what I couldn't do. I never listen to what people say about me. I used it as a stimulus to work harder and show them they're wrong.

Most experts didn't pick the Pittsburgh Steelers to win the Super Bowl. I get a kick out of going back and reading the season previews now.

My mother always told me to never forget where you come from. She doesn't have to work three jobs anymore. She wants to keep her job at the school. We'll be traveling during spring break. It's wonderful how things ended up. This is a great country.

It will be different for us next season. Some guys won't be here. I plan to lead by example. I've had a lot of honors, but I want to continue to be a consistent ballplayer. When I get back I will be totally focused on next year.

"It's truly a dream come true."

My life has changed a lot since the Super Bowl. I went to Disney World with Jerome the following day. We've both been on TV and radio shows all over the nation. It's been non-stop. I'll miss Jerome next season, but I'm happy with the way his career ended for him, going home to Detroit and winning the Lombardi Trophy. It was great for his family, being a part of it. He'll be great in his TV career. He's a natural.

Everybody wants to put their hands on me. I never envisioned it would be this way. It was so great to ride in that parade in downtown Pittsburgh when we got back. This town loves its Steelers, that's for sure.

Losing those championship games in earlier years still hurts the most, but this helps make up for those disappointments.

Winning the Super Bowl was something special. Ninety-five million watching. That's a lot of people. It's truly a dream come true. It's like fantasy football. I never thought about this. I'm speechless. I'm having lunch with the President. It's like Forrest Gump. Things keep happening.

Hines Ward stiffarms Ty Law, a defensive back from Aliquippa.

Note the Korean markings on the tattoo on Hines Ward's right bicep.

A Hero's Return

Hines Ward received a hero's welcome, according to *Associated Press* reports, when he and his mother, Kim Young-hee, who is South Korean, returned to Seoul in early April, 2006.

It was the first time Ward had been in Seoul, where he was born and left when he was a year old, in nearly 30 years. He and his mother were there for a 10-day visit that included a meeting with South Korean President Roh Moo-hyun and receive honorary citizenship for the city of Seoul.

South Korean companies were competing for the privilege to transport him, and provide lodging and clothing for him and his mother.

Their arrival was carried live on local television with broadcasters dubbing it "a hero's return" and calling the Steelers' star receiver "the pride of the Korean people."

Ward was ecstatic over the reception for him and his mother. "It's a dream come true," said Ward. "I just want to thank the Korean community for the support for my mom and me. We're going to catch up on some old traditions."

Among the gifts he received was a plush white bathrobe. Ward wore it in the locker room when he returned and drew smiles from his teammates.

Merril Hoge
It's still fun to be in his company

"I know more about the game than I did as a player."

Merril Hoge had come a long way from Pocatello, Idaho to Pittsburgh, Pennsylvania. Hoge liked to poke fun at himself, telling stories that made him out to be some kind of hick who'd come to the big city. It was like the children's story about the country mouse and the city mouse.

One evening, back when he was playing for the Pittsburgh Steelers, we shared a dais at a fish fry fund-raiser at St. Agnes Church in Bridgeville, not far from my home in Upper St. Clair.

Hoge told a rapt all-male audience about his first year with the Steelers. Pat Hanlon, who had been my assistant when I was the sports information director at the University of Pittsburgh, was then working for the Steelers in their public relations and community relations department, and Hoge had a story that involved Hanlon.

Hanlon had an assignment for Hoge, whom he liked a great deal. "He told me he wanted me to speak at a midget football league banquet," said Hoge.

"I said, 'Man, I knew football was popular in Pittsburgh, but it's incredible that you even have a football league here for midgets.'" Bada boom. The St. Agatha audience laughed at that one and Hoge had them in the palm of his hand for another 15 minutes of similar poke-fun-at-Merril Hoge stories.

It's hard not to like Merril DuAine Hoge, who was born on January 26, 1965 in Pocatello. He's a handsome, warm-hearted fellow who's easy company. He doesn't take himself too seriously, but he has always tackled his challenges and assignments seriously.

Hoge has not carried a football for the Steelers since 1993, yet he remains a popular and familiar figure in Pittsburgh. He continued to maintain a home in the North Hills for many years after he retired as a player, as well as in his native Pocatello. His main residence is in Fort Thomas, Kentucky, just across the Ohio River from Cincinnati. His wife Toni has family and friends there. "I travel a lot and am away a great deal of the time," explains Merril, "so she's comfortable there when I'm on the road. She lived there before we met, and we have many great family and friends there."

They have been married for 13 years and have two children, a 12-year-old daughter named Kori, and a nine-year-old son named Beau.

Hoge does several football-related shows for ESPN and is a sought-after public speaker. He's overcome concussions that caused him to retire from the National Football League sooner than he had planned, and cancer that caused him to take time out and consider his good fortune. He was 41 and had been cancer-free for nearly three years when we spoke over the telephone on Wednesday, March 29, 2006.

"That's the real bonus," he said. "I've got a great family. I love what I'm doing. I'm fortunate to do what I do. I'm still involved in a game I've always loved. I'm passionate about it, and I'm well prepared. I don't take anything for granted. I do my homework. That's what makes the shows special and legitimate.

"I've studied so much film and talked to so many people in pro football through the years since I've been in this position that I know more about the game than I did as a player. I know it from more angles. I have developed some great relationships with some great people. I'm doing what I love and I don't get beat up on Sunday anymore."

Hoge is one of several Steelers from those teams of the '80s who stayed in football by becoming a sports broadcaster. Mark Malone, Tunch Ilkin and Craig Wolfley have flourished in the field. They were friendly and cooperative with the media as players and made an easy transition into working on the other side of the fence.

"I'm the poster boy for the two C's."

Hoge is an analyst for a wide variety of NFL programs on television and ESPN Radio. These include ESPN2's NFL Live; NFL Match-Up, which is aired on ESPN and ESPN2; ESPNEWS Football Friday; The NFL on ESPN Radio, which is heard Sunday afternoons throughout the season; and the NFL Draft Show. Hoge also occasionally provides reports for Sunday NFL Countdown. Hoge joined ESPN in 1996, working as a game analyst and sideline reporter for ESPN2's college football coverage. "This will be my tenth year with ESPN," Hoge said when we spoke. "Our Draft Show is the most highly-watched show on ESPN. We're on for 18 hours of coverage during the two draft days. We'll have 18 to 20 million people watching the show."

He does the show with Ron Jaworski, the former quarterback of the Philadelphia Eagles who came out of Youngstown State to make his mark in the NFL. "No one studies more tape than we do, and that's what makes our observations more meaningful. Otherwise, you're just guessing."

An eight-year NFL veteran, Hoge spent 1987-1993 with the Steelers and was the team's starting fullback for five of those seasons. He set the team record for most receptions by a running back, totaling 50 in 1988. He concluded his career in 1995 in his second season with the Chicago Bears. He'd suffered too many concussions and was advised by doctors to retire.

"I'm the poster boy for the two C's," said Hoge. "I can talk about cancer and concussions with the best of them. If I can remember my own stories."

Hoge was helped relating to his concussions by Dr. Joseph Maroon, a neurological surgeon at Allegheny General Hospital and then UPMC who has served for over 20 years as one of the Steelers' team physicians. He was treated for non-Hodgkin's lymphoma by Dr. Stanley Marks, a renowned oncologist, at the Hillman Cancer Center in Shadyside.

Hoge is currently chairman of the board of the Western Pennsylvania Caring Foundation, a program that assists uninsured children and provides a center for grieving children, adolescents and their families. There are three of these grieving centers — in Pittsburgh, Erie and Harrisburg — called the Highmark Caring Place. Hoge is also a co-captain of the Caring Team for Children, a partnership among more than 200 schools in Pennsylvania that has raised funds for local children since 1989.

Hoge has headed an annual golf outing to raise funds for the Caring Foundation. It is usually held in May at Southpointe Golf Club in Canonsburg. He has been a figurehead for this event along with Carnell Lake, Mark Bruener, Hines Ward and, most recently, Max Starks. These Steelers have recruited their teammates and friends around the NFL to play with the foursomes who pay to play in the golf outing.

Judd Gordon, the director of strategic development and initiatives for Outreach and Development of the Caring Foundation, coordinates an annual golf outing. Gordon is a big fan of Merril Hoge and the other Steelers who have assisted him in making this golf outing such a huge success through the years. "He's great to work with," said Gordon, a good man and a former ordained minister. "He extends himself in every respect to make a positive contribution to what we're trying to accomplish. When he speaks, people listen. He speaks from his heart."

Hoge had a personal experience he can share with kids. His mother died when he was 19, and he remembers how that affected him and his kid brother, Marty, who was 14 at the time. He and Marty are in business together back in Pocatello.

"The Winning Game Plan."

Hoge has been a leading advocate for patients with non-Hodgkin's lymphoma (NHL) — a cancer of the immune system — since he was diagnosed with the disease on Valentine's Day in 2003. At age 38, he was forced to face an opponent tougher than any rival he had ever encountered on the football field. Hoge discussed the problem with Mario Lemieux of the Pittsburgh Penguins, who has fought a similar battle with the same affliction. Lemieux and friends had formed a cancer research foundation that has also raised funds, and Lemieux makes occasional visits to Children's Hospital.

In early 2003, Hoge visited his personal physician to seek treatment for an abnormal back pain that was unlike any of the previous football injuries Hoge had experienced. After undergoing several tests, Hoge learned that his pain was actually the result of a malignant tumor caused by early-stage NHL. Fortunately for Hoge, his treatment regimen, combined with an early diagnosis, a winning football mindset and family support was the game plan Hoge needed to tackle his cancer. He is now in remission and hopes to help others with NHL.

Since his diagnosis, Hoge has become a dedicated advocate for NHL patients. He is a spokesperson for "The Winning Game Plan," an educational program for patients diagnosed with NHL, designed to empower them with the knowledge to manage their diagnosis successfully and encourage them to take an active role in their treatment decisions. "The Winning Game Plan" is sponsored by Genentech, Inc. and Biogen Idec.

He speaks on such subjects as Life in the NFL, Health and Fitness and Setting and Attaining Your Personal Goals. Because of his own battles to overcome physical setbacks, he also speaks about Dealing With Adversity, Overcoming Obstacles, the Power of the Mind and the Body, How to Use Adversity to Become a Better Person and Finding Peace in Your Life.

He was an "Iron Man" with Steelers

Hoge was a standout football player at Idaho State University, where he was a four-year starter, setting 44 school and conference records. He still holds two NCAA records.

He was a tenth-round draft choice of the Steelers in 1987, the same year they picked up Rod Woodson, Thomas Everett, Hardy Nickerson, and Greg Lloyd. They got Lloyd with their second sixth round choice. So it was a pretty good draft class. Getting Hoge so late was a stroke of good fortune for the Steelers and the NFL at large.

Hoge was with the Steelers from 1987 to 1993. He led the team in rushing and receiving in four of his first five years, setting a team record in his third year for receptions by a running back.

Hoge was the kind of good guy that the Steelers now boast about on their Super Bowl championship team. He was the Steelers "Iron Man of the Year" two years in a row (1989 and 1990), and was named to the All-Madden Team in 1989. Hoge went on to play one year with the Chicago Bears before being sidelined by post-concussion syndrome. At the time of his retirement, he had the longest consecutive streak of games played in the league. He admits now that he came back to play too soon after suffering several concussions.

He gained 3,139 rushing yards and 2,133 receiving yards, playing fullback for the Steelers two-back offense. He was one of only two Steelers to rush for more than 100 yards in back-to-back playoff games. The other, of course, was Franco Harris. So he was in good company. When I called Merril Hoge, I caught him, by coincidence, checking videotape of the Steelers' safety Troy Polamalu for a special pre-draft show he was researching.

Merril Hoge:

"Polamalu is a special guy."

NFL Films sends me all of its game coverage every week. Steve Sabol, who runs NFL Films, authorized that I could have this about four years ago. I get everything from Sunday at my door Tuesday morning. To get ready for our Draft Show I have to go over all the college tape I can get my hands on. I have an office and theatre in my home. I check in with Marvin Lewis and his staff in the Cincinnati Bengals' offices from time to time, but I don't do any of my tape work there.

Talking about Troy Polamalu, he's a very unique player. He's unlike any player who's ever played that position.

He's fortunate to have Darren Perry as his position coach and Dick LeBeau as the defensive coordinator. He couldn't ask for better mentors. Dick LeBeau is the master of maximizing a player's skills into his defensive schemes. Polamalu permits him to do things he couldn't do with anyone else back there.

They've had to incorporate special drills in their practice sessions so they know what to do when Polamalu is permitted so much freedom. They have to do drills that are different just so they know how to react.

Polamalu is a special guy. He's a great story for rookies who struggle in their first year. I remember a Steelers' game at Kansas City (second game of the 2003 season) in his rookie year. He looked completely lost. And he was.

Young players nearly always need two years to catch on to what they're supposed to be doing. That's why they ought to sign rookies to two-year contracts. They give them too much money up front. About 70 percent of the time they're not worth it. I think they ought to put more money in the hands of players who merit it. They could write contracts so that they're still not free agents until their fourth year. Teams are forced to spend so much money now. If they're good players you're going to pay them what they're worth, but not up front. That's one of the major flaws, as far as I'm concerned, in the current financial set-up.

Some of those high-priced prospects hold their team hostage. Bryan Leaf was an absolute disaster with the San Diego Chargers. They couldn't cut him. They had to let good players go to stay under the salary cap because his salary was so high. That hurt them and set them back for a few years.

Guys like Troy Polamalu and Ben Roethlisberger will get the big money as they deserve it. It's stupid the way it is now, and the Players Association has gone along with this set-up.

The Steelers wouldn't have gotten to the Super Bowl unless they had Troy Polamalu and Ben Roethlisberger. They had some other special players as well. I had Hines Ward as my MVP in the Super Bowl. I thought the turning play of the game was Randle El's touchdown pass to Ward. It was a perfectly set up play because Randle El and Ward started out on the same side of the field, which helped Ward leak out into the open field. It was a gutsy call that won the Super Bowl for the Steelers.

They're impact players. Polamalu is different, that's all. You can go back to great defensive backs like Jack Tatum and Ronny Lott, but Troy is different from those guys, as good as they were. Donnie Shell was a hitting stud, but he had nothing like the range and athletic skills Polamalu brings to the game. There's no one like him right now.

I like to talk to the defensive coaches. Even when I was playing, I liked talking to guys like Dick LeBeau and Dom Capers on the sideline. I wanted to know why they made the defensive calls they made. What were they thinking? Why are you calling this? I thought it would help me on offense. I wasn't that fast or that athletic, so I had to play smart and I had to play with a passion. I'm still that way.

I never say I can coach a football team. There's an art to coaching and play calling. If we're passionate enough about it, knowing how the game is to be played, I might be able to learn how to be a coach. But I'd never say I could step in and do it now.

So many fans feel like they can coach, but that's strictly Fantasy League thinking. Coaches put in more time than most people are willing to in their jobs. Every day is overtime.

"The coaches brought Ben along carefully."

When Big Ben was a rookie he had the things in place to allow a rookie to be successful. The coaches brought him along carefully. He was asked to do very little early on. They weren't asking him to make plays to win games. They wanted him to manage the offense, not make mistakes, and not do things that might lose the game.

That's hard for a young player to do that. That's harder to do for a rookie than to play to win the game. You have to pull back the reins. A guy like Big Ben knows his ability, and he wants to go for broke. That's how he became a winner in the first place. He's a leader and he wants to take over.

I can tell you that the coaching job done by Ken Whisenhunt, their offensive coordinator, was as great a coaching job as you'll ever witness. He gradually gave Ben more and more, as he could handle it. He didn't force-feed him or ask him to do more than he was ready to do. They did simple things, but they made it look different every week. The way they conducted the development of Big Ben was a masterpiece.

They don't get to the Super Bowl unless Big Ben plays the way he did against Denver. He didn't have the best Super Bowl, but they don't get there without him. In the Denver game he played so exceptionally well. The week before, in the same scenario, Tom Brady of the Patriots broke down against the Broncos. Ben handled all the pass rushes and blitzes, and he executed their game plan perfectly.

When a player performs well there's always a special relationship between coach and player. Ken Whisenhunt and Dick LeBeau are the best, as good as anybody in their profession. They take advantage of the special skills of their star players.

Assistant coaches want to show what they can do. They want to show their stuff. That's how they're going to get a head coaching job. So Whisenhunt had lots of stuff in his playbook that he couldn't use early on with Roethlisberger. He was patient and it paid off. He turned down a head coaching job in Oakland because he knows the Steelers will be good again, and he'll get a better opportunity to be a head coach. The Steelers are lucky he's still with them.

Some coaches ruin young quarterbacks by what they ask them to do. I think that's what happened with Steve Spurrier in Washington with his quarterback, Patrick Ramsey. Ramsey got beat to death. I don't know if he'll ever be able to play well in the National Football League because of what he went through in Washington. He's still flinching.

So many players are ruined because coaches ask them to do too much right away.

> *"A winner is somebody who has given his best effort."*
> — Walter Payton in his autobiography *Never Die Easy*

"You want to play for Bill."

You have to give credit to Bill Cowher for the kind of coaches he has hired since he's been the head coach of the Steelers. His greatest genius was the staff he hired his first year on the job. On the defensive side, he had Dom Capers, Dick LeBeau and Marvin Lewis. Those three guys all became head coaches. I love all of those guys; they're great to be with, and they still help me a lot. On offense, he kept Dick Hoak. He's one of the greatest hidden gems in the National Football League. There's not much fuss made about him in Pittsburgh — he likes it that way — but he's known and respected throughout the National Football League. He brought in Ron Erhardt, and he was the perfect coach for a running team. He had been a head coach. We went from 7-9 in Chuck Noll's last season (1991) to 11-5 in Bill Cowher's first season. Two years later, we improved from 9-7 to go 12-4.

He established the kind of team he wanted to have. We ran to set up the passing game. But we were primarily a running team. Bill stayed consistent with that, except when Tommy Maddox became his starting quarterback and he went with the passing game. That was for one year and then he made the correction. He got back to what won best for him.

Consistency is the most important aspect in pro sports. The Steelers have more stability and consistency than most teams.

Except for that one season, Bill has never wavered from that. If you want to be great in this league you have to establish an identity and a consistency. You have to find what works and stay with it. That's what made Chuck Noll so great. Make first contact. Strike a rising blow. Same foot, same shoulder. You'll never forget that. He taught us the same stuff year after year. Chuck and his staff were all teachers, and they taught us the same techniques year after year. We had smaller offensive lines than most people did, and we trapped more than most teams. You had to be smart to play for Chuck Noll.

Bill established his philosophy. When the Steelers threw the ball more they struggled. It took him only one year to correct that.

I played for Bill and I know what that's like. You want to play for Bill. He's a great motivator. He established a great relationship with his players from Day One. It was like this: "From Monday through Saturday I will take care of you. On Sunday you take care of me."

In short, he was saying I won't beat you up all week, but you'll have to play for me on Sunday. He's always been true to that. His summer training camp isn't as tough or demanding, as it was when Chuck Noll was the head coach. If the Steelers lose two in a row during the season, Bill doesn't have them go hard against each other the next practice as a punishment, or to make a point. Noll wasn't big on long practices, either, but we scrimmaged and had contact more than they do now.

There have been times when I thought the Steelers had the best team in football, but didn't knock down the door. I felt in my heart that this was going to be the year they knocked down the door. Once they got to the playoffs they were unstoppable. What they did at the end is unreal.

The Steelers should still be a strong team. They've kept their coaching staff intact. They're still a young team. The offense should get better. Ben should get better. Losing a playmaker like Randle El hurts. It's hard to find someone with the versatility to throw a ball like he can. He may find it more difficult to do some of the things he did now that he's with a different supporting cast. We'll see.

They still have Hines Ward and he was also a quarterback in college, so maybe they'll call on him to do that. I love him. I don't know of many wide receivers that can set the tempo for a game. He occupies the defensive mindset. They want to keep track of him at all times. He's an impact player.

You have to account for him on every play. If they run the ball he might knock your block off. He's doing what every wide receiver should do when he's not the primary target. He finds a way to do something. He's clutch. He'll catch the ball in traffic and hold onto it after he's hit. He contributes in so many ways. And you've got to like a guy who always comes up smiling, no matter how hard he gets hit. He symbolizes the Steelers today the way Jack Lambert and Joe Greene once symbolized the Steelers.

"It started on top."

I played for two organizations in the NFL. There was definitely a big difference between the Chicago Bears and the Pittsburgh Steelers, and how they treated players. What the Rooneys have established and what they believe in has set the Steelers apart from the pack, as far as being fair and giving and being respectful of the players.

I don't know of any other organization that was as genuine in its approach. It started on the top, first with The Chief and then his son Dan, and then Dan's son Art II. Since I've been around they've had only two coaches — Chuck Noll and Bill Cowher.

No one else in the NFL can say that. That's why they've had such consistency. To be great you have to be able to use your instincts. You can't be thinking about what you're supposed to do; you have to do it. With the Steelers, you know what you're supposed to do. You do it instinctively. You can just play. That makes a major difference.

There's a Steeler way of doing things. I think it still affects my approach to what I do today.

Jim O'Brien

Merril Hoge has hosted a golf outing to raise funds for Highmark Caring Foundation at Southpointe Golf Club.

Mel Blount
Delivers message

"Don't let other people tell you what you can do."

In the summer of 2005, Mel Blount was called to breakfast by his mother at the family's farmhouse in Vidalia, Ga. "It was 5 o'clock in the morning," recalled Blount. "I looked sleepy at the breakfast table, and my mother told me, 'You better get some sleep, Son.' I told her, 'That's what I was doing when you woke me up!'"

Blount's coal black eyes moistened at the mention of his mother. "She's 98 and, God willing, she will soon be 99," said Blount. "She amazes me with her energy. She gets up every morning at 4:30 and goes about her tasks."

Mel Blount is one of my all-time favorite Steelers. He was a great cornerback for them in the '70s when they won four Super Bowls and were the most feared team in the National Football League. Blount, at 6-4, a rock solid 220 pounds, was one of the reasons.

Blount, who shaves his head, is still a formidable figure at age 56. He has some age wrinkles around those piercing, yet warm eyes, but he still looks like he could play. He told me he had been inducted into another Hall of Fame, this one for horsemen of color, just a few months earlier. He was the best speaker at the Coaches Corner Luncheon program at the Boardwalk Complex in October of 2005. He came across as much more sincere than Dick Butkus had at the same event a month earlier.

Butkus was in Pittsburgh because he was playing the role of the head coach of the Montour High School football team for a television reality series called *Road to Glory*. Butkus said he was there to help the kids get better, but it sounded like he was there because he was getting paid for his acting gig. It had to be a test for Lou Cerro, the first-year coach at Montour who had enjoyed great success coaching at Seton LaSalle High School. His kids would have gained a great deal more from spending similar time under the supervision of Blount.

At the Coaches Corner luncheon, Blount followed Pitt's Dave Wannstedt and three area high school coaches. They all spoke about their quest to develop good young men while teaching them to become good young football players. Blount took his cue from the coaches and delivered a stirring talk about his own experience.

"These high school coaches have a chance to make a real impact on their players' lives," said Blount, who operates the Mel Blount Youth Home in Claysville, out in Washington County. It was hard to believe he had been operating this rehabilitation and education facility since 1989. It provides "a structured and nurturing environment" for males 13 to 17 years old.

Among the all-star celebrity cast at Hilton dinner are, left to right, host Mel Blount, Terry Bradshaw, Donnie Shell and Randy Grossman.

Photos by Jim O'Brien

Mel Blount shares spotlight with Steelers president Art Rooney II.

He and his staff provide support for youngsters who have gotten into trouble and need some proper direction. "I remember during my junior year in high school that our coach used to read us newspaper clippings about a kid he'd sent from our school to college. This young man was a running back at Allen University in South Carolina.

"I remember how proud he was of his kid, and when I was listening to him read those stories I made up my mind that some day he'd be reading stories like that about me. I was inspired to want to get a college scholarship, too. And I did. Some people will tell you that you're a dreamer and you can't do this or that. Don't let other people tell you what you can do with your life."

Blount said he was lucky to have the kind of coaches and family he had back in Georgia. "I was the youngest of eleven children," said Blount. "My parents were dirt farmers and they didn't have much. But they managed to send seven of us to college. Seven out of eleven. I think that's a pretty good percentage."

In a follow-up conversation with Blount, after his annual dinner at the Hilton to raise funds for the Mel Blount Youth Home, he offered some other thoughts on his mission over lunch at Legends of the North Shore, next to Allegheny General Hospital on the North Side.

"I went to the Super Bowl this year and I had my three sons with me, and it was a great experience for us," said Blount. "It was a great time. I was happy for the Steelers' organization. When I got back home I wrote notes to Bill Cowher, Dan Rooney and Art Rooney congratulating them on their accomplishment of a great season.

"They have all supported my efforts at the home, as have so many of the Steelers, past and present. I played for four Super Bowl teams and I was surrounded by some great people. I learned how much you need other people if you're going to be successful.

"We're just excited that people are behind what we're trying to do out on our farm. The whole thing is about the kids. We're trying to plant some seeds and, hopefully, see them germinate. We're trying to turn kids around and get them headed in the right direction.

"They get sent to us because they've gotten into some kind of trouble or they're having difficulties in their lives.

"I grew up in a large family on a farm in the South. I grew up when there was still segregation down there. I saw how people in our community reached back to encourage people and to help people.

"It's still with me. It's a part of me, who I am, and what I want to be. I came from a church-going family, and I learned the stories of the Bible. We just try to teach these kids some basics. Chuck Noll told us that if we wanted to win big games we still have to rely on the basics. You have to stick with the basics.

"It's difficult in these times to reach some of these kids. They just didn't have the parents we did. You're teaching them some things — rules and to respect other people — that they should have been learning since birth. You're getting them when they're 14 or 15 and they're hearing some of these things for the first time.

"We've had some real success stories. We had one kid who went on to serve our country in Afghanistan, and he's talked about how what he learned at our Mel Blount Youth Home served him well when he was over there. It was very moving. It's great to know I had an impact on the game of pro football, but it's more important to have an impact on these young kids. I left my mark in pro football and I want to leave my mark in this community."

I've seen Blount hugging some of these kids to let them know how much he cares about them. I can tell you first hand that when Mel Blount gives you a hug you feel safe from any threat in the world. Blount and his good friend John Stallworth, who also comes from a church-going family in the South, both offer hugs to old friends. Both are outstanding individuals. Stallworth is a big success in the business world.

Blount didn't bring it up, but he has endured much more abuse than Tommy Maddox or any of the other current Steelers since he started the Mel Blount Youth Home. Some of his neighbors have objected to him bringing young blacks that have been in trouble into their neck of the woods. He's had crosses burned on his property, racial epithets inscribed on the fences surrounding the property.

I saw some of this stuff when I toured his facility on several occasions in his company. He has persevered and, with the help of a lot of well-intentioned folks, his program has flourished. He has gotten the support of people such as Elsie and Henry Hillman. "I love working with those kids," said Blount. "I believe I'm helping them. I don't think there's a happier retired football player than me." His wife TiAnda does a great job in coordinating his fund-raising dinner. "It was her idea in the first place," says Mel Blount. "She wanted to do something special for my 50th birthday."

I remember the first time I met Mel Blount. It was in July of 1979. Chuck Noll had his veterans scrimmage the first day they reported to camp at St. Vincent College. Blount missed a tackle on the first play, got off the ground, and caught the ballcarrier with a jarring hit from behind. Blount had been on three Super Bowl teams at the time, and in several Pro Bowls. I asked him why he got off the ground to make the tackle, like a rookie trying to impress the coaches. "I learned a long time ago," he said, "that you can't get anything accomplished pounding your fist on the grass." I knew right away that I was going to like Mel Blount.

Mel Blount on working with kids at his Youth Home

"Chuck Noll told us if you want to win big games you have to do the basics. It's different now for these kids. They didn't have the parents we did. You're teaching them things you learned a lot earlier in your home."

Terry Bradshaw
Comes back to embrace Chuck Noll

"All I wanted to do was play . . . and win."

Beads of sweat formed fast on the expansive forehead of Terry Bradshaw. They glistened under the harsh lights of the TV cameras in a VIP reception room at the Hilton Hotel. Bradshaw was speaking to the Pittsburgh media. He was explaining his latest comeback.

Right from the beginning, Bradshaw was sweating real bullets. It was a nervous night for the former Steelers quarterback and Hall of Fame star. He was like a cat on a hot tin roof.

He was back in town as the marquee attraction for a dinner and luncheon sponsored by Dapper Dan Charities. He was to be inducted into the Dapper Dan's Pittsburgh Sports Hall of Fame on Sunday evening, February 9, 2003, and he was to offer reflections the following day at a luncheon in memory of Mike Webster, who centered the ball to Bradshaw most of his stay with the Steelers. Webster had died a month earlier.

Bradshaw had come back to Pittsburgh to pay his respects. It was all part of the process of getting back into the fold. He had failed to attend the funeral of his dear friend and former boss, Art Rooney Sr., and people in Pittsburgh still remember that. They never bought Bradshaw's flimsy excuse that he didn't want to be a distraction, attracting attention by his appearance at the funeral home or St. Peter's Church on the North Side.

Bradshaw saw the Dapper Dan Sports Dinner, one of the most respected sports awards dinners in the country, as an opportunity to make peace with Pittsburgh, the Steelers, the Rooneys, the fans and, most of all, his former coach, Chuck Noll. None of it was necessary, of course, as far as his perceived adversaries were concerned. For the most part, this was Terry's perception of the way things were, not their perception. Bradshaw has always been one of the most respected and popular athletes ever to grace a field in Pittsburgh. Sure, he was booed in the early days, and labeled as being dumb, and all that. At his appearances this time, Bradshaw admitted he didn't know what he was doing in those days, as far as reading defenses and being football smart.

"All I wanted to do was play, and win," he said. "That's what it's all about. So I didn't like it when I was benched, or when Chuck criticized me, or called me out in front of the team. No, I didn't like that at all."

Terry Bradshaw on Ben Roethlisberger:
"The thing you saw in the kid is that all he cares about is winning. Forget stats. He understands — as I did, as I do to this day — that the only thing that matters is winning."

George Gojkovich/Getty Images

Bradshaw, at age 52, had forgiven those who hurt him back then, and now he was asking anybody he'd ever said anything bad about to forgive him as well. Bradshaw has regained his religious roots, and wants everybody to embrace him and know that he never meant any harm.

Noll, age 72 at the time of the Dapper Dan Dinner, was not exactly what he would have liked in the way of a coach back then. He wasn't patting him on the back and assuring him that he was the man. He wasn't a warm, fuzzy type, like say Sam Rutigliano of the Cleveland Browns.

Noll was what Bradshaw needed back then. He was demanding, and difficult at times, but he taught Bradshaw all he needed to know to be one of the biggest winners in pro football history.

"Terry was always there when the chips were down," noted Noll in his introduction of his former quarterback at the banquet. "He was always at his best in the biggest games. He always came through when we needed it the most. That's why we won four Super Bowls."

"What an unbelievable ovation he received."

Basketball winners Ben Howland of Pitt and Swin Cash of McKeesport, an All-American at Connecticut and a WNBA star in Detroit, were honored as the Sportsman and Sportswoman of the Year at the Dapper Dan dinner, but Bradshaw was still the star attraction. He's the reason they sold out the dinner so early, and prompted them to add a follow-up luncheon to handle all the ticket requests. There were over 1500 for the dinner at $125 per ticket, and over 200 for the luncheon at $75 a ticket.

The dinner was five hours long, the luncheon lasted less than two hours. The luncheon program was more compact and easier on the backside. The dinner had some special moments, though.

Howland said he had taken his son to see the Steelers play the Indianapolis Colts in a nationally televised Monday night contest at Heinz Field back on October 21, 2002. Bradshaw was an honorary captain for that night's game. "What an unbelievable ovation he received when he was introduced at halftime," said Howland. "It was impressive."

Pittsburghers were so pleased that Bradshaw was coming back to town again, as he'd done during the Steelers' season, showing he had a change of heart, and wanted to be a part of the Pittsburgh sports family once more. "I'm home; I can't tell you how much that means to me," began Bradshaw in his remarks.

Bradshaw had been talking non-stop to Noll, who was sitting next to him on the dais. Noll was not comfortable about all this fuss. He never thought there was any problem with his regard for Bradshaw. He thought Terry was just being Terry, the ultimate showman, saying anything to cause a buzz. He always admired Bradshaw's athletic ability, and was a bit bemused by his showbiz antics.

"Terry is obviously a man who enjoys life," Noll said of the guest of honor. "But I'd rather talk about Terry, the football player. Terry came out of Louisiana, and he was just a great athlete. He not only had great ability, but the ability to do it when the chips were on the line. To do it in the big games. Terry had great ability to throw the ball deep. He wanted to do it on every play, and that's where we differed a bit.

"But I looked up some records, and in the Super Bowl Terry averaged more yards per pass than any other quarterback. He threw nine touchdown passes in four Super Bowls. He had two receivers who were pretty good. John Stallworth averaged 40.33 yards per catch in the Super Bowls, and Lynn Swann averaged 40.25 yards per catch in the Super Bowls.

"If Terry has just thrown passes, the offensive line would have been at a real disadvantage. But we could run the ball, too. Franco Harris rushed for 354 yards in the Super Bowls. There were people who wanted to stop the run when they played us, but few of them succeeded.

"So Terry could go back and have time to throw the football. It all added up to us having four Super Bowl victories."

He introduced Bradshaw the way Ed McMahon used to introduce Johnny Carson on the Late Night Show. "Here's Terry!" announced Noll, dragging it out as long as he could.

"I'm still trying to please him."

Terry Bradshaw was every bit the TV evangelist in his appearance at the Dapper Dan dinner, but he seemed honest and genuine in his remarks. One never knows for sure whether Bradshaw is just being an actor. One night he showed up for Jay Leno's late night show by dressing as Santa Claus and he just took over the show. Leno became the guest.

Bradshaw was more nervous about this assignment than being on TV with Jay Leno or with Don Imus on his morning show. He was sweating more than ever.

"Even tonight," he confessed about still being nervous around Noll, "sitting next to him, I'm still trying to please him. I've always been that little child around him.

"The problems I've publicized were never really problems," Bradshaw continued. "They were my problems, no one else's.

"In a greater sense, he became my father. He helped me in so many ways, I realize now. I guess I've finally grown up, and matured.

Terry Bradshaw on Pittsburgh:
"We've been separated, gotten back together, and now we're in it for the long run."

He taught us and we listened and we executed. And we won. Hey, I'm so glad to be back."

Terry pointed to John Majors, the former Pitt football coach, sitting in front of him on the dais, and spoke about how they got to know one another in Terry's early years with the Steelers. "He was one of the few people in Pittsburgh who talked like me," said Bradshaw with a big smile. "It took a Southern guy to understand me.

"I remember being on the sideline at Pitt Stadium when Tony Dorsett rushed for 250 and some yards against Notre Dame. I was so lonely for people back home in those days. It's good to see you again, John."

Then Bradshaw showed that he can poke fun at himself for some of his shortcomings. He brooded when anybody questioned his intelligence when he started out with the Steelers. Hollywood Henderson of the Dallas Cowboys had said, "You can spot Terry Bradshaw C-A and he still can't spell CAT!" That stuff was all behind Bradshaw now.

"I'm just so glad to be back," he continued. "I would have liked to have written a speech, but I don't write very well.

"I was a smart boy because I always thanked my Savior and my mommy and daddy. They were always there for me. They're here with me tonight. My mom's pushing 74 and my dad's 75. He had a heart attack last year. He was just going to the lake to troll when it happened and he ended up in the hospital. I'm so glad they're both in good health.

"I've always been a mama's boy. Soon after I reported to the Steelers, I had to have an operation. John Best, the Steelers' doctor, did the operation on me. When I came out of the anesthesia they told me I was saying, 'I want my Momma.'" Bradshaw smiled and took out a handkerchief and mopped his wet brow, something he would continue to do from time to time.

"It's been way too long," said Bradshaw, getting back to his Prodigal Son song. "One of the good things about life is that, as we get old, we get wiser. I've never been one who has had all the answers.

"We were supposed to win Super Bowls. It wasn't easy. It was difficult. I came out of Louisiana Tech, and I wasn't too sophisticated, on or off the field. I couldn't read coverages. It was such a culture shock coming here. All of you were so different.

"I didn't know what you expected of me. I didn't ask to be the No. 1 (draft choice) pick. And you only paid me $25,000! My dad was there when Dan Rooney signed me to a contract on the 50-yard line at Three Rivers Stadium. The stadium wasn't even completed. I never had money like that in my life (Dan Rooney told Bradshaw the next morning that he had made a mistake. Rooney said the contract was for $26,000). I went home with $7,100 in the bank. Then I learned about a thing called taxes. I had a P.E. degree . . . what did I know about stuff like that? I had to sell cars on the side just to get by.

284

"As I settled in with Coach Noll, I had a lot to learn. I was about five years behind everybody else."

Then Bradshaw directed his remarks to Noll, sitting to his left. "I was just a little bit slow about all this stuff," he said, laughing aloud at his own remarks. "I'm sure I drove you crazy. You're trying to pass along your brilliance, but I just wanted to play football. I don't want to run the football. I just wanted to throw it.

"We were being taught the lessons to be successful. I knew more about defense than I did about offense. If you knew the opponent and their weaknesses you could attack it and win.

"I didn't like being benched. I didn't like losing my job. I didn't like it. You have a choice. You can blame somebody else, or you can accept the blame."

Terry Bradshaw embraces Coach Chuck Noll.

Jim O'Brien

Art Rooney Sr.
More stories about "The Chief"

"That's just the way he was."

No sooner do I finish writing one of my books and turning it over to the printer than someone tells me a story that should have been in the book.

I take notes and file the anecdote and tell myself that I will use it in some future book. In a way, it keeps me going.

This happened threefold soon after I finished writing *The Chief — Art Rooney and his Pittsburgh Steelers* in the summer of 2001. The book was on the presses at Geyer Printing in Oakland when it started.

Nellie King, Paul Martha and Dan Lackner — all genuine "Pittsburgh guys" in the words of Art Rooney — offered their own reflections on the founder and patriarch of the Pittsburgh Steelers who had died, at age 87, on August 25, 1988.

King was the former Pirates' pitcher of the '50s and the beloved sidekick to Bob Prince on Pirates' broadcasts for nine years (1967 through 1975). Martha was a classmate of mine at the University of Pittsburgh, an All-America running back on Pitt's 9-1 team that didn't go to a bowl game in 1963, and the No. 1 draft choice of the Steelers in 1964. He played seven years in the National Football League, the last of those years with the Denver Broncos.

Lackner was the president of Paper Products Co, Inc. in the Terminal Building on the South Side. His uncle, Dan Hamill, founded the company in 1913. "My mother was one of 11 children, and Dan was the only boy in the family," said Lackner. Hamill was an old friend and former business associate of Art Rooney in the early days of the Steelers. Dan Lackner followed in his uncle's footsteps and also became a friend of Art Rooney and worked as an office boy at the Fort Pitt Hotel. "When someone bought a season ticket in those days they'd have me run the money to the Potter Title & Trust Company at the corner of Fourth and Grant," allowed Lackner. "It was a big deal. Things were so bad if we didn't have the fights at Hickey Park we'd have been out of business. They were always telling me they were holding checks at the bank (because there weren't sufficient funds to cover them), and to tell Mr. Rooney about that. There wasn't much money to go around in those days.

"Rege Cordic and I used to be let out of school at Central Catholic 20 minutes early so we could catch a 76 Hamilton (street car) that took us downtown so he could go to work at WWSW and so I could get to the Fort Pitt Hotel to help out there. Cordic became a big star in the radio business at KDKA, and then on the West Coast."

Dan Lackner is the father of Rich Lackner, the head football coach at Carnegie Mellon University.

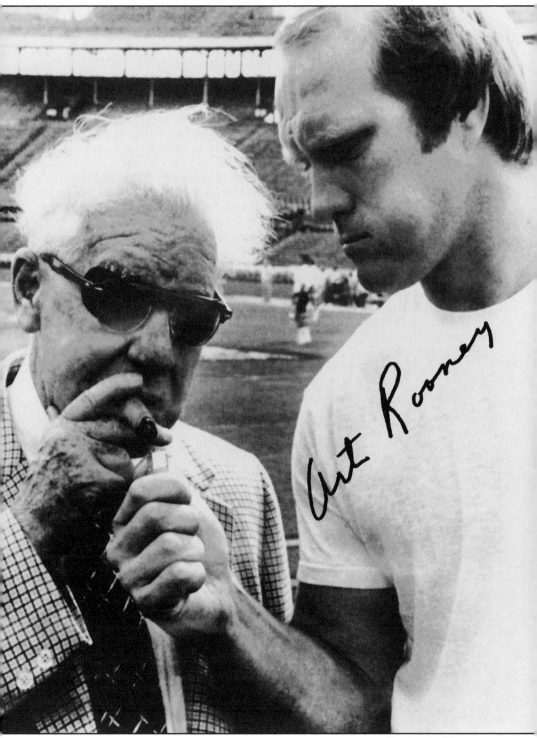

Art Rooney

Terry Bradshaw lights cigar for his boss, Art Rooney Sr.

When I interviewed Dick LeBeau, the defensive coordinator of the Steelers, on Wednesday, March 8, 2006 for this book, as I was leaving the Steelers' headquarters on the South Side, driving down South Water Street alongside the UPMC Sports Performance Complex, I spotted a delivery truck from Paper Products as I was about to make a right hand turn onto the Hot Metal Bridge. I was making a turn to go to the Steelers' offices. I waved to the driver and he waved back, probably wondering who the hell I was. It was good to know they were still providing paper and envelopes for the Steelers. The Rooneys remain loyal to old friends.

I learned later that UPMC is also a customer of Paper Products.

"What are you working on?" asked Nellie King when he called to ask me a question about publishing books. He was writing one about his days with the Pirates and needed some help.

When I told him I had just finished a book about Art Rooney, he said, "Mr. Rooney was a wonderful man. When the Pirates fired me as a broadcaster, the first letter I got came from Mr. Rooney. He told me how much he enjoyed my work, and that he would miss hearing Bob Prince and I doing the games. He offered me best wishes and hoped I'd land another job soon. It meant a lot to me. So the first letter I received with some sincere expression of concern came from the owner of the Steelers. I never heard from John Galbreath, the owner of the Pirates. That tells you all you need to know about the owners of two pro teams in Pittsburgh."

King turned 79 in 2006. He was in fragile health and he and his wife Bernadette, had sold their home in Mt. Lebanon and moved the year before to a senior care facility on Bigelow Boulevard in Oakland.

Martha, who turned 64 in 2006 and was living in San Diego, called me from California about something he was involved in back home in Pittsburgh. Martha and I have always had a good relationship, going back to our days when we attended a few classes, notably Spanish, the bane of both of our existences in our student days, at Pitt. I was the sports editor of *The Pitt News* and he was a star on the football and baseball teams, as well as a starter on the freshman basketball team. "After I was drafted by the Steelers," said Martha when I spoke to him during a visit to San Diego, "I went down to their offices with my father, Al Martha, to talk to Mr. Rooney. That's how simple things were then. I didn't have an agent; no one had an agent. As we're talking, Mr. Rooney asks me what I planned on doing if pro football didn't work out for me.

"It caught me off guard. I told him I was thinking about going to medical school. He advised me to check that out, and see if I could go to school while I was playing for the Steelers. I did and I found out that there was a conflict between the class schedule and the Steelers' practice schedule. I talked to Mr. Rooney again the next week, and told him what I had learned. He said, 'Have you ever thought about law school?' I said I hadn't. He suggested I check that out. He gave me a name and a phone number to call at Duquesne University. I did that a few days later and learned that I had already been accepted to their law school. Everything had already been taken care of. They just needed a copy of my Pitt transcript for their files. That's how I became a lawyer."

"It looked like Phipps Conservatory."

Dan Lackner, who turned 80 in July, 2006, still goes to the office most mornings and puts in an honest day's work. He had a new kidney put in and a knee replacement during the 2005 season, and was up to working six hours a day. He was so proud of his family. Two of his brothers were priests — Paul and Fran — and both had been favorites of Art Rooney, who liked to keep company with priests.

When Lackner's son, Rich, won his first game at CMU he gave him a silver dollar to mark the occasion. When Rich won his second game he gave him two silver dollars. Thus a tradition was begun. Within a dozen years, he was carrying over a hundred silver dollars with him to give to his son after a game. When security measures got tougher at the airports, this caused problems. Then, too, it became difficult for him to buy that many silver dollars. "Now I just shake hands with him after every game," related Lackner. "He had about five thousand dollars worth of silver dollars when he cashed them in."

Lackner recalled what happened when he attended the funeral of Art Rooney's wife, Kathleen, at Devlin's Funeral Home on the North Side. It truly tells you everything you need to know about Art Rooney, and why he was such a beloved figure in Pittsburgh, maybe the most beloved figure in the city's history.

Kathleen Rooney died, at age 78, at Allegheny General Hospital not far from their home on the North Side. She and Art had been married for 51 years and had five sons. She passed away on Sunday, November 28, 1982 following a heart attack. The Steelers were playing a game in Seattle when it happened. Dan Rooney, the oldest of the five sons and then the team president, left the game early and returned to Pittsburgh.

Mr. Rooney once told me it was more important to attend a funeral when a friend suffered a death in the family than it was to attend the funeral of the friend. It makes so much sense. Mr. Rooney was wise in so many ways.

"No sooner had I stepped inside the door of the funeral home," related Lackner, "than this guy comes down the hallway and calls out to me. We'd gone to school together at Central Catholic High School many years before. His name was McNamara, Joe McNamara. He told me his father of the same name had died at the VA Hospital and was laid out in the next room. 'All his friends are gone, and I didn't know whether to have a funeral for him or not,' said his son. 'But I decided to do it, so here we are.' He told me his father had been a city fireman and had lived on Dawson Street in Oakland.

"I went with him to pay my respects. There was nothing in the room but the casket and a kneeler. That was it. It was a sad scene.

"He told me they were only going to be at the funeral home for one day. When I left him to pay my respects to Kathleen, I bumped into Art Rooney in the lobby. He said, 'Dan, who were you talking to back there?' I told him about my boyhood friend and his father. He said, 'C'mon, let's go back so I can pay my respects.' So we went back together and I introduced him to my old friend, whom I hadn't seen in years, Joe McNamara. Mr. Rooney talked to him for awhile, offered his sympathy, and I could tell it meant a lot to McNamara. Art signed the book and took a Mass card with him. He went to more funerals than anyone in Pittsburgh, and he always took one of those Mass cards with him when he left."

I recalled looking through Mr. Rooney's collection of books at his office at Three Rivers Stadium, and most of the books had Mass cards in them. I learned from his secretary Mary Regan and one of his sons, Art Rooney Jr., that he used them for bookmarks. In more recent years, during a visit to Art Rooney Jr. at his office in Upper St. Clair, he showed me some of his books and opened some of them to show me that he, too, used Mass cards for bookmarks.

Back to Dan Lackner's story...

"As we're coming out of the room, a big, powerfully built black man is coming through the door, carrying a big basket of flowers on each arm, said Lackner.

"Art called out to him. 'Where are you taking those flowers?' The man said they were for Mrs. Rooney. Art said, 'We have enough flowers. You take them back to our friend McNamara.'

"I saw Joe Greene and I think Terry Bradshaw coming in behind the man with the flowers. Mr. Rooney also sent them back to see his friend McNamara.

"In the door comes Tom Foerster, the former County Commissioner, with his friend, Tom Flaherty, the former mayor of Pittsburgh. They were two of the top politicians in Pittsburgh, and dear friends. Mr. Rooney greets them, accepts their condolences, and tells them, 'Don't forget to go to the back room and pay your respects to our friend McNamara.'

"Foerster shoots Rooney a look. 'What McNamara?' And Rooney responds, 'Our friend McNamara, the fireman.'

"And Foerster says, 'I don't know any fireman named McNamara.'

"And Rooney rather testily tells him, 'Yes, you do! The one from Dawson Street. Out in Oakland.'

"And Foerster gives in and says, 'Oh, that one.' And he and Pete Flaherty go back to the other room. So Art had everyone go back to pay their respects 'to our friend McNamara' and sign the visitors' book. It went on like that the rest of the day. When I came back the next day my friend McNamara was still there. 'We decided to stay another day,' he told me.

"I went into the room once again to see his father. You could hardly see Joe McNamara. He was surrounded by flowers. The room was full of flowers. It looked like Phipps Conservatory. He showed me the visitors' book and so many famous Steelers, such as Joe Greene and Mel Blount and Terry Bradshaw, had signed the book. Pete Rozelle, the NFL Commissioner, and Al Davis, the owner of the Oakland Raiders, had been there, too. Everybody who was anybody in the National Football League or in Pittsburgh had signed the book. Art had sent more flowers and so many of those who came to pay their respects to Mrs. Rooney. That's just the way he was. That visitors' book might be worth something these days."

It would be worth at least a few silver dollars, no doubt.

Bob Milie

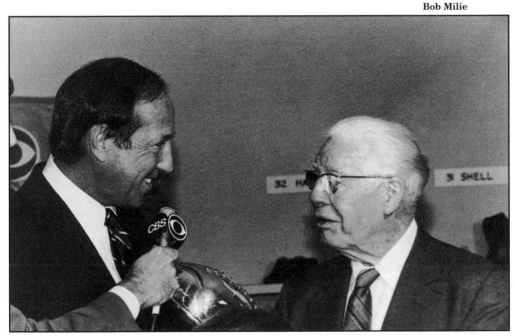

NFL Commissioner Pete Rozell presents Super Bowl IX Lombardi Trophy to Steelers owner Art Rooney Sr. at Tulane Stadium.

"To have a championship team it takes a great coach, great ownership — with the Rooneys — and great teammates."
— **Jerome Bettis**
at ESPY Awards in Los Angeles
July, 2006

Dan Rooney
At Super Bowl XXX

"We're here for the game."

S teelers president Dan Rooney appeared at a press conference in late January, 1996 in Tempe, Arizona prior to the Steelers' game with the Dallas Cowboys in Super Bowl XXX. I was invited by the Steelers to fly to Phoenix on one of their charter airplanes to attend the event and it was great to be there, even though the Steelers came up short in a game they could easily have won. Rooney's remarks still reveal the approach he wants the Steelers to take regarding the way they represent Pittsburgh. His words remain insightful into the Steelers' Way.

Dan Rooney:

"The people in our organization are important."

It's been written that I'm part of the old guard. I consider myself part of the people that think the tradition of the National Football League is very important. I think that includes everyone. There are great new owners in the league. They contribute someone like (Denver's) Pat Bowlen. He goes all-out and participates on committees. He does a fine job. A guy like (Carolina's) Jerry Richardson who just comes in for an expansion team. He's doing quite a bit. Then, of course, you have people like (New York Giants') Wellington Mara who really follows the past and knows the history of the league. I think that our position is that the National Football League really is something that is important.

It's great for us to be back in the Super Bowl regardless of anything else. I have to say that I'm really very, very thrilled about being here. There have been a lot of things written, even the slogan "one for the thumb," which is a problem. This team is its own team. That is a thrill for me to see these young people come of age. It's really their Super Bowl. They're the ones that are doing it. As Neil O'Donnell said, he's looking for one for the ring finger.

We're lucky to have a coach like Bill Cowher. If you will remember back then (when he was hired), everybody talked to us about how young he was. "Do you think he's ready for it? Sure, he's a good coach, but do you think he's ready for it?" I have to say that every time I would talk to Bill, you thought of his age. His enthusiasm, his ability to command a situation and be a leader of people, just came through. I felt here is a guy who can do this job. That leadership and that enthusiasm have come through. He's really shown great leadership for our team.

I think there are differences between the Dallas Cowboys and the Pittsburgh Steelers. I think our approach is a lot different off the field. On the field I think we're similar in that we want the best players. We feel the approach is to get players to come up through your ranks, not go after the big free agent types. Go after people that you are going to bring in and they are going to help you and that everybody is a part of the organization. And I think Dallas does that. Off the field, I think we're totally different. I think their approach is the big sell, the big America's Team, and things like that. The football end of it, which is the important thing, and I think that's important to remember. We're here for the game. We're not here for Nike. We're not here for Pepsi. We're not here for Coke. We're here for the game. I think we're very similar in that regard.

I hated to see Art Modell move his team from Cleveland to Baltimore. I personally think that teams have to stay where they are under most circumstances. I think there are circumstances that could prevail that a team would, should move. They are considerably less than what is happening now. Cleveland is a great football town. It's one of the traditional places like Pittsburgh. Pro football started in Pittsburgh, we say. But it really was developed itself in the nature that we know in the Ohio, western Pennsylvania area. I really hate to see Cleveland without a team.

I think the Steelers' organization personality was set by my father. It goes back to the beginning. The thing always meant so much to him. We're trying. I don't think any of us can do it near as well as he did. It is people that mean something. The people in our organization are meaningful. Every player is important. Every coach is important. Our staff, our fans, you have to consider that. I think that if there is a uniqueness, it's people that are meaningful to us. To get very emotional, I'd say it's love. It's the love that exists among us for everybody. I think that's what counts and I think it came from him and I think we're trying to carry it on.

The Super Bowl has changed since we were last in it. It has gotten a lot bigger. There's more hype. To be quite honest with you, it is more (Cowboys' owner) Jerry Jones. It's more selling. It's more NFL Properties buying maybe with Jerry on some of these things. I really believe the game is the important thing. That should be our principle purpose here, to play a great football game and do everything we can to make that the best it can be. Everything else should be secondary. It's where we are. It's the biggest sporting event in the world.

Dan Rooney at Super Bowl XL

Dan Rooney was interviewed by several writers on Media Day at Super Bowl XL.

Since 1970, only the Cowboys have been to the playoffs more often than the Steelers, who were making their 22nd appearance during the 2005 season.

Rooney was under public pressure to fire Cowher after the Steelers finished 6-10 in 2003, but he extended his contract instead. The Steelers went 31-7 from that time on, including the post-season games. Players talk about how Mr. Rooney always makes the rounds in the locker room, after a victory or defeat, and shakes hands with everyone and offers a pleasant or encouraging remark. At 73, he was the oldest club owner since the death of Giants' co-owner Wellington Mara during the 2005 season. Mara was a close friend of Dan and his father. For the record, Art Rooney Sr. was also 73 when the Steelers won their first Super Bowl back in 1975.

"We're not in this thing to make all the money in the world. We've got to pay the most attention to the game, and what's good about it, and how to protect its legacy," Dan Rooney told the assembled media.

"People who are making a run at it feel, 'We'll do everything we can; we'll shoot for the moon this year.' Our philosophy is, 'If you do that and it doesn't work, where are you?' Changing coaches . . . all that does is make you an expansion team.

"Bill's a good coach, a good person. Everybody has a down year now and then. I was impressed with his knowledge and his enthusiasm. He had confidence he could do the job. Being from Pittsburgh also had a little to do with hiring him, too, because we had coaches in the past who didn't believe in Pittsburgh the way Bill and Chuck Noll do.

"Bill and Chuck thought Pittsburgh was a special place. Some of those other coaches we had didn't think Pittsburgh was too much.

"The biggest thing my father passed on to me was to treat people right. We treat our players as people, not just workers. We're concerned for them away from the field and whatever problems they might have. My father always had a relationship with the players, and I've tried to do the same."

CHUCK NOLL

1969   1991

NATIONAL FOOTBALL LEAGUE

SUPERBOWL   CHAMPIONS

PITTSBURGH STEELERS

© MURRAY CARDS

Illustration by Merv Corning commissioned by Art Rooney Jr.

Chuck Noll watched Super Bowl XL at home in Bonita Springs, Florida

Chuck Noll was invited by Steelers' owner Dan Rooney to be his guest at Super Bowl XL, but he turned it down because his back was bothering him. "His back is terrible," said his wife Marianne over the telephone from their home in Bonita Springs, Florida. "It goes from bad to worse."

Noll had turned 74 on January 5, and this was the latest health problem he had encountered in recent years. He used to attend golf outings and other social events frequently in Pittsburgh, but had to cut back on his traveling and other activities. They still had a home in Sewickley as well.

"You can tell he's uncomfortable and in a lot of pain," said Joe Gordon, the former Steelers' publicist, who visited the Nolls during a winter stay with his wife Babe in Florida. "He can hardly do anything."

Noll was not fielding phone calls leading up to the Super Bowl, but his wife said they would be watching the game on television. "I think he's just proud of anything the Steelers do. It means a lot to us as Pittsburghers. We have lots of friends down here who are having Super Bowl parties, but we'll watch the game by ourselves," said Mrs. Noll.

Seattle
Brings back military memories

"I can always land the plane on a glacier."

I remember when I received my military shipping orders in 1965. I was being sent from Kansas City, Missouri and my orders said something about APO Seattle with some numbers after it. Hey, I thought, Seattle is a nice city. I'd been there before. In my sophomore year at the University of Pittsburgh, I had traveled to Seattle with the Pitt football team. They would play the University of Washington there.

Don James was their coach, Rick Skaggs and Ray Mansfield were two of their outstanding offensive linemen, and both would later play for the Philadelphia Eagles. Mansfield would be traded to the Steelers and be the starting center on their first two Super Bowl championship teams. I remember the press box was so high; second only at the time altitude-wise to TCU's press box. You could see Puget Sound from the press box at the University of Seattle.

I remember visiting the Space Needle and dining in the restaurant that revolved around the top of it. That was the landmark of the World's Fair that was held there in 1962.

Seattle was just a stopover city, however, a departure city from the continental U.S. I was headed for Alaska. A place called Fort Greely, somewhere between Anchorage and Fairbanks. The U.S. Army's Arctic and Cold Weather Testing Center was located there. Terrific. Alaska was the 49th state, but it was considered "foreign duty" and brought extra pay.

There was a blizzard the evening I got off the airplane at Anchorage and I promptly threw up when I got on the landing strip. A soldier had shot and killed himself in the barracks the night before I got there so the fort was in a state of confusion and sadness when I arrived.

When the Steelers played the Seattle Seahawks in Super Bowl XL, it made me remember my days at Fort Greely and in Seattle.

I would learn to ski in Alaska, and it's really the only place I ever skied, except for one or two visits to Boyce Park out near Monroeville.

I was sent there to be the assistant editor of the newspaper at Fort Greely. Two weeks after I got there I became the editor. It was a 12-page paper when I arrived, and a 28-page paper after I became the editor.

We worked out of a little building about a mile from the main barracks area. We had an island to ourselves in a way. Our building housed a radio station and a TV station. I started my own nightly TV sports report, and made a set that included a poster with the Pirates' Dick Groat on it. I filled in once in a while on the radio, doing my best imitation of Porky Chedwick, a popular Pittsburgh deejay who introduced rock 'n roll music to the city over WAMO. We received weekly shipments of film of TV shows that were screened nationally a week or so earlier. We could watch them at our own leisure and often invited our buddies from the main post to come out and join us for an evening at the movies.

I was there for ten months. There were animals everywhere: moose, caribou, elk, bears of all kinds and the lakes were teeming with fish. It was a sportsman's paradise. Unfortunately, I was not and never will be a sportsman. I remember there were large mosquitoes. Everything was large in Alaska. There were few single women on the military post.

I rode with pilots getting airtime on single-engine airplanes over glaciers, mountains and tundra. I remember the engine conking out once and a red light flashing on the dashboard. The pilot didn't panic. He told me he'd catch it in gear, taking the plane downward until it caught hold, much the same way we had gotten cars to restart by popping the clutch on a downhill glide when the engine would quit. "If that doesn't work," the pilot told me, "I can always land the plane on a glacier." That was reassuring.

When I returned to the States, getting out two months early so I could start classes in September in graduate school English Literature studies at Pitt, I had a four-day stopover in Seattle.

I thought I was going to get out on Saturday, but a second lieutenant told me the offices were closed on Saturday and Sunday, and I would have to wait till Monday to depart the military service.

This was Friday. "Why can't you let me out today?" I asked the young officer.

"Because you would be getting out one day earlier than your orders call for," he replied.

I appealed to his good sense and suggested he was smart enough to make that decision on his own. He shrugged his shoulders and said it was out of his hands. In short, he said he was going by the book. Young officers often would say that.

If that wasn't bad enough, I saw my name on the K.P. (Kitchen Police) list for Saturday and Sunday. What a great sendoff — two 12-hour shifts cleaning up in the mess hall. To hell with that, I thought.

I left Fort Lewis and took a taxicab to downtown Seattle and got a room at a hotel there. I went to see Luther Adler starring as Tevye in a stage production of *Fiddler on the Roof* at a local theatre, I reported back to Fort Lewis to be dismissed on Monday. I was docked two days pay. When I think about it now, I could have been put in the clink for two days for being A.W.O.L. You live and learn. You get smarter when you're in your 60s than you were in your 20s.

I would return to Seattle in later years, traveling with the New York Knicks when they went there to play the Sonics, for the NBA All-Star Game, and, eventually, with the Pittsburgh Steelers. I have many fond memories of Seattle.

Elsie Hillman
A special date

"She's a real Pittsburgh guy."
— The late Art Rooney

*T*here were several significant stories that came out of the National Football League's Annual Owners' Meeting that took place in Orlando, Florida in late March, 2006. The owners were celebrating a new labor agreement with the players that had been hammered out two weeks earlier in what had been the most arduous since the league and players' union agreed on a free agent-salary cap deal in 1992. Paul Tagliabue announced that he was retiring after more than 16 years as NFL commissioner, having succeeded Pete Rozelle in the high profile position.

Art Rooney II, in his third year as president of the Pittsburgh Steelers, was voted by the league's general managers as the NFL Executive of the Year. Kevin Colbert, the Steelers' director of football operations, finished fourth in the balloting for the award that is named in honor of the late George Young.

Young was a close friend and fellow traveler on the scouting trail for many years with Art Rooney Jr., who headed the Steelers' scouting department during the glory days of the '70s. Young had been a scout for the Baltimore Colts and went on to become the general manager of the New York Giants.

Dan Rooney was credited by Tagliabue as being one of the owners who helped him steer the owners into voting for the latest labor agreement and for revenue sharing by the NFL franchises.

Art Rooney II related that his father had hinted that he would be getting honored at the league meetings, "and, of course, added immediately that 'you know I've won two of those things.' So there's always a challenge," said the son.

Young Rooney's name came up at the meetings as a possible successor to Tagliabue, but he was not interested, wanting to look after the Steelers. His father was named to the important search committee a week later to find the next NFL Commissioner. Dan Rooney has always been respected and viewed as a voice of reason among the owners.

I spent a special evening back in 1998 in the company of Paul Tagliabue, Dan Rooney, Art Rooney II and Elsie Hillman, the First Lady of the Republican Party In Pittsburgh as well as a power broker on the national political landscape. The Hillmans remain one of the richest families in America, yet everyone who knows them describes them as wonderful, generous, down-to-earth people. The Hillman Foundation gave a gift of $25 million to Children's Hospital. The UPMC Hillman Cancer Center not far from their home in Shadyside is named in their honor.

298

A *Christmas Carol*, Act I:

A special card came in the mail at the outset of 2001. It was from Elsie Hillman and it had a message at the bottom of the card hand-written in red ink. Elsie said she was recovering nicely from a short hospital stay the previous month. She also offered some kind comments about some newspaper columns of mine she had recently read. It made my day.

The message in red ink reminded me of a Christmas card I had received the same week the previous year. It also reminded me of a "date" I had with Elsie Hillman in December of 1998. I'm not a kiss-and-tell guy, but I have to share this story with you.

The Hillmans, for the record, don't do much writing in red ink.

For the few who may not recognize the name, Elsie Hillman happens to be the wealthiest woman in western Pennsylvania. She is also the most politically powerful woman in western Pennsylvania. For a long time, she was the chairperson of the Republican Party in these parts. She has always been a big sports fan, and was a close friend, for instance, of the great boxer, Billy Conn, the original "Pittsburgh Kid," and his wife, Mary Louise Conn.

Elsie's husband is Henry Hillman. He is always referred to in society or "Seen" columns as "an industrialist." I don't know what that means, but let's just say the position pays well. Henry Hillman is one of the richest men in America.

They are an odd couple, but a great team. Henry is reserved. Elsie is not. Elsie is a great lady, but so down-to-earth. She likes to dance. She's a lot of fun. Both are generous with their time and money. They can afford to be. But not everyone who can afford to be does that.

Art Rooney, the late owner of the Steelers, used to say rich people didn't like to spend money. "That's how they got rich," he'd say. Art Rooney would have regarded Elsie Hillman with another of his favorite expressions. He'd say "she's a real Pittsburgh guy."

Elsie has friends in high places. She has been buying ten copies of my newest book annually and having me inscribe appropriate messages on them.

In January of 2000, I received a card with a Houston, Tex. address on the outer flap. I didn't recognize the address. The card read: "Dear Jim, Elsie Hillman sent me 'Hometown Heroes.' I'll read it. Thanks for the good wishes Elsie passed along and for inscribing my copy. Happy 2000!" It was hand-written in red ink, but I couldn't make out the name.

I flipped it over and there was a beautiful portrait photo of the family of former President George Bush. Barbara was behind him. Our next president was to his immediate left. It was dated Dec. 25, 1999. I couldn't get over President Bush taking the time to write me a "thank you" card on Christmas Day. There's a lesson in there for all of us.

I had known of Elsie Hillman since I was a kid because my late mother, Mary Minnie O'Brien, was one of five Republicans in our community in Hazelwood, and she worked the polls every election. I didn't get to know Elsie well, though, until we teamed up at a funeral in Greenfield, of all places.

Elsie was alone at the funeral of Jack Rafferty, a street ruffian of sorts who was a Republican activist. He also booked numbers as a sideline, illegal in some parts of town. "Imagine me and Jack being friends," she whispered in my ear.

Elsie latched onto my right arm in the funeral procession at St. Rosalia's Catholic Church. We made a nice couple. I knew the match had the tongues wagging of all my old buddies and rivals from Greenfield. Elsie called me a few weeks later on the telephone. She said she had to speak at a United Way dinner at the Doubletree Hotel the next week, and she needed some background information on Dan Rooney, the owner of the Steelers, who was being honored at the fete. She asked me to fax her something ASAP.

A few days later, she called me again and thanked me for my help. "Remember that dinner I told you about," she began. "Well, Henry has a conflict in his schedule and he can't make it. You'll be my date." She said a dark suit would be fine. I was to meet her in the lobby at The Doubletree Hotel at 6:15 p.m.

I like the way she summoned me to be with her that night. I wish I had used the same approach when seeking a date during my school days at Allderdice High School. Instead of groveling on the telephone, sweating and seeking the right words, I should have simply said, "You'll be my date."

It's too late now for me to put that wisdom to any good use.

Elsie Hillman has a few words of advice for Pittsburgh Mayor Bob O'Connor. Ironically enough, Mayor O'Connor ended up in the UPMC Hillman Cancer Center in Shadyside for treatment during the Major League Baseball All-Star Week in Pittsburgh in July 2006.

A Christmas Carol: Act II.

Elsie's confidence comes from her status in Pittsburgh social circles. She is also the most pleasant, affable, approachable, good-humored and down-to-earth woman you would want to meet. It's easy to be in Elsie's company.

As soon as I said I would be happy to go with her and hung up the phone, I thought about Kathie. She happens to be my wife. She had met Elsie outside her home in Shadyside when we delivered some books there once, and Kathie was impressed with how personable and gracious Elsie had been with her.

I called Kathie on the telephone to make sure it was OK with her. "Elsie Hillman called me," I began, "and she wants me to go with her to a big dinner. Do you mind if I go with her?"

"Heck, no," Kathie came back. "I hope she adopts you."

I could always count on Kathie for her support.

Elsie met me in the lobby of the Doubletree. She was fashionably late. I was sweating that she was going to stand me up. As she approached, I was wondering how to welcome her. She gave me a little peck on the cheek. She knew what to do.

She showed me a black handbag and opened it slightly to reveal a copy of one of my books, *Keep The Faith*, with Steelers' star running back Jerome Bettis on the cover. "I wanted to show this to my friends," she said with a smile. I followed Elsie wherever she went. I walked one or two steps behind her. I remembered that Prince Phillip did that when he walked with Queen Elizabeth.

People were bowing and genuflecting, or so it seemed, as Elsie made her way through the hallways. They were all happy to see her. She introduced me to everyone as "my writer friend." Then she'd give them a peek at the Bettis book in her little black bag. I felt like a young artist, Raphael perhaps, walking with his patron.

We sat at a table that had to be the "power" table in the room of 800 or so guests at the Doubletree. Dan Rooney and his wife, Pat, were at the head of the table. His oldest son, Art II, and his wife, Gretta, were across from me. David Roderick, a Rooney friend and the former president and CEO of U.S. Steel and USX, was there with his friend, Becky Fisher, along with Helge Wehmeier, president and CEO of Bayer Corp. I was seated next to Paul Tagliabue, the NFL commissioner. Joe Browne, the commissioner's right-hand man, made quite a gesture on his own. He swapped seats with me so I could sit next to Tagliabue. Browne sat next to Elsie Hillman.

I imagined Dan Rooney whispering into his wife Pat's ear, "What's O'Brien doing here?" I was asking myself the same question.

When it was Elsie's turn to speak from the platform above us, reciting Rooney's achievements, she started by showing the audience my book. She then placed my book in front of her on the podium and it showed up on huge screens throughout the room. It was fantastic.

You can't buy that kind of endorsement, especially from Elsie Hillman. I figured some people who knew me were saying, "I can't believe O'Brien got Elsie Hillman to shill for him."

It was an eventful evening. I told Elsie afterward that if Henry ever had another conflict that she could call on me at some future date. She hasn't summoned me since, I must confess. I might have blown it when I drank an IC Light from the bottle. I hope not. She dropped me a card from the Caribbean Islands, written in red ink, after she heard about my concern in this regard. She assured me that another date was on the horizon. Now she sends me cards from different places around the world, the way Art Rooney once did, and I save them all. She's a special woman the way Art Rooney was a special man. Pittsburgh is lucky they both came our way.

George Gojkovich/Getty Images

Dan Rooney, Chairman of the Board

Joe Paterno
Pokes fun at Pittsburgh favorites

"If I didn't live in State College I'd want to live in Pittsburgh."

It was the best of weekends for Joe Paterno, even though Penn State didn't even win a football game. Paterno was honored at two prestigious awards dinners in Pittsburgh on April 28 and 30, 2006, and in between he attended the baptism of his 15th grandchild in Philadelphia. "We're Catholic, of course," explained Paterno in one of his throwaway lines. Paterno poked fun at Franco Harris and Jerome Bettis, the two best running backs in the history of the Steelers, as well as Agnes Berenato, the women's basketball coach at Pitt, and found time to lampoon Italians and Asians with a sharp needle. He referred to Dan Rooney, the chairman of the board of the Steelers, as "Danny," which tells you something about how old Papa Joe is.

Paterno was the least prepared and best received of all the speakers at both banquets. He was just being Joe Paterno, patronizing, poking fun at himself and anyone within earshot, and lecturing, as he must, stumbling here and there at the microphone. All he needed was a wrinkled raincoat to complete the "Colombo" picture. The crowd at both events was happy to have Paterno on the podium, just being Paterno. At age 79, he was happy to just be there, and the crowd responded in kind. They were happy to have him.

A lot of great comedians have come out of Brooklyn and Paterno picked up on their sense of humor and looking at the world differently, especially with his poor vision.

He was one of six to be honored at the 14th Annual History Makers Award Dinner on a pleasant Friday evening at the Westin Pittsburgh Convention Center. A record crowd of over 500 was in attendance for a $500 a plate dinner. One of the other honorees was one of my boyhood heroes and a dear friend for nearly 30 years, Herb Douglas, who came in from Philadelphia for the affair. Douglas, who grew up in Hazelwood and starred as an athlete at Allderdice High School and the University of Pittsburgh, won the bronze medal in the 1948 Olympic Games. I was a guest of Douglas at his table at the History Makers Award Dinner sponsored by the Senator John Heinz Pittsburgh Regional History Center. Douglas and I served on a champions committee to establish the Western Pennsylvania Regional Sports Museum there two years earlier. Four years earlier, my wife Kathie and I were among the 80 guests he invited to his 80th birthday party, a black-tie affair at the Duquesne Club.

Douglas, who is 84 and retired after a distinguished business career, said, "I remember Paterno was at Penn State when I was a kid."

It was that kind of night, where everyone was humbled a little. Franco Harris, who played for Paterno at Penn State and went on to become a big hero with the Steelers of the '70s, toasted and roasted Paterno at both dinners. He was able to use the same notes both nights, and did so splendidly. Harris has become a statesman of sorts in Pittsburgh, and a point of pride to those like Paterno who have witnessed his growth since he left Fort Dix, New Jersey in favor of State College, Pennsylvania. Harris had served as the chairman of the championship sports committee and coordinated all the meetings.

On Sunday evening that same weekend, Paterno was honored with a Lifetime Achievement Award at the 70th Annual Dapper Dan Dinner, while Jerome Bettis of the Steelers and Agnes Berenato, the women's basketball coach at the University of Pittsburgh, were honored as the Sportsman and Sportswoman of the Year in Pittsburgh.

Paterno had fun at their expense, pillorying Harris and Bettis, the two best running backs in the history of the Steelers. Harris is in the Pro Football Hall of Fame and Bettis is expected to be inducted when he become eligible five years after his final season with the Steelers. Paterno also had some fun at Berenato's expense, but, like so many at the Downtown Hilton she was happy to be keeping company with such a legend as well as the other sports and political luminaries on the three-tiered stage.

When I asked Berenato before the dinner if she could imagine coaching the Pitt basketball team at age 79, she smiled. "At 79, do I think I'm going to be coaching? No. I hope I'm in Cape May. I hope I'm in Europe. I might be dead by then." Paterno said he wasn't much of a singer, but he'd be glad to sing at her funeral if she so desired. The message was that he intends to still be around.

Paterno was one of the few in the crowd who could recall some of the sports legends who were honored in the early days of the Dapper Dan Dinner such as boxers Billy Conn and Fritzie Zivic, football's Buff Donelli and "Bullet Bill" Dudley, baseball's Frankie Frisch, Ralph Kiner and Stan Musial, golf's Lew Worsham and Arnold Palmer, basketball's Dudey Moore and Red Manning, hockey's Baz Bastien and harness racing's Del Miller. Paterno also paid tribute to Al Abrams, the late sports editor and columnist for the *Pittsburgh Post-Gazette*, who started the dinner back in 1939. "He was a Dapper Dan," offered Paterno, "and he started all this."

I was born in 1942 and became aware of the Dapper Dan Dinner when I was a young newsboy for the *Post-Gazette* in the mid-50s when the honorees included Pitt football coach John Michelosen, and the Pirates' Dale Long, Dick Groat and El Roy Face. I read Al Abram's column six days a week and wondered what it would be like to have a job like his. He seemed to go to great places, witness wonderful events

Franco Harris, Joe Paterno and Ralph J. Papa of Citizens Bank of Pennsylvania were among speakers at Heinz History Makers Dinner at Westin Convention Center.

Mayor Bob O'Connor welcomes Joe Paterno to Pittsburgh at awards dinner sponsored by Dapper Dan Charities to benefit Boys' and Girls' Club.

and spend time talking to interesting people. It seemed like a great way to make a living. Being invited to sit on the dais at the Dapper Dan Dinner in 2006 was a real honor for me. I had been invited for the first time two years earlier, but had a conflict in my schedule which kept me from sitting on the dais. I did manage to catch the tail end of the speeches that night.

Florida State's Bobby Bowden and Paterno were running 1-2 as the winningest coaches in college football history, having surpassed the immortal Bear Bryant years before. Paterno was praised for that and his outstanding track record for graduating the vast majority of the young men he recruited to Penn State. Paterno is personally blamed, on the other hand, for ending the Pitt-Penn State football rivalry. Paterno was ticked off at Pitt officials for betraying him and going in another direction (the Big East) when Paterno tried to put together a conference that included Penn State and Pitt back in the late '80s.

"They had to turn to a guy named Chuck Noll."

Paterno poked fun at the Italians and Asians in the same breath. Noting the presence of "my good friend" Dr. Freddie Fu, the sports medicine director at UPMC, Paterno said, "The Italians are always using their hands when they speak, and the Asians are always clicking their cameras and taking pictures." Paterno pretended to be clicking a camera so everyone got the picture. Joe Paterno wouldn't be Joe Paterno if he didn't say something he shouldn't have said. He can be wise and funny in front of a microphone, but equally dangerous.

He spared no one. When I posed a question for Paterno at a press conference that preceded the Dapper Dan Dinner, he said, "O'Brien, you were a pain in the butt when you were young, but you were lucky enough to talk a young woman into marrying you and you came out okay." What that remark had to do with what I had asked him, I'll never know, but he wanted to keep things in their proper perspective. He was the coach and I was still a punk student sportswriter on *The Pitt News*.

I remember going to Penn State during my student days and how Paterno held court in a room at the Nittany Lion Inn on the eve of a game between Pitt and Penn State. Back in those days, the early '60s, the host school would entertain the visiting school's administrators as well as the media at a party. It was done everywhere. Things were more civil away from the field in those days.

A writer such as Chester L. Smith, the sports editor and columnist for *The Pittsburgh Press*, would travel to Penn State and stay a few days and be treated like visiting royalty.

Paterno always had points to make, and he prided himself on being a professor on a college campus. He has always been teaching us something. You didn't have to agree with all that he said but you were learning just the same, and he was making you think, something every professor worth his or her salt should do.

I remember picking Paterno up at the Greater Pittsburgh Airport back in the early '80s to escort him to a Coaches Corner luncheon at the Allegheny Club at Three Rivers Stadium. The monthly sessions were then known as the Curbstone Coaches luncheons. En route to downtown Pittsburgh, I told Paterno about my brother Dan's death a month earlier. A year later, at the same site, when Paterno walked in the room and spotted me, he came over to shake hands. While doing so, he said, "How's your sister-in-law and her kids getting along?"

Paterno impressed me with his recall and his concern.

He may not have done right by Pitt or Penn State to end the football series, but there's something about Paterno that remains appealing. Unlike some sports coaches, he's never forgotten that he's working at a university.

Paterno had a chance to coach the Pittsburgh Steelers, but he rejected Dan Rooney's offer. "They had to turn to a guy named Chuck Noll," said Paterno. "I deserve to be honored in Pittsburgh for helping to make that happen."

I mentioned to Paterno that some Pittsburghers expressed unhappiness in him being honored at a Pittsburgh banquet. "I didn't ask to be honored," he replied. "We have a lot of Penn State alumni in these parts, and a lot of kids from this area have made big contributions to our program at Penn State. I've always liked Pittsburgh and its people, and I'm proud to get these honors. At my age, I'm happy just to be here."

I get a kick out of Joe Paterno. He always makes a fuss when we meet, and he can't help but needle me. "I didn't know they let Pitt guys in here?" he'll say as he shakes your hand vigorously and draws you in for a hug. "I haven't seen you in years and now I keep running into you," he said when we crossed paths for the fourth time that weekend.

"They had to have some Pitt people to dress up the event," I told him, giving him some of his own medicine.

The last time we'd seen each other was about four years earlier at the New Castle Country Club where we were both speakers at a golf outing where a lot of former Penn State football players were in the field. It was held for the Foreman Foundation. That foundation was formed when John Bruno, a former Penn State punter, died from melanoma at age 27 in April 1992. His father, John Bruno Sr., was in attendance at the golf outing. I had Paterno sign one of his two autobiographies at that meeting. He seemed touched that I asked.

I always wished that Pitt had its own Joe Paterno, someone who stood the test of time, and stayed the course. Pitt had some legendary coaches through the years, but none provided the stability and permanency that Joe Paterno lent Penn State. There are 18 libraries on the Pitt campus, but none of them is named for a football coach. Penn State takes pride in the fact that it has a sports facility named for one of its former presidents — Bryce Jordan Stadium — and a library, thanks to a $3 million gift he made, named after Joe Paterno.

"I wonder what happened to all those secretaries."
— Joe Paterno

Paterno talked about his first days in Pittsburgh when he was a young assistant coach to Rip Engle at Penn State. "I came to Pittsburgh in 1950, a young bachelor, and I thought I was handsome," recalled Paterno. "I used to hang out with the guys at a place called the Cork & Bottle at the bottom of the Oliver Building. I wonder what happened to all those secretaries who used to go there."

I couldn't help myself. I turned to my wife Kathie at our table and said, "They're probably at Kane Hospital or at nursing homes." I knew I was far enough away from the dais that Paterno couldn't see me, but I started worrying that he might have heard me. Paterno's players insist that if they did anything wrong on the practice field, no matter how far from him and his thick eyeglasses they might be, Paterno would make a squeaky observation about their miscue.

Paterno's players, especially Franco Harris, love to mimic Paterno's squeaky voice. It always draws a laugh. Even Paterno makes fun of the way he talks.

Paterno got serious, too. He was asked about his graduating quarterback, Michael Robinson, and how he was the 100th college player picked in the NFL draft that weekend. "I was amazed he went that late," said Paterno. "I don't know how you build a pro football team, but you can't tell me there are 99 football players better than him. He did as much as any single football player I've had. He did a lot of different things."

He looked over at Franco Harris and was reminded of how pro scouts sought his thoughts about whether Harris or Lydell Mitchell was the best back on his Penn State football team back in the early '70s.

"I don't know, you're going to have to make that mistake on your own," Paterno recalled telling the scouts.

"If I told Lydell Mitchell to run through a wall he would do so without hesitation," Paterno continued. "If I told Franco to run through that wall he'd look for a loose brick somewhere."

Then he recalled a meeting he had with Dan Rooney following the Steelers' 1968 season when Bill Austin posted a 2-11-1 record, his third losing season in as many years on the job. "When Danny and I talked in 1968," said Paterno (the only person in the room who would refer to the Steelers' owner as Danny). "I was tempted to go with the

Photos by Jim O'Brien ⟶

Franco Harris and George Washington are honored with sculptures at Pittsburgh International Airport. They are both captured with likenesses as 22-year-old men.

Dapper Dan Sports Dinner lineup featured Franco Harris, Jim Tracy, Joe Paterno and Dave Littlefield. Pirates' personalities were excited about meeting Harris and Paterno.

pros. The offer was a good one. I just didn't want to leave Penn State. I thought I could get some good things done there.

"I went to Penn State 56 years ago (at age 23) because I needed $2,000. I thought I'd coach for a while, and then go back to Brown. I wanted to go to Law School. I owed money and I didn't want to spend any more of my father's money. He was upset with me. 'Why'd you waste your time going to college?' he asked me. Two years later, when I told him I thought I had found something I'd like to do. He told me, 'If you're going to do this, then make a difference.' And that's what I've always tried to do.

"You never know how much of an influence you are on anyone, but I'd like to think I helped some of these guys like Franco to find their way. I remember his dad Chad telling me he hoped I'd get Franco to get rid of his mustache. Look at him. Does it look like I had an influence on him?"

Franco offered a smile through a bearded face, one so familiar to his fans in Pittsburgh. Andy Masich, the president and CEO of the Heinz History Center, had mentioned that he had returned to Pittsburgh earlier that day and knew he was in the right place when he saw the recently erected statues of Franco and George Washington in a Heinz-sponsored exhibit at an entryway at the airport.

Franco is shown bending over to catch the football in that famous "Immaculate Reception" sequence. "My back hurts from leaning over so much out there at the airport," offered Franco.

When Franco reflected on his playing days at Penn State, he mimicked Paterno's squeaky voice. "Franco, go to the ball . . . go to the ball." Franco let that line float for awhile, before adding, "I didn't really learn that lesson, of course, until I got here to Pittsburgh."

Harris also reminded us that it had been 21 years since he retired from the National Football League, being released at mid-season by the Seattle Seahawks after going there in a salary dispute with the Steelers. Guess who Franco was rooting for in Super Bowl XL?

"I find that the older I get the smarter Joe Paterno gets. We were lucky to have Joe Paterno in our lives. He had a great experiment going to show that school and football could co-exist and flourish."

Ralph J. Papa, regional president of Citizens Bank of Pennsylvania, served as dinner chairman and emcee for the Heinz event. He had spent years heading Mellon Bank's regional center in State College, and had a chance to catch a fellow Italian Joe Paterno up close and personal. "Joe's greatest accomplishment," offered Papa, "was the level of class he has brought to collegiate athletics and the example he has set for so many to follow — on and off the football field."

Joe Paterno

"Something positive is going to happen."

Joe Paterno said he had found a lot of talent in Pittsburgh and Western Pennsylvania through the years. He found his wife Sue in Mt. Pleasant, out near Latrobe. They have five children and remain a happy and contented couple.

Paterno said he thought Pitt made a wise decision in picking Dave Wannstedt to direct its football fortunes. "Something positive is going to happen," he said.

Paterno also said he's happy doing what he's doing at Penn State, and planned to stay a while longer. If his Penn State team would play in a post-season bowl game after the 2006 season, Paterno would be 80 years old when he stood on the sideline for a holiday season contest. That's unreal.

"I've never had a bad football team," he said. "I'm doing what I did when I was six, seven and eight years old. I'm playing games. You can't beat that. If I can keep my staff I'll be fine. We've got great kids to work with. Bobby Bowden and I have talked about this, and we're not thrilled about the alternatives. What do you do after you've coached a college football team? I don't like what happens then."

Paterno probably felt at the top of his game as he had won several Coach of the Year awards after the 2005 season when Penn State won the Big Ten title and defeated Bowden's Florida State team in the Orange Bowl.

Paterno has posted a 354-117-3 record. He is second all-time in games coached (474) and is tied for fifth among Division 1-A coaches with a .750 winning percentage. He is the all-time leader among coaches in bowl appearances (32) and post-season victories (21). He's won two national championships, had five undefeated and untied teams, won five American Football Coaches Association Coach-of-the-Year plaques, and had 20 finishes in the Top Ten.

"My heart bleeds black and gold."
— Jerome Bettis

Joe Paterno picked up the dinner plate of Jerome Bettis at the beginning of his remarks. "I wanted to show you that Jerome has the only clean plate up here," said Paterno, drawing an easy laugh.

"I remember when he was in high school, and our coaches were high on him. They thought he'd be a great linebacker. I saw him and I saw that fat ass, and, to me, he didn't look like a linebacker. He looked like a nose guard.

"All I know is, this guy I thought would be a nose guard is playing fullback for Notre Dame the next time I see him. I said to my guys, 'If that son of a gun gets by the line of scrimmage, the first guy that hits him high, I'm gonna yank him out of the game.' But then I looked at another couple of tapes, and I said, 'You know, he's got pretty good feet.' So I said, 'Don't wait for him.' I never thought I'd say that about a big, fat guy."

Bettis kept his head bowed and laughed off most of Paterno's pointed remarks. He knew the Coach was having fun at his expense. But he breathed a sigh of relief when it was his father's turn to talk.

John Bettis introduced his son Jerome at the Dapper Dan Dinner. He praised him for being a great son and a great family man as well as a great football player. "This year was a fantastic ride," said Jerome's father, who was along for the ride with his wife and two other children. "It was something we had hoped for, something we didn't know was possible. The ride is not over; it's a continuing trip."

He mentioned that his son's success enabled the family to go to Disney World for the first time, attend the Grammy Awards event in Los Angeles for the first time, and to go to the Olympics in Turin, Italy for the first time. "I've enjoyed the ride," said John Bettis. "It's been a blast."

His son seconded his father's feelings. "It's hard for me to understand the magnitude of it all," said Jerome Bettis. "I know what the Dapper Dan means to Pittsburgh. I want to say thank you. I've been helped in a lot of ways by a lot of people.

"I want to thank my teammates. I really rode their shoulders. This season didn't turn out the way I wanted it to as far as individual success. But they gave me an opportunity to leave this game a champion. I thank the Pittsburgh Steelers for taking a chance, as the Coach (Paterno) says, on a fat kid with good feet. The organization gave me a chance to have success. I went to talk to Mr. Rooney before the Super Bowl and told him you believe in people and not just winning. They believe in people first and stats second. I want to thank Coach Cowher for knowing when to put me on the bench. I want to thank Dick Hoak for letting me be the assistant backfield coach and helping some of our young guys. I want to thank Bob Pompeani for getting me involved in the Jerome Bettis Show. At first, I said, 'What am I doing?' Bob gave me an opportunity for getting prepared for life after football. I thank the City of Pittsburgh. You have let me into your hearts and let me into your homes. You've taken me into your hearts. My heart bleeds black and gold. I'll always be with you.

"I went over to talk to Franco Harris. He gave me advice when I first came here. He said, 'When the season is over, be sure to take care of those injuries. Get well before the following season.' After 13 years, I can tell Franco that I took pretty good care of myself. And I want to thank NBC for giving me a job. I'm working now. It's a beautiful thing.

"I want to thank Coach (Paterno) for not taking the job (with the Steelers). He'd still be coaching and I wouldn't be here. I have to say thank you to me . . . for not being stupid enough to go to Penn State."

He also thanked his wife for presenting him with such a beautiful baby daughter, and thanked his family for their support.

In earlier interviews, Bettis offered some observations about his final season. "It's been an incredible ride," Bettis said after the Steelers defeated the Seattle Seahawks, 21-10, back on February 5, 2006. "I decided to come back to win a championship, and mission accomplished. So with that I have to bid farewell."

In his final game at Heinz Field, Bettis scored three touchdowns against the Detroit Lions, his boyhood team. He has a sense of theater. Jerome Bettis was aware that the Dapper Dan Dinner raised significant funds to support the Boys and Girls Club. He had his own Bus Stops Here Foundation in his native Detroit. He was named the 2001 Walter Payton NFL Man of the Year for his community service. He credited his parents for raising him properly, and showing him the way. "Without them, I wouldn't be the man I am today," he said.

Jerome Bettis poses with Dr. Freddie Fu of the UPMC Sports Medicine Performance Complex.

Penn State's Paterno provides inspiration for seniors

A minister friend of mine shared a story about how Penn State football coach Joe Paterno provided him with inspiration to return to work.

Dr. Pat Albright has been serving as the interim pastor at Westminster Presbyterian Church in Upper St. Clair for several months. He had previously served for 16 years at Mt. Lebanon United Methodist and for a spell at nearby Southminster Presbyterian.

He remembers receiving a telephone call from a member of the personnel committee at Westminster asking if he would be willing to fill the void created when Rev. Stu Broberg left to assume a similar post in downtown Pittsburgh.

"I was 74 and quite content with my retirement and my wife Betty Lou and I were looking forward to doing some of the things you're able to do when you're not working," recalled Dr. Albright. "I thought I was too old to take on this task.

"I said I'd like a day to think about it and pray on it. When I did that the first images that came to my mind were those of Joe Paterno, the Penn State football coach, and Cardinal Joseph Ratzinger, who is now Pope Benedict XVI.

"They were both 79 and were willing to take on greater challenges. That did it. I agreed to serve."

Dr. Albright is an avid reader and he finds inspiration and the right words for his sermons in many places. He's also an avid sports fan and finds great enjoyment as a fan of the Steelers, Pirates and Penguins, as well as the Penn State and Pitt football teams. He still manages to get to a Pitt and a Penn State football game at least once a year, thanks to the kindness of friends with tickets.

He says his favorite Theology Journal is *Sports Illustrated*. He believes that there are many stories in sports that translate to our lives and meeting the challenges therein.

Joe Paterno was in Pittsburgh this past weekend and was honored at two awards dinners I attended. Paterno was a big hit at both events.

I told Paterno privately what Dr. Albright had told me, and he loved the story. "That's great," he said, giving me a high five to show his joy.

One of the History Makers was Stephen Flaherty, who grew up in Dormont and graduated from South Hills Catholic (now Seton LaSalle) High School. He's best known for winning a Tony Award as the composer of the Broadway musical "Ragtime," and he played a number from that score on the piano to complete the program. He also put in a pitch to raise funds to save the Dormont Pool.

Big Ben is Big Kid
Enjoys himself on golf course

"I like to get out with the guys
and have some fun."

Ben Roethlisberger took a short cut and came rambling down a steep grassy knoll in a golf cart. He came to a screeching halt on the cart path, his golf cart taking a 180-degree spin. He smiled at everyone who was staring at him and his burgundy buggy. Cart No. 38 was still standing upright. I looked back up the hill from whence he came. The drop was the same angle as a stairway, about 30 yards' worth of hillside.

I thought it was a good thing Bill Cowher wasn't where I was, riding shotgun next to Max Starks of the Steelers on the edge of my seat. Cowher might have killed Big Ben right on the spot. Or he'd have had a stern word or two with him in the clubhouse.

Big Ben can't help himself. He's 24 years old and he's a bit reckless. Cowher and Terry Bradshaw have both been critical of Roethlisberger for riding a motorcycle and, worse yet, riding a motorcycle without a helmet. That was old news.

Then again, maybe Big Ben wouldn't be the sensational football player he is without walking or riding on the wild side from time to time.

This was a Monday, May 22, at the 13th annual Hoge-Starks-Ward Celebrity Golf Classic for Children at the Southpointe Golf Club in Canonsburg. It was for the benefit of the Highmark Caring Foundation.

I had seen Roethlisberger playing basketball a month earlier with the Steelers' basketball team at Canon-McMillan High School in the same Washington County Community about 25 miles south of Pittsburgh.

This was at the 18th tee and there was a backup of three fivesomes. Maybe Ben got impatient, or maybe he just wanted to amuse everyone.

I had been interviewing Max Starks, the 6-8, 340-pound offensive tackle while accompanying him across nine holes at the Southpointe Golf Club course. Big Ben, by coincidence, was playing behind us.

I had an opportunity, by happenstance, to observe Roethlisberger at play. There is, indeed, playfulness about Roethlisberger that is very appealing. He positively skipped across some of the greens. When he'd see Starks crush an occasional tee shot, Roethlisberger would call out — like a radio or TV broadcaster — something to accompany the shot.

"Catch the houses! Catch the houses!" he hollered on one hole when a grand slam by Starks looked like it might carry into a cluster of homes at the edge of the course. "It's a high fly ball to deep center," Big Ben called out on another hole. He was just having some fun.

He had played in another fund-raising golf outing three days earlier at the Fox Chapel Golf Club. That was hosted by Marc Bulger, the Pittsburgh born and bred quarterback of the St. Louis Rams.

I learned a few days later that in between he had offered a message at a school program at The Chadwick Restaurant in Wexford and received rave reviews.

The day after I had seen Roethlisberger at play at the Southpointe Golf Club, I heard a good report on him when I was conducting an author's program at the West View Elementary School in the North Hills School District. Dr. Joseph Clapper, the district's school superintendent, attended a luncheon where I spoke to faculty members and administration prior to conducting some writing workshops.

Dr. Clapper told me that nine northern Allegheny County school districts had joined together to combat a serious adolescent drug and alcohol problem in a group called The Alliance.

"On Saturday, Ben spoke to a group of 200 students, teachers and other adults," said Dr. Clapper. "He impressed upon them the dangers of using drugs and alcohol. Ben did a fine job. Ben was extremely generous with his time and he was very personable with the students. He signed autographs for anyone who asked."

Ben Roethlisberger has been a busy boy ever since he signed with the Steelers out of Miami (of Ohio) University in 2004. "Everyone has wanted a piece of him — including me — since he first stepped foot in Pittsburgh," said Ed Bouchette, the veteran Steelers' beat writer for the *Pittsburgh Post-Gazette*. "I think he's handled it pretty well."

He was a hot topic in Pittsburgh. Most had good things to say about Big Ben. Others said he was "stupid" for his daredevil ways with his motorcycle. A man who refereed some of the Steelers' basketball games thought he should have been friendlier with people, and thought he was a bit of a jerk. Some spoke of getting a cold shoulder from him.

Personally, I thought Ben was doing the best he could to please everyone. But that's an impossible task. Yes, there are times when he walks with his head down so as not to make eye contact. He can't smile and sign an autograph for everyone who approaches him. I think he has embraced many worthwhile causes, and tried to use his celebrity in the right way.

May was "sweeps month" and the local television stations were trying to outdo one another in an effort to boost ratings. They were covering the Steelers' mini-camp and "coaching sessions" as if they were pre-Super Bowl events. They carried a story where Terry Bradshaw, in town for a charity golf outing, renewed his criticism of

Signs in nearby windows drew attention of Ben Roethlisberger as he played golf in Highmark Caring Foundation outing at Southpointe Golf Club. Below, Ben Roethlisberger submits to interviews at halfway point of Highmark Caring Foundation golf outing at Southpointe Golf Club.   Mike Longo

Big Ben's dangerous behavior on his bike. They did a full story on Big Ben's spring vacation to his ancestors' homeland of Switzerland, and a full report on Big Ben's new pooch. Everything about Big Ben was big news.

He had managed to stay out of trouble. That's not easy for some Steelers. Since the Steelers won the Super Bowl all of their actions attract more attention and media coverage. Before May was completed, Santonio Holmes, the Steelers' No. 1 draft pick out of Ohio State University, managed to get arrested by police in Miami for disorderly conduct. The incident occurred at 3:30 a.m. on Collins Avenue, a street I was familiar with from when I covered the Miami Dolphins for *The Miami News* back in 1969. I was also familiar with a sage comment my mother had made from time to time, that is, "Nothing good happens after midnight."

Jake Plummer, the quarterback of the Denver Broncos, was arrested for a road rage incident in which he was accused of banging his car into a car whose driver had honked a horn at him.

There were other familiar names in the news. Craig "Ironhead" Heyward, a former Pitt and NFL star running back, died at the age of 39 from a brain tumor. Jim Trimble, who came out of McKeesport to become the head coach of the Philadelphia Eagles for four years (1952 through 1955) and later a personnel man and scout for the New York Giants, died from emphysema at age 87. I had a good association with both men in earlier years. They would be missed.

"I try to do what I can."

I had occasion to ask Roethlisberger a few questions when he took a food break at the clubhouse midway through the golf outing for the Caring Foundation. He picked up a hamburger and a cold drink at the break. He was asked to do some television interviews. One of the requests came from WPXI-TV, Channel 11. When a young woman asked Roethlisberger about that, he turned and looked to a cluster of media people nearby. "Channel Eleven!" he hollered out. "Channel Eleven . . . boo!"

Bill Phillips, a sports reporter for Channel 11, came over to talk to Roethlisberger. Several weeks earlier, Channel 11 had sent a camera crew to Roethlisbrger's residence on Washington's Landing, just off Route 28 near Millvale. He had caused a stir there because he had parked one of his cars in the street instead of his driveway — a no-no with the homeowner's association. Roethlisberger didn't think it deserved news coverage, and he resented the media coming to his doorstep. Roethlisberger was right about this infringement on his privacy.

Phillips apologized profusely. "It wasn't the sports department that did this," he explained to Roethlisberger. "It was the news side.

I told them they should never go to your house again unless it's on fire."

Roethlisberger repeated his unhappiness about the incident. "I heard a rumor," he said, "that Dan Marino wouldn't do interviews with Channel Two because of something they did to him."

For the record, Roethlisberger submitted to the interview request at the Southpointe Golf Club. Then, too, I spoke to J.D. Fogarty, an old friend who was one of the charter residents at Washington's Landing, and is the president of the neighborhood association.

"Ben has been a good neighbor," offered Fogarty, a spotter for Bill Hillgrove in the broadcast booth. His father, Fran Fogarty, had been Art Rooney's business manager for many years with the Steelers. "Ben has treated everyone out here in a positive manner. There's never been any problems at his place like late or noisy parties, or anything like that."

There were also reports that Ben was about to move to a new locale in the Pittsburgh area.

When I spoke to Roethlisberger, he said, "I try to do what I can to contribute to good causes in this city. My father was a generous man and he taught me to try and make a difference when I could. I like to play basketball with the Steelers because it's just fun — no pressure — and I like to get out with the guys and play some basketball. Or golf. It's a chance for people to see you do something besides playing football."

At the 14th tee on the golf course, there was a sign in one of the windows of an office building that is part of the Southpointe complex. It read "BEN, WILL YOU MARRY ME?" Another sign read "HI, BEN" and "GO HINES MVP." A woman in the window held up a telephone number. One of the people in Ben's fivesome called the number of his cell phone, "It turned out he had gone to school with her," reported Roethlisberger when I asked him about the incident. "He handed me the phone and she said, 'Ben, I love you.' It was all in good fun."

When Roethlisberger went by the building on the other side, several women had taken a timely smoke break to be there as he passed. They yelled at him and he smiled and waved to them. Starks said, "You never see signs like that for offensive linemen. But I can do without that kind of attention."

Roethlisberger was wearing a ballcap, a black windbreaker, khaki knee-length shorts, black golf shoes over white anklets. He looked like a young man having a good time.

"You think you're bulletproof."

Tunch Ilkin and Craig Wolfley were talking about Big Ben on their "Inside The Locker Room" show on Fox Sports Radio one morning.

They were talking about how when they were young Steelers they frequently rode dirt bikes and three-wheel vehicles through farm fields. I talked to Tunch Ilkin on the telephone about this later in the day. "We were just out having fun," he said. "You should have seen us when we went out skiing together. We did some wild things. I'm not saying what we did was right or wrong. It's what you do when you're that age. It's the difference between being a kid and being a parent. When you're that age you think you're indestructible. You think you're bulletproof. One of the reasons Ben is such a good football player is because he's a risk taker. It's in his blood. You don't want to take that away from him."

Mike Longo

Ed Joyner, off-duty state trooper, serves as bodyguard for Big Ben who signs autographs for youngsters who attended Steelers' basketball game in Canonsburg promoted by Wayne Herrod.

Antwaan Randle-El

Chris Hope

They'll be missed

Kimo von Ohlhoffen

Montana & Rooney a winning parlay
at Pro Football Hall of Fame

It was the best day ever to enter the Pro Football Hall of Fame. There had never been a gathering of great football players to match this one. NFL Commissioner Paul Tagliabue thought it would be a good way to start off a new century by inviting every living member of the Hall of Fame to the sport's shrine in Canton, Ohio. That's located just 100 miles west of Pittsburgh, but it was a trip back in time, to when many of those football heroes were hale and hardy, when they were bubble gum cards stored in a drawer in my boyhood bedroom. It was a great way to celebrate the NFL's 80th anniversary.

Everyone who was there should have felt honored by the occasion. There were 111 of the 136 living members of the league's elite who came to Canton last week. Sid Gillman, who taught Chuck Noll so much about football, came in a wheelchair. A half dozen walked with the aid of a cane. Many more moved with great difficulty — up and down the steps of the building with a football-shaped façade. We chose to see them as they were when they were stars.

We were, as former 49ers owner Eddie DeBartolo Jr. put it when he introduced the most popular of all the inductees, Joe Montana, surrounded "by the very best of the best." The Class of 2000 was heralded as one of the best classes of inductees as well. It was a class that made anyone from Pittsburgh or Western Pennsylvania feel particularly proud. It was headed by Montana, a hometown hero from Monongahela, and Steelers president, Dan Rooney.

They were the last to be inducted in the three-hour-long ceremonies. They saved the best for last. They were preceded by Dave Wilcox and Ronnie Lott, two of the hardest hitters in pro football history, representing two different eras of excellence for the 49ers. Lott had been a teammate, close friend and admirer of Montana during the great run when the 49ers won four Super Bowls in the '80s.

Howie Long of the Oakland Raiders, who wore No. 75 because of his admiration for the Steelers' Joe Greene, was the other member of the high-profile class. Greene was there, too, as a former inductee and as the man chosen by Dan Rooney to present him in the induction ceremonies. Seeing them and the rest of the Hall of Famers stirred different memories for those in a record crowd of 18,000. In his recent fan's memoir, *Home and Away*, Chicago-bred writer Scott Simon wrote, "Sports stories can be memories and daydreams by which we measure our growth, like a parent's strokes inching up the unseen insides of a doorway."

I go to Canton every July to enjoy these gatherings. It has become a rite of summer. I love this stuff. I go there with two good friends, Bill Priatko and Rudy Celigoi, who played the game in college. Priatko spent enough time over a three-year period with the Browns, Packers and Steelers to serve him in good stead the rest of his life.

When the formal ceremonies were concluded, I was ready to go home. I'd been out in the sun too long and knew I would be punished for it. As Wellington Mara, the owner of the New York Giants, once told me through winced blue eyes, "The Irish were not meant to be out in the sun."

Priatko never gets enough of this scene. He wanted to look for Mike Ditka. I didn't think there was a chance we could find Ditka in the crowd. Priatko persisted and Rudy and I followed him, reluctantly.

We showed our credentials to get through three different lines of security guards and, before we knew it, we were at a party for Hall of Famers and their families. We spent a half-hour with the likes of Mike Ditka, George Blanda, Joe Greene, John Henry Johnson, Tony Dorsett and Al Davis. Oh, if only Joe Namath and Montana and Dan Rooney and his late father, Art Rooney, had been there.

I had two ice-cold beers that helped take the burn out of my forehead. Mixing with so many personal favorites, catching up with their current activities, seeing Dorsett mimic the way John Henry Johnson once punished would-be tacklers with a fierce forearm was a priceless experience. Any fan would have loved to be in their company.

Jim O'Brien

Joe Montana and Dan Rooney are heralded on banners at Fawcett Stadium during Pro Football Hall of Fame induction ceremonies in early August of 2002.

Milestones are reminders of
a road well traveled

August 7, 2002

I circled two dates on my August calendar. Kathie and I will celebrate our 35th wedding anniversary on August 12. I will be marking my 60th birthday on August 20. I'm prouder of the first; it's an achievement. The second just happened, and I have a hard time believing it to be so.

I was a lucky young man the day I discovered Kathie. It was at a party in Oakland when we were both in graduate school at the University of Pittsburgh. Kathie was completing her studies for a master's degree in social work, and I was taking some post-graduate literature classes after coming out of a two-year commitment in the U.S. Army. Kathie has kept me on my toes, and sometimes my heels, ever since. She has had the greatest impact on my life of anyone I have known.

Kathie is demanding and often difficult to please. She set the highest standards for our daughters, Sarah and Rebecca, and for me, and we have all benefited from that. She keeps the three of us humble.

I came back a week ago from speaking at the grand opening of a new library in Plum Borough and told Kathie that a woman told me she could listen to me all night. Kathie came back, "I do, and it's no great shakes."

Our house has been in an upheaval in recent weeks as we had some painting and wallpapering done in rooms upstairs. I couldn't find my wedding ring for two days and I got anxious about its absence. I didn't tell Kathie because I didn't want her giving me any flak. This is my third wedding ring. Kathie keeps track of stuff like that. When I finally relented and told her, she told me that she had put it away in my dresser. When I saw the ring it was like finding the huge gemstone in "The Lord of the Rings." I was out de-thatching our front yard — raking the dead stuff out of the grass — when Kathie came upon me, probably to inspect my work. It was a task she had been after me to do the last three years. I told her I had a story to tell her. A fellow from Brookline named Barry Foley, who was retired from being the head groundskeeper at Three Rivers Stadium, had died the day before. One of his sons told me they put a copy of my book about Art Rooney, *The Chief*, in their dad's coffin because he was so proud of the chapter I had written about him in the book.

I told Kathie that was the fourth casket I knew of that one of my books had been placed in for the funeral service. Kathie came back, "I'll tell you another casket your book is going to be in . . . your casket! When you go, all your stuff in the garage is going with you. There will be a few boxes of books in your casket."

See what I mean. Kathie keeps me humble, and on the straight and narrow. Sometimes I wish she'd let me up for air. Sometimes I feel like I'm walking through a minefield, afraid of a misstep.

The saving grace is I realize that her discipline has been good for me. It has kept me out of trouble for the most part.

Our daughter Sarah sent me an e-mail last week in which she said she was surprised that I referred to us as "seniors" in my last column. I told Sarah that, like it or not, we are, indeed, seniors. We have had our AARP cards for a couple of years, we get senior discounts at stores, hotels and movie theaters. I've got a 95-year-old mother, and that's a reminder that I'm not a kid anymore. More people call me "Mr. O'Brien" these days.

Kathie keeps our home and me clean and looking our best at all times. She even irons my T-shirts and undershorts. That puts her in my Hall of Fame right there. I went to the Pro Football Hall of Fame last Saturday to see John Stallworth of the Steelers and Jim Kelly of East Brady and the Buffalo Bills get inducted.

Everyone spoke about the important role their families had played in their success. The inductees were all grateful for the support they had received through the years. It reminds me of how lucky I have been. Stallworth and the Steelers of the '70s always speak about having those four Super Bowl rings, and how that is a testament to their success. If I hadn't found that wedding ring last month I might have had my fourth wedding ring by now.

Stallworth is still married to Flo, and they are one of the few couples from those Steelers of the '70s who remain married. Kathie has a locket from the Steelers' fourth Super Bowl triumph, back when I was covering the club for *The Pittsburgh Press*, and she still has her first wedding ring. I'm glad it's the one I gave her. To me, my wedding ring is better than any Super Bowl ring.

HOF 02

Jim O'Brien

John Stallworth swaps tall tales with former teammate John Banaszak at Mel Blount Youth Home dinner at downtown Hilton. Banaszak was boasting about his two new titanium knees.

Doug Miller was one of the lucky ones
who will never forget Sept. 11

*T*he Steelers and Shanksville were linked shortly after the tragedy of 9/11. Those are numbers that will never need explaining in our lifetime. Images of airplanes steered by terrorists into the Twin Towers of the World Trade Center in New York and the Pentagon in Washington, D.C. are etched in our minds forever.

Shanksville is a small community in central Pennsylvania , just east of Somerset. United Flight 93 crashed in a field outside of Shanksville, and the 40 passengers and crew resisted the four hijackers, preventing the airplane from being crashed into an unknown national landmark, most likely The White House or Capitol in Washington, D.C. Three days later, Steelers' officials, Coach Bill Cowher and a number of players traveled 80 miles by bus from Pittsburgh to express their sympathy and gratitude at a candlelight vigil in Somerset.

"People felt good that they wanted to be a part of it," said Paula Long, 59, a volunteer at the Flight 93 temporary memorial located near the crash site, in an interview with The New York Times. "These big, tough Steelers that people put on a pedestal — they were letting go of their emotions. It humanized them."

Later in the interrupted 2001 season, the Steelers invited a group of firefighters and other rescue workers who responded to the plane crash in Shanksville to attend a game as their guests at Heinz Field in Pittsburgh. The Steelers had them seated in the owners' box and presented a check to Red Cross on their behalf.

My wife Kathie and I visited Shanksville two years later, while driving to Ligonier to attend "Fort Ligonier Days" in mid-October. We checked out all the tributes placed in an open field to mark the event. It was so quiet, an almost eerie stillness, and images of September 11 came to mind. Yet one felt at peace with the scene. There was a certain serenity to the pastoral setting, quite a contrast to what happened there on 9/11. The movie "United 93" came out in late April of 2006 and it brought back all the shock and horror and sadness we experienced on September 11, 2001.

I picked up a new Cadillac Seville that same afternoon at Baierl Cadillac in Wexford, just north of Pittsburgh. I had been having second thoughts about buying a Cadillac. I didn't know if it would send out the wrong message. When my wife Kathie gave me the green light — "you deserve it," she said — after I was looking at less costly automobiles one afternoon the week before.

I watched much of the 9/11 events unfold on the television in the waiting room at Baierl Cadillac, I was convinced that the sky was *falling and someone was sending me a message. It also reminded me of one of my proteges, Doug Miller, and how "United 93" would strike him if he saw the movie.*

September 4, 2002

A young friend of mine is one of the lucky ones who survived September 11, 2001. Doug Miller, the 32-year-old media relations director for the New York Jets, was scheduled to be on Flight 93 that morning.

He was one of the few people in New York who had ever heard of Shanksville, where Flight 93 crashed that day after some of its passengers heroically rushed the terrorists aboard rather than be part of a missile that was bound for Washington D.C. and U.S. government buildings. All 40 passengers and members of the crew, as well as the four hijackers, were killed.

Doug Miller's mother, as Barbara Emerick, was born and spent the early part of her life in Shanksville, in Somerset County. Miller had visited Shanksville as a kid to visit relatives. His mother's family later moved to Johnstown.

Miller was scheduled to depart Newark Liberty International Airport on United Airlines Flight 93 at 7:45 a.m. on September 11. The plane was to fly to San Francisco. Miller was going there to do advance publicity work for an NFL game in Oakland that Sunday between the Jets and the Oakland Raiders.

There was a problem with his laptop computer the night before the flight and he was unable to complete work he had to get done before he could leave New York. So he had to call United Airlines and change his flight. He didn't make that rescheduled flight, either, because the NFL canceled its games that weekend in the wake of the tragedy of September 11. Miller accompanied the Jets on a trip to Pittsburgh last month when the Jets opened the Steelers' pre-season schedule at Heinz Field. I picked him up at the Marriott City Center and we had lunch at Del's in Bloomfield. We were joined by another young friend of mine, Keith Maiden, 25 at the time, from Geyer Printing in Oakland.

Maiden and Miller had both become fathers for the first time in July and were so excited to share stories about their infant sons. "I can't believe how I feel about him," Miller said, referring to Tyler Emerick Miller. "I hated to leave him when I came here."

I told Doug that now he can appreciate how his mother and father, Barbara and Don Miller, feel about him and his sister, Becky. They are a very close family. They lived a block from our home in Upper St. Clair for over 20 years before Don retired and they moved to Celebration, Florida to be near their daughter Becky and her family. In his early teen years, Doug Miller liked what I was doing for a living, and I mentored him and helped land him his job with the Jets as a student intern. He has been with them for 11 years. I am so proud of Doug Miller.

His wife, Carolyn Bodnar, grew up in Bethel Park. They met in New York, connecting interestingly enough through a computer dating service. They are so proud of their baby. The Millers are still shaken by what might have happened if Doug's laptop computer hadn't failed him. He shakes his head now when he remembers how that caused him great anxiety over having to change his travel plans.

Miller remembers accompanying the Jets on a trip by ferry to Ground Zero, the ashes of what had been the World Trade Towers. "I'll never forget the smell," said Miller. "You think about 9/11 every day when you live in New York. There are still so many reminders. I think about my situation, and what might have happened, what I might have done if I'd been on that airplane.

"I don't like being the guy who could have been on Flight 93. There were 2800 killed in New York that day and everyone knows someone who was lost. I was just lucky. My life was spared. We sat around in stunned silence that day, watching the tragic events transpiring. None of us will ever forget it.

"Some day we'll tell Tyler about it."

"You read about it every day in New York," Doug Miller told me during his recent visit to Pittsburgh. "There's some story about Ground Zero in the paper every day. When I'm driving from New Jersey to New York I can see the absence of those buildings on the New York City skyline. It still haunts you."

Miller family, from left to right, include Don and Barbara, with son Doug and daughter Rebecca. Doug is public relations director of NFL's New York Jets.

Joey Porter on the Pittsburgh Steelers:
"Don't ever count us out. People definitely wrote us off in December, and when you tell somebody they can't do something, proving it wrong is the sweetest joy of all."

There are different strokes
for different folks in sports

October 22, 2002

A flimsy black and gold seat cushion that was given away free to all fans that attended the Steelers' final game at Three Rivers Stadium had a price tag of $30. The two-year-old cushion was now considered a "classic" item.

An 18 x 26 framed color photograph of "Pittsburgh's own" Johnny Unitas, with his signature across the chest of his light blue Baltimore Colts jersey, was for sale for $499. The price has gone up since Unitas died.

The same was true for a similarly sized print of Mike Webster that he signed. It was now selling for $169. It, too, had increased in value since Webster's recent death. A vendor was wearing an "Iron Mike" T-shirt, in Webster's honor, no doubt. Such T-shirts were also for sale.

This was at a sports memorabilia and card show that filled the bottom floor at Century III Mall in West Mifflin this past weekend. Caputo's Collectibles had lined up a team of Steelers to sign autographs, and that drew thousands of die-hard Steelers' fans. You'd never know there was a challenging economy to see the line of fans waiting to get their autographs.

They had to purchase a ticket for $35, for instance, to get the signatures of Hall of Famers such as John Stallworth, who was there on Saturday, and Jack Lambert, who was there Sunday. That was for a simple signature on a flat item. Of course, they could buy large color photographs or helmets. It cost a little more to get a signature on a helmet or a football. It could cost nearly $100 for some signatures, depending on the "personalization" request.

Most Steelers' fans showed up in their Sunday best, black and gold jerseys with their favorite Steelers' name across their shoulders. This is considered formal attire in some parts of Pittsburgh. They were getting revved up for the Monday Night football game with the Indianapolis Colts at Heinz Field.

There were several Steelers signing at the same time inside Caputo's Collectibles, but if you wanted to get the signature of a second or third player, you had to go back and get at the end of a line of several hundred people. And the die-hard fans, like so many sheep, did exactly that.

Personally, I don't get it. I treasure a biography of Muhammad Ali that he signed for me, and I wish I had asked for autographs when I was interviewing the likes of Joe Louis and Joe DiMaggio and Joe Namath. But I wouldn't get a similar charge from getting the signature of Kimo von Oelhoffen, a Steelers' defensive lineman, though he is a terrific guy with a great smile.

They didn't have signing sessions by sports personalities when I was a kid. I collected sports cards and memorized the stats and info on the back of them, flipped them, played with them, scuffed them up. Today, kids buy them and never open the pack. They remain unread under plastic protective slipcovers.

I don't understand the public's fascination with bobble-head dolls of sports personalities or having a football helmet atop a coffee table in the family room. As much as I hated the Atlanta Braves' fans waving those plastic red tomahawks, I detest even more the Anaheim Angels' fans banging those plastic red bats — they call them "Thunder Sticks" — and making so much noise. What does that have to do with baseball? Such fans turn a baseball park into an amusement park, and the teams promote the ludicrous idea.

David Stern, the savvy NBA commissioner, was asked in a radio interview last week what kind of basketball memorabilia he had in his home. He said he wasn't into memorabilia. "I don't even think it's appropriate," said Stern, who is considered a sports-marketing genius. "I collect memories." That's what I do, of course, and I chronicle the achievements of the Steelers, Pirates and Penguins, among other athletic marvels, in my books. I must admit I was jealous of the long lines in the mall for the signatures of Steelers such as Joey Porter, Kendrell Bell and Tommy Maddox. It was a good payday for them. Stars like Lambert and Stallworth were paid $5,000 to $10,000 just for showing up, with incentives depending on the number of signatures.

Few of those autograph-seekers strayed my way for books about the Steelers. Most of my customers come to me on a different path. They smile about the idea of paying $35 for Stallworth's signature.

Those who dig that stuff should be alerted to another signing show that is scheduled at Robert Morris University's Coraopolis campus. Two of the greatest running backs in pro football history, Hugh McElhenny of the 49ers, and Tony Dorsett of Pitt and the Cowboys, will be there. So will another Hall of Famer, Bill Mazeroski, one of this city's most popular ballplayers.

Brookline's own Bobby Del Greco will be there. I bumped into the former Pirate a few weeks back and he bought me an IC Light at Tambellini's Restaurant in Bridgeville. I should've asked him for his autograph as well.

Popularity comes at a high price

Several months after Super Bowl XL, Jerome Bettis was commanding $150 and more for his signature at a signing at Ross Park Mall and Troy Polamalu was getting $125 for his signature at The Mall at Robinson Township. That was for a signature on a flat item.

Ray Downey is recalled at
St. Bernard's memorial Mass

December 11, 2002

I was having dinner at DeBlasio's Restaurant in Mt. Lebanon when I spotted Ray Downey with his wife, Elizabeth, and friends, at a nearby table. I went over and said hello and put my hand on Ray's round shoulders.

I had heard the Downeys were moving in to Asbury Heights, the senior care complex on Bower Hill Road nearby, where my mother has been living the last five years. I told Ray I would stop by to see him someday when I was visiting my mother. I told him I wanted to interview him. That was about four or five months ago.

Ray Downey, who made his home in Mt. Lebanon for many years, had been associated with sports in Pittsburgh most of his 93 years. He knew a lot about what went on behind closed doors. He was the public address system announcer for the Pittsburgh Steelers games for 48 years, at Forbes Field, Pitt Stadium and Three Rivers Stadium. He had done the same at Duquesne Gardens for hockey games, basketball games and ice shows.

He was a retired vice-president of Western Maryland Railroad, but he had moonlighted in front of a microphone most of his adult life. Win or lose, good times or bad, he was the calm voice over the p.a. system. He had announced for the Ice Capades and six-day bicycle races at the Gardens. He also had a pre-game show on KDKA radio for awhile, broadcast Hornets hockey games on KDKA-TV and filled in occasionally for Steelers' broadcasts on WWSW. He loved to play golf, and served as president of the Chartiers Valley Country Club and of the Western Pennsylvania Golf Association.

It was often a family affair as his brother-in-law Bill Oxenreiter would drive and Bill's son, Mark, and Downey's son-in-law, Mike Linn, would serve as spotters in the booth. Bill is the father of sportscaster Alby Oxenreiter, another familiar sports voice in Pittsburgh.

"I tried not to let my voice change, whether it was the Immaculate Reception or an automobile commercial," related Downey during an earlier interview. "I went to a party after Franco Harris made that catch and scored the game-winning touchdown against the Oakland Raiders, and a man told me how he saw the play from the sixth level of the stadium. It made me laugh, because everyone now says they saw it. I was sitting at the 50-yard line and never saw the play."

He had seen it all, in truth, and he had good stories to tell. I had talked to him from time to time, but never at great length, not for the record. I was dismayed when I read in the obituary section a few weeks back that Ray Downey had died of heart problems.

I never got around to interviewing him again. That's a problem in what I do as a sports author and historian. Some times the people I want to talk to and when I want to do it aren't compatible. We're not always on the same schedule.

Downey died too late in the year to get on the list of those associated with sports in Pittsburgh who are memorialized at an annual Mass and breakfast meeting on the first Saturday in December at St. Bernard's Catholic Church in Mt. Lebanon.

Father George Wilt, who hosts the reunion of sports officials and sports enthusiasts, mentioned Downey in his remarks. He had conducted a funeral service for him at the same church only a few weeks earlier.

There were 108 names on the list, two of them prematurely. Brian Wisniewski and Tom Bigley were both present in the church, sitting near one another in the same row. The reports of their respective deaths in the St. Bernard's listing were erroneous. Someone gave Ducky Kovach, the keeper of the list, some bad information.

I had the task of reading the list of the dead, and offering commentary when I knew something about the individual. It was the most impressive listing I can recall in recent years.

I personally knew or was aware of the achievements of 32 of them, and that was too many as far as I was concerned.

It was headed by Johnny Unitas, my boyhood hero, and Byron "Whizzer" White. Unitas came out of St. Justin's High School to become the greatest quarterback in pro football history for the Baltimore Colts. He had been cut by the Pittsburgh Steelers at their 1955 training camp. White played one season for the Steelers in 1938 and then went off to Oxford as a Rhodes Scholar. At 45, he was the youngest man ever named to the Supreme Court. He was sworn in by President John F. Kennedy.

Leon Hart came out of Turtle Creek to be a big part of a string of national championship football teams at Notre Dame and won the Heisman Trophy in 1939. Following him on the list was Jack Fitzhenry, a boyhood friend of mine I had played CYO basketball with before he moved on to play at St. Francis of Loretto, Duquesne University and a team that traveled with the Harlem Globetrotters.

Three other former Steelers running backs, Sam Francis, Fran Rogel and Joe Geri were on the list, along with a lineman, Willie McClung. I had called McClung when I was working on my latest book, but his wife told me he was ill and in the hospital. I never got to talk to him either. Mike Webster, the Steelers Hall of Famer, who died at 50 a few months back, was on the list. What a shame.

Two men from my childhood were on the list. Frank Casne was the recreation director in my hometown and took me to my first Pirates games at Forbes Field with the Knot-Hole Gang. Sam Hoak was from my hometown and was a football official. He officiated sandlot games for the same $7 that Unitas made when he was playing briefly for the Bloomfield Rams here after he was cut by the Steelers, before he got the call from the Colts to join their team.

All of the names on that list had left their mark, even if it was on Pittsburgh's sandlot fields or area church gyms.

Ray Downey was the public address announcer at Duquesne Gardens as well as wherever the Pittsburgh Steelers were playing.

Regulars at sportsmen's memorial Mass at St. Bernard's Church in Mt. Lebanon, left to right, were Frank Casne, Bob Shearer, Al Zellman and Fred Yee. All were teachers and coaches in City of Pittsburgh schools. Casne and Zellman are now deceased.

Hall of Fame celebration
in Canton worth the trip

August 6, 2003

I was sitting on a soft bench somewhere in the middle of the football-shaped building that is the Pro Football Hall of Fame. I was watching many of the greats of the game go by, settling for a hello on the go, a brief handshake, a few words, a photo.

My friend Rudy Celigoi was sitting next to me, pointing out some former players or coaches I might have missed. Our friend Bill Priatko was outside, under an umbrella, saying hello to old friends as they boarded a bus to go to nearby Fawcett Stadium for this summer's Hall of Fame induction ceremonies.

Priatko played for the Steelers for a single season in the mid-50s, and went to training camps with the Cleveland Browns and Green Bay Packers, and felt like he was in his twenties again as he embraced Bart Starr, Joe Schmidt, John Henry Johnson, George Blanda and Mike Ditka. Bill got to talk to the widow of Paul Brown, one of his all-time favorite coaches and a big influence in his approach to the game.

They were celebrating the 40th anniversary of the founding of the Hall of Fame in Canton, Ohio — billed as the birthplace of pro football — and over 110 Hall of Fame members were present for the activities. It was thought to be the largest gathering of Hall of Fame players in one place at one time in history.

It rained most of the 110-mile trip from Pittsburgh to Canton on Sunday. This was the first time the induction was held on Sunday. It rained most of the day. They wouldn't permit anyone to enter the stadium with an umbrella, so only family and the closest of friends and football fanatics sat out in the rain. Blame it on 9/11. We left early, knowing we could catch some of the activities on television along the way home.

We drove to an Applebee's Neighborhood Grill & Bar in Alliance, Ohio — the hometown of Hall of Famer Lenny Dawson — and watched some of the induction on television. They had a wall devoted to photos, jerseys, shoulder pads, pennants, you name it, signed by Dawson. One of the photos showed him in a Steelers uniform, others when he played at Purdue and when he starred for the Kansas City Chiefs. We were driving into Alliance when, by coincidence, Dawson was heard in a radio broadcast introducing his former coach Hank Stram for induction in the Pro Football Hall of Fame. I spent ten months as an editor at the U.S. Army Home Town News Center in Kansas City in 1965, and did spotting for the TV announcers at the Chiefs games at old Municipal Stadium. So I had a history with Dawson and Stram, two of the nice guys in the business.

We go to the Hall of Fame induction every summer, and we all liked it better when it was on Saturday, followed by a pre-season football game the same day. Now the game is played on Monday night. The whole thing, like most sports activities, is done to suit the needs of network TV, and that's a shame. It was better for the fans when they got in for free and watched the ceremonies on the front steps of the Hall of Fame on George Halas Drive. It was more intimate, more like a summer picnic outing.

As soon as we arrived on the grounds outside the Hall of Fame on Sunday we went into a large white tent to get out of the rain, and ended up being the first to go through the buffet line. The food, catered by Giant Eagle, was outstanding. Being first in the buffet line might have been the highlight of the trip. We got to see some Steelers who are in the Hall of Fame, such as John Henry Johnson, Bullet Bill Dudley, Mel Blount, John Stallworth, Lynn Swann, Joe Greene, Franco Harris, Chuck Noll and Dan Rooney. Former Pitt players similarly honored included Ditka, Schmidt and Tony Dorsett.

"I walk bad, but just look around here," declared Ditka. "We all walk bad." Ditka is now a well-paid spokesman for Levitra, a new drug that will compete against Viagra. If a tough guy like Ditka needs some help it will lessen the shyness on the part of other men to use such a product. That's the sales pitch anyhow.

We also got to see Joe Namath, Lenny Moore, Sam Huff, Gale Sayers, Chuck Bednarik, Mike Munchak, Frank Gifford, Pete Pihos, Frank Gatski, Randy White, Bobby Bell, Dante Lavelli, Willie Wood, Lem Barney, Don Shula, Bill Walsh, Al Davis, Alan Paige, Dave Robinson, Paul Hornung and Merlin Olsen. The oldest Hall of Fame member there was Ace Parker, 91, who quarterbacked the Brooklyn Dodgers. Steve Van Buren, a tough running back for the Philadelphia Eagles, was the earliest inductee, as a member of the 1965 Class. You have to wonder when you're seeing some of these old-timers if you'll ever see them again. I went up to the Steelers' training camp at St. Vincent College in Latrobe last Thursday, but it rained that day, too, and spoiled things for the fans who flocked there. It's been a tough year for outdoor activity. Wonder how many of these Steelers will make it to Canton someday? Jerome Bettis is regarded as the best bet. It would be nice if he had the kind of season that would make him a shoo-in.

Sam Huff, as pictured at Pro Football Hall of Fame.

Art Carney was also cast
as Art Rooney in his career

November 19, 2003

There is a buzz in Pittsburgh about the Public Theater's current offering, *The Chief*, which is drawing record crowds downtown. Pittsburgh-bred actor Tom Atkins is getting rave reviews from those who've seen the one-man show, a 140-minute monologue without intermission. There are two Pittsburgh treasures on the stage at the O'Reilly Theater, Art Rooney and Tom Atkins. Art Rooney spent most of his life on the North Side and Atkins had relatives who lived there. He grew up in Carrick and now resides in Peters Township.

"It's a challenging role, and I was nervous about playing the part of a man so well known to Pittsburghers," said Atkins. "But it's been one of the most satisfying experiences of my stage career. I really enjoy it. He'd have been fun to be around. He led an interesting life."

The stories of the Steelers' popular patriarch are insightful, and say as much about Pittsburgh and its history as the wonderful man who brought pro football and so much joy and pride to this city.

There was a touch of irony to the death of actor Art Carney as *The Chief* was getting its five-week run underway here. Carney played the role of Art Rooney in a 1980 movie about Steelers' running back Rocky Bleier, based on his book *Fighting Back.*

Atkins told me he knew that Carney had been *The Chief* in an earlier theatrical production, but said he had never met Carney during their respective acting days on Broadway.

Carney was best known, of course, for his role as Ed Norton, the sewer worker who lived upstairs of Ralph Cramden, the bus driver played by Jackie Gleason, in a dreary New York apartment in the classic TV series *The Honeymooners.*

When Bleier was growing up over his dad's saloon in Appleton, Wisconsin, he watched *The Honeymooners*. So it was a big thrill for Bleier to meet and mix with Carney when he came to Three Rivers Stadium right after the Steelers had won their fourth Super Bowl in six years.

I felt the same way. I was 14 and had just started my duties as the sports editor of the weekly newspaper in my hometown when *The Honeymooners* came on TV in the mid-50s. It was a must-watch show on the weekly TV schedule.

Jackie Gleason and Art Carney were lovable characters, and they were important in our lives because they made us smile and they made us laugh, and sometimes they'd even make you laugh so hard you'd cry.

I never met Carney, but I did interview Gleason when he was in Pittsburgh during a national tour to promote his TV show *The Great One*. That was back in 1962 when I was a summer intern writer at *The Pittsburgh Press*.

Gleason had been in a movie *The Hustler*, in which he played the part of a legendary pool player. I was going to play an exhibition match with another legendary pool player, Willie Mosconi, at the newly opened South Hills Cue & Cushion on Route 51, for a story that same week.

Mosconi was a fifteen-time world straight-pool champion who once ran 526 consecutive balls, calling the ball and pocket before every shot. "I never did miss," Mosconi told Steve Bushin of *Sports Illustrated*. "I just got tired and quit." You had to love keeping company with Willie Mosconi. I spent considerable time in my misspent youth in pool halls in Hazelwood, Greenfield and downtown Pittsburgh. There were always so many colorful characters in those hangouts. It was part of my education as an aspiring writer. I asked Gleason to give me some tips on how to beat Mosconi.

"You should complain about the lighting, say the pool table is tilted, and swing your cue stick around," said Gleason, mimicking the motion he had in mind. "You might hit him in the ankle with the cue stick and it's tough to shoot pool through flinched eyes."

When I sank my first few shots against Mosconi, he said, "What are you doing? You hustling me?"

I still remember Mosconi and those special moments I spent with him that afternoon every time I pick up a cue stick and shoot pool when I'm at a party and someone wants to play. I always think to myself, "I wonder if this guy realizes I played pool with Willie Mosconi."

Gleason and Carney could make everyone laugh, even though it's reported they really weren't pals off camera. Gleason was a tough act to follow.

Carney died in Connecticut after a long illness at the age of 85. Ed Kiely recalled how Carney asked him questions about Art Rooney so he would know how to play the part. Atkins also called on Kiely, and Dan Rooney and Art Rooney Jr., and others for the same reason. Kiely was the public relations director of the Steelers for many years before giving way to Joe Gordon.

Kiely recalled his conversation with Carney. "One day Carney asks me, 'What fingers does he use to hold his cigar?' I told him I would be damned if I knew, but that we could go visit with Art and he could see for himself. I was impressed that he wanted to know details like that so he could properly depict him in a movie.

"Carney was a frightfully shy guy. It was hard to believe the guy was so funny on TV in those Jackie Gleason shows," continued Kiely. "After he visited with Art for awhile, he was about to leave when he asked me, 'Do you think you could get him to sign some photos of himself for me?' I told him he could ask Art, but he didn't want to do that. Art signed some photos for him, and — just as I knew he would — he asked Art Carney, 'Say, Art, do you have any pictures with you? You ought to be autographing photos for me.' That was just like Art Rooney."

Art Rooney and Art Carney compare cigar-smoking styles in 1980.

Michael Chikiris/The Pittsburgh Press

Bill Jerome/Pittsburgh Weekly Sports

World champion pool player Willie Mosconi is careful not to get hustled by young Jim O'Brien of *The Pittsburgh Press*.

Jim Boston
Behind the scenes Steeler

"He never got the credit he deserved."
— Art Rooney Jr.

December 3, 2003

Jim "Buff" Boston was taking a turn as a substitute bartender at Dante's Restaurant when I first met him. He was helping out the owner, Dante Sartorio, when the regular bartender didn't show up on time. This was back in 1961, when I was 19 and he was 27. He was moonlighting at Dante's, a popular hangout on the Brentwood-Whitehall border.

Bobby Layne and Ernie Stautner frequented Dante's. They were the two best ballplayers on the Steelers in those days. So did a dozen or so other Steelers. Sportswriters and sportscasters were among the regulars. There were some colorful characters there, many of them sports bettors.

What a mix. Boston was working during the day as the equipment manager or assistant trainer with the Steelers. So you had a man who worked for the Rooneys, who spent many of his evenings in the company of the players. There were usually enough players at Dante's on any given evening to field a team, and the sports media and gamblers drinking and, at times, dancing in the same nightspot.

It's hard to imagine anything like that these days. Trust me that it will never happen again. I was at Dante's with my brother, Dan, who was five years older and lived nearby. I wanted to meet and mix with the media guys like Myron Cope, Pat Livingston, Doc Giffin, Bob Drum, Tom Bender, Ed Conway, Dave Kelly, Tom Hritz and, on occasion, Roy McHugh.

Those days came to mind last week when Jim "Buff" Boston died after a year-and-a-half bout with liver cancer. Boston, who'd been living in Peters Township, was 68. He retired in 1994 after working 45 years with the Steelers. He started out as a ballboy during his student days at North Catholic High School, and ended up as the club's chief negotiator in player contracts.

"He never got the credit he deserved for his contribution to our championship run," related Art Rooney Jr. on the day that Boston died. I was a guest of Art Rooney Jr., one of the team's owners, for lunch at the St. Clair Country Club last week. "Buff and my brother Dan kept that team together through some difficult challenges."

Rooney was telling me that Boston was in bad shape, and wasn't expected to live that long. When I returned home after lunch, I received a phone call from Tom Rose, the sports editor of the

Washington Observer-Reporter, telling me that Boston had died. Rose was a fellow traveler during the glory days of the Steelers.

When I was a sports reporter, we flew on the same airplanes as the Steelers, rode in the same chartered buses, and had a great deal of freedom at their training camp at St. Vincent College, and could even visit the players in their dorm rooms to interview them. We joined them for dinner when they had a Family Night picnic at camp each summer. We joined the coaches for happy hour following the second practice of the day. All talk was off the record, but it provided insight and perspective to the proceedings.

None of the media today are able to do that. The ground rules have changed. There are more media than ever before, but they are kept at a distance. They interview the players, for the most part, before and after meals, standing outside the dining rooms for a few minutes, grabbing those precious sound bites.

I love those sound bites. Casey Hampton and Plaxico Burress are the best ones. I never know what they're saying. They rival Aleksey Morozov of the Penguins for difficulty to determine what they said.

I was in the press box at Heinz Field for the Pitt-Miami mismatch on Saturday night. In the third quarter, when Pitt quit competing, I turned to the game notes provided by the sports information departments of the respective schools. The Miami notes contained a page of rules for the media. Pitt and the Steelers have similar restrictions. It mentioned all the places that were off limits to the media. It's easier to visit and interview inmates at the city's jail.

It was better in the old days. Bobby Layne and Ernie Stautner and those other Steelers at Dante's discussed their day at practice. They told stories, and shared their opinions about everything.

The older writers mentored me. I learned what I could write, and what I shouldn't write, and no one was poorer for the omissions. I contend that you were better informed and so were the readers if the athletes were relaxed around you, and trusted you. In the long run, you wrote better stories.

It helped me develop journalistic judgment early in my career. As Dick Young, a great New York writer, told me when I was on a bus one day with the New York Yankees, "Remember that you're their guest."

I got stories you would miss if you were traveling on your own.

"Buff" Boston was a big guy. His nickname was given to him by Jim Rooney because he likened him to a buffalo. Boston was about 6-3, 300 pounds. He kept law and order at Dante's and on the sidelines during Steelers' games. He was a brassy guy, one of those North Side figures that Art Rooney attracted to his organization. "Baldy" Regan and his sidekick Bernie Stein were two others that come to mind. Boston was street smart, and it helped him and the Steelers survive their early struggles.

He knew who to let in and who to keep out of the best of parties.

I'm grateful to folks like him who helped show me the way in the sports world. They opened doors to an exciting life.

These sports heroes
had such memorable names

I was back in my bedroom on Sunnyside Street in Glenwood, a mill-town in the southeastern end of Pittsburgh. I was checking out the piles of publications I kept in the corner on my side of the room I shared with my older brother Dan.

There were tall stacks of *Sport* magazine, *Sports Illustrated*, the *Police Gazette* and *Classics Illustrated*. The first three had great sports stories in their pages, the latter were comic book versions of the classic books such as *Tom Sawyer, The Count of Monte Cristo* and my all-time favorite, *Swiss Family Robinson*. I swear those comic book versions were more interesting than the real versions of those books at the local library.

What sent me back in time was reading a necrology in the sports pages of a year-end newspaper. Necrology. Now there's a good word to file. It means a list of recent deaths. These were deaths in the sports world in the year 2003.

The list included several of my favorites. There was Valery Brumel, 60, a Russian high jumper who won the silver medal at the 1960 Rome Olympics and gold at the 1964 Tokyo Games. I loved reading about Olympic athletes and track and field was my favorite. Those two Olympic Games came after my senior year at Allderdice and my senior year at Pitt, respectively.

There was Dave DeBusschere, 62, a Hall of Fame basketball star with the New York Knicks. I was visiting in Los Angeles when DeBusschere died. I had traveled with the Knicks to Los Angeles in 1970 when they beat the Lakers to win their first NBA title. DeBusschere was a starting forward, teaming up with Willis Reed, Bill Bradley, Walt Frazier, Dick Barnett, Cazzie Russell and Phil Jackson to win that championship

Althea Gibson, 76, the first African-American woman tennis player to be ranked No. 1 in the world, was on the list. I had seen her up close when she was on the grounds of the West Side Tennis Club in New York to check out the U.S. Open Tennis Championships. I saw a memorial to her in her hometown of Wilmington, North Carolina a couple of summers ago.

Sid Gillman, 91, a Hall of Fame football coach who gave Chuck Noll his first coaching opportunity with the Los Angeles Chargers, had died. I last saw Gillman sitting in a wheelchair during an induction ceremony at the Pro Football Hall of Fame in Canton. That was on the day that Joe Montana and Dan Rooney were inducted.

Otto Graham, 82, a Hall of Fame quarterback of the Cleveland Browns. He led his team to the championship game in each of his ten pro seasons. He also played one year in the NBA. Graham was so great. He was a contemporary of Bobby Layne, who led the Detroit Lions to championships in that same era, and then came to Pittsburgh and put some life into the Steelers for several seasons under Buddy Parker.

Otto Graham and Bobby Layne had great names. So did some of their teammates, such as Mac Speedie, Dante Lavelli, Dub Jones, Horace Gillom, Mike McCormack, Doak Walker, Dick LeBeau, Lou Creekmur, Bill Stanfel, Hunchy Hornschmeier, Tobin Rote, Jack Christiansen, Dorn Dibble and Les Bingaman. The latter weighed over 300 pounds, which was rare then. How about Bob St. Clair, a 6-7 lineman. St. Clair ate raw meat; I remember that. There was Cloyce Box and the Rams had two quarterbacks, Norm Van Brocklin and Bob Waterfield, Waterfield was married to film star sexpot Jane Russell.

The Steelers had Jim Finks, Lynn Chandnois, Fran Rogel, Dale Dodril, Bobby Gage, Pat Brady, Jack Butler and Jerry Shipkey. Those names just had a ring about them. They were real football names.

Charlie "Choo-Choo" Justice, 79, a University of North Carolina running back, was twice runner-up for the Heisman Trophy. Ballplayers had great nicknames back then, and none had a better one than "Choo-Choo" Justice, unless it was Dick "Night Train" Lane. "Night Train" was married to soul singer Dinah Washington.

In those days, there was also Clyde "Bulldog" Turner, Elroy "Crazy Legs" Hirsch, Gene "Big Daddy" Lipscomb and Vito "Babe" Parilli. Maybe you remember a particular favorite.

George Plimpton, the writer, and Tex Schramm, the president and general manager of the Dallas Cowboys, Willie Shoemaker, the jockey, and Warren Spahn, the great left-handed pitcher for the Braves, also died last year. I interviewed Schramm for two hours about Art Rooney at the Super Bowl in Tampa a few years back. Now he was gone.

I attended the annual Old Timers Memorial Service at St. Bernard's in Mt. Lebanon on the first Saturday in December. Among the more than 100 local sports personalities who were remembered were the following:

Ray Downing, Andy Dugo, Dan Galbreath, Josh Gibson, Jr., Johnny Hopp, Pat Livingston, Alex Medich, Joe Moore, Dick Phillips, Billy Reynolds, Scoops Saulsbury, Leo Skladany, Dick Stuart, Jim Theodore and Fran Webster.

If you grew up around here and followed sports closely all those names, or many of them anyhow, will mean something to you. There was a magic about those names. When I went into the U.S. Army in 1964, my mother tossed out all my magazines, comic books and bubble gum cards.

I wish I still had them, but in a way they have stayed with me.

Breakfast with "Bullet Bill"
beats NFL draft any day

April 28, 2004

I had breakfast on Sunday morning with Art Rooney's all-time favorite Steeler. I spent three hours in the company of "Bullet Bill" Dudley, who was inducted into the Pro Football Hall of Fame in 1966, one of its earliest classes. He is a legendary sports hero, and a good, down-to-earth individual.

This was the second day of the much-ballyhooed National Football League draft, which got more coverage than the War in Iraq. The Steelers' equipment manager Rodgers Freyvogel was figuring out how they could fit the name of the team's No. 1 draft choice — Miami of Ohio quarterback Ben Roethlisberger — across the shoulders of a Steelers' jersey. Hey, Chris Fuamatu-Ma'afala had one more character in his hyphenated last name, so it can be done.

Steelers' fans were trying to figure out whom the team would draft next. I was more excited about being with "Bullet Bill" Dudley. He turns 81 this year and, frankly, he's achieved more and led a more interesting life to talk about than any of the present-day prospects.

Dudley was in Pittsburgh to sign autographs on Saturday at a Sports Card and Memorabilia Show at Robert Morris University. We met the following day at the nearby Embassy Suites. After breakfast, I drove Dudley to the airport for his return trip to Lynchburg, Virginia. He was still going to the office several days a week to look after his insurance business.

An NFL team would have to draft eight players to do what Dudley did for the Steelers when he arrived in 1942, the year I was born. Dudley was on the small side, even in that era, at 5-10, 176 pounds, but he could do it all. The Steelers drafted him on the recommendation of Art Rooney's good friend, George Halas, who owned and coached the Chicago Bears.

The Bears didn't need any running backs, so Halas passed along a tip he had received from Dudley's coach at the University of Virginia. Things were a lot less sophisticated in the draft in those days.

Dudley was an outstanding rusher. He returned kickoffs and punts. He could pass, even though his form wasn't pretty. He played defensive back, made many interceptions, and was regarded as a fierce tackler. He was the team's punter, and kicked-off and handled placement-kicks. He did so without taking a step, just a pendulum motion with his right leg.

In his first game with the Steelers, Dudley raced 55 yards for a touchdown. The following weekend, he returned a kickoff for a touchdown. He led the league in rushing as a rookie and made All-Pro.

He spent the next two seasons, 1943 and 1944, piloting B-29 bombers in the Army Air Corps in the South Pacific.

In 1946, Dudley led the league in rushing, punt returns and interceptions — a Triple Crown — and was named the NFL's MVP. He didn't get along with dictatorial and dour head coach Jock Sutherland, and was traded to the Detroit Lions the following season. He later starred with the Washington Redskins as well. He was a captain with both clubs. With the Skins, he once returned a punt 96 yards for a touchdown against the Steelers.

I was signing books one day at South Hills Village when a customer told me he was at Forbes Field the day "Bullet Bill" Dudley returned a punt 96 yards for a touchdown. Just for fun, I pulled out my personal telephone book and looked up the home phone number for "Bullet Bill." I called him and told him about the fan that was standing next to me.

Without hesitation, Dudley declared, "Yes, Joe Geri was the Steelers' punter. I caught the ball near the sideline and my momentum almost took me out of bounds. But I stopped a step short of the sideline and hesitated a second. When I did that everyone came to a stop. I think they thought I stepped out of bounds. But I just turned and went straight up the sideline, and I took it all the way."

I asked "Bullet Bill" if he thought he could still do that. He was in his 80s at the time. "I don't think I'm that fast anymore," he said.

"I wasn't really fast," added Dudley. "The nickname just sounded right. I forget the sportswriter who gave me that name. But I was determined. I wasn't very big, but I think I had a big heart. I told my wife, Libba, that I wanted her to put these words — 'He tried' — on my tombstone."

My wife Kathie and I visited the Dudleys at their Virginia home in October of 2003. They are gracious hosts and a winning team.

Steelers' founder Art Rooney once told me: "I believe Bill Dudley was as good as any football player in the National Football League. He wasn't fast, even though his nickname made you think he was, but nobody caught him. He couldn't pass, but he completed passes. He was one of the top kickers in the game. He was the best all-around ballplayer I've ever seen, right up there with Sammy Baugh."

Dudley's kickoff return average was an unbelievable 30.05 yards for 58 returns, second only to Gale Sayers in NFL history.

He didn't care for Jock Sutherland, though, and asked to be traded. Dudley told me about a time that he was walking through the lobby of the Pittsburgh Athletic Association (PAA) where Sutherland resided, and that Sutherland snubbed him as he passed. "Like I had no business at his club," Dudley recalled. "I was the league's MVP under him, so he couldn't have been all bad. I just didn't care for his manner.

"In one game, one of our players who was struggling was stretched out on the field, injured on the last play before the half, and Sutherland stepped right over his body on the way to the locker room."

"Bullet Bill" Dudley
Pro Football Hall of Famer
at his home in Lynchburg,
Virginia

Jim O'Brien

I could tell Dudley didn't want to talk any more about Sutherland, so I switched subjects. Dudley went to Mass at a Catholic church in Moon Township on Saturday evening so we could get together on Sunday morning. He was born into the Baptist religion, and converted to Catholicism soon after he was married. He says he prays a lot, and that he always did. "I think all our prayers are answered," he said, "but not always the way we want them."

Dudley said that "responsibility" is the most important word in the dictionary. He served in the Virginia legislature for eight years, and was a trustee at his alma mater — "we call it The University" — for eight years as well. He took pride in serving his country during World War II. We had another bond. Our daughter, Sarah, had graduated Phi Beta Kappa from the University of Virginia in 1996. I had breakfast with Libba and Bill Dudley at the Boar's Inn in Charlottesville on the morning of the day that Sarah and I first visited the University of Virginia for a tour four years earlier.

"Where is she going to school?" Bill Dudley asked me that morning.

"We visited North Carolina yesterday," I said, "and she really liked that. That's No. 1 right now."

"Has she seen the University yet?" asked Dudley.

I didn't know what he meant. What University?

"We call Virginia simply The University," Dudley explained.

That tells you everything you need to know about the University of Virginia. Oh, yes, it's also Thomas Jefferson's University. There are more images of Jefferson than Dudley to be found on the campus grounds, but Dudley is still a Big Man on Campus.

When you're with Bill Dudley, and listen to him talk about God and country and family, you know you are with a man of good values. It's not something I take for granted. I saw three of the Pirates of the 1960 World Champions at that same RMU show — Dick Groat, El Roy Face and Bob Skinner — and a former West Virginia All-American and All-Pro in Sam Huff. I had breakfast the day before with Lynn Chandnois, and talked to Ernie Stautner, Frank Varrachione, Gary Glick, John Reger, Bill Walsh and Dale Dodrill. Seeing them and having breakfast with "Bullet Bill" Dudley was better than watching the NFL draft any day of the week.

'Bullet Bill' Dudley

> **"I told my wife I want her to put these words on my tombstone: HE TRIED."**
> **— Bill Dudley**

346

Father's advice stayed
with these sports stars for life

June 16, 2004

I always enjoy attending the Mario Lemieux Celebrity Invitational and the Three Rivers Arts Festival. Stargazing and hobnobbing with the rich and famous is fun for all of us. It's a shame that bad weather seems to stalk these annual events and that you have to tip-toe around the puddles.

Many of the sports celebrities were complaining about having to play in the rain — that's no fun — but they smiled through it and still found time to talk to fans and sign autographs. "It's about being nice, that's all" said Joe Theismann, the former Notre Dame and Redskins quarterback who is now an ESPN football analyst.

I asked several of the sports celebrities to share some words of advice their fathers offered that has served them in good stead. Father's Day is being celebrated this coming Sunday.

"My dad's name was Joe," said Theismann, "and he always said, 'Never give up on your dream.' He's 82 and he's my hero."

Tommy Maddox, the Steelers' quarterback who just signed an improved contract, was playing with Mario Lemieux and Michael Jordan, the marquee attractions at The Club at Nevillewood. "My dad told me to give it your best effort and don't worry about it," said Maddox. "After that, let's go fishing. My dad, Wayne Maddox, was a senior vice president with Allstate Insurance. He's done great.

"My dad preached that you should work as hard as you can. He worked hard and he was an honest man. He grew up fighting the odds. He grew up in a log cabin in Laurel, Mississippi and worked in the fields. He's the one who had to overcome adversity.

"I always had an earlier curfew than all of my friends. I was urged to do the right thing and to stay out of trouble. I think parents are too concerned with how their kids are going to view them. I respected my father. I loved him then and I love him even more now. He's my best friend now. He wasn't my best friend when I was growing up.

"Growing up he wasn't a best friend figure. He was a father figure. We go golfing just about every Saturday when I'm home. My brother and a friend of mine go together. We're too worried about whether our kids are going to like us. When we do that we're doing them an injustice."

Ben Roethlisberger, the No. 1 draft pick of the Steelers, had the longest name across the back of his caddy. He's big, but not as broad-shouldered as Maddox. He seems like an agreeable fellow and should fit in well here.

"My father told me he would always be proud of me no matter what I did in sports," recalled Roethlisberger. "He said you'll get out of it what you put into it." He said his dad was the vice-president of a company that provided automotive parts for Honda.

As the season progressed, and Big Ben took Pittsburgh by storm, I wished I had asked him if I could ride with him in his cart for a few holes that day at Nevillewood. He would have obliged me, I'm sure, just as Tommy Maddox had done when I made a similar request when he was playing in the Caring Foundation's annual golf outing at Southpointe the previous year. I would have had Big Ben all to myself, for a meaningful interview. Once he became a star with the Steelers, it was nearly impossible to get a one-on-one interview with him.

Mike Eruzione, the captain of the 1960 ("Do you believe in miracles?") Olympic hockey team, said his father Eugene "Jeep" Eruzione held down three jobs to put food on the table for his family in Massachusetts. "My father always told me if you understood the value of hard work at some point in your life you'll be successful."

Richard "Digger" Phelps, the former Notre Dame and Fordham basketball coach and ABC/ESPN analyst, got his first name and his nickname from his father and his occupation as a funeral director in Beacon, New York. He got much more, just as Max Starks of the Steelers did in growing up in the funeral business. "He and my mother made me understand that you have to care about people. Because they need you when they lose a loved one. They said you had to care about them beyond the three days they were grieving at the funeral home.

"I've been around death all my life. You also learn that, at the end, we are all alike. There are no different colors, no ethnic groups. We're all the same. I've traveled the world, and I know that to be true. That's helped me in a lot of ways."

Eddie Johnston, the assistant general manager and former coach of the Penguins, is known best as the man who drafted Mario Lemieux. "There'd be a parking lot down where the Mellon Arena is if we hadn't done that," said Johnston, who lives around the corner from me in Upper St. Clair. Then again, to hear Lemieux lament the lack of progress in building a new arena, that could still happen.

Johnston's dad, David, came over from Ireland, and worked at a cigarette-making company in Montreal. "There were six of us boys," Johnston said. "My dad said it's nice to be nice and it doesn't cost you anything."

I asked my daughter Sarah the other day if there was anything she and her sister Rebecca recall me telling them along those lines. "When we asked you what you wanted for Father's Day," said Sarah, "you'd always say, 'I just want you girls to behave. That's the best present of all — just being good kids.'" My father, Dan O'Brien, a machinist and drill press operator at Mesta Machine Co. in West Homestead, took pride in showing up for work. He and my mother always said, "Stay busy and stay out of trouble."

"I play golf. I'm not a golfer. You're not going to see me on the PGA Tour any time soon."
— Steelers tackle Max Starks

Here's the book on Big Ben
and the 2004 Steelers

November 10, 2004

I plan on waiting a while before I write a book about Ben Roethlisberger, the Steelers' wunderkind quarterback. Few athletes have ever generated the kind of early excitement as "Big Ben," but let's take time out and see how this all plays out. Remember when this town was crazy about Kordell Stewart? Remember how Stewart advised us that he'd be in the Pro Football Hall of Fame someday?

Remember two years ago when Tommy Maddox was the toast of the town? I remember doing a book-signing at Waldenbooks at The Mall at Robinson Township one Sunday afternoon, and sneaking across the hallway to watch the Steelers' game at Tennessee on television.

Maddox connected with Hines Ward for a big gainer early in the game. When I returned to my table, I thought that perhaps I should write a book about Tommy Maddox. He was so hot. Ten minutes later I returned to the TV action and saw Maddox stretched out on the turf. He'd been knocked unconscious. There was a time when we wondered whether he'd ever play again. So I scratched the idea of a book about Tommy Maddox.

It's safer to write about the Steelers of the '70s. That won't change next Sunday. By the way, the 2005 official Steelers' calendar has a cover photo showing Maddox handing the ball off to Jerome Bettis. How about that?

In recent weeks, passersby have been hollering out to me that I should be writing a book about "Big Ben" and the current Steelers. I cautioned them that it might be a good idea to hold that in reserve. Then came upset victories at Heinz Field over the previously unbeaten New England Patriots and then the previously unbeaten Philadelphia Eagles. Fans are throwing caution to the winds and making travel plans for Jacksonville in February.

Somewhere in between there were signs hailing Roethlisberger for President. His name is now on the backs of so many authentic Steelers jerseys worn by fans around here and across the nation. "We haven't had anybody this big since the Steelers of the '70s," said my friend Ed Nuttall, who operates a sports memorabilia store at The Mall at Robinson Township. "We can't keep his stuff in stock, and I'm getting calls from all over the country. We'll soon be getting more T-shirts, a wastebasket, a bobble-head doll, window stickers and decals and a few other things with his name on it. It's unreal."

349

Yet, for all we know, the current Steelers' quarterback who could end up in the Pro Football Hall of Fame someday might be Brian St. Pierre. Hey, don't snicker.

The Steelers have a history of hiding Hall of Fame quarterbacks. They cut Johnny Unitas at his rookie camp, of course, and they ignored Lenny Dawson and Jack Kemp. Unitas and Dawson are in the Hall of Fame and Kemp was a championship quarterback in the American Football League and is now in Congress.

Earl Morrall and Bill Nelsen went on to stardom elsewhere in the NFL. We know something about great quarterbacks in this town. We've had Bobby Layne and Terry Bradshaw behind center for the Steelers. When they open the new Western Pennsylvania Sports Museum at the Heinz Regional History Center this weekend there will be much tribute to some of the great quarterbacks who were born and bred here.

As a young man, I enjoyed the company of Bobby Layne and Bill Nelsen at some watering holes in the South Hills, and Johnny Unitas was my boyhood hero. I played a little quarterback for a sandlot football team called the Hazelwood Steelers and wore No. 19, high-top black shoes, and tried to throw with the same just-pass-the-ear throwing motion. We played on some of the same football fields in Bloomfield and Lawrenceville and Polish Hill where Unitas once played after he was cut by the Steelers.

Besides Unitas, there's Joe Montana, Danny Marino, George Blanda, Jim Kelly and Johnny Lujack. Lujack is not in the Pro Football Hall of Fame, but he did win the Heisman Trophy in 1947. Marino is a cinch to go in next summer at Canton ceremonies.

Chuck Noll used to say that "football takes on a life of its own," and that's certainly true this season. Bill Cowher will be up for Coach of the Year honors, something Noll never won even though he took home four Super Bowl titles in as many outings, yet Cowher's hand was forced to play Roethlisberger so early and Jerome Bettis rather than Duce Staley this past Sunday.

Outstanding players such as Casey Hampton and Kendall Simmons have also been lost to injuries, yet Chris Hoke and Keydrick Vincent have stepped up to take their place and then some. There have been forced changes in the secondary. Thank goodness Dick LeBeau came back as the defensive coordinator.

I want to stop all those people wearing the Roethlisberger jerseys and ask them to pronounce and spell his name properly. Danny Marino admitted he had to do his homework and memorize the proper pronunciation before he returned home a week ago to interview Roethlisberger for a feature for the HBO show "Inside the NFL."

Hines Ward and Jerome Bettis jerseys are still popular around here, but they've given way to Roethlisberger as the chosen uniform of the day. Don't forget about Maddox, by the way. Maddox will make a big contribution to the Steelers before the season is over. Maddox has mentored "Big Ben," and both are deserving of our respect.

350

Rocky Bleier deserves
ringing endorsement from us

"I like to give back to the community."

*R*ocky Bleier's handsome likeness appeared on billboards throughout Pittsburgh during the spring of 2006. He was being honored — sort of — at the Mel Blount Youth Home's 8th Annual All-Star Celebrity Roast on Friday, April 28, 2006 at the Downtown Hilton.

"How do you roast Rocky Bleier?" asked emcee Chris Berman of ESPN fame. "He's a war veteran, a hero, a good guy, a Notre Damer!" Even so, some of Rocky's former teammates such as Andy Russell and Randy Grossman did their best to humble one of their favorites.

Asked if he liked roasts, Bleier said, "Not really. Sometimes people go too far, say something they regret. You're expected to be funny, and that's not easy. But it's for a good cause. We all respect the work that Mel is doing for the kids at his farm and we want to support his efforts. When Mel asks you to do something you can't refuse. I'm honored to have been selected. I've emceed the dinner, as you know, for many years." Asked about the Steelers' current club, Bleier said, "I get the impression that there are a lot of good guys on the present Steelers' team. That's why Pittsburgh has embraced them. They made a tremendous comeback to win the Super Bowl and bring a lot of pride back to Pittsburgh."

Bleier turned 60 a month earlier and still had a spring in his step. "Rocky is a great guy and he's got a great story," said Blount before the dinner. Bleier is best known, of course, from overcoming leg wounds he suffered in combat in Vietnam to return to the Steelers and become a star running back alongside Hall of Famer Franco Harris when the Steelers won four Super Bowls in the '70s.

Rocky and his wife, Jan, who have been married ten years and reside in Mt. Lebanon, were an attractive couple at the black-tie affair. When I spoke to Rocky at the pre-dinner reception at the King's Garden, he said, "I guess I like to give back to the community because of my Catholic upbringing. Plus my parents owned a restaurant and bar and you learned early to treat the public right and with respect. I'm like I am because of some insecurities, I suppose, and always wanting to be liked."

"I have three heroes in life: John Wayne, Ronald Reagan and Rocky Bleier."
— J.R. Wilburn, Steelers receiver (1966-1970)

I felt badly for Rocky Bleier last week. Someone had stolen three of his four Super Bowl rings while he was delivering a speech at the 116th Moose International Convention in Charlotte, North Carolina. To make matters worse, the story in the Pittsburgh newspaper about the incident dredged up some difficult days in Bleier's life.

There was something mean spirited about the story, delving into Bleier's divorce and personal bankruptcy filing back in 1996 when he sold the four rings to a friend, attorney Herb Conner, an Upper St. Clair neighbor of mine at the time. Bleier later bought them back. Conner was helping him through a challenging time; that's all. Then, too, the newspaper report included a string of tales about how other NFL players had lost or sold their rings. What that had to do with Bleier's misfortune is hard to fathom.

Bleier has made another comeback in his life, one that's not quite as stirring as his return to star for the Steelers in the '70s after suffering disabling wounds in a rice paddy in Vietnam, but one that's been quite satisfying for Bleier.

He's remarried and he and his wife Jan, a jewel of a woman from West Mifflin, have adopted two little dolls from the Ukraine that anyone would love to have in their own home. The Bleiers live in one of the nicest neighborhoods in Mt. Lebanon, and no one is going to have to throw a fund-raiser on Rocky Bleier's behalf.

But how many fund-raisers has Bleier lent his name and talents to through the years in this town, and so many others? Doesn't he deserve better treatment from the media here? Someone stole his Super Bowl rings. They have great significance to him and so many other Steelers. It's a time to reflect on his accomplishments, his contributions to our community, not his difficult days, not family breakups or bankruptcy reminders.

I remember what John Banaszak, a teammate of Bleier who lives in McMurray, said at the Dapper Dan Sports Dinner at the outset of this year. Banaszak has three Super Bowl rings. "Sometimes I take them out and look at them," said Banaszak, who was representing the Steelers of the 1979 championship season, "and I get tingly all over."

It's hard to believe it was 25 years ago that the Steelers, as well as the Pirates, last won a championship. But we'll never forget that year, or the '70s, when Pittsburgh was hailed everywhere as the "City of Champions," and we loved being citizens of such a winning town. Banaszak won't forget, either. ("Ask me what's new?" he said when we bumped into each other at the Blount Dinner. "I've got two new titanium knees. They feel a lot better than my own.")

Bleier was understandably upset by the treatment his personal loss received in media reports here. It reminded him of the hurt he felt when tell-all stories surfaced about his family difficulties six years earlier. "Now I know why Terry Bradshaw feels the way he does about Pittsburgh," Bleier told me when I telephoned him last week.

Jim O'Brien

Rocky Bleier, with his wife Jan, was honored at the 2006 Mel Blount Celebrity Roast Dinner at the downtown Hilton.

Memories are Made of This

Hall of Fame quarterback Terry Bradshaw donated his four Super Bowl rings, his College Football Hall of Fame ring, Pro Football Hall of Fame ring, his Hall of Fame bust, four miniature Super Bowl trophies and a helmet and jersey from one of his Super Bowl victories to his alma mater, Louisiana Tech University. "I don't need them to remind me of anything," said the former Steelers' star performer. "I played in those games, and that's all the memories I need."

Bleier will think better of that remark. I know what he meant. But he and Bradshaw also realize that most of the people in Pittsburgh have great affection for them. They are still treasured icons in this city, more valued than any Super Bowl rings. Bradshaw is back in the fold. Rocky has remained here right along. He's been happy here.

"Those rings stand for something special," Bleier continued in our conversation. "I wasn't expected to walk right again, let alone play football. I didn't win those Super Bowl rings. Our team won them. We were the first team to win four Super Bowls, the first team to win back-to-back championships twice. No one had done what we'd done."

Bleier said he called the Charlotte newspapers to report the loss of his rings, hoping it might help him recover them. He said the Pittsburgh newspapers called him, and that's why he felt betrayed by the stories that emerged after he returned the calls — as he always does — only to be blind-sided by what he read. His loss became the stuff for editorial cartoons. It was embarrassing.

I've gotten to know Bleier better over the last five years, and I have come to admire him even more than I did when I was covering the Steelers when they won their fourth Super Bowl in six years. Bleier is one of the best Pittsburgh has to offer. He makes a lot of money telling his personal success story across the nation. But he lends his name and time to so many local charities and fund-raising efforts without any pay at all.

I traveled with Rocky to Canton, Ohio two years ago when he represented all the former NFL players who'd been in the military service and were being honored at a special display area at the Pro Football Hall of Fame. Bleier did a bang-up job with appropriate and humble remarks.

Bleier remains one of the favorites of football fans everywhere. He did me a favor two years ago by speaking at my "Keeping The Faith" dinner at Asbury Heights in Mt. Lebanon. The event raises money — over $220,000 in five years — for benevolent care, to subsidize senior residents who might run out of money so they can stay there. Everybody who meets Rocky Bleier is impressed with his friendly manner and personal warmth. That night, while posing for a picture, I realized that, at 5-8½ inches, I was just as tall as Rocky Bleier. I told him, "What's the deal, Rocky? Coaches always told me I was too small to play football." Rocky smiled and poked a stiff finger into my sternum several times. "Your problem," he said, "is that you believed them."

Rocky has so many motivational messages. I hope his rings are returned to him soon. He earned them the hard way, and he's never forgotten how tough they were to come by. We shouldn't forget either.

This is a time of the year when we celebrate Memorial Day and the Fourth of July and recall those who served their country. Rocky Bleier participates in many of these events. In so many ways, he is still serving his country and certainly this community.

Big Ben strikes the right chord
at every opportunity

November 24, 2004

I can't remember when this community was more excited about a rookie sports star than it is about Ben Roethlisberger of the Steelers. Once we all — including me — learn how to spell his name and pronounce it properly he'll be even more of a topic of dinner conversation.

The Pirates produced their first National League Rookie of the Year this season in Jason Bay. There's an easy name to spell and pronounce; yet there's no comparison in the talk around town.

Tyler Palko of Pitt, who also has an easy name that fits nicely into one-column headlines, made a good run at Roethlisberger last week on all the sports talk shows, but for all the wrong reasons. It wasn't because Palko passed for five touchdowns, the first opposing quarterback ever to do so at hallowed Notre Dame Stadium, but rather because of ill-chosen remarks in the post-game TV interview.

That's a shame. I saw the interview and I asked the guy next to me, "Did I just hear what I thought I heard?"

Many have rushed to Palko's defense and have advanced the thought that it was TV's fault for pushing a mike to his mouth when he was so caught up in the excitement of a last-minute victory over Notre Dame.

Sorry, but that doesn't wash with me. Palko takes great pride in being the voice of this year's Pitt Panthers football team, so he has to be especially careful how he phrases his enthusiasm. He has to think before he speaks. I wonder if he ever took a class in public speaking at Pitt. It would serve him well.

The same could be said for all athletes. I cringe when I hear some of the "sound bites" that pass for insights on some of the sports reports on radio and television in our town. They are peppered with such pithy phrases as "you know" and "like" and offer little in the way of wisdom. So many fans call in to sports talk shows and start a sentence with "I seen..." The hockey sound bites are the worst.

Palko's coach, Walt Harris, has a bad habit of saying the wrong things in interviews, pre-game and post-game, and difficulty in phrasing a simple sentence. Harris, for instance, cannot properly say "Pittsburgh." The same is true of at least two of his assistant coaches. It makes one wonder why Steve Peterson, the athletic director, wants everyone to refer to the school as Pittsburgh rather than Pitt.

The same is true for Bill Cowher, the coach of the Steelers, who also mispronounces many words and mixes up the order of the most cliched phrases. They don't take time to think out their thoughts, and to watch what they say, and how they say it. Expressing themselves properly should have a higher priority on their personal agenda.

Pittsburgh has a chance to have two outstanding quarterbacks carrying the day over the next few seasons and, in Big Ben's case, for many more years. In time, Palko could put Pitt into a major New Year's Day bowl game. In time, not this year I suspect, Roethlisberger could lead the Steelers to a Super Bowl or two.

It's highly unlikely, no matter how good Big Ben turns out to be, he can match Terry Bradshaw's record of winning four out of four Super Bowls. And, believe me, the Steelers never win four Super Bowls without the combination of Chuck Noll and Terry Bradshaw.

Palko practices at the same complex as the Steelers, and even eats in the same cafeteria — how the NCAA permits such a situation is unfathomable — so he has a chance to keep an eye on Big Ben. Palko would be wise to model Big Ben's mechanics and how he handles himself on the field, but he'd be just as wise to see how Ben handles himself in interviews, especially network interviews.

Roethlisberger has impressed everyone with his poise under fire. "He's made some plays only the good ones can make," said Art Rooney Jr., the head of the Steelers' player personnel department during the Super Bowl run of the '70s.

"He's big and strong, and has a sense or feel for the rush, and how to get away from it," remarked Rooney during lunch at the St. Clair Country Club last week. "He's three years ahead of Terry at this time. But Bradshaw was the best once he settled into the job."

Andy Russell has become a fan of Big Ben, but he agrees with what I wrote here last week that we should wait awhile before we induct him into the Hall of Fame. Pittsburgh's Danny Marino will be going in this summer, and Roethlisberger has a big job ahead of him in matching Marino's numbers.

"Before declaring Roethlisberger the next greatest, I'd like to see him deal with some adversity," remarked Russell during dinner at The Club at Nevillewood, near his home on the 18th hole of the club's magnificent golf course. "So far it's been kind of easy being a front runner. All athletes have bad days and his will come. It's how he deals with it that will determine whether he's got the ability to forge a career that will put him in the Hall of Fame. My guess, however, is that he does have the right stuff. But let's wait and see."

I caught Rocky Bleier putting up Christmas lights outside his home in the Virginia Manor section of Mt. Lebanon last week. He was impressed with Roethlisberger and Palko, though he wasn't pleased that Palko beat his old Notre Dame team.

"Both of them have a lot of ability and poise," said Bleier. "The Steelers are playing better because guys are stepping up and coming through in a big way when they have to take someone else's place. I like the way Roethlisberger handles himself."

Bleier has taken the time to work on his speechifying. He's always been concerned about his image on and off the field. He likes the way Roethlisberger always seems to say the right thing. Some on the media are happier when a player makes a gaffe like Palko did. TV likes to shine its bright lights and hold its microphones to the too-wide mouths of Ray Lewis and Terrell Owens and Chad Johnson. Controversy sells.

Perhaps Palko has learned his lesson. He's a good kid, I know that from personal experience. He just has to think before he speaks — a rarity in the sports world these days. We wish Palko and Big Ben the best of luck. At this time of year, I'm thankful for my family and friends and my teachers and mentors. I'm also thankful we have Tyler Palko and Ben Roethlisberger to root for in Pittsburgh.

Big Ben has fun with Chris Hoke during introduction of Steelers' basketball team at Canon-McMillan High School.

One day Ben Roethlisberger is playing basketball in Shaler Township, Moon Township or Canonsburg and the next thing you know he's seen playfully riding a bicycle in Berne, the capital city of Switzerland.

I was visiting my daughter Rebecca in Los Angeles and enjoying the luxury of reading some of the best newspapers, like the Los Angeles Times, The New York Times, The Washington Post, USA Today and The Wall Street Journal, and all of them contained photos and stories showing Big Ben on a bike in Berne. It was Tuesday, May 9, 2006.

Big Ben was big news everywhere he went. It was amazing how far and how fast he had become a big-time sports star. Big Ben visited Lauperswil, a town of about 2,800 people about 20 miles east of Bern, where his ancestors once lived. He was also pictured sampling for a large loaf of Emmental cheese, a point of pride where his great great grandparents grew up. Schools were closed and diplomats celebrated Big Ben's arrival. His great great grandfather lived in Lauperswill in the Swiss cheese-producing region of Emmental. He left for the U.S.A. in 1873.

"It's something out of a dream or a movie," remarked Roethlisberger during a weeklong trip to discover his family's roots in Switzerland. "I'm starting to feel more Swiss the longer I'm here."

Roethlisberger went to Switzerland soon after one of his teammates and favorite receivers Hines Ward went to South Korea with his mother to learn more about his heritage and to visit places familiar to his mother. Ward was a year old when his parents departed South Korea to come to the U.S. While Roethlisberger was in Switzerland, Ward announced that he would soon return to South Korea to champion efforts to improve the environment for racially mixed children there.

Michelle Wie, the teen golf sensation, had also gone to South Korea in May to play in a pro golf tournament there, and she was astounded by the reception she received. Her parents were from South Korea. She was born in Hawaii.

Roethlisberger was recruited to come to Switzerland as spokesman for Swiss Roots, a campaign with the slogan "How Swiss Are You?" intended to help Americans of Swiss origin reconnect with the Old Country.

Big Ben never misses a beat. He always seems to do the right thing, make the right move, and make something out of nothing. It's a trait that has marked his short stay with the Steelers and helped him attract a lot of fans.

In Los Angeles and San Diego, I visited several sports memorabilia stores. There were pictures, plaques, signed helmets and all sorts of Steelers' stuff prominently displayed in all the stores. Big Ben, Hines Ward, Jerome Bettis, Troy Polamalu and Bill Cowher were all for sale.

It's easy to be rooting
for Peyton and Tyler, too

*P*eyton Manning was the enemy when the Steelers faced the favored Indianapolis Colts at the RCA Dome in the first round of the AFC playoffs.

We were happy when the Steelers sacked or pressured Peyton. The victory at Indianapolis was the key to the Steelers' successful post-season run. Manning merits our adulation, however, for his football ability and, more so, for the manner in which he conducts himself off the football field.

Sometimes the Mannings are hard to take, but consider this:

Peyton Manning received the NFL's Walter Payton Man of the Year Award at ceremonies linked to Super Bowl XL in Detroit in February, 2006. The award recognized his work with children and Hurricane Katrina victims in his native Louisiana.

The award is named in honor of Walter Payton, a great running back for the Chicago Bears who died of cancer in 1999. Payton's coach, Mike Ditka, has said that Payton was one of the greatest and toughest football players he was ever around.

When Manning was presented the award, he said, "I challenge each and every player in the National Football League to consider the impact they have just because they play the game of football. Then go do something about it. There's more to the game."

Payton and his brother Eli, a quarterback for the New York Giants, and their father, Archie, who was the quarterback of the New Orleans Saints for 11 years, are all involved in philanthropic activities.

December 1, 2004

A friend of mine, George Schoeppner, an insurance man in Mt. Lebanon, told me a Thanksgiving story that grabbed my heart and wouldn't let go.

Schoeppner spent the holiday last Thursday with his grandson, nine-year-old Tyler, and Tyler's parents, Pam and Eric Frenzel, at their home in Carmel, Indiana. Pam is George's daughter.

George and Tyler sat on a couch together and watched Tyler's favorite football player, Peyton Manning, throw six touchdown passes to lead the Indianapolis Colts to a convincing 41-9 victory over the host Detroit Lions. Manning has thrown 41 TD passes so far this season and is closing in on Danny Marino's league record of 48 TD passes in a season.

Marino and Schoeppner share a distinction. They were both All-America ballplayers at the University of Pittsburgh. Schoeppner was an All-America infielder on Pitt's baseball team back in the late '50s, and Marino was an All-America quarterback for the Panthers in the early '80s. Schoeppner and Fred Mazurek were Pitt's only two All-America performers in baseball for a long time. Then George and Tyler watched Pitt beat West Virginia 16-13, winning the game on a late touchdown run by Panthers' quarterback Tyler Palko. George's grandson liked the fact that he had the same name as the Pitt quarterback.

"Before I left, Tyler just sat on my lap for about ten or fifteen minutes and we just hugged one another," George told me when he returned home. "It was great. I was happy to be there. I missed my wife Barb and our family, but I was so happy I was out there. We don't know if he'll be here for Christmas."

Tyler Frenzel has leukemia. He has lost his hair to chemotherapy treatments. He had a bone marrow transplant and appeared to be doing well, but then things went poorly. His prognosis is not good. Peyton Manning and some of his teammates on the Colts have spent a great deal of time with Tyler, trying their best to cheer him up and lend encouraging words to his war with cancer. Tyler wears his No. 18 blue Colts' jersey with great pride. He was a big fan of Peyton Manning even before he learned he had leukemia.

The diagnosis came on December 20, 2002. "He's been through hell," said his father, Eric Frenzel. It's important to hear about what Manning and some of his teammates have done. He plays in the same town as another pro athlete, Ron Artest of the Indiana Pacers of the NBA who got a lot of publicity recently when he raced into the stands at a game with the Pistons in Detroit and started fighting with fans. We've heard about the Clemson and South Carolina football teams fighting with one another, and other negative news in the world of sports. It's refreshing to hear about Peyton Manning and his personal concern for Tyler Frenzel.

When Tyler was six years old, his parents took a picture of him in front of his bedroom mural of Peyton Manning. They had the picture enlarged and sent it to Peyton Manning. Tyler wrote and asked for an autograph and got it on his blown-up picture. A year-and-a-half later, Tyler was a patient at Riley Hospital for Children in Indianapolis, and received a telephone call from Peyton Manning. Manning made the connection that this was the kid who'd sent him the picture to be signed. They became fast friends, frequent pen pals. "I have a lot of his cards and autographs," Tyler tells everyone.

"Peyton has been wonderful," said Pam Frenzel, Tyler's mom. "He sent Tyler a cake when he turned 9 in March. He also gave him a $200 gift certificate for the Colts' team store."

On a larger scale, Manning provided funding for four football-theme rooms for young patients at the hospital. Blue and white is the color, of course, with lots of Colts' paraphernalia all over the place. This is Peyton's major project in the community.

"I've enjoyed watching the hospital grow," Manning told Sara Scavongelli of the *Indianapolis Star*. "We wanted to show each kid that there are people looking out for them."

In a similar vein, I learned something of a special gesture by Jack Lambert for a cancer-stricken child during Lambert's days as a player for the Pittsburgh Steelers. A woman in North Syracuse, New York, sent me an order for a copy of my newest book, *Lambert: The Man in the Middle*, and it was accompanied by a beautiful note.

"My grandson was 16 years old and in the Make-A-Wish program," she wrote. "His wish was to go to Dallas to see the Steelers play the Cowboys in a pre-season game. But he was too weak to go. So Make-A-Wish arranged for a Steeler to call him. That turned out to be Jack Lambert. He called and told my grandson he would wave to him during the game. And he did. My grandson died later that night. So Jack Lambert will always have a special place in our hearts."

It's refreshing, even if painful, to hear these stories. It's nice to know that athletes can put their celebrity to good use, and spread some cheer. Such efforts make so much more sense than all the chest thumping and dancing in the end zones after touchdowns.

No one in Pittsburgh wants to see Danny Marino's records broken. Danny does a lot of good with the children at a hospital he has funded generously in his backyard in South Florida. But if someone has to do it, Peyton Manning seems like a worthy successor. When it comes to children, he has a huge glad hand and a heart as big as Danny Marino's.

Tyler Frenzel died at age 9 on December 11, 2004, five days after he had attended a holiday party hosted by Peyton Manning.

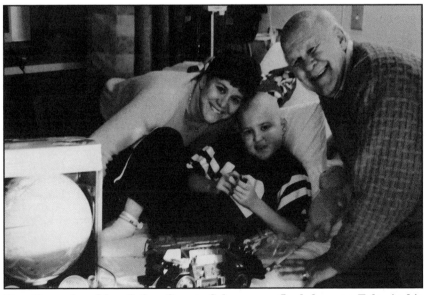

Photo from Frenzel family

Pam Frenzel and her father George Schoeppner flank her son Tyler in his room at St. Vincent Children's Hospital in Indianapolis. Tyler is shown wearing No. 18 jersey of his favorite Colt player, quarterback Peyton Manning.

Letter from Pam Frenzel:

January 30, 2006

(This is a letter from Pam Frenzel, the mother of Tyler Frenzel, and the daughter of George Schoeppner of Mt. Lebanon. Schoeppner, a retired insurance salesman, still holds the one-game scoring record of 55 points in a basketball game for Mt. Lebanon High School, and is one of the few All-American baseball players in the history of the University of Pittsburgh, back in 1959.)

Dear Mr. O'Brien,

Enclosed you will find several articles about my son, Tyler, and Peyton Manning. I also enclosed my favorite photo of the two together, when Peyton presented Tyler with his own jersey. I wanted to give you a history of the relationship between Tyler and Peyton.

Tyler was a fan of Peyton Manning from the start. In the summer of 2001, when Tyler was six years old, we had his room painted with a football mural. One scene on the wall has Peyton Manning at the line of scrimmage. We took a photo of Tyler, dressed in his Manning jersey, sitting in front of the mural. Tyler wrote to Peyton and drew a picture, and we sent it along with the photo, asking for an autograph. Peyton signed the photo of Tyler and returned it. That was the beginning.

A year and a half later, on December 20, 2002, Tyler was diagnosed with Leukemia at the age of 7½. He was treated at St. Vincent Children's Hospital in Indianapolis. Peyton Manning does a lot of charity work with this hospital. The staff at the outpatient cancer clinic knew Tyler was a fan and asked Peyton to call him in the hospital. Peyton called Tyler in the hospital on December 23. We were amazed, because it was a very busy time in the season as the Colts were gearing toward the playoffs. Even more amazing was the fact that Peyton remembered Tyler. When my husband, Eric, asked Peyton if he remembered a little boy who had sent him a photo and picture a year and a half earlier, Peyton recalled receiving the items.

In June 2003, Tyler was invited to play in a flag football game at the Colts Complex with kids from different organizations that Peyton sponsors. Tyler was in a lot of pain from his chemotherapy treatments, but he was not going to miss the opportunity to play football with Peyton Manning! The last play of the game, Peyton decided to play quarterback for his team of kids. Tyler was the rusher and he chased Peyton from sideline to sideline several times, trying to catch him. It was a thrilling time for Tyler, and the relationship between Tyler and Peyton just blossomed from there.

Tyler started a maintenance chemo regimen in July 2003 and life mostly returned to normal, until the end of January 2004, when the cancer returned. Tyler began a three-month chemo protocol to prepare him for a bone marrow transplant. In March 2004, Peyton had a cake sent to Tyler in the hospital for his 9th birthday and gave Tyler a gift card to shop at the Colts store. Tyler achieved remission and went to another hospital (Riley Hospital) for his bone marrow transplant. While

Peyton Manning poses with Tyler Frenzel, one of his biggest fans.

Tyler had pillow cases and covers with Colts' logo on them during his hospital stay in Indianapolis.

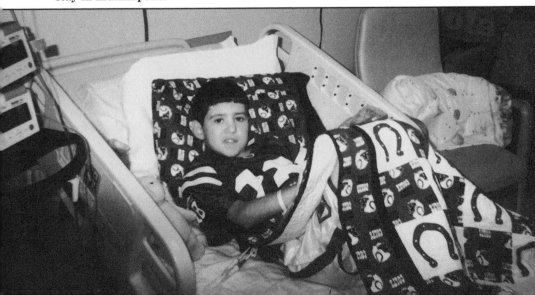

Tyler was recovering from the transplant at Riley, Peyton was to unveil four Peyton Manning rooms at St. Vincent Children's Hospital. He wanted Tyler to be a part of the ribbon-cutting ceremony. The doctors worked together to make it happen, and on June 28, 2004, Tyler participated in the ribbon-cutting ceremony with Peyton. Tyler had to return to Riley Hospital immediately following the ceremony. It was his first time out of the hospital in five weeks.

Again, Tyler did well, reaching his 100th day post-transplant with relative ease. Then at the end of September 2004, the cancer returned. Tyler started chemo at Riley Hospital, and then we asked that he be transferred back to St. Vincent Children's Hospital to be closer to home. Tyler got to stay in one of the Peyton Manning rooms while at the hospital! After his release from the hospital in early October 2004, Peyton Manning arranged a private meeting with Tyler at the cancer outpatient clinic and surprised him with an official #18 Colts jersey with "Frenzel" on the back. The jersey hangs proudly on our basement wall.

The chemo did not work for Tyler, and on November 2, 2004, doctors told us there were no more treatment options available for Tyler. Again, Peyton Manning stepped in to help cheer Tyler up. Tyler was invited to a Colts practice on November 5, 2004. At the end of the practice, Peyton huddled his teammates together and obviously shared Tyler's story with them. Then, every player came over to Tyler, shook his hand, chatted with him and signed his Colts quilt. It was a wonderful experience for Tyler!

Peyton then offered Tyler three tickets to sit in a suite at the upcoming Monday Night Football game. Furthermore, on December 2, 2004, Peyton sent Tyler on a shopping spree at the local Toys 'R Us. Tyler purchased a football game, where you throw small footballs at targets for points.

On December 5, 2004, Tyler was selected as a Coin Toss Kid for the Colts game. He got to go out to the center of the field and watch the coin toss with the captains of the team, one being Peyton Manning.

Then, on December 6, 2004, after a very long day of chemotherapy and transfusions, Tyler insisted on attending Peyton Manning's holiday party at the Indianapolis Children's Museum. We walked in an hour late, and there was Peyton Manning, waiting to greet Tyler! Tyler died five days later. We buried him in the Colts jersey of his favorite player — Peyton Manning — a tribute to a bond between one caring, famous athlete and one special little boy.

A few days after Tyler died, Peyton Manning visited our home to see the room where Tyler spent so much of his time, and a room filled with photos and autographed memorabilia of himself, one of Tyler's favorite heroes.

On December 21, 2004, the Colts and a local radio station hosted an auction to help raise money for "Tyler's Treehouse" at Camp Emma Lou in Bloomington, Indiana. The camp is being built by Scott Rolen of the St. Louis Cardinals, another great friend to Tyler. Scott and Peyton worked together on the auction. Close to $200,000 was raised for the treehouse. It was incredible that Peyton Manning was using his contacts/resources to help a fellow athlete with his charity, and he was doing it for Tyler. Our family will forever root for the Colts because of the compassion and care shown by Peyton Manning for our son.

Big Ben a big hit
at 'Breakfast With Champions'

April 27, 2005

They say that no two snowflakes are alike, and that must be especially true when those snowflakes fall in late April. It was football-like weather over the weekend when the NFL held its annual two-day draft of college prospects. Most of the draftees drew high praise, and everyone expressed sheer delight with their draft picks.

It's unlikely that any of the teams made a selection that will turn out as well as Ben Roethlisberger of the Steelers. Big Ben was the biggest first-year sports phenomenon ever to hit Pittsburgh. From a marketing standpoint, no one else came close.

Not only was he a terrific quarterback, but he was the kind of humble, self-effacing "I'll take the blame if things go badly" leader we love. Everybody was enamored of Big Ben. What's not to like?

I have an exclusive of sorts as I was the only reporter present for what Ben said was his first outing as a featured speaker since he joined the Steelers and won NFL Rookie of the Year honors.

This was at Foodland's 9th annual "Breakfast With Champions" at the Marriott City Center in downtown Pittsburgh on Saturday, April 16. It was for the benefit of the Leukemia & Lymphoma Society.

Roethlisberger captured the ballroom crowd immediately when he confessed, "I'm a little nervous. I'm still a rookie. This is my first speaking engagement. I'm more nervous than before a game. My hands are a little sweaty. I kinda need a football here."

Roethlisberger was honored as the Athlete Champion, and Amy Katz, a 12-year-old 7th grader at Jefferson Middle School in Mt. Lebanon received the Patient Champion Award. Miss Katz is challenged by leukemia that has caused her to put her sports activity on hold. She had previously participated in soccer, swimming, softball and tennis.

"Amy is the real champion here," remarked Roethlisberger.

He was now an honorary member of Amy's Army. Miss Katz had been diagnosed with chronic myelogenous leukemia in autumn of 2003. Since that time she has been in and out of hospitals, and must take daily medication. Her father, Michael Katz, is a financial officer for a Green Tree engineering firm. I learned from others that Michael Katz was one of the top platform tennis players in Pittsburgh. Mr. Katz and his family told me that they knew my daughter, Dr. Sarah O'Brien, then a pediatric oncology fellow at Children's Hospital, because she had checked Amy from time to time. My wife Kathie knew the folks from the Leukemia & Lymphoma Society because she is a social worker in the Cancer Center at Allegheny General Hospital.

Amy's mother, Lisa Katz, talked about Amy's Army, a volunteer group of more than 100 people, who held fund-raisers over a two-year period to help defray the cost of testing for a bone marrow transplant for Amy. A transplant is Amy's best chance for a cure. Along the way, they have added 6,000 more people to the national registry and ten patients from across the nation have found life-saving perfect matches as a result of their efforts. But none for Amy. So the march continued.

Big Ben seemed to be everywhere, lending his name to many worthy causes. His heart seemed to be in the right place. He had appeared the previous evening at the Mel Blount Youth Home Celebrity Roast, and would be honored the next evening as the Sportsman of the Year at the annual Dapper Dan Sports Dinner. Arnold Palmer was presented with a Lifetime Achievement Award at that fete.

Big Ben joined "Arnie's Army" and "Amy's Army" in the same weekend and continued to say all the right things that have endeared him to Pittsburgh sports fans. He stands tall for all the right things.

He knows his place in Pittsburgh. The company he was keeping that weekend humbled him. He said he was nervous at that same time a year ago, wondering where he'd go in the NFL draft. "My dream was to play in the NFL," he explained, "and I wanted to make the most of the opportunity. I knew I was going someplace, and I could be going east or west. I knew I wasn't going to stay in Findlay, Ohio because it wasn't big enough to have a pro football team.

"I came to the best city in the country. I got to play with all great guys like Jerome Bettis, Hines Ward and Tommy Maddox. I wasn't expecting to play much. I thought I'd start out standing on the sidelines, helping Tommy any way I could. When Tommy got hurt, I knew he was a tough guy, and he'd be back at quarterback. I was expecting Tommy to be back for the next game. I never doubted he'd be all right. But I kept the job and it's been great.

"So you never know what is coming your way. I'm inspired by the people I've met here today. I have new friends like Amy and Christine out there. They are an inspiration to me. People here have dealt with real challenges. I play a game. I go out and entertain you guys on Sunday. What I do is nothing compared to these kids and their families."

Big Ben was joined at the breakfast by Kevin Spencer, a special teams coach with the Steelers; KDKA Radio's Larry Richert, former Pirates Nellie King and Bob Friend, former Penguins' star Pierre LaRouche, golfer Carol Semple-Thompson, former Steeler Mike Wagner, former NFLer Rob Holmberg and Pitt's mascot and cheerleaders.

I was saddened the following week to learn that a former No. 1 draft choice of the Steelers had died at age 76. Bobby Gage came out of Clemson in 1949 and starred for two seasons. He was one of the first Steelers I was aware of as a child, and I always liked his name. As a rookie, he raced 97 yards for a touchdown against the Chicago Bears. It's still the record for the longest run in Steelers' history.

That same weekend, while driving to Tennessee for a week's vacation, I drove through Bluefield, Va., the hometown of the Steelers' No. 1 draft choice in 1942, the year I was born. "Bullet Bill" Dudley of the University of Virginia has stood the test of time and he's in the Pro Football Hall of Fame.

I also drove through Bristol, Va. on the way to and from Tennessee. That's where Ron Necciai of Monongahela struck out 27 batters in the minor league baseball game, the only time that's ever been done in professional baseball history. If I knew the Steelers were going to select Heath Miller, a tight end from Virginia, with their first draft pick I'd have gone off the highway to find his hometown of Whiskey Creek nearby.

Hopefully, Miller will match up well with Mark Bruener, the last tight end the Steelers selected in the first round (1995). Bruener, much like Big Ben, was a terrific guy on the field and in our community.

Amy Katz enlisted Big Ben to be in "Amy's Army" during "Breakfast With Champions" sponsored by Leukemia & Lymphoma Society.

From the Katz family

Children's Hour

Ben Roethlisberger resented it when people questioned his intelligence for riding a motorcycle without wearing a protective helmet. It was no longer the law in Pennsylvania to do so at the outset of the 2005 football season. Ben was just 23 at the time and didn't feel the need to wear a helmet unless he was on the football field as quarterback of the Pittsburgh Steelers.

His coach, Bill Cowher, wasn't thrilled about him riding on a motorcycle in the first place, but was especially critical of him doing so without taking safety precautions. Terry Bradshaw heard about the story and suggested it wasn't very smart. "Park the motor-cycle," he advised Ben Ben on national television.

As a young quarterback, Bradshaw's intelligence was often questioned. Thomas "Hollywood" Henderson of the Dallas Cowboys once suggested that you "could spot Terry C and A and he still couldn't spell CAT." Bradshaw bristled at such comments, and now it was Roethlisberger's turn to resent such parental-like interference.

Roethlisberger must have given Bradshaw a cold shoulder somewhere along the way since then, perhaps at a celebrity golf outing. Bradshaw came to Pittsburgh in mid-May, 2006 to head up the celebrity lineup for a fund-raising golf outing at The Club at Nevillewood, just outside of Bridgeville. KDKA's Bob Pompeani posed a question for Bradshaw, asking him what he thought of a recent remark by Roethlisberger that he was hoping to start passing more in the Steelers' offense. Bradshaw brushed aside that question to continue criticizing Roethlisberger about his penchant for continuing to ride motorcycles.

"He has to be responsible as a team leader," said Bradshaw.

He also hinted that Roethlisberger had not been friendly to him since he offered his critical remarks. "My remarks were tough," Bradshaw said, "but people who know me will tell you that I say what I think, but I'm really behind you.

"He's a grown man. I'm just disappointed with him. He's a great talent. He doesn't owe me an explanation. He doesn't have to like me. I don't care if he's a friend."

It all seemed so silly. Like kids feuding in a playground. One had to wonder why Terry was getting into a hissing contest with Ben Roethlisberger. After years of offering public criticism of Chuck Noll, Terry finally made peace with his old coach and seemed relieved to do so. Terry should know better than to keep throwing logs on the fire this time out, especially when there's enough love in Pittsburgh for both of its Super Bowl-winning quarterbacks. Ben should know better, too, now that he was 24.

This was all before Ben was injured in the motorcycle accident.

Tom Atkins fills in for
late Art Rooney at golf outings

May 25, 2005

I ran into and talked to Tom Atkins on three occasions last week. He was a celebrity participant in two golf outings that raise money to assist children and adults who are challenged by health issues.

Atkins is the popular Pittsburgh-born-and-bred actor who's best known these days for portraying Steelers' founder Art Rooney Sr. in the Public Theater's production of *The Chief*. He grew up in Carrick and now lives in Peters Township.

Atkins has portrayed Pittsburgh's most beloved figure at the O'Reilly Theater the past two holiday seasons, and will do so again for a one-week run this January.

So now Atkins gets invited to celebrity golf outings that include Steelers, Pirates and Penguins and former Pitt players. He participated last Monday in the 12th Annual Hoge-Ward Celebrity Golf Classic for Children hosted by Judd Gordon of Highmark Caring Foundation. That was held at the Southpointe Golf Club in Canonsburg.

Atkins also attended the party on the eve of the 29th Annual Andy Russell Celebrity Classic, and played with a foursome on Friday at The Club at Nevillewood. This event is so well supported that half the participants played at Southpointe Golf Club.

"I'm honored to be invited," said Atkins. "When I was living in New York and Los Angeles, I was still a Pittsburgh sports fan, so I enjoy mixing with these men and women as much as anybody."

He never met Art Rooney, though he saw him as a young man. "It was an intimidating role, playing someone people in Pittsburgh knew so well," he said. "It's been my most satisfying role."

Art Rooney is known to have played some golf in his early years, but made his mark mostly in baseball, boxing and football. "Tom played better than Art Rooney would have," said Carl Dozzi, a golf equipment salesman who helps in a big way with many of the local golf outings. "After all, if Mr. Rooney were still alive he would be 104 years old."

Atkins was able to smile at the joke. He's never been confused with Arnold Palmer while playing golf. But he blended well with all the ballplayers and businessmen at the Hoge-Ward event. Hines Ward was out there, with Bill Cowher and Ben Roethlisberger leading the way.

Andy Russell rounds up some of the great football players of the past, especially linebackers, for his event every year. Russell resides just off the 18th green at The Club at Nevillewood. There are lots of Hall of Famers in his field.

369

"I like people and you meet a lot of great people out here," said Atkins. In that respect, Atkins is a lot like Art Rooney, comfortable and at ease with everyone. He is naturally gracious and greets everyone with a smile and easy conversation. "I never enjoyed a show as much as *The Chief*," he continued. "I'm having the time of my life up there on that stage." Atkins says Dan Rooney, the chairman of the board of the Steelers, has seen the show six times, and that Art Rooney Jr. of Mt. Lebanon has seen it four times. "Art Rooney Jr. told me, 'You really got him. It's like going down to the old man's office and hearing him tell stories. I've heard all the stories before, but it's great to hear them again.'"

Pittsburgh born and bred actor Tom Atkins mimics boxing great Harry Greb, whose picture hangs in back room of Atria's Restaurant & Tavern in Mt. Lebanon. Greb was known during his heyday as "The Pittsburgh Windmill." Greb was from Garfield and Atkins came from Carrick.

Father's Day is reminder
of importance of that role

June 16, 2005

I wish I could take my father to Atria's Restaurant & Tavern to meet my friends this Friday afternoon. We could toast him at the popular Mt. Lebanon establishment for Father's Day. My dad would be 100 years old if he were still alive, and perhaps a bit frail, but I think he'd still have a thirst for the occasion. He was a little guy, about 5-7, 145 pounds and liked to tell people he was a jockey when they asked him what he did for a living.

That would get a laugh. He had an easy way about him, an easy smile. He had a bit of Will Rogers in him, with a twist. Dan O'Brien never met a bar he didn't like. There were 34 of them in a mile stretch between the bank and our home in Hazelwood, a community at the eastern end of the inner city of Pittsburgh.

That was a veritable minefield when he cashed his paycheck on Friday and made his way home, slaking his thirst and paying off his tabs along the way. My mother never knew how much she'd be getting by the time he got home. I was the youngest of four children, and the one most willing to go get Dad and bring him home for dinner.

I enjoyed meeting his friends. They liked my dad and they liked his boy. They'd buy me orange soda and potato chips or pretzels, and slip me quarters. It was a good gig. I've always enjoyed being with good guys at a good bar.

When I was about ten years old, I started delivering the morning newspaper to many of those bars on my paper route. In truth, my dad was a drill press operator at Mesta Machine Company on the other side of the Glenwood Bridge in West Homestead. He worked the graveyard shift, from 11 p.m. till 7 a.m. That made life a little different at our home. He worked there over 30 years, as did his two brothers, Rich and Robbie, and, later, my older brother Dan. My dad had dropped out of school after seventh grade to go to work, originally, at the Baltimore & Ohio Railroad. He lied about his age back then to get the job.

He took great pride in always showing up for work. I have met men who worked with him, and they told me he was good with the "greenhorns" — the new workers — and lent them tools, and taught them how to do things easier and more efficiently. I'd like to think I'm like that.

The older I get the more I appreciate my father. He drank too much and smoked too much, and that did him in way too early. He spanked me twice in my life, and quit when I cried. He had caught me smoking cigarettes, when I was 9 and 13. He didn't want me smoking. I haven't smoked since. I didn't want to get spanked a third time. He got his point across, and I hold no grudge. It didn't scar me for life.

He didn't pressure me about anything, just to be good and stay out of trouble, just like my mother did. He was never in my face. We didn't play catch with a ball except maybe once. It's not a void in my life. Our parents didn't watch us play every game in those days. We didn't expect them to be there. It was a bonus when they showed up. We weren't playing for their amusement or approval.

He told some good stories. He swore that he was traveling over the Glenwood Bridge one day and saw an airplane that had crashed into the Monongahela River being pulled out of the drink. Remember the story about the airplane that disappeared into the Mon? My dad said the government wanted that airplane pulled out of there before anybody investigated what happened.

When we'd watch an occasional Steelers' game on the black and white screen — this was before color TV — my dad would insist that the J.J. Doyles, one of our local sandlot football teams, could beat the Steelers. And he was serious about that. I remember watching bowling with him on TV. Buddy Bomar comes to mind. I remember watching Buddy Bomar bowling against Andy Varipapa on TV one Saturday afternoon.

My dad liked us, and he liked our mom. Even when she was scolding him about something, usually from downstairs in the kitchen when we'd be sitting in the front room watching TV, he'd smile at me and say, "I still love her." Sometimes he'd sing a song, and sometimes he talked too much. I don't sing, but sometimes I talk too much.

There's more Dan O'Brien in Jim O'Brien than I was willing to admit when I was younger, and knew so much. Now that I am older, I have learned to appreciate my father. He tried. He did his best. I learned a lot from my dad — things to do and not to do — and try to be the best father to my two daughters, and the best husband to my wife. It's a responsibility and a full-time task.

The last time I took him out to meet my friends at a bar, I was 19 and not of legal age. He and my brother went with me to Dante's on the Brentwood-Whitehall border. I told my dad to pace himself, and he did that by ordering an Iron City and an Imperial for starters. They almost got into a fight with Bobby Layne and Ernie Stautner of the Pittsburgh Steelers. Both are in the Pro Football Hall of Fame.

"Bobby Layne and Ernie Stautner are giving Dad a bad time," my brother Dan declared. "We're not going to put up with that!"

"Yes, we are," I shot back.

They say God invented whiskey so the Irish would not rule the world. I think there's something to that. My dad died of emphysema when he was 63. I will be 63 this August 20. That's scary. I will be eager to turn 64.

Mel Blount on his Youth Home in Claysville:

"The whole thing is about the kids. We're just trying to plant some seeds, trying to germinate good things. It's a hard job, but somebody has to do it. It's part of me, who I am, what I want to be."

Remembering those
who are still in harm's way

June 15, 2005

W hat would it be like to have a son or a daughter in Iraq these days? The bombing, shooting and killing continues, and it seems to be getting worse. It's difficult to distinguish enemies from allies.

Maureen and Bob Milie of Mt. Lebanon and their friends, Helen and Bill Priatko, know what it is like. Valerie Milie, a 41-year-old Seabee in the U.S. Navy, recently returned from a tour of duty in Iraq, and David Priatko, who will turn 39 next month, is in the midst of his second year-long tour there. Priatko is a major, and a battalion executive officer with the 3rd Infantry Division.

Miss Milie also did a previous stint during Desert Storm. During that period, she rescued four Marines that were lost in the desert and got a citation from the Secretary of the Navy. Better yet, she was made "an honorary Marine" by those she rescued. She is a Chief Petty Officer, the equivalent of a staff sergeant in the Army.

Valerie was a pretty good all-around athlete during her days at Mt.Lebanon High School.

The Milies and Priatkos sat at a table at Gaetano's Restaurant in Banksville last month and swapped stories about their family experiences in this regard. "My Maureen was beside herself," observed Bob Milie. "We had lots to be concerned about with our family."

Their son, Bob, a federal agent, had just gotten over a cancer scare and a stay at Bethesda Naval Hospital. He is now accompanying an American general in Greece.

"Worry doesn't solve anything," said Helen Priatko, who has battled cancer for over 18 years. "It only makes things worse. I just pray on it, and ask The Lord to look over him."

On Memorial Day we honor those who have served our country in the military service. We tend to think of the old-timers, the veterans of World War I and World War II, of Korea and Vietnam, the ones we see marching in their often too-tight uniforms in holiday parades. But we ought to keep the kids in mind that are presently serving to restore order in various parts of the globe. Especially in the Mideast.

The Milies count their blessings that Valerie has returned safely, and the Priatkos are proud of what Major David is doing, and they will be smiling broadly when he comes marching home again. Bob Milie and Bill Priatko got to know each other through the Pittsburgh chapter of the National Football League Alumni Association.

Milie was an assistant trainer to Ralph Berlin of Bethel Park for all four of the Steelers' Super Bowl championship seasons. Priatko played for the Steelers in the late '50s, and also saw time with the Cleveland Browns and Green Bay Packers. He served in the U.S. Air Force and remained on Reserve duty for a 20-year stint. He has an older son, Danny, who, like his brother David, is a graduate of West Point. Robin Cole of Eighty Four, and the past president of the Pittsburgh NFL Alumni chapter, led a contingent of former Steelers who showed up for Valerie's homecoming celebration. Rocky Bleier of Mt. Lebanon, who was wounded in Vietnam and made a heroic comeback from injuries that threatened his ability to walk let alone run, was present, along with Lloyd Voss of Scott Township and Mike Wagner of Moon Township. Wagner was wearing a tuxedo, as he had another party to attend, and Cole and Bleier both looked handsome in coat and tie.

These Steelers really are special men, as I have written here before. They continue to make a contribution in the community. Tony Parisi of Mt. Lebanon, who was the Steelers' equipment manager for more than 30 years, also attended, along with former Pirates' pitcher and broadcaster Nellie King of Mt. Lebanon.

"It was great to be with my family, our relatives and our friends," said Valerie. "And I was surprised at how many celebrities showed up. It made me feel good, and happy to be back in Pittsburgh."

Two days after I attended Valerie's party, I was in a church near Los Angeles on Mother's Day. They said a prayer for those serving in the Mideast. They asked everyone in the church who had served in the military to stand up and be recognized.

I will admit I was not happy when I received my draft notice shortly after I graduated from Pitt in 1964. I served for two years in the U.S. Army, at stations in Fort Knox, Ky., and the U.S. Army Hometown News Center in Kansas City, and at Fort Greely, Alaska. I was not in harm's way, and don't think of myself as a veteran. Now I appreciate the experience, and am glad I can stand up and be counted among those who served. I was one of the lucky ones. Keep our men and women in mind and in your prayers.

Rocky Bleier welcomes Valerie Milie back from military duty.

Mario Lemieux's golf outing
still star-studded event

June 22, 2005

I am looking forward to the Mellon Mario Lemieux Celebrity Golf Invitational this Thursday through Sunday at The Club at Nevillewood. It turns little Presto into a Community of Champions each June.

That's where I first met Ben Roethlisberger a year ago. I talked to the Steelers' No. 1 draft choice at the No. 1 tee. He was instantly likeable. I was asking a dozen of the celebrities to tell me something special their fathers had told them as youngsters that had stayed with them. The event was held earlier last year, and I was working on a Father's Day column.

Big Ben boasted about his father and what a great impact his parents had on his life. Other celebrities would do the same. As the Steelers' season progressed, and Big Ben got even bigger — as big as any star in the National Football League last season — I scolded myself for not spending more time with him that day at Nevillewood.

Who knew he was going to be so big — as big as any NFL rookie ever — and capture the city like Lemieux and even Clemente never did? Then I wished I had asked him if I could ride around with him in his cart for a few holes, and interview him at greater length, as I had done a year earlier with Tommy Maddox as well as Rocky Bleier and J. C. (Richmond) at a similar charity-related outing at the Southpointe Golf Club in Canonsburg.

Last year, I talked to Joe Theismann for the first time at the Lemieux Invitational. Theismann had been a star quarterback at Notre Dame and with the Washington Redskins, and a TV football analyst. It was raining a little, and Theismann invited me under his umbrella.

He repeated my name when I introduced myself. He put his arm around my shoulder and drew me nearer. He not only answered my question regarding his father, but he added a couple of thoughts on the same theme. Theismann thanked me for seeking his opinion. He said it was nice talking to me. He repeated my name once more.

I knew he was a professional motivational speaker, and a pro at this stuff, but I still complimented him the next day on the way he had handled our first meeting. "It's not about motivational speaking or anything else," said Theismann. "It's the way you ought to treat people."

Most of the men and women Lemieux and his staff seek out for this outing that raises a million dollars each year for cancer research in this area are like that. They know how to treat people right. They get it. They know how to mix with the people who pay big dollars to play golf with them for a good cause, and they know how to treat the fans that fill the fairways to watch them. It's been a great event.

Some guys never get it. Johnny Bench, Mike Schmidt and Andy VanSlyke, for instance, still think they're hot stuff and are rude to patrons and volunteers. It's a chance to see Michael Jordan and Danny Marino, two of my all-time favorites. I go back to their high school and college days with both of them. Jordan knows me as the editor of *Street & Smith's Basketball* magazine, and never lets me forget that my prep basketball expert left him off the pre-season All-American list before his senior high school year in Wilmington, N.C. I've always been impressed with the way Jordan and Marino regard their parents, and how family is important to them.

That's why it's disappointing to learn that this will be the last Lemieux Invitational to be held at The Club at Nevillewood. The event has worn out its welcome and too many green paths in Presto. Next season it will be staged at Laurel Valley in Ligonier, and it will be a corporate affair. It will not be open to the public. That's a shame, but rumors have been flying like Charles Barkley drives in that direction the past two years.

A few years back, Frank Fuhrer held his Family Invitational at the St. Clair Country Club and that brought some of the world's greatest pro players to our backyard. But that got chased away as well and later disappeared altogether. It was our loss.

It's nice for golf fans and sports fans to have a chance to see some of these outstanding sportsmen and sportswomen in action up close. It's a chance to get to know them a bit better, and find out, in most cases, that they're pretty good people. So savor the Lemieux Invitational one more time. We won't have Mario too much longer on the ice, either, so we had better cheer him on while the opportunity still exists.

Mario Lemieux and Michael Jordan are among the celebrities who compete regularly in the Mellon Mario Lemieux Celebrity Golf Tournament.

Eddie Johnston still known best
for bringing Mario to town

Here's a story that's particularly insightful in light of the retirement of Mario Lemieux during the 2005-2006 National Hockey League season, and the drafting and signing of Sidney Crosby as his heir apparent on the Pittsburgh Penguins.

June 29, 2005

A biographical sketch of Eddie Johnston said he is best known as the man who drafted Mario Lemieux. I suggested to Johnston, a long-time neighbor of mine in Upper St. Clair, that this would also be in the first paragraph of his obituary. He smiled. "It was a no-brainer," he said of his decision to draft Lemieux.

Johnston will turn 70 this November, but he was out there in sweltering heat for four demanding days at the Mellon Mario Lemieux Celebrity Invitational at The Club at Nevillewood this past weekend.

He was one of many Penguin representatives at the event that has raised millions of dollars for cancer research. If you wanted to see Penguins play this past year you had to go to an area golf course. With the season cancelled because of the owners' lockout, anyone associated with the Penguins had plenty of time to play golf.

"It was a crazy year," Johnston said. "You didn't know what to do with yourself."

Last week you would have had to go to the Highland Park Zoo to find more penguins than were at Nevillewood. Pierre Larouche, who lives in Mt. Lebanon, took home the first prize purse of $40,000 for the second year in a row, edging four-time winner Rick Rhoden, a former Pirates' pitcher, with a final round 65.

Larouche was Lemieux for the Penguins before they drafted Mario with the first overall pick in the 1984 draft. Larouche could play and score with the best of them during his All-Star career. He was the Penguins' first pick in 1974 and a year later was the youngest player to score 50 goals and 100 points in a season. It was a record later broken by Wayne Gretzky.

Joe Mullen and Randy Hillier of Upper St. Clair, Jay Caufield, Mark Recchi and Craig Patrick also represented the Penguins at Nevillewood. Former Steelers' coach Chuck Noll, who was a neighbor of Johnston in Upper St. Clair for over 20 years, often played in similar charity-related golf outings at Nevillewood.

Johnston was the general manager of the Penguins when they picked Lemieux. "I knew what we needed to do," he said, wiping sweat from his brow during a break at Nevillewood. "I had a lot of good offers from other teams who wanted to trade for that pick, but I never considered them seriously."

Johnston said that Bobby Orr and Gretzky were two other prospects that everyone recognized would be immediate impact players in the National Hockey League. "There's another kid right now who's regarded in the same way," Johnston said. "His name is Sidney Crosby and he comes from Nova Scotia."

Johnston should also be remembered as the winningest coach in Penguins' history. He was the goaltender when the Boston Bruins won two Stanley Cup championships, and he was the last goalie in the NHL to play every minute of a season (1963-64).

When another old friend, Myron Cope, announced his retirement last Tuesday, he said he wanted to be remembered as a writer. "When I die," cracked Cope, "I can see a newspaper obituary on me with the headline 'Towel Inventor Dies.' You betcha."

It was Cope who created "The Terrible Towel," of course, but he figures he accomplished a great deal more during his 35 years as the color man and analyst for Steelers' football and, before that, as a nationally sought-after sportswriter for many first-rate magazines. Cope lived in Scott, Upper St. Clair and Mt. Lebanon during that span.

Cope and Johnston have always been good company. They knew how to play to the gallery, and how to have a good time, and how to treat people properly.

That's the way most of the headliners behaved at the Mellon Mario Lemieux Invitational. Tommy Maddox, Mike Eurzione and Joe Theismann treated everyone the best, according to an informal poll I took, and Charles Barkley was right behind with being popular with the crowd. This was the last go-round for the event at the green layout in Presto. Next year they will be playing in private at Laurel Valley. That's our loss, just as it would have been Pittsburgh's loss if Eddie Johnston had never brought Mario to Pittsburgh in the first place. Imagine that.

Chuck Noll and Eddie Johnston have played in their share of Pittsburgh-area golf outings to raise funds for various causes.

The Emperor knows how
to Cope with retirement

July 13, 2005

Myron Cope might be wise to place a call to his old friend, Chuck Noll. Cope announced last month that he is retiring after 35 years as the colorman on Steelers' radio broadcasts, and he is concerned about what he is going to do with himself.

"It's my life," he told his good friend Joe Gordon, the former public relations director of the Steelers, who's been retired about eight years from his post.

"It was my life, too," said Gordon. "It was Chuck Noll's life. You've got to get a new life."

Cope has been challenged by health issues the past two or three years, but he was hopeful of getting better and being able to continue to be part of the Steelers' broadcast team. Cope has been the heart and soul of the Steelers' broadcasts since their glory days. For some, he is Steelers' football more than Terry Bradshaw, Franco Harris, Joe Greene, Jack Lambert, Jack Ham, Mel Blount, Jerome Bettis or Big Ben.

When Gordon told Cope, as he had agreed to do years ago, that he was slipping that's all Cope needed to hear to make his decision. He didn't want to go on if he wasn't on top of his game.

Remember how Cope called Noll "Chaz" and "The Emperor" when he was on the air? It was such name-calling and other crazy stuff that made Cope so colorful and unique. What also set him apart was that he was trained as a reporter and he had a gift as a writer and observer. He knew a good story when he saw one and he knew how to tell that story. He had a sense of humor, and often poked fun at himself. Most people liked him and he had good news contacts and inside sources.

I know few people who have retired as successfully as Chuck Noll. He never looked back. He and his wife Marianne found other ways to amuse and entertain themselves. His name never surfaced when an NFL job came open. He simply wasn't interested. He had played and coached in the NFL for 39 years and he was ready to walk away from it before he turned 60.

He is 73 years old now, faced with health issues of his own — that's often the biggest challenge in retirement — but he's happy with his life. He once defined retirement to me this way: "When you wake up in the morning you have nothing to do, and when you go to bed at night you have half of it done."

Noll used to tell his players that they should prepare for their "life's work" — what they would be doing when they were done playing football. When I asked him what his "life's work" had become, he smiled and said, "Fund-raising."

379

He got involved with many Pittsburgh-based causes, especially the Guild for the Blind in Bridgeville, and headed its board of directors when it became Pittsburgh Vision Services. He's retired from that now, too.

Cope, who is 76, has been active throughout his professional career with many good causes. He's done so much for charitable entities. He's been a big fund-raiser for Allegheny Valley School, where his son Danny has resided for years. Cope succeeded the late Bob Prince as the school's prime fund-raiser. Cope raised money for autistic care and research. Like Prince, Cope became a Pittsburgh icon. Both had their critics — who doesn't? — but more people enjoyed and cherished them than otherwise. Cope will have more time to spend with his daughter Elizabeth.

We will miss Cope's voice as we have Prince's voice. Both cheered for Pittsburgh teams, and did so in a warm and generous way. When Cope had his own sports talk show, he made every caller feel as if he or she had done him the biggest favor in the world by tuning in and being a part of the show.

Steelers' management was concerned about Cope's status and wasn't sure how to handle the dilemma. No one wanted to tell Cope it was time to call it quits. They didn't want to have a repeat of the situation that still haunts the Pirates and that was the firing of Bob Prince. Cope and Prince were Pittsburgh treasures. Some fans were still crazy about Cope. Some thought he was making too many mistakes, and rambling with his stories. Gordon saved the Steelers from an embarrassing situation by convincing Cope it was time to walk away from the broadcast booth.

At his best, Cope was a tremendous asset to the Steelers. Cope could be critical when necessary, and needled Noll and Bill Cowher when it was called for. Cope has called it quits. He and Stan Savran set the standard, and it was a high one, for sports talk shows and commentaries in this town. Cope doesn't need or deserve derisive comments from any of the young wolves that have followed in his footsteps. They're in business because of him.

They would do well to adopt his style and aim at being credible and having integrity and good taste in their offerings. Cope's been a class act.

Cope's biggest concern right now should be getting well, regaining his voice. Most Pittsburghers cherish Cope and will miss him during Steelers' games. Bill Hillgrove, Tunch Ilkin and Craig Wolfley will work out fine. They have their special skills as well. They have always played off Cope and will enjoy the freedom to set their own tone.

Cope wants to be remembered as a writer, not the inventor of "The Terrible Towel" or anything like that. He felt he had a gift in that respect. During his career, he has been a gift to Pittsburgh, a local treasure. We hope he gets well soon, and enjoys the rest of his new life.

Myron and Marino
Pittsburgh parlay at Canton

August 3, 2005

It seems fitting somehow that Danny Marino and Myron Cope will be honored on the same weekend at the Pro Football Hall of Fame in Canton, Ohio. Marino grew up in South Oakland and Cope grew up on the other side of Schenley Park in Squirrel Hill. Both were drawn to the ballparks and stadiums and arenas in between. Now they are being honored for what they accomplished along the way. They are two of Pittsburgh's most popular sports personalities, indeed, civic treasures.

Both have given back to the community and then some.

Pete Rozelle, the late commissioner of the National Football League, liked to say that the two best weekends in professional football were the Super Bowl and Hall of Fame festivities.

Cope, who recently retired after 35 years as the analyst/color man for Steelers' radio broadcasts, will receive the Pete Rozelle Award that recognizes a distinguished career in NFL radio-television. It will be presented to him at the enshrinees' dinner this Saturday evening.

Marino, who rewrote the NFL passing record book during his 17 seasons as quarterback of the Miami Dolphins, will be inducted into the Pro Football Hall of Fame on Sunday afternoon at ceremonies at Fawcett Stadium. There will be over 21,000 fans in attendance and many of them will be making the 110-mile trip from Pittsburgh.

Cope lives in Mt. Lebanon these days, and previously lived in Upper St. Clair and Scott Township. Marino's wife, Claire Veazey, grew up in Mt. Lebanon and still has family there.

I plan on being in Canton. I go there every summer for the Hall of Fame festivities. I drove there a month ago to do some research at the HOF Archives. I had to smile when I saw a picture of Danny Marino on the wall in the lobby of the Hall of Fame, not far from the 7-foot statue of the legendary Jim Thorpe.

Marino was pictured with Steve Young, the quarterback best known for his heroics for the San Francisco 49ers, and two deceased pro football pioneers, Benny Friedman and Fritz Pollard — the 2005 HOF Class.

It brought to mind two personal memories from 1982. I had dinner that year with Danny Marino and his family at their home on Parkview Drive, not far from a sandlot football field that now bears Marino's name. It's where he starred for the St. Regis Catholic Grade School football team, before he went to Central Catholic High School and the University of Pittsburgh.

His mother, Veronica, cooked a spaghetti dinner and his dad Dan was a great host. Dan's two sisters, Cindi and Debbie, were there. It was evident their parents held all three children in the same regard.

That same year I was invited to a party at the Greenfield home of Sal Sunseri, a senior teammate of Marino, then a junior at Pitt. Sal and his buddy Emil Boures had both been drafted by the Steelers that day. The Marinos were at the party. So was Myron Cope. Before the evening was over, Cope was dancing with Veronica Marino, Danny's mother. Cope had taken dancing lessons as a child from Gene Kelly's mother, and takes great pride in his dance floor ability. "If I had stayed at it," Cope often kids, "no one would have heard of Gene Kelly."

Cope has been challenged by several health issues in recent years, including a balky back and a throat ailment, but I'll bet he's capable of dancing with Mrs. Marino in the streets of Canton this weekend. What company he and Danny will be keeping. Cope is receiving an award that has previously been given to the likes of Lindsey Nelson, Curt Gowdy, Pat Summerall, John Madden, Frank Gifford, Jack Buck and Charlie Jones.

Marino will be in there with quarterbacks from Western Pennsylvania or the Steelers that he grew up admiring, such as Joe Namath, George Blanda, John Unitas, Jim Kelly, Joe Montana, Bobby Layne, Lenny Dawson and Terry Bradshaw. Marino's bust will be in the same room as Sammy Baugh and Sid Luckman and Art Rooney.

Jim O'Brien

Dan Marino fans donned their No. 13 jerseys to show their support at Pro Football Hall of Fame induction ceremonies in Canton, Ohio in August of 2005.

Record crowd attended 2005 Pro Football Hall of Fame induction ceremonies. Class included Steve Young, Benny Friedman, Dan Marino and Fritz Pollard.

Pro Football Hall of Fame
theme is all about family

August 10, 2005

A friend was critical of the induction speeches at the Pro Football Hall of Fame. He felt they should have been more about football and less about family. "This isn't the Family Hall of Fame or the Father's Hall of Fame," he said.

The speeches were all too long, and we agreed on that, but I felt the content was appropriate. "You can't get anything accomplished alone," said Steve Young, the former 49ers quarterback and one of the four new Hall of Fame inductees.

That's why I like to hear that family is foremost in the minds of Young and Dan Marino, the former quarterback of the Dolphins and a popular representative of his hometown of Pittsburgh. I have always respected Marino for the way he treated and spoke about his family.

Young was introduced by his father and Marino by his oldest son, Daniel. Two pioneers of the National Football League, both deceased, were Fritz Pollard and Benny Friedman. Pollard was represented by a grandson and Friedman by a nephew. So it was difficult not to talk about family at these festivities.

I have never been in favor of having family members, sons and wives and fathers, presenting the players for induction, but this time it seemed okay. Normally, I feel that important football figures should do the honors. They've earned the right to be at the Hall of Fame.

Daniel Marino was the best presenter by far. He touched his father's heart — it was clearly evident — with his proud remarks. "No one could have asked for better examples than my parents," said the young Marino. "They're so grateful for everything in their lives. I was so lucky to be raised by such wonderful parents."

Glancing toward his father, he spoke about wise decisions his father made. "And the smartest decision he ever made off the field was when he chose my mom."

That had to move his mom, Claire Veazey, who grew up in Mt. Lebanon and was sitting in the first row with the rest of her children.

Marino and Young, two of the most handsome guys ever to be inducted into the Pro Football Hall of Fame, both spoke of the influence of their family and friends and coaches and teachers in their lives. That is a staple of all Hall of Fame induction speeches, and it should be.

I always come away from Canton and the Pro Football Hall of Fame with my mind full of thoughts, thinking about what I heard and how I can apply it to my own life. I sat in an air-conditioned press box with cold soft drinks nearby, and didn't have to endure the heat of a long afternoon. So I thought about my good fortune in being afforded such comforts because I am a writer and a newspaperman. I have never taken such treatment for granted. There were about 50 Pro Football Hall of Fame members at Fawcett Stadium on Sunday. I love to see the old-timers, the ones I idolized in my youth, as well as contemporaries whom I admired for their athletic achievement and, in some cases, for the kind of people they are.

The thoughts expressed in the speeches are often reminders of the approach we all need to take to the challenges in our lives. It's like a revival meeting, a religious pilgrimage. My mother always said you will be judged by the company you keep, and I was in good company.

The stories about Friedman, who was Jewish, and Pollard, who was one of the few blacks in pro football in his time, were enlightening and enriching. They both overcame racial and religious prejudice to succeed and help keep the pro game alive. All the stories are compelling in their own right.

Few of us will ever experience what these men accomplished as athletes, but we can learn from them how to succeed in the game of life. This is August and I have two big dates coming up in the next two weeks. This Friday, Aug. 12, is the 38th anniversary of my marriage to Kathleen Churchman. I will be 63 on Aug. 20. That's a Saturday so I hope to be playing basketball that morning to celebrate being alive and doing something I love to do. While writing this column, I got a call from Kathie and she told me that Peter Jennings, the TV news anchorman, had died from cancer. Such news always catches you off guard. I'm glad to strike the next key on my computer and I'm grateful Kathie has kept the flame in my heart going this long. I think our daughters would agree that the best decision I ever made was marrying their mother. "She's the only one who'd have you," my Rebecca reminds me. Sarah just smiles at Rebecca's remark.

Jim O'Brien

Steve Young speaks at Hall of Fame press conference as Dan Marino looks on in gymnasium at Fawcett Stadium.

Steelers' fans sound off
at St. Vincent College

August 17, 2005

A mighty roar went up from the crowd covering a hillside above one of the football fields at St. Vincent College. The Steelers' training camp was in session, and Bill Cowher was conducting what amounted to a touch-football game.

Yet the fans were roaring for every run and every successful catch as if they really counted for something. The Steelers were shadowboxing, sparring in the hot summer sun, but the fans were serious in their shouting and applause.

The crowds have come back in earnest to St. Vincent College in Latrobe. I haven't seen this kind of crowd or heard this kind of noise from the surrounding hillsides since 1980. That was the summer after the Steelers had won their fourth Super Bowl in six years.

For Steelers' fans, going to St. Vincent College was always a rite of summer, a pilgrimage to a religious shrine of sorts, but the attraction dimmed when the Steelers stopped winning Super Bowls. It wasn't as much fun when security measures made it more difficult to get close to the players.

The Steelers have tried to find a middle ground in this age of security-crazy tactics, and have done things to regain fans for their summer scrimmages and practice sessions. A 15-1 record is really at the root of this return to glory days at the Laurel Highlands retreat. There are great expectations for the 2005 season.

Ben Roethlisberger and Jerome Bettis and their smiling familiar faces are two big reasons for the increase in crowds. Both play well to the crowds, and take the time to sign autographs when possible. The fans were also hopeful they'd be there on the day when Hines Ward ended his contract holdout and joined the Steelers in the summer sun.

Ward, one of the Steelers' most popular players in history, had managed to get his name in the same sentence as the Eagles' Terrell Owens, and that's not where he wants to go. Everyone was hoping the Steelers and Ward could work out a deal and get him back on the field.

Three out of four kids and adults seemed to be wearing Big Ben's No. 7 jersey. He signed autographs for many of them, especially the little ones. I was wondering when he saw that sea of 7s whether he saw 7s or $s. His popularity is unreal. Seeing Ben & Jerome was as close to giving away Ben & Jerry's ice cream on this sultry summer day.

"I had been warned about what life can be like for a quarterback in this town," remarked Roethlisberger after practice last Thursday. "So far so good. But I can't go out of the house and do some of the things I'd like to do. That's the downside of this."

When Bettis and Roethlisberger and a few other of the Steelers' outstanding players made the long walk from the field up those cement steps that lead to the locker room there were more roars from the fans. They were the kind one expects whenever Tiger Woods hits a drive shot in a major golf tournament.

Like many of the fans, I didn't recognize half the players out on the field. They hadn't cut anyone yet. I could still see some of those players that were on the field that summer of 1980, and I am not talking about Steelers' analysts Tunch Ilkin and Craig Wolfley, who were both rookies that summer, and now roam the sidelines seeking inside information.

I can still see Franco Harris and Joe Greene and Terry Bradshaw and Mel Blount and Jack Ham and Mike Webster sweating in the sun. I saw Sandy Roma, a Point Park senior from Upper St. Clair, interviewing Big Ben as a summer intern at WTAE-TV, working alongside Andrew Stockey, the station's sports director who lives in Cecil. It was good to see Miss Roma chasing her dream, something I had encouraged her to do when I caught her act on the high school's student TV a few years back.

She is as eager to make it in the big-time as all those prospects out on the football field. It will be difficult for the Steelers to have a 15-1 record again — make that highly unlikely — but they could go deeper into the playoffs. The fans have high hopes, that's for sure. That roar at St. Vincent is a giveaway.

Art Rooney Jr. shares scouting insights with Kevin Colbert.

New Orleans
is best sports title site

"I've already seen it!"
— Weeb Ewbank

September 14, 2005

I know New Orleans too well. I have visited the Crescent City at least a dozen times in my career. It's not a city you like at first glance; you have to get to know it.

It was a unique city, different from all others. I know its streets, its beats, its beauty, its bad side, its smells, good and bad. I've heard the music of Al Hirt and Pete Fountain and the jazz band at Preservation Hall. I've walked the streets that are still being shown on television round the clock, ever since Hurricane Katrina came to town and tore it apart and flooded its homes and historic buildings. I've never been to Biloxi, or any place in Mississippi for that matter, so I can't relate to what's happened there.

Through the years, New Orleans has been the best town to hold a major sports championship or title of any kind. Everything was confined to a few blocks and you could walk to everything from your hotel. The streets were full of sights and sounds unlike any back home. There was a show of some kind on every street corner. I've been to eight Super Bowls, but the three I attended in New Orleans prompts me to say it was the best site of all. No city has hosted as many Super Bowls as New Orleans.

I remember walking down Bourbon Street behind Weeb Ewbank, the coach of the New York Jets, when the Super Bowl was played in New Orleans in 1970. His team had upset the Baltimore Colts in Miami to win the Super Bowl the year before.

A barker in front of a strip bar was inviting passersby to come into the bar to see Ricki Covette, billed as the tallest exotic in the world. She was 6-7, I recall. "See the biggest bust in the country!" the barker hollered to Ewbank. "I've already seen it," replied Ewbank. "It was my ballteam this year!"

I first visited New Orleans that year as a writer for *The Miami News*. I was covering the Super Bowl match-up of the Minnesota Vikings and Kansas City Chiefs. Lenny Dawson, who had been a quarterback for two seasons with the Steelers, led the Chiefs to a victory. I interviewed him before and after the game at Tulane Stadium.

One of the things I enjoyed the most about that first Super Bowl experience was having an opportunity to meet and talk to some of the great sportswriters and columnists in the country, such as Red Smith and Dave Anderson of New York, who would both win the Pulitzer

Prize for sportswriting. I also met Milton Gross and Stan Isaacs of New York, Blackie Sherrod of Dallas, Edwin Pope of Miami, Furman Bisher of Atlanta, Jim Murray and Melvin Durslag of Los Angeles, Joe Falls and Jerry Greene of Detroit, Jerry Izenberg and Dave Klein of Newark, John Camichael, Brent Mussberger, Bill Gleason and Ray Soens of Chicago, Hubert Mizell and Tom McEwen of Tampa. I sought them out and talked to them as much as I could. I admired these men.

I would later cover two Super Bowls at the Superdome, and the Steelers vs. the Saints in New Orleans. At my first Super Bowl, when the Kansas City Chiefs beat the Minnesota Vikings, I interviewed Lenny Dawson of the Chiefs, the game's MVP, in the locker room after the game. You could go to the locker room in those days. In one of the Super Bowls in New Orleans, Mike Ditka, a former Pitt All-American end from Aliquippa and Carnegie, caught a touchdown pass in that victory over the Miami Dolphins. That same weekend, I covered a heavyweight championship bout in which Joe Frazier defended his title against Terry Daniels, scoring a third round TKO.

I arranged to meet a former light-heavyweight champion who grew up in New Orleans, Willie Pastano, at a local dive called The Bastille.

The last time I was in New Orleans was in early April, 2003 when I went there during the NCAA men's basketball championship. I was inducted into the U.S. Basketball Writers' Hall of Fame, and I took my wife Kathie with me.

She had been there with me once before. We toured the town, visited the Louie Armstrong Museum, and I took her to a hotel where Frazier and his sparring mate, Ken Norton, later a heavyweight champion himself, had trained on the top floor. I remember that Norton was helping Frazier prepare for the fight. I recall one day on the top floor of the Hotel Monteleone watching a trainer slam a medicine ball repeatedly into the stomach of Norton as he laid on a table. The trainer was standing over the table and slamming that medicine ball as hard as he could onto Norton's stomach. It was tough to watch.

Famous writers had stayed there, at the Hotel Monteleone.

New Orleans was the hometown of Tennessee Williams and Anne Rice, and writers were always drawn there, such as Mark Twain, Erskine Caldwell, Sherwood Anderson. Truman Capote came into his own there.

We toured Royal Street and looked at the artwork, antiques and books that were displayed in one little shop after another. As I watch the Hurricane Katrina coverage, I wonder what's become of all that stuff in the storm that has devastated the area.

I prefer my favorite images of New Orleans to the horrific photos and images that continue to disturb us. My New Orleans remains intact. Like Preservation Hall.

"You can't get much done in life if you only work on the days when you feel good."
— **Jerry West**

Watching TV sports
a family affair

September 28, 2005

I have a recurring dream — a nightmare really — that I am reporting on a football game and afterward I cannot find the locker rooms to interview the coaches and the players.

It ranks right up there with dreaming about having a test in school the next day and not being properly prepared.

I was glad I didn't have to go to the locker room on Sunday evening to interview Bill Cowher and Ben Roethlisberger and the Steelers after their frustrating 23-20 last-second loss to the New England Patriots. It wouldn't have been much fun.

I was home watching the game on television in our family room. I was watching the game with my son-in-law, Dr. Matthew Zirwas. My wife Kathie, our daughter Sarah and our granddaughter Margaret, now 16 months old, came and went. I love every moment with Margaret, and am so glad her parents moved to Mt. Lebanon. I was pushing her on our neighbors' swing set and missed the Patriots' first touchdown. We had dinner during the fourth quarter, believe it or not, and had a birthday cake to celebrate Sarah's 32nd birthday. Kathie had prepared Texas steak on rice at the request of Sarah. We sneaked peeks at the TV in the next room while we were dining.

Sarah's birthday was on Sept. 20, but we missed it because we were visiting our younger daughter, Rebecca, and her fiancé, Quinn Carlson, in the Los Angeles area. We visited the Los Angeles Zoo and walked Rebecca's dog Bailey about three times a day for a week, and watched a lot of sports on television. I read the *Los Angeles Times* and the *New York Times* every day, a sure sign that we were on vacation.

I watched the Dodgers' games on TV, and got to see Barry Bonds of the Giants hit two home runs in his first few games back since being out most of the season with knee ailments.

It's great to be able to watch sports on television three hours earlier in the day because of the time difference. We watched a Monday night football doubleheader and the second game was over around 9 o'clock, about the same time Monday night football begins when you're in Pittsburgh.

Rebecca could care less about sports — what did I do wrong in raising her? — whereas Sarah is interested, especially if it's Pitt basketball.

During dinner, Kathie mentioned that we had watched a spirited boxing doubleheader on HBO on Saturday night, which prompted Matt to observe, "I'll bet you are the only suburban couple to watch boxing on TV together on Saturday night." To which Kathie countered with, "I like boxing. I've always enjoyed it."

394

Kathie has never been an ardent sports fan, but she never objects when I'm watching it, and she checks in from time to time for the score, and a highlight or two. Sometimes, during the boxing doubleheader, or a Pirates' game, for example, she will do her ironing in the family room. Kathie finds ironing relaxing, and it makes her feel like she's not wasting her time. Kathie is most relaxed when we are both working.

As for that Steelers' game, it wasn't well played, but it was good theater. Tom Brady and the Patriots played well when they needed to, and Roethlisberger and the Steelers didn't. Adam Vinatieri remains the best clutch place-kicker in the game. That's all you need to know.

Jim O'Brien

Dan Rooney speaks to Dr. Matthew Zirwas at North Side Hall of Fame induction dinner at Three Rivers Stadium.

"Dealing with people representing things bigger than yourself, it's the subtitle of being an NFL quarterback. I'm still growing to accept all of this. There are times when it does feel like, hey everybody, I'm only 24."
— Ben Roethlisberger

Deb & Digger real characters
in Steelers' scene

October 12, 2005

A female police officer and a male mortician and former coroner are seldom found in the same sentence. They are linked, however, because they have been behind-the-scenes characters in the colorful sports setting of the Steelers and Pittsburgh, and shared their stories with me last weekend.

I awake each day in search of stories and welcome meeting the likes of Deb Stickis of Morningside and Bill "Digger" Young of Butler. I met them at area shopping malls, the main streets of suburbia, Century III Mall and South Hills Village, respectively. Their stories brought a smile to my face and I hope they do the same for you.

"Digger" Young, 72, owns a funeral home in Butler, and once served as its county coroner. His son now holds that latter position. The elder Young drove an ambulance and assisted the team doctor and trainers for the Steelers when they played at Forbes Field, Pitt Stadium and Three Rivers Stadium. The ambulance was a black hearse from Digger's funeral home.

Bill Belichick, the coach of the New England Patriots, and Ben Roethlisberger, the quarterback of the Steelers, should hear Young's stories. Belichick chased Steelers' trainer John Norwig when Norwig went to the aid of an injured Patriots' player in a recent game at Heinz Field. Belichick swore at Norwig when he did so. Roethlisberger has a reputation for being a well-behaved, caring citizen, so he would be amused by some of the stories Young tells about Bobby Layne, a Hall of Fame quarterback for the Steelers (1959-1962).

"I used to go to the other team's bench before the game and tell the trainer where the stretchers and wheelchairs were, stuff like that," said Young. "The only coach who ever chased me away was Paul Brown of the Browns. Like I was a spy and was going to tell the Steelers something about the Browns."

Billy "White Shoes" Johnson, a receiver and kick-return specialist for the Houston Oilers, once told "Digger" Young not to touch him when he asked "Digger" how he got his nickname, and learned he was a funeral director. "I think it scared him," Young said.

Young also brought some of those small whiskey bottles they used to have on airplanes with him to the games. For proof, he provided a copy of a letter from the late Jim Boston of McMurray, when he was the business manager of the Steelers, that read: "It was brought to my attention by the Three Rivers Management that a complaint was lodged against you for bringing in whiskey to the stadium in a brown attaché case. Let's make sure that we do not do that from now on."

He enclosed a parking pass for the Nov. 8, 1970 game at Three Rivers with his warning. "Bobby Layne used to come up to me and ask me, 'Do you have anything on your hip?' He usually took two of those bottles, sometimes three, and drank them during the game," said Young.

Deb Stickis, a youthful looking 54, provides security in the parking lot for the Steelers' players at Heinz Field. She caught my eye because she was wearing a Steelers' windbreaker, a brand new No. 87 Sidney Crosby Penguins' jersey and bright gold sweatpants. "I have a Pirates' tattoo on my right hip," she revealed, "and I'm thinking about getting a Steelers' tattoo over my heart. Ike Taylor, Troy Polamalu and James Farrior are my favorites.

"I'm thinking about getting a tattoo with their numbers somewhere else, but I don't want to upset my husband with any names on me. Farrior's mother called him 'Poopsy' because she was a big fan of 'Happy Days.' Someday I'll wash up in the Allegheny River and they'll say, 'She must have been from Pittsburgh.' I just love my Pittsburgh sports teams."

George Gojkovich/Getty Images

> **"A person doesn't really become whole until he becomes a part of something bigger than himself."**
> **— Jimmy Valvano**

Cliff Stoudt understands
Steelers' quarterback situation

November 16, 2005

I called Cliff Stoudt on the telephone to get some insight into the Steelers' quarterback situation. "Same old, same old," said Stoudt from his home office in Dublin, Ohio. "I've been there, done that. Pittsburgh hates quarterbacks, that's all there is to it."

I could see Stoudt smiling in my mind's eye. Stoudt should know about these matters. He was a backup to Terry Bradshaw for six of his seven seasons (1977-1983) with the Steelers, and for Troy Aikman of the Dallas Cowboys at the close of his 13 seasons in the NFL. He also put in two seasons with the Birmingham Stallions of the USFL.

He played against the Pittsburgh Maulers at Three Rivers Stadium and was badly abused by the fans for leaving the Steelers to sign with the other league. They threw stuff at him from the stands and verbally abused him from start to finish. Steelers' owner Art Rooney arranged for his parents to eat in a private dining room in the Allegheny Club after the game. "Mr. Rooney always treated me well," said Stoudt. "I was still welcome in his office."

Stoudt is now 49 and is an investment broker. We've gotten to know each other better in recent years and he is good company. He developed a great sense of humor during his NFL career and is quite the comic.

"The best job in Pittsburgh is backup quarterback," he said. "It's actually playing that ruins the relationship."

Stoudt spent his first four seasons with the Steelers on the sidelines and qualified for an NFL player pension without playing in a regular season game. "After the third game of the exhibition season," he recalled, "I never took a snap in practice with the first team offense. I quarterbacked the scout team. I knew the other team's plays better than the Steelers' plays. The same was true with Mike Kruczek and Mark Malone. It's hard to be ready to play when you're the backup quarterback."

Stoudt made these statements before the Steelers beat the Browns in a nationally televised Sunday night game. Charlie Batch, the pride of Homestead, started for the second week in a row and redeemed himself, but suffered a broken hand on his throwing arm. He gave way to Tommy Maddox as the starter for the second half. Maddox, once the most accurate of passers, didn't throw the ball any better than he had two weeks earlier in a bad showing and loss to the Jacksonville Jaguars. He was booed.

Maddox may have to start this Sunday in Baltimore because Ben Roethlisberger isn't fully recovered from a knee injury. Ben hopes to be back for the big showdown with the Colts in Indianapolis. It's a real soap opera.

Cliff Stoudt and his wife Laura relax at Bob Evans Restaurant near Pickerington, Ohio.

Cliff Stoudt enjoys reunion with Bill Hurley at Andy Russell's celebrity golf tournament at The Club at Nevillewood. Photos by Jim O'Brien

"Some things don't change," said Stoudt. "The receivers are more vocal these days in their complaints, but when Terry and I were there the receivers all wanted the ball. Lynn Swann and John Stallworth both wanted to be the go-to guy; they just didn't get in each other's faces or the quarterback's face about it. Swann and Stallworth wanted it every down, and they were always open.

"I'm glad I never had to play with anyone like Terrell Owens. I feel for Donovan McNabb. It's not his fault. T.O. was off to his best season ever, but he's never going to be happy. He may be the biggest superstar to go unsigned in the National Football League."

He said Chuck Noll would not have allowed anyone to go off on a fellow player the way T.O. did on McNabb. "Whatever Noll didn't police, Joe Greene looked after in the locker room."

Stoudt volunteered another observation:

"I was surprised by how quickly the fans came down on Tommy," said Stoudt. "Three years ago, Tommy was the toast of the town. He was the NFL's Comeback Player of the Year."

Stoudt believes Maddox and Batch deserve better. Even Roethlisberger was criticized for his substandard post-season showing his rookie season. "People forget we're human," said Stoudt.

He was reminded of this side of his stature two years earlier when his wife Laura underwent surgery for the removal of a large tumor on her brain. She's fine now. Brett Favre of the Green Bay Packers suffered several losses in his family the past two years; his wife Deanna survived a breast cancer scare. Some famous quarterbacks, Danny Marino, Jim Kelly, Boomer Easiason and Doug Flutie all had sons with serious health challenges. Trent Dilfer, the Browns' quarterback, suffered the loss of a five-year-old son a few years back. (Kelly's son has since died.)

Things change. Stoudt comes back to Pittsburgh frequently and plays in charity golf outings with other Steelers alumni. Friends of mine recall seeing Stoudt driving golf balls at Point State Park once, and how impressed pro golfing legend Lee Trevino, who was also there, was with Stoudt's driving ability and distance.

Mickey Graziani, the locker room manager at Diamond Run, where the Steelers hold the annual Ray Mansfield Memorial Golf Outing, said Stoudt is still an impressive performer on the golf course. "He can strike that ball off the tee with some of the top pros," said Graziani.

Cliff's daughter Cydnei is on scholarship for basketball at UNC-Wilmington. His older son Zachary is a promising freshman quarterback on the high school team in Dublin, and younger son Cole is quite the athlete, too. Wife Laura is doing well.

"Tell Tommy and Charley to hang in there," said Stoudt. "They'll be popular again in twenty years."

"Now people are going to figure I can't come back (from his accident) and play as well, so I have incentive to prove them wrong. I never think that I can't get even better."
**— Ben Roethlisberger,
on interview with Jim Rome, July 13, 2006**

Writer thankful for the Princes
of the sporting world

November 22, 2005

I could hear soft rain striking the windowpanes of my bedroom. I wasn't sure whether I was dreaming or just thinking in the night. Mel Blount, one of my all-time favorite Steelers, was speaking. He was saying he thought that they should leave a chair empty on the dais at sports dinners and luncheons where sports broadcaster Bob Prince once performed his magic. It would be a proper tribute to Prince. That would surely include the Dapper Dan Dinner at The Hilton, the Coaches Corner luncheon at The Strip, and the Thompson Club Sports Night Dinner in West Mifflin. Maybe they should also leave a seat open for Prince in the TV and radio broadcast booths at PNC Park.

There is a lounge at PNC Park with lots of Prince photos and memorabilia, including one of his infamous loud sports jackets. Maybe there ought to be a statue outside the ballpark the way there's a statue of broadcaster Harry Carey outside Wrigley Field in Chicago.

It's hard to believe it's been 30 years since Bob Prince was "The Voice of the Pirates." Lanny Frattare has been in the booth that long, surpassing Prince's run of 28 years at the mike. It's been 20 years since Prince died. Yet Prince lives on. When his voice is heard on a taped broadcast on some reflection piece it still commands our attention and stirs our hearts. There was something special about the way Bob Prince talked. His voice said baseball.

Only last week at South Hills Village, someone asked me why the Pirates fired him. I still get that question a lot. I tried to explain, but it still made no sense. Prince admitted he contributed to his own dismissal, failing to adhere to admonitions from the brass at both KDKA and the Pirates to alter some of the things he did, at the ballpark and away from the ballpark.

In the end, however, it was a firing in which everyone lost. Bob Prince lost, the Pirates lost and those of us who cared about baseball and the Pirates lost the most of all. It was a triple play, a triple killing. Many insist they quit caring about the Pirates when Prince was fired.

A man came up to me at the mall and told me that his father had immigrated to America from Czechoslovakia and claimed he learned to speak English by listening to Bob Prince doing the Pirates' broadcasts. I asked the man what his father's friends thought about him saying, "Bug on the rug" or "can of corn" or "we need a bloop and a blast."

I was just kidding the Czech's son, of course, but those are some of the phrases we associate with Prince. He was a pure delight. I also hear stories of how Prince picked up someone who was hitchhiking, and how great it was to be in his open Cadillac convertible, riding through the streets of Pittsburgh. He was a generous man, quick to pick up a bar tab. As Thanksgiving approaches I am reminded of how fortunate I have been, how thankful I am for my family, my real friends, and for the people I have associated with in the sporting world.

Prince has to be in my Top Ten list. It is headed by Art Rooney, the founder of the Steelers, and Frank Gustine, the former Pirates' infielder who owned and operated a popular restaurant on the Pitt campus for over 30 years, and Doc Carlson, the director of the student health service at the University of Pittsburgh when I was a student there in the early '60s. Carlson had been an All-America football player at Pitt, the basketball coach and a member of the charter class of the Basketball Hall of Fame.

I learned from all of them. I recently had a few telephone calls with Angelo Dundee in South Florida. He was Muhammad Ali's trainer. Talking to him reminded me of his kind acts through the years. One of the calls came when I was out for a walk near my younger daughter Rebecca's apartment in Woodland Hills, California. I sat down on a bench and couldn't believe I was talking to Angelo Dundee on my cell phone. Dundee rates in the Top Ten as well.

Many of us long for the glory days of the Steelers, and what wonderful fellows played on those teams in the '70s. There are a lot of good guys on the current club as well. Some of them would be wise to tame their acts. It's important to pick your models. Even the best of models have flaws. You have to find the best they have to offer and do your best to behave similarly. Former Steelers' star Mike Wagner would like to see more sportsmanship in the games we play. Isn't that supposed to be what it's all about? Prince always put baseball and fun and games in their proper perspective. We can still see his smile, and hear the gaiety in his voice. It's summer at Forbes Field once again.

Bob Prince poses with Gold Glove winners, left to right, Bill Mazeroski, Gene Alley and Roberto Clemente.

'Who's Big Ben?'
she asks with a Straight face

December 15, 2005

I may have met the only person in Pittsburgh who doesn't know about Big Ben. Her name is Debbie Straight, and she's the red-headed waitress at the Olive Garden in Green Tree.

I stopped there for lunch last Thursday, getting off the Parkway West midway between stops in Monaca and downtown Pittsburgh. I was wearing a black and gold tin button that says simply "BIG BEN 7" that a friend had pinned on my jacket lapel a week earlier. The button is as wide as the lapel. It's been a good conversation-starter.

A lot of people think I should write a book about Big Ben Roethlisberger, the boy wonder quarterback of the Steelers. Like tonight.

He is a marketing and sports phenomenon unlike anything we have ever experienced in Pittsburgh. That button is one of about 150 or so items that are available about Big Ben. Everybody wants to know where I got it, and some even want to buy it from me.

Gerry Hamilton of Oakmont, a friend of mine who helps me with my books and book-signings, gave it to me. She buys bobbles, bangles and beads everywhere she can find them. She especially likes earrings and pins. She's 82 and deaf and she's even heard about Big Ben.

Getting back to the Olive Garden and Debbie Straight . . . she approached me to get my order. I wanted the daily special — ravioli with shrimp and crabmeat — and pasta fagiola. Eyeing my black and gold button, she asked, "Who's Big Ben?" with a Straight face.

I must have blinked a few times. "You're putting me on, aren't you?" I asked Debbie, doubtful about her inquiry.

"No, I'm not," she said sincerely.

"He's the quarterback of the Pittsburgh Steelers," I said.

"I'm not into sports," she said. "I'm into the arts and stuff like that."

"You don't have to be into sports to know about Big Ben," I went on. "You just have to get up in the morning in this town to know about Big Ben."

"I'm sorry," she said. "I thought it was some kind of political button."

"Where do you live?" I asked.

"In Heidelberg," she came back.

"In Germany?" I came back, being a smart aleck.

"No, near Carnegie," she said.

So I gave in and told her a little bit about Ben Roethlisberger and how our city may soon be called Roethlisburg and we will be known as Roethlisburgers. I have eaten a Roethlis-burger at one of the restaurants that feature them around town, and I jumped on Big

403

Ben's bandwagon weeks ago. He's so poised under fire, so competitive, and I like what he appears to be all about.

I spent four hours before Sunday's 4 p.m. game with the New York Jets at the Station Square Shops. I like to go there because that's where all the out-of-town fans flock. Business was brisk at both Hometowne Sports and Pro Images, two stores at opposite ends of the complex that sell all those replica football jerseys, T-shirts, hats, mittens and scarves.

They both ran out of Roethlisberger jerseys before the game. "We got 200 of them Friday," said Frank Meyer of Baldwin, owner of Hometowne Sports. "We can't keep any of his stuff in the store long. It's unreal." Not that he's complaining, mind you.

Most of the people who paraded past me were wearing black and gold attire. Roethlisberger's jersey was the most popular, with Jerome Bettis right behind him. That turned out to be prophetic about the day's game. Most of the Jets' fans were wearing the jerseys of Chad Pennington, their quarterback, and Curtis Martin, their star running back, who just happened to play for Allderdice and Pitt, my alma maters.

I thought how if we had picked Pennington in the draft five years ago, like a lot of pundits thought we should have, Pittsburghers would be in love with him rather than Roethlisberger.

By the way, the jerseys of Tommy Maddox, Charlie Batch and Kordell Stewart, all Steelers' quarterbacks, were on sale, reduced from $64.99 to $44.99. Jerseys for Jason Gildon and Amos Zereoue were also on sale. Fame can be fleeting, Big Ben should be warned.

Steelers fans were there, from as far away as Portland, Oregon, to see their team in action. It always fascinates me how people in distant places, with no roots here, are such stellar Steelers' fans. I met two fans an hour apart that live in Detroit, but detest the Lions in favor of the Steelers.

As everyone knows, except maybe Debbie Straight, Big Ben and Big Jerome Bettis combined to lead the Steelers to a 17-6 victory over the Jets to clinch the AFC North title. So many expect Big Ben to lead us to the Super Bowl. We'll see.

The next time I saw Debbie Straight she was standing before me when I was doing a booksigning at Waldenbooks at South Hills Village. She was wearing a black and gold blouse, and she had Big Ben pins on her. She had been teased unmercifully by her co-workers at Olive Garden, and they'd given her some Steeler stuff to make sure everyone knew she really was a Pittsburgher at heart.

> *"I'm not even thinking about it, about riding (a motorcycle) or not, about wearing a helmet or not. The only helmet I am thinking about right now is my football helmet, getting it back on and playing for the Steelers."*
> **—- Ben Roethlisberger at celebrity golf outing at Lake Tahoe, Nevada June 13, 2006**

Cowher's parents root for 'Billy'
in new digs in Mt. Lebanon

January 25, 2006

A gentleman from Mt. Lebanon was eager to tell me about his new neighbors. "Bill Cowher's parents live in our apartment building," he said. "It's on Washington Road, across from Southminster Presbyterian Church. We get a kick out of his mother talking about her 'Billy' in the halls."

One of the many "feel-good" stories about the upcoming Super Bowl, matching the Pittsburgh Steelers against the Seattle Seahawks, is about Jerome Bettis going back to his hometown of Detroit for the championship game that may conclude his distinguished playing career.

A Super Bowl victory for the Steelers would be the icing on the cake to celebrate a Pro Football Hall of Fame career for the popular Pittsburgh sports celebrity. His parents, Johnny and Gladys Bettis, have been on TV almost as much as their son. Gladys and Jerome will be doing one of those "Chunky Soup" commercials before you know it.

It's a family success story. The Cowhers can make a similar claim. Bill or "Billy" needs a Super Bowl victory even more than Bettis to assure him an induction spot someday in the Canton, Ohio shrine. His parents prefer to stay in the background. They didn't make the trip to Arizona when the Steelers played in the Super Bowl there at the end of the 1995 season.

It's been ten years since the Steelers last played for the Super Bowl and they are still seeking that elusive fifth Lombardi Trophy as well as a ring. That fifth ring, by the way, would only count as "one for the thumb" for Dan Rooney, Dick Hoak and Joe Greene in the Steelers' organization.

We all know that Bettis bought his parents a new home with some of the early money he made in the NFL. Hines Ward did the same for his mother. Without any fanfare or publicity, Bill Cowher helped his parents move from his boyhood home in Crafton to a condominium complex in Mt. Lebanon this season.

Laird and Dorothy Cowher are in their early 80s now. One of the reasons Bill was finally able to convince them to move was because his dad's arthritis got too bad for him to handle the stairs in their three-story brick home on Hawthorne Street. I recall Laird having difficulty on those demanding steps when I visited him and his wife at their home the last time the Steelers played in the Super Bowl. Their condominium has an elevator.

When I listened to his proud parents at their previous home in Crafton — where they have since named an alley after their son — I learned a lot about why Bill Cowher became such a big success in his favorite sport. He was raised right. "When he comes in this house, he's not Coach Cowher," allowed Laird Cowher. "He's still Billy to us. He sits in that same chair you're in; that's his seat. He likes to go into the living room and watch TV. He'll lie down on the floor, prop a pillow under his head, have a beer and just relax."

Bill and Kay Cowher and their three girls live in Fox Chapel. They make the trip to Mt. Lebanon frequently and there are Bill Cowher sightings in the South Hills the way there were once Chuck Noll sightings during the glory days of the Steelers in the '70s. Noll lived in Upper St. Clair, and the Steelers stayed at the nearby Sheraton Hotel (now Crowne Plaza) on the eve of home games.

Speaking of Noll sightings . . . someone told me they saw the former Steelers' coach recently riding one of those motorized carts through the Pittsburgh International Airport, saying his back wasn't up to the long walk.

Noll and many of his assistants, Dan Rooney and Art Rooney Jr., and many of the players lived in the South Hills in those days. Dan and his wife Pat now live in his boyhood home on the North Side, and most of the Steelers live in the North Hills.

Bill's parents have been married for 58 years. Laird is a long-limbed 6-4, with large hands and a long jaw. His full name is Laird Gifford Cowher and he is Scotch-German and fits the thrifty-stubborn stereotype. That's why it took him so long to move to Mt. Lebanon. He taught Bill a lot about sports, and about staying the course. He had more bromides to offer than Vince Lombardi about the proper approach to competition.

He and Dorothy will probably stay back here in their condo when the rest of the Cowhers head for Detroit. "It's Billy's time," he'll say. Laird likes his new digs, though he misses the home on Hawthorne Street. He'd rather stay home, so he can go to the bathroom when he wants to, grab a beer when he wants to, and settle in and root for his son to win the big one. The Steelers can beat the Seahawks.

Dorothy and Laird Cowher share thoughts on their son Billy with one of his biggest boosters, Marty Schottenheimer, coach of the San Diego Chargers. Schottenheimer came out of McDonald, Pa. to star at Pitt in early '60s.

"What do you think Bill Cowher was like when he was 24?"
— Anonymous

Sean Casey and Pirates pulling
for win by Steelers in Super Bowl

February 1, 2006

S ean Casey was doing double duty this past weekend. He was promoting the Pirates and the Steelers, and saying it was a great time to be back home in Pittsburgh.

Casey, the pride of Upper St. Clair and the Pirates' newest first baseman, was one of the star attractions at the annual Piratefest. This event is meant to stoke fires in the hearts of Pirates' fans during the often-gray days of winter. Casey was doing that, but he was also wearing a Steelers' jersey celebrating their AFC championship.

He was talking about the Pirates and the Steelers in the same breath, and talking about both so loud he didn't really need a microphone. Pirates' broadcaster Lanny Frattare, a former neighbor and fan of Casey in Upper St. Clair, was still calling Casey "the mayor," a moniker he picked up while playing for the Reds in Cincinnati. They say that Sean Casey was the most popular ballplayer there since Pete Rose.

Bob O'Connor can concede that there is room for another mayor in Pittsburgh, especially someone who is going to be so popular here, and help in the latest Renaissance effort.

There was a long line of Pirates' fans waiting patiently to get an autograph from Casey, or Jason Bay, Zach Duke and Jack Wilson at the David L. Lawrence Convention Center. This was at the same time Friday evening as an estimated 30,000 fans were filling the bottom bowl at Heinz Field on the other side of the Allegheny River for a pep rally for the Steelers. Despite the competition, the Piratefest drew record crowds.

The surprising Pitt basketball team would run its record to 17-1 on Saturday afternoon before a sellout crowd at the Petersen Events Center in Oakland, rallying to defeat a similarly surprising Marquette team.

"This is a great time to be a sports fan in Pittsburgh," said Kevin McClatchy, the Pirates' principal owner, capturing the city's frenetic feeling.

Some media observers misunderstood the situation. They expressed sorrow for the Pirates to be running a promotion at the same time as the town had gone Steelers' crazy in anticipation of the Super Bowl match-up with the Seattle Seahawks.

Those who were here during the glory days of the '70s, when Pittsburgh was hailed as "The City of Champions," ought to remember that one team's success created a citywide energy that engulfed all our sports teams. The Steelers won four Super Bowls in that decade and the Pirates won two World Series, and Pitt won a national football championship. Hey, Bruno Sammartino was hailed as the "world's

Sean Casey shows his Steelers' allegiance at 2006 Piratefest.

Steelers tops in NFL merchandise

For the first time since 1980, NFL-licensed Pittsburgh Steelers merchandise was the top seller among the 32 teams in the league. The No. 2 team was the Philadelphia Eagles, the first time two teams in the same state could make that boast.

The popularity of Steelers such as retired tailback Jerome Bettis, quarterback Ben Roethlisberger, Super Bowl MVP Hines Ward and Troy Polamalu has enhanced the team's image on an international basis. In 1980, the Steelers were coming off their fourth Super Bowl victory in six years. The teams split the revenues from such sales so this does not represent a personal bonanza for the Pittsburgh club, except for the increase in sales through its own marketing efforts.

wrestling champion," and native sons such as Johnny Unitas and Joe Schmidt were inducted into the Pro Football Hall of Fame.

It wasn't long before the Penguins won back-to-back Stanley Cups in the '90s. The NHL's latest wunderkind Sidney Crosby & Co. could do that before long and, hopefully, they'll be doing it while playing in Pittsburgh. Mario Lemieux retired in the midst of the madness over the Steelers, but we should celebrate his career and contribution to our city rather than mourn his absence in the lineup.

Sean Casey is such a pleasant and engaging young man and an all-star caliber .300 hitter at his position, that he will brighten the local sports scene. He scolded Jason Bay, who grew up in Canada and has ties to Seattle, for saying he was rooting for the Seahawks in the Super Bowl. "We'll have to work on that," promised Pirates' GM Dave Littlefield.

Casey is hosting a Super Bowl party at his southern home in Jupiter, Florida this coming Sunday. He says he has all sorts of black and gold decorations, and Terrible Towels for his guests who are coming from as far as Boston to celebrate the day.

"It all works together," claimed Casey. "The Steelers' success can be a springboard for the Bucs as well. We can feed off one another, as the teams here did in the '70s. I see a passion that people have for the Steelers and Penguins and Pirates . . . the bottom line is Pittsburgh wants to see winning teams.

"I've got my brand new 'AFC Champions' T-shirt. I've actually been wearing Steelers shirts under my (baseball) uniform for years. I hope they can win another ring. And I hope we'll do what we're supposed to do this season, and the fans will rally around that.

"I've seen it happen here. I saw what it was like when Barry Bonds and all those great players were here in the early '90s. It can be like that again. And I think we can feed off the atmosphere in Pittsburgh sports. It was a great time to be a Steelers fan, obviously. And I think it's a great time to be a Penguins fan, with Sidney Crosby here. But I think it's going to be a great time to be a Pirates fan very soon, too."

Casey, by the way, rented a home in his native Upper St. Clair, just two blocks from my home. It was great to have such a classy guy move into the neighborhood. During the 27 years I had been living there, many coaches and players lived in our plan. Eddie Johnston, Chris Steele, Frank Lauterbur, Dick Walker, Craig Wolfley and John Fox were among them. I thought about that when I saw that Fox had signed a new five-year contract to coach the Carolina Panthers of the NFL for $5 million a year. My daughters used to baby-sit for his kids.

A Steelers' hat-trick in Washington, D.C.
Ben Roethlisberger received the NFL Quarterback of the Year award at the 21st National Quarterback Club Awards Dinner in Washington, D.C. on July 22, 2006. Jerome Bettis was presented with the Lifetime Achievement award and Bill Cowher received the NFL Coach of the Year award.

Down on Smallman Street

Steelers' fans are the real story for Super Bowl XL

February 8, 2006

Bobby Faloon is a big fan of the Steelers. So he is still smiling about the Steelers' Super Bowl victory over the Seattle Seahawks. A fifth Lombardi Trophy has been added to the Steelers' collection.

Faloon is in his 40th season as a vendor at Pittsburgh ballparks, beginning as a youth selling peanuts and popcorn and hot dogs at Forbes Field, and going through Three Rivers Stadium to PNC Park and Heinz Field, where he now hawks beer most of the time. Faloon is first in the union seniority ranks.

Faloon, who coaches kids' football teams in Mt. Lebanon, was selling Steelers' T-shirts and beads and souvenirs on the sidewalk on Smallman Street in the Strip District last Saturday. I went there on the morning before the Super Bowl to catch the scene.

"I've never seen anything like it," offered Faloon. "It was even crazier last Saturday. They're buying everything that's black and gold."

Smallman Street looked like Bourbon Street in New Orleans, as I recalled it when I was there to report on previous Super Bowls. The street was filled with Steelers' fans, most of them in black and gold costumes, with wild hats on their heads, black and gold beads draped around their necks. There was a festive atmosphere, Pittsburgh's answer to a Mardi Gras celebration.

I never noticed that so many of the storefronts had balconies, with black wrought iron fences, just like the ones in the French Quarter. I'd been to Detroit during an Arctic blast back in 1982 and I decided to stay home and watch this one on TV.

The usual commerce was going on in the stores that line Smallman Street, regular customers buying fresh fish and meat and vegetables, baked goods, Italian and Asian groceries. The sidewalks were crammed with tables piled high with Steelers' garb of one kind or another.

There was music playing over p.a. speakers on every block, most of them playing the "Steeler Polka" or updated fight songs. Everybody was talking about their favorite football team, and their chances of beating the Seahawks in the Super Bowl.

John Jesiolkiewic — now there's a real Pittsburgh name — who hails from Heidelberg, had a dog on a leash that was getting a lot of attention from the passersby. The dog, usually called Disney, was wearing a home-made sweater with MILLER and 83 on its back. She was part Chow Chow and German Shepherd, and paying tribute to the Steelers' outstanding rookie tight end, Heath Miller. She and her owner were sharing some beef cubes on a stick.

I thought about Bobby Faloon and John Jesiolkiewic when I was watching post-game TV reports of fans filling East Carson Street on the South Side and Forbes Avenue in Oakland after the nail-biting battle with the Seattle Seahawks. It was not an easy game to watch, so everyone was eager to celebrate.

Thousands of people poured into Pittsburgh from distant places over the weekend to be part of the Super Bowl weekend. There may have been 50,000 to 60,000 who traveled to Detroit and occupied the city for several days. Motown became Steeltown. Even the natives were rooting for the Steelers, according to the Detroit newspapers.

There were lots of fans wearing black and gold outfits and waving Terrible Towels, and this wasn't lost on the Steelers' players as they came out on the field. It felt like a home game, they said.

It was a great day for the Rooneys and Bill Cowher, Hines Ward, Jerome Bettis, Joey Porter, Alan Faneca, Deshea Townsend and Co. Dan Rooney paid tribute to his coaches and players and administrative staff, but most of all he thanked the fans. He said the Steelers won this one for Pittsburgh.

Dawn Dunlap and her husband Shawn, who live in Mt. Lebanon, had planned on attending a Super Bowl party on Sunday evening. They were watching the game on a small TV instead in the maternity ward at Mercy Hospital. Dawn had delivered baby Luke, 6 pounds 14 ounces, in the lobby at Mercy Hospital on Saturday at 9:10 a.m., about the same time I got out of my car on Smallman Street.

Mercy Hospital was the favorite hospital of Art Rooney Sr., the founder and patriarch of the Pittsburgh Steelers. He was surely smiling down on all the weekend's events in his hometown.

He always said that Pittsburgh was a great sports town and that its fans were particularly special. This Super Bowl proved that and then some. I thought about the guys who were called out on Sunday afternoon to salt our snow-covered streets and how bummed out they must have been to miss watching the Super Bowl.

Dan Rooney Jr., a Steelers' scout

Dan Rooney Jr. was a teenager when the Steelers won their previous Super Bowl in 1980. He was coaching high school football in North Carolina the last time Bill Cowher's team made it to the Super Bowl. Rooney Jr. was credited for finding Fast Willie Parker, the blazing running back from the University of North Carolina, who had been a key contributor to the team's successful run. He urged the Steelers to sign him as a free agent.

"I really believe that Coach Cowher is our undisputed leader," said Rooney Jr. "And everybody knows, whether they believe what he says or whatever they think, we are here to do what he wants.

"We're trying to provide him with an organization to win a Super Bowl. Everybody in the organization has to have one goal, and that's to win a Super Bowl. And the only way to do that is to support the guy that's running the show, and that's Bill."

> ## "It's fair to say that I'm our Old Reliable."
> ## — Jerome Bettis

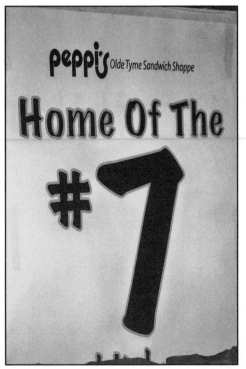

Photos by Jim O'Brien

Bobby Faloon, at left on facing page, and fellow vendors created New Orleans-like scene on Smallman Street before Super Bowl XL in Detroit.

Ernie Stautner symbolized
the Steelers of the '50s

"He was the toughest football player I ever met."
— **Andy Russell**

February 23, 2006

A Steelers' fan should know something about Ernie Stautner. He symbolized the Steelers of the '50s and early '60s. He was their star performer from 1950 through 1963. They had a winning record in only four of his 14 seasons.

Back then the Steelers were known as a tough, hard-hitting football team, but they didn't have enough good players. They'd give opposing teams a tough afternoon, but they usually came up on the short end of the scoreboard at Forbes Field and Pitt Stadium and road stops in the National Football League. Opposing teams paid dearly when they defeated the Steelers.

There was none smarter or tougher than Ernie Stautner, who was born in Bavaria and went to school at Boston College. He was a 6-1, 235-pound defensive end/linebacker, and he represented the Steelers in nine Pro Bowls. I had several of his bubble gum cards in my collection. We loved the Steelers in those days even though they seldom won.

I first met him back in 1961 when I was 19 and the sports editor of *The Pitt News*. He and his buddy Bobby Layne, the Steelers' quarterback, hung out with another dozen or so Steelers at Dante's, a restaurant/bar on the border of Brentwood and Whitehall. Another dozen media types were there on any given night of the week. Imagine a nightspot where Steelers and sportswriters and broadcasters enjoyed each other's company.

I went there to meet, even when I wasn't old enough to be there, and gain wisdom from the likes of Myron Cope, Pat Livingston, Bob Drum, Dave Kelly, Ed Conway, Roy McHugh, Doc Giffin, Tom Bender and other guys in the news business.

If you're going to call yourself a Steelers' fan you need to know about Ernie Stautner. His No. 70 is still the only Steelers' jersey that is officially retired. Being a fan should mean more than wearing your favorite player's official jersey or a ballcap or T-shirt or having a Terrible Towel draped over your television set on game day. Someone asked Dick Hoak, who had been with the Steelers as a player and coach, who came to mind first when he thought of all the guys he'd known on the Steelers. "Ernie Stautner," said Hoak. The Steelers' backfield coach recalled how he first met Stautner when he was attending a banquet to honor his midget football team in Jeannette

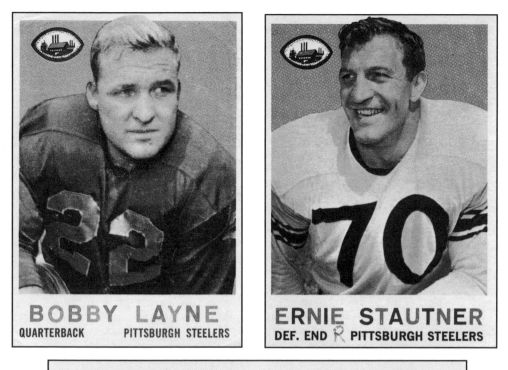

BOBBY LAYNE
QUARTERBACK   PITTSBURGH STEELERS

ERNIE STAUTNER
DEF. END ℞ PITTSBURGH STEELERS

> *"People have invented themselves, public characteristics for themselves, invented whole careers. Their whole life is fiction."*
> — Wallace Stegner, biographer

STEELERS

Lynn Chandnois
HALFBACK   PITTSBURGH STEELERS

JACK BUTLER
HALFBACK   PITTSBURGH STEELERS

and Stautner was the speaker. "When I joined the Steelers as a rookie, Stautner was still on the team," said Hoak. "When I told Ernie about that earlier meeting, he told me not to tell anybody else that story."

Stautner, who had suffered with Alzheimer's Disease the past eight years, died in a nursing home in Carbondale, Colorado last Thursday. He was 80. I last visited with him in April of 2002 when he was in Pittsburgh for a reunion and autograph-signing session with Steelers of the '50s. His family said he watched with pride as the Steelers beat the Seattle Seahawks in Super Bowl XL.

Jack Butler, a great defensive back of the Steelers in the '50s and one who deserves to be in the Pro Football Hall of Fame, remembers Stautner well. Butler, who lives in Munhall and heads an NFL scouting combine, said of Stautner: "He was one of those Germans, know what I mean, a tough dude. Quick off the ball, he'd explode off the ball, make great contact and pound the hell out of offensive tackles. And he could chase. He was all football and a team player all the way, a good guy."

Bill Priatko, who grew up in North Braddock, and played linebacker at Pitt and with the Steelers in 1957, takes great pride in playing with the likes of Stautner and Butler and knowing the Rooneys.

"I always termed him a smaller Joe Greene," said Priatko, who lives in North Huntingdon, and had the pleasure of going to Detroit with his daughter Debbie and having an insider's view of all the activities surrounding Super Bowl XL. "He had the same type of quickness and strength to dominate a football game like Joe Greene. He was just a durable, tough, tough football player."

Andy Russell was a rookie in Stautner's last season of 1963 when the Steelers lost to the Giants in New York in the final game when they had a chance to win the NFL's East Division title for the first time. Russell, who played 12 seasons as a linebacker with the Steelers, and played in seven Pro Bowls, remembers Stautner well and loves to tell stories about him.

Russell, who resides near the 18th hole and clubhouse at The Club at Nevillewood, said, "I remember a game when Stautner broke his thumb, and it was back against his wrist. It was just dangling there. He came to the sideline, grabbed some tape from the trainer, and wrapped it back in place. Then he returned to the game. He had a compound fracture.

"I had something like that happen to me a few years later, and I tried to do the same thing. But I fainted. Stautner was the toughest football player I ever met."

I remember one evening when I went to Dante's with my brother Dan, who was five years older than me, and our father, also Dan O'Brien. I told my Dad to pace himself, that it would be a long evening. So he starts off by ordering an Iron City and Imperial whiskey as soon as we were seated at Dante's.

About an hour later, my brother Dan comes to me at the bar and says, "Bobby Layne and Ernie Stautner are picking on Dad. We're not going to put up with that!"

I looked my brother in the eyes, and said, "Yes, we are." And, like a bouncer, I escorted him and Dad out the door of Dante's and drove them home. Layne and Stautner ended up in the Pro Football Hall of Fame. Stautner was the defensive coordinator for the Dallas Cowboys, helping Tom Landy shape the "Doomsday Defense." It was as highly regarded as "The Steel Curtain Defense." Now they're gone. So are my dad and brother. I thought about that when I heard that Ernie Stautner had died.

Ernie Stautner stood tall for Steelers in the '60s. That's "Boots" Lewis, Buddy Parker's good luck charm, kneeling on sideline.

A former Steelers star
is honored in his hometown

March 29, 2000

A wail of a passing train and "Amazing Grace" played on bagpipes are the sounds that stay with me. They framed an hour-long program to pay tribute to former Steelers star running back Fran Rogel in his hometown this past Saturday. They set a funereal-like tone to what was both a celebration and a memorial service. Rogel turned 72 this past December and is in declining health physically and mentally. He suffers from Parkinson's Disease and dementia. His family, friends and fans wanted to make sure he knows how they feel about him before it's too late. About 60 of them showed up to share his special day.

I followed Fran Rogel into the North Braddock Borough Building, 18 miles east of Pittsburgh. His younger brother Bernie brought him there from Fran's farm in Bakerstown, about 30 miles away. Bernie helped Fran get out of the automobile, and supported him as he shuffled through the glass doors.

Another younger brother, Elmer, entered the hallway in a wheelchair later on. The oldest brother, Bill, begged off, saying the only way he could come would be in an ambulance. There was a solid chair set out in the hallway especially for Fran Rogel. He was seated in front of a showcase that contained jerseys and caps from the glory days of the Purple Raiders of North Braddock Scott High School.

Rogel wore a blue and white Penn State warmup suit and ballcap that had been sent to him by Nittany Lions' football coach Joe Paterno nearly two years earlier when Rogel was honored at a dinner at the Churchill Country Club. He seldom spoke, and only offered a word or two when he did. It was difficult to discern what was registering in Rogel's mind, but he smiled and sang and wept when appropriate. He wept when they sang his school's fight song.

This was a man legendary quarterback Bobby Layne once called "the toughest man I've ever known in the NFL."

Rogel was a star running back at North Braddock High, at Cal State, Penn State and with the Steelers for eight seasons (1950-1957). He set records that were later surpassed by the likes of John Henry Johnson, Dick Hoak, Franco Harris, Rocky Bleier and Jerome Bettis.

He was the first pro football player I ever met in person. My father introduced me to him at Frankie Gustine's Restaurant in Oakland, just across the street from Forbes Field where the Steelers and Pirates played in those days. It was 1952 and I was ten years old.

My father hoisted me onto a barstool so I could be at eye level with Fran Rogel. He was a husky 5-9 or 5-10 at the time. He's even shorter now.

The Forbes Field faithful used to chant "Hi, Diddle, Diddle, Rogel up the middle!" It was often chanted to criticize the Steelers for their predictable offense. Today, they call it smash-mouth football. Art Rooney, at the request of sportswriter Bob Drum, asked Coach Walt Kiesling to call a pass on the first play of the game instead of having Rogel run up the middle. Kiesling told one of the linemen to jump offsides because he didn't want the play to work. He said if it worked then Rooney would be making more suggestions about what plays to call. The Steelers surprised the opposing team so much with the opening pass play that it went for a touchdown. But it was called back because a Steelers' lineman was off-side.

On Saturday, Rogel was seated in a hallway at the North Braddock Borough Building that had many trophies, jerseys, dried-up and flaking footballs, vintage photographs — so many mementos and memories. Like Rogel, they had rough edges.

There was a framed photo of the 1937 North Braddock Scott team that won the WPIAL Class AA football title. Bill Rogel was an all-state guard on that team. There was a plaque commemorating the school's PIAA basketball title in 1939. Now there would be a new plaque on the wall, this one acknowledging the outstanding career of Fran Rogel, a hometown hero.

Two of Rogel's greatest admirers, Bill Priatko and Rudy Celigoi, organized this tribute. Priatko presided over the program, citing the highlights of Rogel's career as a player, coach and teacher. Rogel later returned to Braddock Scott as a football coach and teacher, and did the same later on at Valley High School in New Kensington.

I arrived about an hour before the kickoff for the Rogel tribute and had a chance to tour North Braddock and nearby Braddock. Like Rogel, they have seen better days.

I checked out what was once Scott High's stadium. You can see Kennywood Park across the river from there. The first time I was ever in North Braddock was as a benchwarmer with the Hazelwood Little League All-Star team. We lost to North Braddock. I was 12 at the time. Going back to North Braddock can make you young again.

* * *

I went to Fran Rogel's viewing at the Ronald V. Lucas Funeral Home at the corner of Bell and Jones Avenue in North Braddock, near the football field where he was once a scholastic star. Rogel died on Monday, June 3, 2002, and was laid out on June 5 and 6. I was there on Thursday, June 6. Among the football people I recognized who were present to pay their respects were: Art Rooney Jr., Jack Butler, Billy Reynolds. Jim Gilhooley, Chuck Heberling, Rip Scherer, Chuck

---

Lynn Swann received the Republican Party's nomination for governor of the state of Pennsylvania. Swann, 53, was hoping to become the state's first African-American governor. "I haven't cried this much," said Swann at the announcement, "since I was inducted into the Hall of Fame."

Klausing, Lou "Bimbo" Cecconi, Nick DeRosa, Tony Romantino and Tom Stabile, and several members of Penn State's 1947 Cotton Bowl team. I spoke with my pal Bill Priatko and his buddy Rudy Celigoi. Priatko would deliver the eulogy the next day at Sacred Heart Church.

I was introduced to all the Rogels. They pronounce their name differently than Fran did. The family prefers the emphasis on the first syllable. I was struck by how small he looked in the casket. His skin was dark. He didn't look like Fran Rogel. As Art Rooney once said of funerals in general, "No one looks good in the box."

Jim O'Brien

Fran Rogel is honored in his hometown of North Braddock back in 2000.

"There's a lot of Chuck Noll in Tony Dungy, and there's a lot of Terry Bradshaw in Peyton Manning."
— **Tom Moore, offensive coordinator of Indianapolis Colts and former assistant coach of PittsburghSteelers**

Kilroy was here
He played for the Steagles

"My dad used to go to all the big races."
— **Art Rooney Jr.**

August 13, 2003

A loyal reader of my column complimented me for a story I wrote about Seabiscuit. A week later, the same fellow asked me, "Was there really a horse named Seabiscuit?"

He thought the story was too good to be true. Yes, indeed, there was a Seabiscuit, and he was the biggest story in the country in the late '30s and early '40s. The book by Lauren Hillenbrand about Seabiscuit and the movie by the same name captured the hearts of many. It was a wonderful comeback story.

Art Rooney Jr., who lives in Mt. Lebanon and works out of an office in Upper St. Clair, read the book and saw the movie. He believed his father saw Seabiscuit beat War Admiral in a much-ballyhooed match race at Pimlico Race Track in Baltimore back then. He said his dad and his mother went to Santa Anita Racetrack and to racetracks in Tijuana, just like in the story of Seabiscuit.

"My dad used to go to all those big races," related his son during a luncheon meeting at the St. Clair Country Club in the fall of 2003. "He knew all those guys in racing, and he raced horses himself."

Art Jr. also knows that his father did some of the same things with his horses that are part of the Seabiscuit saga, such as working out horses in the middle of the night, or on different tracks, so no one else could time them and know how fast or slow they might be running.

Art Rooney Sr. was regarded as one of the best handicappers on the horseracing scene. The story is not true, however, that he bought the Steelers with money he made on a big winning streak at Saratoga. He bought an NFL franchise in 1933 for $2,500 and called his team the Pittsburgh Pirates. Three years later, he had the big two-day winning spree at racetracks in New York where he won an estimated $300,000 — big money in those days.

The Philadelphia Eagles also entered the NFL in 1933, and their history is intertwined with the Steelers. During an off-season period in the early '40s, Art Rooney Sr., sold his Steelers to a New York playboy-steel baron named Alexis Thompson. Not many know that.

Thompson then decided he'd rather have a team closer to home, so he swapped the Steelers for the Philadelphia Eagles. Bert Bell, who owned the Eagles, talked Rooney into going into a partnership with him and they became co-owners of the franchise in Pittsburgh. Rooney had second thoughts and regretted selling his team. He welcomed

Bell's offer. So the Steelers never missed a season. For years, the Steelers operated with franchise papers first granted to the Eagles.

When Bell became the commissioner of the NFL he had to relinquish his ownership in the Steelers.

The Steelers and Eagles got together for a pre-season game at Heinz Field on a Saturday night in August, 2003. It marked the 60th anniversary of the 1943 season when they joined forces during World War II because of a shortage of able-bodied pro football players.

That team was called the Steelers-Eagles when they played two games at Forbes Field that year, against the Packers in September and the Lions in November, and they were called the Eagles-Steelers when they played in Philadelphia. Chet Smith, the sports editor of *The Pittsburgh Press*, called them the Steagles, and the name stuck. Jack Lambert would have fit right in with those Steagles or, later, the Pitt-Cards, a joint venture with the Chicago Cardinals.

The Steagles wore black and gold uniforms in Pittsburgh and green and blue (those were the Eagles' colors in those days) when they played four games in Philadelphia. Walt Kiesling of the Steelers and Earle "Greasy" Neale of the Eagles were co-head coaches, each taking the lead on his home field. There was even a team in the NFL that year called the Brooklyn Dodgers. I actually met a Steagle in my student days at the University of Pittsburgh. His name was Frank "Bucko" Kilroy, a 6-2, 240-pound defensive tackle from Temple who was originally with the Eagles. He's still active in the NFL as head of the player personnel department for the New England Patriots. He was a terror and played in three Pro Bowls.

As a freshman at Pitt, I helped out in the office of Beano Cook, the school's sports information director. I was there on the day of a football game when people were coming into Cook's office to pick up credentials to sit in the press box.

In order, the following came by: Al Davis, a coach and scout for the Los Angeles Chargers of the newly-formed American Football League, Emlen Tunnell, an assistant coach and scout for the New York Giants, Kilroy, a scout for the Eagles, and Red Smith, a sports columnist for the *New York Herald-Tribune*.

The busts of Davis and Tunnell are now in the Pro Football Hall of Fame. So are the busts of Bell, Rooney, Kiesling and Neale. I usually see Davis in the flesh and, of course, in black attire, there at the annual induction ceremonies. Smith went on to win a Pulitzer Prize. I shook hands with all of them that day in Cook's office.

One of the good guys in the National Football League, Jim Trimble of McKeesport died at age 87 on May 23, 2006. He had worked as a personnel consultant and scout with the New York Giants for many years. At age 34, he became the head coach of the Philadelphia Eagles for four years (27-20-2). Adrian Burk, Chuck Bednarik and Bucko Kilroy were some of his players. He once played for the McKeesport Olympians.

Pete Dimperio
Coaches could still learn from him

"You're lookin' good."

March 9, 2006

Many of the area's finest football coaches were at a gathering in Green Tree. They were assembled at the Radisson Hotel for the 44th Annual Pittsburgh Coach of the Year Clinic that ran Friday through Sunday, March 3-5, 2006.

This event began back in 1963 when Pete Dimperio, the famed football coach of the perennial City League champion Westinghouse High School team, joined forces with two of the most famous college football coaches in the country, Bud Wilkinson of Oklahoma and Duffy Daugherty of Michigan State, to conduct a series of clinics for high school coaches here.

Those three are all gone now, but the clinic continues under the direction of Pete's children, Peggy and Pete Dimperio Jr. of Squirrel Hill, with the help of a consultant staff of area high school football coaches and administrators, with Nike as the lead sponsor.

The clinic speakers included Kirk Ferentz, who grew up in Upper St. Clair and became the highly successful head football coach at the University of Iowa, and Al Groh, the former head football coach of the New York Jets who is now the head coach at the University of Virginia.

Joe Bugel of Munhall, the assistant head coach for offense of the Washington Redskins, was on the clinic staff. He's still regarded as one of the best line coaches in the National Football League.

Tom Bradley, the popular defensive coordinator at Penn State University, and Matt Cavanaugh, the handsome offensive coordinator at Pitt, were among the speakers. There were high school coaches conducting clinics as well, and they included Jim Render of Upper St. Clair High School and Ray Braszo of Steel Valley High School.

Bradley, by the way, was wearing a white dress shirt and tie with a dark blue V-neck sweater and looked like a fine representative of Penn State. I was struck by how many of the high school coaches, especially the younger ones, had shown up dressed so slovenly. They were wearing outsized or baggy sweatpants and sweatshirts with their ballcaps on backwards. If I were a young coach, I thought, I'd want to look good and make the best possible impression on the established coaches. I'd want them to see me in the most favorable light.

I noticed that most of them spent their time in the lobby in the company of the same coaches they came with. What could they learn new from them? I had a chance to chat for twenty minutes or more with Dave Robinson, a former Penn State and Green Bay Packers linebacker who lives in Akron and was at the clinic representing a synthetic turf company.

We talked about Vince Lombardi and some of his theories on football. I wondered how many of the coaches had ever heard of Dave Robinson. Or Vince Lombardi. When I went to big sports events such as the Super Bowl, I always wanted to spend time with the top sportswriters in the country, and hear what they had to say. I figured I could learn something from them. Hanging out all the time with the other sportswriters from Pittsburgh was incestuous behavior, as far as I was concerned. What could they tell me I hadn't already heard a hundred times in the press boxes in Pittsburgh?

The speakers' roster at the Coach of the Year Clinic through the years was an impressive one and had included the likes of John McKay of Southern Cal, Rip Engle and Joe Paterno of Penn State, John Michelosen, Foge Fazio, Walt Hackett, Mike Gottfried and Walt Harris of Pitt, John Majors of Pitt and Tennessee, Jackie Sherrill of Pitt and Mississippi State, Jake Gaither of Florida A&M, Darrell Royal of Texas, Bob Devaney of Nebraska, Frank Broyles of Arkansas, Bo Schembechler of Miami of Ohio and Michigan, Tom Prothro of UCLA.

Also in the listing of former clinicians were Tom Cahill of West Point, Eddie Robinson of Grambling, Chuck Klausing of Indiana (Pa.) and Carnegie Mellon, Dan Devine of Missouri and Notre Dame, Woody Hayes of Ohio State, Ben Schwartzwalder of Syracuse, Frank Kush of Arizona State, Bobby Bowden of West Virginia and Florida State, Lou Holtz of North Carolina State and Notre Dame, George Welsh of Navy, Tom Osborne of Nebraska, Don Nehlen of West Virginia, Gerry Faust of Notre Dame, John Robinson of Southern Cal, Bobby Ross of Maryland, LaVell Edwards of BYU, Barry Alvarez of Wisconsin, Don James of Washington, Bill McCartney of Colorado, Tom Coughlin of Boston College, Rich Lackner of Carnegie Mellon, Howard Schnellenberger of Louisville, Gene Stallings of Alabama, Dave Wannstedt of the Chicago Bears, Steve Spurrier of Florida, Rich Rodriguez of West Virginia, Bob Stoops of Oklahoma, Nick Saban of LSU and Larry Coker of Miami

Pro players and coaches such as Steelers' standouts Roy Jefferson, Ray Mansfield, Lloyd Voss, Tony Dungy, George Perles were speakers, and Frank Ryan and Bill Nelsen of the Cleveland Browns also appeared. That's quite a distinguished alumni group.

Most of the clinics were devoted to x's and o's, and all sorts of sophisticated stuff. The Pete Dimperio who founded this clinic never bothered with too much of that. He kept it simple and he still won. He grew up in my hometown of Hazelwood and he was a terrific lineman at Thiel College. The Dimperios lived on Tecumseh Street, near my Uncle Everett and Aunt Kathleen Burns. They owned and continue to operate a super market on the main street, Second Avenue. I remember my brother Dan played for a sandlot football team called

Pete Dimperio

the Tecumseh Street Indians. Every neighborhood had a football team of one age group or another, usually supported by local merchants. The most generous givers were usually the local numbers writers, an illegal activity in some respects. The cops knew the numbers writers, too, but tended to look the other way, especially when someone was pressing a $20 bill in their hands.

Before he taught health classes and phys ed and coached the football team at Westinghouse, Pete Dimperio was on the faculty staff at Herron Hill Junior High School, now the Milliones Middle School. He was asked to coach basketball and tennis teams there. He didn't know much about either sport. He had winning teams, though. Jazz musician Walt Harper played tennis for Pete at Herron Hill Junior High and continued to enjoy the game in his adult years.

Some of the coaches who have been involved in WPIAL and PIAA basketball tournaments, and post-season play such as The Big East Tournament and NCAA Tournament would be wise to do what Dimperio did in that regard.

He was famous for calling time out once in a game, and telling his players, "Hey, I want you to start putting the ball in the basket!"

Like I said, Pete Dimperio liked to keep it simple.

Pete Dimperio knew something about winning. He started coaching at Westinghouse in the late '40s and coached into the late '60s. In 21 years as coach there, he won 17 City League championships and posted a league record of 123-5. He ran the single-wing, thought to be an outdated offensive system by most of his contemporaries. (The Steelers, by the way, were the last team in the NFL to employ the single-wing when Jock Sutherland and his disciple John Michelosen were coaching the team). But Pete preferred a simple power game. He was the City League's answer to Vince Lombardi.

His teams always booked pre-conference games with the best WPIAL teams such as Altoona, Johnstown and New Castle. He often played against Mt. Lebanon. His players were mostly black inner-city kids, with a few of Italian and Irish heritage, and they learned how to tackle and block and outrun everybody. One of those Italian kids was Tony Liscio, who later played for the Dallas Cowboys. Liscio was a tackle on one of his championship teams, and he regarded Dimperio in the same class as Tom Landry.

Pete's teams practiced on an 80-yard oil-coated patch in the East End of town, where the Silver Lake Drive-in Movie Theatre was located. That is a Pittsburgh landmark, and a favorite for teen lovers of that period. Pete portrayed the Mt. Lebanon kids to his players as rich kids from the suburbs. "They drive Cadillacs to and from school," Dimperio told them.

One day during practice, Dimperio spotted a low-flying airplane over his team's practice field. Dimperio shouted to his players, "Stand still! Don't move! That's Mt. Lebanon scouting us!"

There was another time when Pete set a newspaper on fire during his pre-game talk. "You've got to have that kind of fire in your belly if you're going to be a winning ballplayer," he told his Bulldogs.

As a pre-teen, I remember playing midget league football against two teams, the Homewood-Brushton Bulldogs and the Homewood Scorpions, who ran Pete's single-wing offense. They were two of the best teams we played. Our team, called the Hazelwood Steelers, once shared the midget league football crown with the Homewood Scorpions. Those teams were feeder programs for Westinghouse High School's team. Dimperio was definitely ahead of his time.

Dimperio had a great sense of humor and he was a terrific after-dinner speaker. He was a regular for years at the annual Thompson Club AA Sports Night Dinner coordinated by Darrell Hess. He made fun of himself and his players in his remarks.

He also used to be a regular at the Curbstone Coaches lunches at the Roosevelt Hotel. Dimperio was named to that group's Hall of Fame in 1967. I attended those luncheons as a schoolboy at Taylor Allderdice High School and at Pitt, often playing hooky or cutting classes to be there. It was part of my education. Art Rooney's office was on the first floor at the Roosevelt Hotel, and he attended those Curbstone Coaches gatherings religiously. He often sat next to Pete Dimperio, one of his favorites. There were times he thought of asking Pete to coach his Pittsburgh Steelers. Dimperio had been a lot more successful than the old friends Rooney had hired to lead his team.

One of Dimperio's favorite lines was: "There are three stages in life. You're young, you're middle-aged and you're lookin' good."

He got himself into trouble with some of the stories he told about his mostly black football team. "We have a lot of freshmen and sophomores on this year's team," he'd tell the audience, "but you wouldn't say we're green."

Dimperio loved his kids, however, and he was a good influence on most of them. He taught them about how to survive in the streets. He had street smarts. There's more to sports than the x's and o's, and not enough coaches or fans recognize that. Too many coaches pride themselves on how complicated their systems are and how their playbooks are demanding. What good are difficult strategies if they don't work, if you won't win?

They need to recognize that character, sportsmanship, dedication and perseverance are often more important. A football coach can learn something from reading about Washington and Lincoln and FDR and MacArthur, Patton and Eisenhower that might help them teach young people how to prosper and succeed in life. Dimperio knew how to coach and he knew how to win. And he helped a lot of young people stay out of trouble and find their way in life.

That's what good coaches and teachers do.

"Joey Porter said some dumb things (after the playoff victory at Indianapolis) about the officials cheating Pittsburgh, but he can blitz for me anytime."
— **Peter King, Sports Illustrated**

The last interviews
with Pitt's Marshall Goldberg

"He was a football player's football player."
— Dr. Jock Sutherland

April 12, 2006

I called Marshall Goldberg on his 85th birthday at his apartment in Chicago. His wife, Rita, answered the telephone. She told me that Marshall was not doing too well, and that he had memory lapses.

"I don't know how reliable his responses will be," she said, when I told her I wanted to interview her husband.

I told her my experience had been that old ballplayers could remember their glory days well, even if they couldn't tell you what they had that morning for breakfast.

Marshall Goldberg had been the most famous football player in the history of the University of Pittsburgh until Mike Ditka and Tony Dorsett came along in the '60s and '70s, respectively. He was known as "Biggie" and "Mad Marshall," and "The Elkins Express." He came to Pitt from Elkins, West Virginia, where his father owned a movie theatre and a clothing store.

"Biggie" Goldberg was an All-American running back who led Pitt to national championships in 1936 and 1937, and was the runner-up for the Heisman Trophy as college football's best player in 1938. The Panthers, coached by the legendary Dr. Jock Sutherland, posted a 25-3-2 in Goldberg's three varsity seasons. "He was a football player's football player," Dr. Sutherland once said of Goldberg.

He was a favorite of national sports columnists such as Grantland Rice as well as Steelers' owner Art Rooney.

Pitt played Fordham in three scoreless ties in that decade and Goldberg, who played in two of those contests, was heralded in the New York newspapers for his ability. He was one of the few Jewish sports stars of that era and many of the sportswriters were Jewish. He was once referred to in a national wire service report as "a Jewish hillbilly from West Virginia."

Goldberg died last week at a nursing care center in Chicago at the age of 88.

I had printed Goldberg's name on a legal pad the day before I learned he had died. I was visiting a friend of mine, Gerry Hamilton, who proofreads my books. She had been ill and had to leave her home in Oakmont for a stay at Sunrise, a personal care residence about a mile from my home in Upper St. Clair. She is 83 and deaf, so I must write messages to her. I was with her in the lobby when Judge Emil Narick entered the facility. He lives there. I wrote a few lines to Gerry Hamilton when I introduced her to Judge Narick. I mentioned that he had been a quarterback on the Pitt football team back in the late '30s, and that he had been a teammate of Marshall Goldberg. "Now I heard of *him*," Ms. Hamilton told me with a smile.

When I heard of his passing, I thought about that phone call I had made to Marshall Goldberg on his 85th birthday and two subsequent calls over the following two months. He spoke slower than I had remembered him speaking, but he made sense. Sometimes he startled me by the details of his recall. His coach was regarded as dour and aloof by many, but he treated Goldberg like a favorite son. Goldberg recalled this one instance of Sutherland putting his hand on his shoulder and saying to him, "Marshall, I'm counting on you to lead the way for our team." Goldberg remembered these details from nearly 70 years ago. At the end of our interview, I asked Goldberg, "What's your wife's name?" There was a pause and he said, "You got me there. Hold on a second. Oh . . . it's Rita."

The year before I had visited the College Football Hall of Fame in South Bend, Indiana. The football player portrayed at the entrance is Tony Dorsett of Pitt. Bernie Kish, who was the director at the time, took my friend Alex Pociask and me on a personal tour. He showed me some large well-preserved scrapbooks that Marshall Goldberg had given him a week earlier. He lent me those scrapbooks so I could read the stories.

They contained newspaper clippings and photos from the '30s and '40s, when Goldberg played for Pitt and then the NFL's Chicago Cardinals. He was a three-time All-Pro defensive back for the Cardinals. To my surprise, I found a loose tear sheet from *The Pitt News* inside the cover of one of the scrapbooks. It contained a column I had written about Goldberg's son, Marshall Goldberg Jr., who tried in vain to follow in his father's footsteps at Pitt during my student days at Pitt in the early '60s. I had won a national collegiate journalism contest with that column. I smiled when I saw it.

A Pitt professor told me he asked his finance class of 35 or so students last week if they had ever heard of Marshall Goldberg. Two of them said they had. All Pitt students should know about Marshall Goldberg and Jock Sutherland and Dr. Jonas Salk and Dr. Thomas Starzl, so they can appreciate better where they are going to school. Their success stories might prove inspirational.

The Pitt family suffered another setback last week when Maggie Dixon, the sister of Pitt's basketball coach Jamie Dixon, died of a heart problem at the age of 28. She had coached the women's basketball team at Army to its first NCAA tournament at the same time her older brother's team at Pitt was in the men's tournament. It was a good story. It hurt to hear what happened to her. So suddenly. She was younger than both of my daughters. Goldberg was 88 and had led a full life. He'd become a millionaire in business after his ballplaying days.

"I prefer to live in the present," Goldberg once said. "To me, playing sports should be a stepping stone to a career. It's not an end in itself." There's a valuable lesson for young people who play games.

Art Rooney had seen Goldberg play at Pitt, but got to know him even better when Goldberg played pro football with the Chicago Cardinals over a ten-year span, interrupted by a three-year stint as a line officer in the U.S. Navy during World War II. Goldberg closed his career when the Cardinals won their first National Football League title in 1948. The Cards beat the Steelers that season, 24-7, at Forbes Field. The Steelers played the Cards eight times during that ten-year period. The Cardinals were combined with the Bears in Chicago during one of those years, the way the Steelers and Eagles were combined during World War II because of the shortage of players.

As a pro, Goldberg led the NFL in interceptions (seven) and kickoff returns (12 for 290 yards) in 1941, and was selected for the All-Pro Defensive Team in 1946, 1947 and 1948.

During his days at Pitt, he was a member of "The Dream Backfield" that included Johnny Chickerneo, Dick Cassiano and Curly Stebbins.

Goldberg's career rushing record of 1,957 yards stood as a school record for 36 years until Tony Dorsett became the leader in 1974.

Goldberg was named to *Sports Illustrated's* Team of the Decade. He was also honored by *Sports Illustrated* Silver Anniversary Team for his success on and off the playing field.

Dan Jenkins of *Sports Illustrated* did an opinion piece once in which he tried to determine who should have won the Heisman Trophy each year, and he wrote that Goldberg had the best credentials in 1937 (when he finished third in the balloting).

His No. 42 jersey at Pitt was retired at halftime of Pitt's 21-17 victory against Miami on September 18, 1997. He was one of only eight football players at Pitt to receive that honor.

During my lifetime, Marshall Goldberg was the noble face of Pitt football. He remained involved in alumni activities and fund-raising. He often returned to the campus for different events where his presence would add to its attractiveness. He was always well dressed and looked the part of a successful businessman when I'd see him.

When he died, I was surprised to read that his wife Rita attributed his death to head injuries he had suffered as a football player. I found that difficult to accept. I had spoken to Marshall Goldberg in his 60s, 70s and 80s and always found him to be a vibrant, confident, self-assured and smart individual. He became a millionaire with a machinery company he purchased and directed in suburban Chicago.

Fabulous Five Survivors
Only five players lasted from the previous coaching regime when Chuck Noll directed the Steelers to a Super Bowl championship in 1974. They were Bobby Walden, Rocky Bleier, Sam Davis, Andy Russell and Ray Mansfield.

I called Dr. Joseph Maroon at UPMC where he is a renowned neurosurgeon, to seek his opinion on the matter. Dr. Maroon has been one of the Steelers' physicians more than 25 years and has done respected studies on concussions and player-related head injuries. He helped develop a test that is now a standard in pro sports to determine the extent of such injuries, and recuperative periods required for such concussions.

"I saw that," Dr. Maroon told me over his cell phone, just before he performed an operation at UPMC that day. "I don't believe that either. That's not a progressive development. He would have shown signs far earlier if he had suffered severe head injuries. It reminded me of how Dr. Cyril Wecht initially said that Terry Long had died from head blows he had suffered during his playing career. Turned out he had swallowed anti-freeze fluid."

I believe that Marshall Goldberg led a full and productive life. My mother, Mary O'Brien, incurred dementia when she was in her 90s. It's something that happens to old people. It can be part of the aging process.

My mother could mouth the words of songs from the '20s and '30s when she would hear the music, but couldn't tell you what she had for breakfast or lunch.

MARSHALL GOLDBERG   **Halfback**

Ben Roethlisberger reflects on his recovery from motorcycle accident: "This was a scary event, but not in the way that it makes me want to change who I am or be afraid to live my life. I look at it as this . . . God had a plan for me and he did this to make me take a step back and see what his plan for my life is. I'm taking that and running with it — I'm thankful for every day. I look at every day as a blessing."

Andy Russell's roundup
Golf outing stirs up good memories

Andy Russell **May 24, 2006**

A friend from Cincinnati sent me a newspaper clipping last week that stirred up some good memories, but made me think of the swift passing of time. It was a tear sheet from a copy of the May 7th issue of *The New York Post* and it had a feature in it called "Blast from the Post." The reprinted story was under my byline and it originally appeared in the May 11, 1974 issue of *The Post*. It was a story I'd written about Julius Erving — Dr. J — and the New York Nets winning the ABA title. It struck me that this story appeared 32 years ago, and I was three months away from my 32nd birthday when I wrote it. That was half my life ago. I will turn 64 this August. "Which half went the fastest?" asked my wife Kathie. I replied without hesitation. "The second half, no doubt about it."

My daughter Sarah and her husband Matt are 32. That helps put it into its proper perspective for me. I was reminded of those days in my life when I attended the 30th annual Andy Russell Celebrity Classic last Friday at The Club in Nevillewood. Russell rounded up such a large field that they also played golf at Diamond Run out by Wexford. Some of the celebrities included Matt Bahr, John Banaszak, Bobby Bell, Craig Bingham, Steve Blass, Rocky Bleier, Mel Blount, Ralph Cindrich, Robin Cole, Jack Ham, Franco Harris, Randy Hillier, Sam Huff, Tunch Ilkin, Roy Jefferson, Pierre Larouche, Louis Lipps, Gerry Mullins, Edmund Nelson, Ted Petersen, Max Starks, Lynn Swann, Bruce Van Dyke, Lloyd Voss, Mike Wagner, Dwight White, Craig Wolfley and Dwayne Woodruff. Russell has raised more than $5 million dollars through the years for local charities dealing with prostate cancer research and with ailing children.

Russell was kind enough to list me among the celebrity guests. But someone else misidentified me in the press notes as Jim O'Brien, the former wide receiver and place-kicker for the Baltimore Colts. I spent several hours looking for the other Jim O'Brien at Nevillewood before Russell told me about the error one of his volunteer staff had made. I was still reminded of an incident involving that Jim O'Brien.

I was in Miami on Jan. 15, 1971 two days before the Super Bowl V matchup between the Colts and the Dallas Cowboys. I interviewed former heavyweight boxing champion Floyd Patterson who was fighting Levi Forte the following night on Miami Beach. Patterson scored a second round TKO. I had been at ringside at the Civic Arena in Pittsburgh back in late March 1967 when Patterson decked Bill McMurray in the first round. McMurray's head struck the floor with such vehemence that I thought he had been killed.

When I was in Miami, I was watching a television interview in which Jane Chastain, one of the first female sports broadcasters, was talking to Jim O'Brien, one of my favorite players for some reason. In the middle of the interview, O'Brien said he had a dream about the upcoming Super Bowl. Chastain went to the next question on her pad. I went crazy. "What was the dream about?" I hollered at the television set. I called Ernie Accorsi, a public relations executive with the Colts and an old friend from his Penn State days, and asked him if he could get the other Jim O'Brien on the phone with me. And he did.

"What was the dream about?" I asked Jim O'Brien. "I have this dream," he said, "and someone kicks a field goal to win the Super Bowl, but I don't know if it's me or the Cowboys' kicker who does it."

Another Jim O'Brien scored the game-winning field goal for the University of Maryland the night before, and another Jim O'Brien was the hero in a Boston College basketball game. I tied this package all together for a column for Saturday's *New York Post*, the day before Super Bowl V.

Talk about good timing. Rookie Jim O'Brien, a year out of the University of Cincinnati, kicked a 32-yard field goal with five seconds to go to break a 13-13 tie in the championship game the following day. O'Brien should have been the game's MVP, but that honor went to Chuck Howley of Wheeling and WVU, a linebacker who had two interceptions and several solo tackles. It's the only time in 40 Super Bowls that a player on the losing team was named the game's MVP.

By coincidence, Floyd Patterson, a popular boxing figure because of his mild-manner approach to a violent sport, died last week at the age of 71. He had been battling Alzheimer's Disease and prostate cancer for years. He was 21 when he knocked out Archie Moore to become the heavyweight boxing champion of the world.

> *"Quarterbacks get too much credit and too much blame. They're cheerleaders more than anything else. A Ben Roethlisberger signed jersey should not draw a higher bid than Joe Greene's autographed jersey from North Texas State."*
> — **Andy Russell**

Jim O'Brien

Andy Russell's Celebrity Classic for Children drew many former teammates, including, left to right, John Banaszak, Mike Wagner, Rocky Bleier, Gordon Gravelle and Dave Reavis.

'Ironhead' Heyward
An irrepressible star in Pitt days

June 7, 2006

I liked Craig Heyward right from the beginning. His four-year stay as a star running back on the University of Pittsburgh football team coincided with my stay as assistant athletic director and sports information director at the Oakland school. He sat out his sophomore season and then departed Pitt after his junior year when he was the No. 1 draft choice of the New Orleans Saints.

He played for five different teams during an 11-year career in the National Football League. He played against the Steelers several times. He came to Pitt in 1984.

All incoming athletes at Pitt were asked to fill out a questionnaire with personal information for their files in the sports information office.

Heyward wrote that his nickname was "Ironhead" and that his hometown newspaper was *USA Today.* We got a lot of national play on that latter note. He not only had a big head, but he had big aspirations as well.

He was 5-10, 260 pounds and an athletic marvel. His coaches were always after him about watching his weight. But he had great athletic ability and could do things others couldn't do, no matter what he weighed. He was one of Pitt's greatest rushers, right up there with Tony Dorsett, Curtis Martin and Marshall Goldberg.

There are images that remain like snapshots in my mind of "Ironhead" Heyward. He had a bubbly personality and was fun to be around. In his freshman year, during an intrasquad scrimmage under the lights at Belle Vernon High School, he went downfield about 15 yards, scooped a low pass off his shoe-tops, regained his footing, took two more strides and then hurdled a defensive back cleanly and continued to run another dozen or so yards. His classmate, Olympic hurdles champion Roger Kingdom, never cleared a barrier any better.

I heard that Heyward could dunk a basketball from a standing jump. One day I came upon him shooting a basketball with some of his buddies on the basketball court under Pitt Stadium. It was called the Pavilion when Doc Carlson's teams played varsity basketball games there in the '30s and '40s. Heyward grabbed a basketball, at my request, and dunked it for me on his first try. Then he offered me a slam dunk smile.

He shared a story about how two rival gangs exchanged gunfire across the football field at one of his high school games back in Passaic, N. J. He came from a rough background and he never quite shed some of his heritage in that respect.

Heyward got into several scrapes with authorities during his student days at Pitt. In one of the episodes, he got into a shoving match with a newspaper boy and tossed him onto a car hood. That didn't look too good. Heyward was sent to my office a few times by the athletic director to discuss the public relations aspects of his behavior. I remembered going to the high school vice-principal at Allderdice High School. He was in charge of discipline. Now I was the vice-principal.

I caught Heyward one day soliciting handouts from alumni and boosters by Gate 3 of Pitt Stadium following a football game. That was in violation of NCAA rules. I didn't report him to the athletic director. I learned the hard way that no one wanted to hear about misbehavior or rules-breaking on the part of the coaches or athletes. The messenger would be slain.

I enjoyed my job at Pitt for the most part, and particularly the interaction with student athletes. I enjoyed mentoring them. I never forgot I was working at a school, a university. In many instances, I was simply passing along bromides about good behavior that I had learned from coaches and administrators during my student days.

No one who looked out the window of the stadium offices and saw Salk Hall on Sutherland Drive should have thought they were the most important person ever to step on the campus.

I had a soft spot for "Ironhead" in my heart. I grew up in an inner-city neighborhood nearby. I learned a long time ago that every young person who gets into trouble isn't necessarily a bad kid. One day I was jogging around the quarter-mile track at Pitt Stadium during lunchtime. Heyward joined me at some point midway through my run. He sidled up next to me. He did this, though I'm sure he knew he would be lectured on every lap. I told him he reminded me of a kid from my old neighborhood. Let's call him Paddy Murphy. I told him that a group of kids could all be doing the same thing but that every time the police came they picked up Paddy Murphy. We jested that they named the Paddy Wagon after him. I told Heyward that he was Pitt's Paddy Murphy.

Later on, Heyward was one of the finalists for the Heisman Trophy. He was invited to the award dinner at the Downtown Athletic Club in New York with the other finalists. A friend of mine there, a fellow named Rudy Riska, told me that Heyward would return months later, around 1 a.m., pounding on the door to get in. Heyward had a few drinks earlier that evening and was feeling no pain.

They closed Pitt Stadium down with a final game with Notre Dame on Saturday, November 13, 1999. I was down on the oval track before the game looking for old friends. Heyward was one of over 400 former Pitt football players on hand for the special event. Herb Douglas, an Olympic medalist in the long jump in 1948 and one of the first blacks to play football at Pitt, was the first to offer a hug. Then came Bill Fralic, an All-American offensive lineman when I was working there in the mid-80s. Heyward sneaked in behind me and gave me a bear hug. That meant a lot to me. He and Fralic could have avoided me, considering me someone who'd always been lecturing them.

Heyward has been plagued with a brain tumor in recent years. He was getting around in a wheel chair. He died at his home in Atlanta on May 27, 2006. He was only 39 years old. It hurt to hear that news. Pitt Stadium is gone and now so is "Ironhead" Heyward. They both seemed indestructible. They were part of what made Pitt so special.

Jim O'Brien

Two of Pitt's greatest running backs, Tony Dorsett and Craig "Ironhead" Heyward, meet on eve of McGuire Memorial Golf Outing coordinated by Danny Rains of McCarl's in Beaver Falls.

"Troy Polamalu is the best big-game defensive player in football. If his diving pick of Peyton Manning hadn't been overturned, it would have gone down as the greatest interception in Steelers history."
— Peter King, *Sports Illustrated*

Epilogue
Big Ben gives us a big scare

A season that began with a promise and a dream nearly ended in a nightmare. Ben Roethlisberger and his Steelers' teammates had made good on a promise to get Jerome Bettis to the Super Bowl in his hometown of Detroit. It was a dream come true for Bettis.

The Steelers beat the Seattle Seahawks in Super Bowl XL and all of them, especially Bettis and Roethlisberger, became the toasts of the town. No one got more fan mail than they did, though Troy Polamalu and Hines Ward were close in that category.

Everything the Steelers did became big news in Pittsburgh and Western Pennsylvania. No one drew more media attention than Big Ben. Quite often it seemed like overkill, turning nothing into news. Some of his critics felt Big Ben was getting a Big Head. When Terry Bradshaw got into the fray, scolding Big Ben a second time in a television interview about how risky and foolhardy it was for him to be riding a motorcycle, a Steeler insider suggested "Terry and Ben both ought to park their egos at the door."

Personally, I thought Big Ben was a bit overwhelmed by all the attention he was getting and was doing his best to accommodate everyone. He was brusque with some who crowded his space and I saw him blow off an interview request from WPXI-TV because its news producers had the temerity to dispatch a television truck out to his townhouse on Washington's Landing. They had heard his auto had been towed for violating an on-street parking ban.

I heard that Ben had bought a $3.2 million mansion in Hampton because he wanted more privacy. It has six bedrooms and four full bathrooms on 4.5 acres. The annual taxes are $47,000.

Then Big Ben really grabbed the spotlight and then some when he was involved in a scary accident riding a motorcycle to the Steelers' training facility on the South Side one Monday morning. This was real news. In truth, it was more surreal than real. The Steelers' story was incredible enough without this. The 24-year-old quarterback struck an automobile that had turned into his path as he was riding along Second Avenue at the intersection with the 10th Street Bridge. Witnesses said his head hit the car's window and then struck the pavement. His head was a bloody mess. He asked a woman who came to his side where he was; he didn't even know what city he was in. He asked the paramedics if he was dreaming.

He was rushed by ambulance through the Armstrong Tunnels to Mercy Hospital, just a few miles away. This accident happened at 11:10 a.m. on Monday, June 12, 2006. It was only ten days since Roethlisberger had spoken on behalf of his teammates at a reception held by President Bush at The White House. It was only eight days since Big Ben joined his teammates at a special private dinner at Heinz Field where they were given their Super Bowl rings.

Big Ben had looked terrific throwing the ball at workouts. He was wearing his hair longer, á la Erroll Flynn in one of his swashbuckling roles, and he had the world in his gifted hands. Life for Big Ben couldn't have been better. And then his world went bang.

Mercy Hospital had been the favorite hospital of Steelers' founder Art Rooney. He got the best room in the house when he was a patient there, the same room that was reserved for the Catholic bishop by the Sisters of Mercy. It was the hospital where Dan Rooney was taken when he was involved in an auto accident the day before Thanksgiving in 1980. His car slid on an icy stretch of Banksville Road as he was driving to work one morning and he crashed into a hillside and suffered facial lacerations and a broken hip. It was the hospital where Dan's daughter, Kate, died from Lupus. Roethlisberger, ironically enough, was stopped by police at a speed trap they conduct on that same road for speeding in an automobile only days before his motorcycle accident. Ben wasn't driving his Harley-Davidson. He was driving a Japanese built bike that could rocket from zero to 180 miles in next to nothing. It's referred to as a "crotch rocket." Ben didn't have a license to drive a motorcycle. He was not, according to eyewitnesses, driving fast.

I was at home writing what I thought was the next-to-the-last chapter for this book when my wife Kathie called me from Allegheny General Hospital where she is a social worker in the Cancer Center.

"Did you hear what happened?" she asked me. "Ben Roethlisberger was in a bad accident on his motorcycle. You had better turn on the television."

I left my computer station and went to my family room and turned on the television. The entire noon news segment was devoted to live coverage of the Roethlisberger story. Local stations even pre-empted soap operas that normally follow the news and stayed with the story for two more hours. It was compelling theater. It reminded me of when I received a similar telephone call when I was working on another book and a neighbor told me that two airplanes had crashed into the World Trade Center in New York City.

This wasn't 9/11, of course, but you wouldn't know it by the media coverage in Pittsburgh. Stories relating to Roethlisberger filled several pages of the Pittsburgh newspapers, and he was the subject of every sports talk show in town, and even on the network versions.

Roethlisberger, ironically, was the cover boy on most of the pro football preview magazines that had hit the newsstands and bookstores in the Pittsburgh region in early June, and now he was the lead story on the front page of newspapers in Pittsburgh and New York, as well as *USA Today*. He was also on the cover of this book that was getting readied to send to the printer. What to do?

Many Pittsburghers and the Steelers Nation were praying for his recovery. My dear friends, Alex and Sharon Pociask, stayed with us while attending a wedding in Pittsburgh the following Saturday.

ESPN's Mike Golic on Ben Roethlisberger:
"Like most athletes, he feels invincible."

Big Ben was featured everywhere in Pittsburgh when he became the city's most popular citizen. Sam Vuick and Steve Kingsland of Brentwood Express on Rt. 51 did bonanza business with a burger named after Steelers' quarterback.

Photos by Jim O'Brien

"When they said prayers the priest mentioned several people from the church and then they mentioned Ben Roethlisberger," said Sharon. A friend told me they prayed for Ben at his synagogue. He was the talk of the town. He could have been killed in this collision. He wasn't wearing a protective helmet when it happened. As soon as it was learned that he would recover from his multiple injuries the criticism started coming in over his foolhardiness in riding a motorcycle, and especially for riding a motorcycle without a helmet. It's the way parents act after their kids survive close scrapes. They want to kill their kids for doing something stupid once they know they're going to be all right. There were callers on the talk shows who defended his right to do what he wanted to do.

Roethlisberger underwent seven hours of surgery by a team led by Dr. Larry M. Jones, chief of the Division of Multisystem Trauma at Mercy Hospital. He broke portions of his upper and lower jaw, his nose, an orbital bone underneath his eye, and lost and damaged several teeth. He suffered a mild concussion but tests revealed no brain damage. He didn't hurt his legs or arms. Lucky Ben. It wasn't long before Big Ben jokes and cruel caricatures showed up in e-mail messages.

It was reported that he would probably be delayed in getting to summer training camp with the Steelers, but he would probably be able to play in the season opener. Even so, the odds on the Steelers repeating as NFL champions were changed in Las Vegas from the Steelers being 8-to-1 to 20-to-1 shots.

I felt a knot in my stomach for two days after learning of Roethlisberger's accident. I had seen him about a dozen times at several sites over the previous two months. I had talked to him, always briefly, getting bits and pieces for this book. I recalled seeing him racing recklessly in a golf cart about the course at the Southpointe Golf Club only a few weeks earlier. It wasn't up to me to say anything to Ben about his reckless bent, but the father in me wanted to tell him it would be wise to be more careful. I couldn't afford to offend Ben Roethlisberger. He wasn't happy when Terry Bradshaw told him to park the bike until his career was over, and he wouldn't welcome my criticism either.

The day after Ben was hurt, I had a date to sign books for Father's Day gifts in the lobby of Fifth Avenue Place. That's the headquarters for Highmark Blue Cross Blue Shield. Judd Gordon of Highmark's Caring Foundation just across the street in the old Horne's Department Store, came by and we talked about Ben Roethlisberger. Ben had played in a fund-raising golf tournament Gordon had coordinated two weeks earlier. Ben had been to a lot of fund-raising events since the Super Bowl when he might have gone into hiding to have some time to himself.

When I was coming out of the basement parking area after my signing, I came upon a line of traffic. I wanted to make a left turn. A fellow on a motorcycle waved for me to come out. I noticed he was wearing a black Steelers' jersey. He wasn't wearing a helmet.

I slowed my car and lowered the window on the passenger side as I passed in front of his motorcycle. I couldn't help myself. I hollered out to him, "Hey, thank you. But get a helmet!" He offered a big smile.

As I passed in front of him, I looked in my rear view window. He was wearing No. 7. When he passed me on the next street I saw ROETHLISBERGER across his back. It was unreal.

Roethlisberger was released three days later from Mercy Hospital and was expected to recover from his injuries and be able to resume playing football for the Steelers. He was a surprise visitor to the team's headquarters in less than a week. Art Rooney used to say, "I'd rather be lucky than good." Big Ben was, indeed, a lucky young man. He lived to, hopefully, learn from his mishap. He remains the man with the magic arm and he's continued to make us pull for him.

Roethlisberger's brush with death reminded many Steelers' fans of what happened to Gabe Rivera, a great rookie prospect in 1983. The Steelers passed on local hero Dan Marino of Pitt and picked Rivera, a defensive lineman from Texas Tech, with their first draft choice. The Steelers thought they were solid at quarterback and that their prime need was for a defensive lineman.

Rivera looked terrific in his early outings. Then Rivera was severely injured in an auto accident on the North Side. He was drunk and driving a sports car above the speed limit when he crashed into a car driven by a Steelers' fan. Rivera's 290-pound body was jettisoned through the back window of his car, a Datsun 2802X. He was not wearing a safety belt. He landed in the woods 20 yards from the collision. He suffered broken ribs, a bruised heart and a bruised lung, nerve damage to his right shoulder and, most seriously, a crushed spinal chord. He was unconscious.

Rivera was left paralyzed by his injuries. He has been confined to a wheelchair ever since while living in San Antonio.

Police charged Rivera with drunken driving, speeding, reckless driving and driving on the wrong side of the road. Twenty-three days after the accident, his wife, Kim, gave birth to a son, Timothy. Rivera had bouts with depression and the marriage turned sour. They have since divorced.

Several people once associated with the Steelers had died in 2005. "It was a rough year for us Steelers," said alumnus Mike Wagner.

Terry Long, a former lineman, had committed suicide, drinking anti-freeze. Bud Carson, the brains behind "The Steel Curtain" during the glory days of the '70s, had died at age 74 from emphysema. Bud blamed smoking for his illness and the need for a breathing-assistance machine when I interviewed him over the telephone in 2004. Steve Courson had a tragic death at age 50. He was cutting down trees on his outpost in Farmington, deep in the woods outside Uniontown, when an ill wind blew a tree in the direction of one of his dogs. Courson was crushed by the tree as he attempted to rescue his dog. Theo Bell, a wide receiver and punt returner on two Super Bowl winners in the late '80s, died on June 21, 2006 after a long bout with kidney disease and scleroderma. He was 52.

The death of Steelers' lineman Justin Strzelczyk, at age 36 on September 30, 2004, had an even closer correlation to what happened to Roethlisberger. Strzelczyk was a likeable character who played for the Steelers for nearly a decade and was a real clubhouse favorite. He rode a Harley-Davidson motorcycle with great gusto.

Strzelczyk was killed in his pickup truck when he led state troopers on a 40-mile chase along the New York State Thruway during the morning rush hour before dying in a fiery head-on collision with a tanker carrying corrosive acid.

Troopers said Strzelczyk crashed his pickup truck into the westbound tanker just moments after swerving around a tractor-trailer that had pulled across the highway to block its path in the eastbound lane. There was quite an explosion and flames soared into the sky. Strzelczyk drove 15 miles on three tires and a rim after one of his pickup's tires was punctured by metal spikes thrown into the road by troopers.

"It could have been so much worse," said state policeman Jim Simpson. "We're fortunate that only one person died."

Strzelczyk, who lived in McCandless Township in the North Hills of Pittsburgh, had been involved in another minor accident about an hour earlier, just west of Syracuse, which started the bizarre turn of events. No one ever figured out what was going on with Strzelczyk that fateful day.

Some of his teammates were upset with me for writing a critical column about Justin's wild behavior. He was their friend, their buddy. But they never saw that his behavior was often ill-thought-out and was not in his best interest. Hey, I liked the guy, too.

When I was interviewing him for an earlier book, *Dare to Dream*, Strzelczyk boasted that he would have a few beers with his biker buddies at Smitty's, a neighborhood bar in Turtle Creek, and then drive to Johnstown and Altoona on treacherous winter highways to play with the Steelers' basketball team. I had one auto accident in my life, and it was during my college days at Pitt, when I lost control of a new Volkswagen Bug on a highway near Altoona. Road conditions are always unpredictable in the mountains of Cambria County during the winter. Strzelczyk was always coaxing me to take a ride with him on his Harley, and go out and choke back a few beers with the boys at Smitty's. I begged off. I was tempted to take a ride, to see what it was like, to better appreciate Justin's joy of the open road for the book. The literati call it "immersion journalism." But I remembered a boyhood promise to my mother that I would never get on a motorbike or motorcycle.

A kid named Butchie Buffo, who lived across the street from my boyhood home, had a motorbike and had frequently offered me a ride. "I don't want to EVER see you on a motorbike or motorcycle," Mary O'Brien told her baby boy more than once. It was one of the rules I had obeyed and I thought I'd like to keep it going. Why blow it at age 53?

Then I heard how Strzelczyk had taken Tom Pratt, a cameraman at WTAE-Channel 4, on such a bike ride, and scared the hell out of

Pratt when he hit speeds of 80 miles per hour. "I like Tom; he's a good man," Strzelczyk said, when I mentioned the incident to him.

"Don't be a wuss!" Strzelczyk scolded me. "Live a little! You must have been the well-behaved kid in your neighborhood. Break out!"

Strzelczyk was the youngest of 18 former Steelers — ages 35 to 58 — who had died since 2000, including seven in a 16 month stretch. "There is no explanation," said Joe Gordon, a Steelers executive from 1969 through 1998. "We just shake our heads and ask why." The numbers are startling. Of the NFL players from the 1970s and '80s who have died since 2000, more than one in four — 18 of 77 — were Steelers.

I had driven through the intersection of Second Avenue and the 10th Street Bridge about a dozen times during May and June of 2006 while attending practice sessions of the Steelers. I know the streets of Pittsburgh well, but that is an intersection I have always approached warily. The Parkway West ramp runs above it and casts a large shadow on the intersection. You have to check out the traffic in every direction because a lot of cars are making left-hand turns there. I have often gone through the Armstrong Tunnels because it's a shortcut to Mellon Arena or to get out to Pitt.

When I was about eight or nine years old, I remember watching a river show from a ramp near the 10th Street Bridge. I remember that Mesta Machine Company in West Homestead, where my father worked, had a sternwheeler boat in a race with a big boat from another mill company along the Monongahela River.

They had two automobiles crash head-on on the dock below and something went wrong and one of the drivers was killed in the collision. I saw a teenage girl I knew get killed in an auto accident when I was in high school on that same stretch. I can still see blood seeping out of her ear and streaming over the gray mill dust at the side of the road.

I am familiar with that stretch of Second Avenue. Before the city's jail was built nearby there was a stretch of buildings that housed the Western Newspaper Printing Company. I oversaw the production of *The Pitt News* and later *Pittsburgh Weekly Sports* during my college years.

If you continue east on Second Avenue it will take you to my hometown of Hazelwood and then Glenwood, about four to five miles away, close by the Monongahela River. I was involved in a bad auto mishap when I was nearing my fourth birthday in August of 1946.

I was riding in an Iron City Taxi with my mother, father, brother and sister. We were traveling across the Glenwood Bridge. It was raining. The tires of the taxicab got caught in slick streetcar tracks on the wooden bridge and swerved violently. I shot out of the back seat of the cab and went headfirst into the top of the steel railing and fell back into streetcar tracks. If I had gone a foot higher I would have soared straight into the Monongahela River. A streetcar could have run right over my body.

I was taken to Mercy Hospital. I was born there on August 20, 1942 and I was reborn there on this visit. I also had seven doctors performing surgery on me, just so you don't think Big Ben got special treatment. Some of the doctors had told my mother that my chances of surviving the surgery were slim. My parents were told to talk to me non-stop so I didn't fall asleep. They were afraid I might lapse into a coma. I had 48 stitches on the crown of my head and a few more in my upper lip where I had a hole the size of a quarter, just below my nose. I still have the scars. I survived the accident.

I turned 64 this August. I can assure Big Ben that for the rest of his life, every time he drives by the 10th Street Bridge, he will be reminded of the day he was nearly killed there. He will tell himself, "I'm lucky to be alive. God must have been looking after me." The lesson to be learned from Big Ben's debacle is that if you are going to play football or ride a motorcycle it's a good idea to wear a helmet.

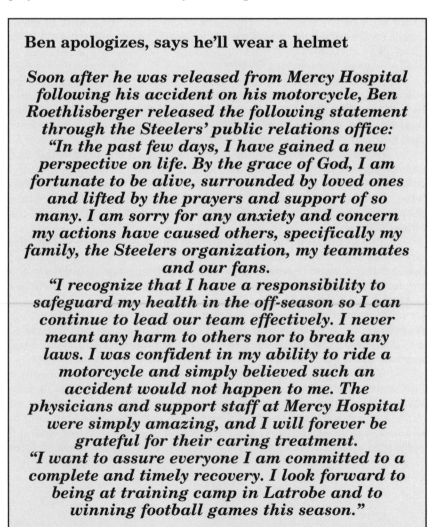

Ben apologizes, says he'll wear a helmet

Soon after he was released from Mercy Hospital following his accident on his motorcycle, Ben Roethlisberger released the following statement through the Steelers' public relations office: "In the past few days, I have gained a new perspective on life. By the grace of God, I am fortunate to be alive, surrounded by loved ones and lifted by the prayers and support of so many. I am sorry for any anxiety and concern my actions have caused others, specifically my family, the Steelers organization, my teammates and our fans.

"I recognize that I have a responsibility to safeguard my health in the off-season so I can continue to lead our team effectively. I never meant any harm to others nor to break any laws. I was confident in my ability to ride a motorcycle and simply believed such an accident would not happen to me. The physicians and support staff at Mercy Hospital were simply amazing, and I will forever be grateful for their caring treatment.

"I want to assure everyone I am committed to a complete and timely recovery. I look forward to being at training camp in Latrobe and to winning football games this season."

Another Promise

"I'm going to try and be better than I ever was"

No sooner had Pittsburghers quit praying for Ben Roethlisberger — his recovery was speedy and promising — than they turned their attention to Mayor Bob O'Connor. It was revealed on Friday, July 7, 2006 that Mayor O'Connor had a rare form of cancer that was invading his brain and spine.

Big Ben and Bob O'Connor had both been participants in the downtown parade that celebrated the Steelers' Super Bowl XL victory back in February. Both were on top of the world at the time. No one could have known what life-threatening episodes were on the horizon for both of these popular Pittsburgh figures. Bob O'Connor once introduced me to Roy Rogers when he was working for the national restaurant chain of that name. O'Connor grew up in Greenfield and graduated from Allderdice High School, just like the late Mayor Richard Caliguiri.

The following Thursday after the disturbing news came out about Mayor O'Connor, we learned from Ben that he had come close to death in his motorcycle accident. Credit four Pittsburgh paramedics — Danny Capatolla, Scott Everitt, Brian Markovich and John Archer — with administering emergency care that probably saved Ben's life. "I was maybe a minute or so away from dying," Roethlisberger revealed in an interview with ESPN's Jim Rome.

They noticed a slit vein in his throat and sealed it off shortly after his June 12 accident. He was bleeding into his stomach and could have drowned in his own blood. A few weeks later, Ben had come to realize how lucky and blessed he was to be able to be on the road to recovery. He was optimistic that he would be with the Steelers at the start of training camp in late July. "People ask me if it's going to change the way I play. Am I going to be more cautious?" said Roethlisberger during a celebrity golf outing in Lake Tahoe, Nevada. "No, that's not who I am. I'm not going to slide instead of dive. I'm not going to step out of bounds instead of trying to get that extra yard. I have every intention of getting out there and playing to the fullest of my ability and still being that free spirit that makes me who I am. I'm going to try and be better than I ever was. Maybe it's going to make people doubt me and put more fire in me. I'll prove them wrong."

He said he had not been doing any soul-searching and second-guessing about riding his Suzuki Hayabusa without a helmet. He said he didn't know whether he'd be riding a motorcycle again soon, but said he'd wear a helmet while he's playing for the Pittsburgh Steelers. He appeared to be a humbler and more gentle Ben.

"I just want everybody to know that, yes, I'm sorry. I'm just so thankful for all the support I've gotten from everyone in the Steelers' organization and everyone in the Steeler Nation. The fans have been great. We have the greatest fans in all of sports, hands down. But I'm going to be OK. They can count on me."

Acknowledgments

I have been fortunate to have friends and patrons support my book writing and publishing efforts over the last 25 years. I am grateful to the Steelers players, coaches and administration that granted me interviews and assistance on this project. I had an opportunity to meet a lot of nice people.

Loyal patrons include John Zanardelli of Asbury Heights; Louis Astorino and Dennis Astorino of LD Astorino Associates, Ltd.; Nancy and Pat McDonnell of Atria's Restaurant & Tavern; Ronald B. Livingston Sr. of Babb, Inc.; Bill Baierl of Baierl Automotive Group; Rich Barcelona of Bailey-PVS Oxides LLC; Ingar Lesheim, Michael Schuler and Andrew F. Komer of Bowne of Pittsburgh; The National Baseball Hall of Fame and Museum; Howard "Hoddy" Hanna of Hanna Real Estate Services, Robert C. Buzzelli, Daniel Koller, Jr. and Jeffrey Todd of Fifth Third Bank.

Don Carlucci of Carlucci Construction Co.; Kenneth F. Codeluppi of Wall-Firma. Inc.; Tom Sweeney and Joe Reljac of Compucom, Inc.; James T. Davis of Davis & Davis Law Offices; Armand Dellovade of A.C. Dellovade, Inc.; Don DeBlasio of DeBlasio's Restaurant; Suzy and Jim Broadhurst of Eat'n Park Hospitality Group; Everett Burns of E-Z Overhead Door & Window Co.; James S. Hamilton of Federated Securities Corporation; Frank Fuhrer of Frank Fuhrer Wholesale; Inc., David J. Malone of Gateway Financial

Jack McGinley of Wilson-McGinley Co.; Steve Fedell of Ikon Office Solutions; Lou Grippo of the Original Oyster House; Frank Gustine Jr. and George Jordan of Armstrong Gustine Development, Inc.; Ed Lewis of Oxford Development Co.; Mike Hagan of Iron & Glass Bank; William V. Campbell of Intuit; Judge Jeffrey A. Deller; Jack Mascaro of Mascaro Construction; Joseph A. Massaro, Jr. of The Massaro Company; Clark Nicklas of Vista Resources, Inc.

Robert Santillo and Danny Rains of McCarl's, Inc.; David B. Jancisin of Merrill Lynch; Angela Longo of National City Bank of Pennsylvania; Jack Perkins of Mr. P's in Greensburg; Dan R. Lackner of Paper Products Company, Inc.; A. Robert Scott of *Point*; Joseph Piccirilli and Tony Ferraro of Pittsburgh Brewing Company; Andy Russell of Laurel Mountain Partners, LLC.; Dan Bartow of Legends of the North Shore Restaurant; the Leukemia & Lymphoma Society.

Pat and John Rooney of Palm Beach Kennel Club; Patrick J. Santelli of Pfizer Labs; James Rohr and Sy Holzer of PNC Bank Corp.; John Seretti of Seretti Chevrolet, Inc.

Daniel A. Goetz of Stylette, Inc.; Dick Swanson of Swanson Group Ltd.; Robert J. Taylor of Taylor & Hladio Law Offices; Jim, Barbara and Ted Frantz of TEDCO Construction Corp.

Thomas J. Usher of USX Corporation; Stephen Previs of Waddell & Reed Financial Services; Ralph J. Papa of Citizens Bank; Judd Gordon of Western Pennsylvania Caring Foundation; Ray Conaway of

Zimmer Kunz, PLLC; Bob Randall of TRACO, Inc.; Bill Tillotson of Hefren-Tillotson, Inc.

Friends who have been boosters include Dr. Edwin Assid, Aldo Bartolotta, Mel Bassi of Charleroi Federal Savings Bank, Jon C. Botula, Miles Bryan, Dave and Frank Clements, Art Cipriani, Joseph Costanzo Jr., Ralph Cindrich of Cindrich & Company in Carnegie, Todd Cover, Mrs. Elsie Hillman, Gregory L. Manesiotis, Robert F. McClurg, Dennis Meteny, George Morris, Andy Ondrey, John Paul, Alex Pociask, Art Rooney Jr., George Schoeppner, Len Stidle, and Rudy Zupancic of Giant Eagle.

Friends who have offered special encouragement and prayer and those who have opened up doors for our endeavors include Tony Accamando, Thomas J. Bigley, Rocky Bleier, Rudy Celigoi, Jack Chivers, Herb Douglas, Stan Goldmann, Dr. Haywood A. Haser, Harvey and Darrell Hess, Debbie Keenan of Reed Smith Shaw & McClay, Pete Mervosh, Bob Milie, Tom O'Malley Jr. of the Bob Purkey Insurance Agency, Sally O'Leary, Bill Priatko and Bob Shearer.

Gerry Hamilton of Oakmont handled the proofreading for this book, and provided kind assistance in many ways.

I do all my work with Pittsburgh firms. All of my books have been produced at Geyer Printing. Bruce McGough, Tom Samuels and Keith Maiden are great to work with each year. Denise Maiden, Cathy Pawlowski and Rebecca Fatalsky of Cold-Comp Typographers did their usual outstanding job.

The *Almanac* newspaper in the South Hills, for which I have been writing a man-about-town column for the past 15 years, has promoted my book signing appearances through the years, as has *The Valley Mirror* in Homestead-Munhall.

Photos were provided by George Gojkovich of Getty Images, Mike Fabus of Pittsburgh Steelers, Dave Arrigo and Kerri McMullen of Pittsburgh Pirates, Mike Longo, Dan Ranker and Wayne Herrod, as well as Duane Rieder of Rieder Photography. Illustrations are by Kevin-John Jobczynski (www.Kevin-john.com) and Merv Corning. The Steelers' communications staff was of special help, with Dave Lockett, Burt Lauten, Michele Rosenthal and Vicky Iuni providing assistance.

My support team begins with my wife of 39 years, Kathleen Churchman O'Brien, and our daughters, Dr. Sarah O'Brien-Zirwas, Rebecca O'Brien and Rebecca's dog, Bailey O'Brien. My son-in-law, Dr. Matthew Zirwas, is also a point of pride, as is Rebecca's fiancé, Quinn Carlson. A child star on the block is our granddaughter, Margaret Harvey Zirwas. They make it all worthwhile.

— *Jim O'Brien*

Peter King of *Sports Illustrated* on Bill Cowher:

"There are few coaches who can motivate players and have the kind of coaching staff that Cowher has assembled."

Author's Page

This is the 22nd book written by Pittsburgh sports author Jim O'Brien. He is on the advisory board for the Sports Museum at the Heinz Historical Center in Pittsburgh, and the board of the Asbury Heights Foundation. He has been inducted into the western chapter of the Pennsylvania Sports Hall of Fame and has won the Bob Prince Award for his journalism efforts and the David L. Lawrence Award for "promoting Pittsburgh in a positive manner on a national level" from Vectors. He was cited as a "Legend" by the Pittsburgh chapter of the Italian-American Sports Hall of Fame.

He was inducted into the U. S. Basketball Writers Association Hall of Fame at ceremonies at the Regency Hyatt in New Orleans on Monday, April 7, 2003. The event was held in conjunction with the NCAA Final Four men's basketball championship. During a three-year span, O'Brien also served on the nomination board for the Basketball Hall of Fame in Springfield, Mass. He votes for the Baseball Hall of Fame in Cooperstown, N.Y.

He writes a column for two suburban weekly newspapers, *The Almanac* in the South Hills and *The Valley Mirror* in the Steel Valley.

O'Brien was also a contributing writer for *Basketball Times, Basketball News, Basketball Digest, Baseball Digest* and *The Sporting News*. He was a staff writer for the *Philadelphia Evening Bulletin, The Miami News, The New York Post* and *The Pittsburgh Press*. He served as assistant athletic director for sports information at his alma mater, the University of Pittsburgh. He has a degree in English from Pitt, and did graduate studies in English Literature.

He has been married for 39 years to Kathleen Churchman O'Brien and they live in the Pittsburgh suburb of Upper St. Clair. They are the parents of Dr. Sarah O'Brien-Zirwas of Columbus, Ohio and Rebecca O'Brien of Woodland Hills, California.

Kathleen Churchman O'Brien

Author Jim O'Brien talks to Ben Roethlisberger at "Breakfast With Champions" event sponsored by Leukemia & Lymphoma Society